UNDER TWO MASTERS

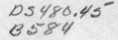

UNDER TWO MASTERS

N. B. BONARJEE

With a foreword by

PHILIP MASON

OXFORD UNIVERSITY PRESS

1970

Oxford University Press, Ely House, London W.1

GLASGOW NEW YORK TORONTO MELBOURNE WELLINGTON
CAPE TOWN SALISBURY IBADAN NAIROBI DAR ES SALAAM LUSAKA ADDIS ABABA
BOMBAY CALCUTTA MADRAS KARACHI LAHORE DACCA
KUALA LUMPUR SINGAPORE HONG KONG TOKYO
Faraday House, P/17 Mission Row Extension, Calcutta 13

Neil Bruniat BONARJEE, 1901

PRINTED IN INDIA BY S. N. GUHA RAY AT SREE SARASWATY PRESS LTD. CALCUTTA-9
AND PUBLISHED BY JOHN BROWN, OXFORD UNIVERSITY PRESS, FARADAY HOUSE, CALCUTTA-13

To

my daughter Reva

in affection

Preface

THIS book requires an explanatory note. It is not intended to be autobiography in the full sense of the term, for a one-time relatively small cog in a large imperial machine is not entitled to it. Nor again have I sought to write a day-to-day or coherent record of work and general life in the Indian Civil Service. Had either been in my mind, I should have included the lighter side of Service life and spiced up the whole dish with amusing anecdotes—of which there was no dearth. But I have not written of the beer and skittles, as it were, of life during my twenty-two years in the I.C.S. because my purpose has been a more serious one. In essence my theme is not personal, and the first few chapters of pure autobiography are there not for their intrinsic interest but rather as an explanation for what follows. They are the background scenery for the stage. I have then selected certain broad lines, sometimes particular episodes, in order to work up to a general estimate of British rule in India; not, indeed, as I saw it in my Service days under that rule, when, like everyone else, I took its basic principles and practices so much for granted that I thought them to be immutable, but as I now see it in retrospect. I do not claim that my appraisal is necessarily correct. It is that of one individual, and is only one of the many evaluations that can be made, according to the number of different angles of vision.

British administrative principles were so entirely foreign to the traditions handed down by previous rulers that they went against the Indian grain. It is true that they were gladly accepted by Indians who could recall the intellectual stagnation of the country in the eighteenth and nineteenth centuries and the political chaos which followed on the decay of the Mughal Empire. But when such memories were dimmed with the passage of time, the very virtues of British administrative ethos made it unpalatable to the taste of later generations. The term 'good government' is susceptible to many interpretations, and as the author of *Many Worlds*, writing in the nineteen sixties about the forties, has said: 'The time had come when good government was not only no substitute for self-government but could not be had without the latter.' It is here, I think, that the key to much of what is happening in contemporary India lies; for 'good government' and 'self-government' have become synonymous in Indian estimation. The disappearance of British administrative ethic and its replacement by Indian have produced, I should say, a general feeling of satisfaction and even contentment in the *upper* strata of society. Independence has cleared away the frustrations and inhibitions which were so manifest everywhere during the last thirty years of the British Raj, and, although others of a different kind have projected themselves, it can be correctly said that among those who at present count for anything in the political, administrative and economic life of the country there is little real dissatisfaction with the working of independence. Politicians as a class, big and small, in the Ministries, in the Legislatures or tucked away in the Party cadres in the rural areas, the higher officials in the various government Services, industrialists, large-scale traders, small shopkeepers, the higher ranks of the expanding professional and middle classes, the wealthier peasants and the men with a political pull in the villages, all have far greater opportunities for worldly advancement and a wider material life than ever before. That these classes constitute only a small proportion of India's near six hundred millions is of relatively small importance, *at least for the time being*, in the light of the political and economic power they are able to exercise.

The new upper class urban generation between the ages of twenty and thirty-five literally has the world, with its financially and socially most rewarding component, the U.N.O., before it. Opportunities of all kinds are numerous with the great expansion of commerce and industry and the enormous growth of official activities. Nor is it difficult for young people of this class with influence—and only the very unfortunate do not possess this in some degree—to hook and land lucrative positions. Much has been done to make life relatively easy for the post-1947 generation in such matters as education and foreign travel; and scholarships are far more plentiful and easier to obtain than before. Political emancipation has brought with it not merely the 'four freedoms' but also quite a few of which the late President Roosevelt had never thought, and the ancient social punishment of 'outcasteing' for breaking the rules of the game is as dead as the dodo amongst the intelligentsia.

Grumbling is inevitable, and it is here in plenty—but where in the world is there no grumbling? Riots and a varied assortment of disturbances for an equally varied assortment of reasons are a daily occurrence in some part of the country, often enough even in the numerous Legislatures. So much so, indeed, that they are taken for granted as being normal elements of Indian democracy. Although under the surface there are ominous rumblings of deeper discontents, *carpe diem* has become the motto of the upper intelligentsia, especially the younger section with that 'enjoy yourself, it's later than you think' feeling which covers over a multitude of unpleasant, and perhaps not very distant, possibilities.

From the psychological standpoint there can be no doubt that independence is a necessity for every subject people—in fact it would have been better for both India and Great Britain had India been given freedom on the Irish model by 1929 at the latest—and to a subject people is of far greater significance than good administration. The thesis that administration in free India has deteriorated from the high standards of the British era has no bearing on contemporary affairs and is of historical interest alone. It is certainly neither of interest nor importance to the new generation which has been educated into different standards and which in any case has had no experience of the past as a criterion for judging the present.

Many of the views I have expressed are unorthodox and are likely to provoke dissent on one or other side of the hill. They are those of an individual in his progress from a strong, though only emotional and sentimental, objection to the presence of the Englishman in India and to the latter's sometimes unpleasant attitudes to a more rational assessment of the manner in which the British actually governed and administered the country. On this last subject, that of British rule, everyone will have his own opinions: but if there are any lynx-eyed persons who seek to spot the cloven hoof of the C.I.A. in anything I have written—and I know of one at least—I can assure them that to the best of my knowledge and belief that organization, ubiquitous though it may be, is totally unaware of my existence.

A word as to my use of certain terms and the spelling of Indian place names. I have used the term 'Great Britain' throughout to cover England, Wales and Scotland, and similarly, for the most part, the word 'British'. I dislike 'Briton' to cover individuals, as it smacks too much in my eyes of the ancient Briton clad in skins dyed in woad: and 'Britisher'—a word once popular among Indians—even more. In the few places where 'English' or 'Englishman' has seemed more appropriate the context will show the connotation. So far as Indian place names are concerned, I have retained the spelling common during the British period, except where the use of new designations has been essential as, for example, in the case of Uttar Pradesh for the former United Provinces or Madhya Pradesh for the Central Provinces, in the later portion of the book.

I am especially indebted to the following: my daughter for the help she has given me throughout; Mr V. S. C. Bonarjee, of the Indian Administrative Service, Bengal; and Mr P. Sondhi and Mr R. Lal for giving me the benefit of the opinions of a younger generation on chapters 9, 10 and 11.

Contents

Illustrations

Foreword

How fascinating, and sometimes how painful, it is to observe the growth of a man brought up in two worlds. N. B. Bonarjee came of a Bengali Brahman family but his grandparents became Christians and adopted many British Victorian values, though always critical of much in British administration in India. After a varied life as journalist and lawyer, Bonarjee's father retired to rural India where he lived as the squire of a small estate in a backward part of Oudh. He was a land-owner very different from most of those who surrounded him, living a simple life and deeply concerned about the welfare of his tenants and cultivators—a Tolstoy with the conscience of a Nonconformist Minister, but a deep understanding of the good in Indian peasant life.

His son was educated in England at the preparatory school for Dulwich, then at Dulwich and finally at Hertford College, Oxford. He was successful in the examination for the Indian Civil Service, and went back to India almost completely anglicized. He had clapped and waved when troops marched by in 1914 and had at first been thrilled to belong to this great Empire. It had been quite late in his school life before he began to perceive that he was not altogether a part of the country with which he had so completely identified himself. By the time he reached Oxford, he was already beginning to rebel against the propaganda of the war years, against the vindictive peace and against the idea of British rule in India.

Yet for twenty years he served the Raj in India, frankly expressing his views, which were often critical, and earning himself a slight reputation as a rebel. It is only later and in retrospect that he pays a tribute to the fairness of his superiors who did not let his views count against him. But his criticism was made invariably from the point of view of an English liberal who happened to have been born in India; he had not yet perceived the depth of the gulf—on which he now insists—between English ethical and administrative standards and those of Hindu India. The difference of approach was borne in on him when he became Chief Secretary under the second Congress Ministry in the U.P. shortly before independence, and he

xiv   *Foreword*

resigned from this important post, thinking that he might
be happier in a district once more.

In the central part of his book, there is scathing criticism of
Indian political leaders, of the world of make-believe about
which they make speeches, and of the Indian capacity for
self-deception. It is with generosity that he turns back to
assess British rule. Indeed there are moments when it is positively embarrassing—to the present writer at least—to read
an appraisal of British rule with so much of which one so
exactly concurs. This is still more the case when Bonarjee comes
to compare British rule in India with any hypothetical alternatives—German, French, Russian or American; particularly
as regards America, I could not go with him all the way.
American treatment of the Amerindians is something to which
many British officials in India often referred without taking
so much trouble as Bonarjee has done to find out what
happened, but I think he has missed a point of importance.
The Red Indians were on the Americans' doorstep—just
as the Nagas and the Lushai were on India's; British rule in
India got under way at a time when letters from London
often took more than a year to arrive in Calcutta. And the
British official in India did not mean to stay; he could afford
to be Olympian and just. Further, the Indian Empire dates
from after the loss of the American colonies and all that Burke
had had to say about little minds and great empires had not
been forgotten. Political decentralisation had become a part
of the British way of thinking.

Mr Bonarjee's book ends with perhaps the most interesting
section of all, an attempt to assess British rule in the light of
Hindu philosophy. He is far from dogmatic but suggests,
I think, that Queen Victoria will be merely one of many
Sultans of whom each, one by one, 'Abode his destined hour
and went his way'. All is illusion and there is no true change
until change ceases to have meaning. It is a view which might
in a modified form be taken even by an historian who was not
in the least sympathetic with Hindu philosophy. In the long
record of India's rulers, how few there are whose names have
any meaning and whose actions have had any influence. But
it is not true of all. Bonarjee himself quotes Asoka and Akbar,
both of whom surely influenced India's institutions for many

years; indeed Akbar's revenue system, modified by the British, persisted till today. In the opposite sense, surely the character of Aurangzebe had a profound effect on history. The influence of the British was greater than any of these Emperors'. As Bonarjee says himself, the criticisms today directed at a largely British political and administrative system are many of them based on British values. The Raj, however, should be compared with dynasties, not with individuals, and I would argue that the Mauryas, the Guptas, the Mughals and the British have left their mark on India. But then I do not believe that all is *maya* and see little point in reading or writing history if you do.

Mr. Bonarjee has now returned to the Hindu fold but seems to accept many of its characteristic tenets with a certain intermittency, perhaps believing that they have validity of varying degrees in various dimensions of thought. It is an attitude that is valuable to anyone who accepts in general a traditional religious system. His book has more in it of Dulwich than of the Bhagavad-Gita.

This is essentially a just book, fair, clear and honest, and I hope it is read with the attention it deserves.

4 August 69

PHILIP MASON

The author

I

Westward Ho!

SITUATED close to the banks of the river Ganga as it flows through the central portion of Uttar Pradesh, the United Provinces of the British, is the ancient and once very sacred town of Kanauj. When I knew it in 1927, it was a somewhat derelict, though picturesque, township, with many old temples and archaeological remains, the mournful relics of former magnificence: but thirteen hundred years earlier, as Kanyakubja, it was the capital city of Harsha, the ruler of a vast empire stretching from the river Sutlej in the north-west to a portion at least of modern Bengal in the east, and from the mountains of Nepal in the north to the wooded hills of central India.[1] Well-planned, and beautified with many tanks and gardens, its inhabitants were more or less equally divided between followers of Brahminical Hinduism and Mahayana Buddhism. It was in short an imperial city of opulence and splendour, well befitting its emperor.

On the death of Harsha his empire disintegrated, and with its dissolution Bengal came into its own again. Bengali tradition has much to say about one Raja Adisura of Gaur or Lakshmanavati, who ruled about A.D. 700. Adisura, a staunch adherent of orthodox Brahminism, noted with disfavour the inroads made by Buddhism, and determined to restore the former power and influence of orthodoxy. In need of erudite Brahmin scholars for his purpose, he turned for assistance to Kanyakubja, where there had been a widespread revival of Brahminism after the death of Harsha. Tradition has it that under orders from Raja Vir Singh, who was in sympathy with the policy of Adisura, five Brahmins, prospective missionaries, left their ancestral temples in Kanyakubja, and accompanied

---

[1] There is uncertainty amongst modern scholars regarding the boundaries of Harsha's empire in Bengal into which it is unnecessary for me to enter. According to the *Oxford History of India* his dominions included 'at least the greater part of Bengal', and the map on p. 166 takes the frontiers up to the kingdom of Kamarupa. Moreland and Chatterjee in their *Short History of India* (1945) seem to have accepted this in general, but point out that 'there is some doubt as to the position of the Kingdom of Gaur in Bengal'. The question is of no importance in my context.

by an equal number of attendants of a less favoured caste, the
Kayastha, started on their long journey to Lakshmanavati in
Bengal. It is to these ten that most Bengali Brahmin and
Kayastha families trace their origins.

In the middle of the 12th century Raja Ballalasen is said to
have conferred on some members of the families of the original
five priests the status of Kulins, or Brahmins possessing the nine
virtues such as piety, scholarship, spiritual experience and the
like. Fifty six were honoured in this manner, and in addition
were given grants of villages. Thereafter they took names derived
from their villages (*gain-nama* or *gramina-nama*), such as
Bandurjya, Chaturjya, Mukhurjya and so on, which in the 18th
century came to be written in English as Banerjee, Chatterjee,
Mukherjee. During the same century the names were Sanskri-
tized into Bandyopadhyay, Chattopadhyay and Mukhopadhyay,
in order to give a touch of antiquity to which their owners
laid claim.[1] In the case of ourselves, Bandurjya completed
its linguistic metamorphosis by being finally anglicized into
Bonarjee; and I once heard of a Chatterji who went a step
farther and chose to call himself Chattairj! Such were the
minor consequences of the impact of the West.

In his *Oxford History of India* Vincent Smith holds that there
is historical basis for the original tradition; and Marshman
fifty years earlier had already accepted it in its entirety.[2] Whatever may have been their origins, however, whether the tradition is mere legend, or, as is more probable, a combination of
legend and fact, the Kulins became an integral and important

---

[1] The story of the origins of the Kulins in Bengal is by no means clear, and
the one I have given is, I understand, the most modern theory. I am indebted to
Prof. S. K. Chatterji for it. There are, however, many other traditions, as for
example, that Raja Adisura, who had no son, invited the Brahmin priests from
outside in order to perform a *Putreshti Yajna;* and again that there were two groups
of Brahmins, one of which, consisting of nine 'ga-ins', was subsequently honoured
by Raja Ballalasen. Here, too, the matter has no bearing on my subject matter
and is really of interest only to antiquaries.

[2] Vincent Smith, *The Oxford History of India* (1920), p. 185. Marshman in his
History of India (1872), vol i, p. 26, records the following: 'The only authentic
event to be further recorded previous to the irruption of Mahmud of Ghazni
relates to the Kingdom of Bengal. Cunouj, the cradle and citadel of Hinduism,
had recovered its importance under a new dynasty. Adisur, of the Vidyu or medical
race of kings, then ruling Bengal, became dissatisfied with the ignorance of his
priests and applied to the king of Cunouj for a supply of Brahmins well versed
in the Hindoo shastras and observances. That monarch about nine centuries ago
sent him five Brahmins from whom all brahmin families trace their origin, while
the Kayasthas, the next in order, derive their origin from the five servants who
attended the priests.'

part of Bengal's life and culture. Peaceful obscurity seems to
have been the lot of our particular section of Bandurjyas for
generations, for I do not know of anyone who achieved anything
spectacular in his day save perhaps for one Sabarnanda who is
said to have made a name for himself as an astrologer and
after whom the family were designated Sabarnanda Brahmins
for some time. From the practical, as opposed to the purely
antiquarian standpoint it was not until Pitambar Bandyopadhyay,
several generations after Sabarnanda, that the family launched
out into deep, hitherto uncharted and even dangerous waters.
Pitambar was my great-grandfather. His span of seventy two
years, from 1783 to 1855, covered a crucial period; for his birth
coincided with the gathering in Europe of the ominous clouds
heralding the French Revolution, and by the time of his death
the British had not only completed their supremacy over the
whole of the Indian subcontinent but had also extended their
empire securely over all five continents.

Pitambar broke with family tradition. Drawn by the pull of
Calcutta, now no longer the centre of a mere trading company
but the headquarters of one of the many contenders for political
power in India, he moved there from Baganda with his family
at an early age. Here he took up employment with an English
attorney and solicitor, Mr Bird (soon to form the partnership
of Collier and Bird), who was attached to the East India
Company's Supreme Court. Rising to the position of Banian or
Superintendent—a post of influence, and even of some authority
at a time when English judges were not very conversant with
the complexities of Hindu law, Pitambar made sufficient money
to be very comfortably situated in life. The earthiness of his
profession, however, was not allowed to kill all his religious
instincts, for he dissipated his competence freely in charitable
gifts of all kinds, thereby earning the title of 'Raja Mahasaya'
from his friends and acquaintances at a Caste Panchayat, but
apart from that gaining nothing whatsoever.[1]

By marriage Pitambar became the son-in-law of the well-
known Pandit Jagannath of Tribeni who was commissioned by
the East India Company to translate into English the various
laws, rules and customs embodied in traditional Hindu law.

[1] Raja Mahasaya or Mahasay signifies a very highly esteemed person.

A competent linguist, he had added a good knowledge of English to his Sanskrit and Bengali, and he joined his father-in-law in the work. It was thus my great-grandfather who was the first to turn the attention of the family in some degree towards the West.

The tide of events was now moving rapidly and by the time Pitambar was thirty years of age British dominion was supreme over a large part of the country. Its apparently irresistible expansion led inquisitive sections of the quick-witted Bengali community to ponder deeply over the reasons why a small band of traders sailing in wooden ships from an island ten thousand miles away should have been able to accomplish so much so easily and so rapidly. What, they asked themselves, was wrong with the Hindu that he succumbed with little resistance to all comers, irrespective of whether the invaders came through the north-western passes or by way of the ocean? The critical, intellectual movement which had already been set in motion by Raja Ram Mohan Roy now commenced to spread. Unorthodox in content, it devoted itself to a serious examination of the harsh, unbending framework of caste in which the Hindu had encased himself for centuries, and of its possible consequences.

One of Pitambar's eight sons, Shib Chunder, my grandfather, was to become revolutionary in his religious ideas, while a nephew of the latter, the son of Girish Chunder, attracted more by English political and social ideas, was destined for eminence in India's political life. This last was Womesh (originally Umesh) Chunder, who abandoned the traditional Bandyopadhyay and then by-passed Banerjee for Bonnerjee. Possessed of a rebellious and adventurous spirit, young Womesh resolved at an early age to break with caste by crossing the unholy seas and going to England. Coming up against vehement opposition from his father, from some of his immediate relations and from the Kulin community in general, he had recourse to subterfuge. Taking advantage of the Bejoya ceremony during the Durga Pujas he ran away from home and was given shelter by an English lawyer, Cockerel Smith, who sympathized with the boy's spirit and smuggled him off to London. Here he was in great financial difficulties for some months. He had already been awarded a scholarship for study in

England from a fund established by a wealthy Parsee, Jamsetjee Jeejeebhai, but what with the surreptitious mode of his hasty departure on the one hand and the seemingly uncompromising opposition of his father on the other, much time elapsed before funds materialized. It took even longer for Girish Chunder and the die-hards of the family entirely to forgive and forget, and to agree that on his return the customary purificatory ceremonies would be sufficient to wash away the original sin of crossing the ocean.

Called to the English Bar in 1864, Womesh returned home to amass a considerable fortune as a barrister and in due course to become not only the leader of the Calcutta Bar, but also of political India. Together with Allan Octavian Hume,[1] Surendranath Banerjea, Dadabhai Naoroji and several others, English, it should be noted, as well as Indian, he took a leading part in the foundation of the Indian National Congress, of which he was twice President, first at the opening session in 1885 and again in 1892. At a later stage of his life during a stay of some years in England he stood for election to the House of Commons as a Liberal candidate. Undeterred at his failure at the first attempt, he intended to try again when death took him away shortly before the General Election of 1906 while he was on his way back to India to lead the agitation against the partition of Bengal. He had considerable influence with many Liberal members of Parliament and other sympathizers with the Indian cause such as the very radical M.P., Charles Bradlaugh; and he spent money freely on India's behalf, the expenses of the Parliamentary Committee in London being paid entirely from his own pocket. On his death he was the recipient of many well-deserved tributes, in the light of which it is a pity that his name and selfless work in the national cause (he twice refused a High Court judgeship to avoid giving up his work for the Congress) have long been buried in oblivion along with those of many other patriotic men who laid the foundations of national revival.[2]

---

[1] Allan is the spelling given in Buckland's *Dictionary of Indian Biography*.

[2] At a memorial meeting held on the death of W. C. Bonnerjee, G. K. Gokhale, the eminent Congress leader from Maharashtra, said: 'Mr. Bonnerjee's claim to our admiration and gratitude rested, of course, on a much wider basis than his pre-eminent attainment as a lawyer. He was in addition an ardent patriot .... and since that time (the foundation of the Congress) to the moment

W. C. Bonnerjee was not the first of the family to be outcasted, for Shib Chunder had forestalled him by many years
by an act of even greater impiety than crossing the ocean.
Womesh Chunder had turned to the political and material
West, but had remained a Hindu, in theory at least, although
his wife and two of his daughters were eventually to adopt
Christianity. But my grandfather felt the call of the religious
West. Nearly a century earlier the valiant Ram Mohan Roy,
in the face of tribulations which amounted almost to persecu-
tion, had fathered a break from Brahminical Hinduism with
the foundation of the Brahmo Samaj, an organisation which
followed a kind of Unitarianism mixed with elements of Vedic
Hinduism and which had attracted many adherents in Bengal.[1]
In Shib Chunder's case a combination of emotional and intellectual revolt pushed him the whole way in his religious deviation.
Born in 1830, he came at an early age under the influence of
Alexander Duff, the famous Scottish missionary and educa-
tionist, and was received into the Christian faith in 1847. His
conversion, along with three other Kulins, the first in that
inflexible community, was no mere ceremonial, and touched
off a great commotion which took time to die down.[2] But Shib
Chunder had now burnt his boats and by thus rejecting once
and for all the shrines of the Kali Bari Temple in favour of the
Chapel—Alexander Duff belonging to the Free Church of
Scotland—completely broke the restrictive bonds of a long
tradition. Inevitably prompt outcasteing followed as a natural
course. Expelled from the family residence and property, Shib
Chunder faced considerable privation at an early age. His
financial hardships were temporarily alleviated somewhat by
Alexander Duff himself, but it was the Bengal Government
which finally came to his rescue by giving him a post in the
Finance Department. This enabled him to live in modest
comfort and in due course to give his children a good education.
Many years later on retirement, by which time reconciliation

---

of his death, Mr. Bonnerjee, with two or three others, was the life and soul of
the movement. *He ungrudgingly gave to the cause his time and his resources — and this far
more than is generally known*' (my italics).
    [1] Ram Mohan Roy (1774-1833) turned against orthodox Hinduism as a boy
when he witnessed the unwilling death of his brother's widow on the funeral
pyre of her husband.
    [2] William Paton, *Alexander Duff: Pioneer of Missionary Education*, p. 138.

with his relations had taken place, he entered the Ministry and with the passage of time became one of the recognised leaders of the Christian Church in Bengal. He died in 1897 after a long illness, his tenure as Pastor of the Scottish Church in Cornwallis Square being commemorated in a memorial tablet there. In the meantime the Bengal Government continued to treat him with great consideration, and even went to the generous, though incongruous, extent of offering him the title of Raja. But Shib Chunder having chosen his God, rejected mammon on principle, preferring to remain an unadorned Reverend and devoting the remainder of his life to his calling and, like his father before him, to philanthropy.[1] His linguistic attainments were remarkable; for in order to delve more deeply into the Old and New Testaments he acquired a working knowledge of Hebrew for the first and Greek for the second in addition to his Sanskrit, Bengali and English.

The punishment of 'outcasteing' having fallen into disuse, its possible consequences mean nothing today, and it is difficult for the modern generation of trippers and commuters to the West to realize their debt to the first generation of pioneers. But a century ago the revolutionary few who were prepared to risk the hazards of foreign travel even became the recipients of an honourable mention in the English-owned newspapers. In the 'One Hundred Years Ago' column of the *Times of India*, for example, there appeared recently an extract from the issue of April 3rd 1867 which referred to 'the hardships of caste expulsion' in the case of the departure of a handful of Indians to visit the Paris Exhibition. 'The terrors of excommunication from caste,' continued the extract, 'far more instant in their action and dread than the thunders of Rome, have already been held over these, but they persevere in their intention.'[2] A far cry, indeed, from the time when the problem was not how to persuade people of all sorts to travel abroad, but owing to the lack of foreign exchange to prevent them from doing so.

After a short period as a widower Shib Chunder married a

---

[1] Buckland, *Dictionary of Indian Biography*, p. 48. This contains a short note on Shib Chunder.

[2] The grand total, excluding two Parsees, to whom Caste did not apply, was eleven and the list as shown in the paper sounds quaint to modern ears! 'One Panjabee, three Purboos, one Brahmin from Gujarat, two Baniyas, two Bhattias, and two Bhousalees.'

second time, and once more fell foul of orthodox Bengal. Not
content with having changed the family religion, he now
changed its blood, his new bride being a Sikhni. My grand-
mother, orphaned in early life, had been in charge of her two
brothers, who in their turn died fighting in the Sikh wars against
the East India Company. The young girl, now guardianless,
was given a temporary home by a kindly officer of the
Company's Forces, Colonel Anderson. Finally placed under
the care of missionaries in Calcutta she too not unnaturally
adopted Christianity. She married my grandfather in 1866
and died in 1915 or 1916 in her eighties. A handsome woman,
reputed to be of very strong character, her family always stood
in considerable awe of her; and from what I recall of a portrait
once in our possession I can well believe it.

There were five children of the marriage, four sons and
a daughter. Something of the split personality found in all
educated Indians to this day appears to have come to the front
in the names given to them. The two eldest sons were
Debendranath (my father) and Pitambar; but the third was
named Alexander Duff after the missionary and the youngest
Vernon Mackay after an old family friend. The girl was always
Aunt Grace to us. To complete the picture I may add that the
call of Christianity had become so strong by this time that my
uncle Pitambar, after a spell in the Military Accounts Department, retired from Government service and followed his father
into the Ministry, on entering which he settled in England.
During my Oxford days he held an incumbency in Reading,
and thereafter in Brighton. My uncle Duff, on the other hand,
though staunchly Christian, never felt the 'call'. He appreciated
the less austere aspects of life such as good food (he was no mean
cook of Bengali dishes), good wine and good company, and was
much addicted to Epsom Downs, Newmarket, Goodwood and
similar pleasure resorts, a pastime which not infrequently
brought him into mild conflict with my father who disapproved
of such frivolities. The last of the brothers, my uncle Mackay,
whom I met in my infancy before we sailed for England but do
not remember, was a Deputy Collector and Magistrate in
Bengal. All died many years ago.[1]

[1] Of the three sons of my uncles, one is now with the B.B.C. Another is also
in London with the Indian High Commission, and the third, after retiring from the

Western influences in the family continued. In 1885 my father proceeded to London to sit for the I.C.S. examination. This was a far more difficult hurdle for young Indians then than it was to be later, the age limit being fixed at nineteen. Young Englishmen took the examination straight from school, and, if successful, spent the next two years at Oxford or Cambridge. Since the subjects were closely related to the ordinary curriculum of the public schools with its emphasis on Greek and Latin, the handicap for the Indian was present from the start. Although my father was not successful, one of his achievements was remarkable. He headed the list in English. For this reason, perhaps, it was not altogether surprising that on his return home with a small feather in his cap he tried his hand at journalism, a profession for which he retained his liking throughout his life.

Coming to the notice of two veterans of the Indian journalistic world of the period, James Wilson of *The Indian Daily News* and Robert Knight of *The Statesman*, two good friends of India, he was appointed editor of the first paper. The vast difference between the times, the hiatus between then and now, was well exemplified by the attitude of another English-owned daily. *The Englishman*, one of the most important and influential newspapers of the day, found it 'regrettable that a native should occupy the editorial chair of so important and well-known a paper'. This not very eulogistic comment, however, not only misfired but also turned out to be an excellent certificate; for its first effect was to bring my father to the attention of Sir George Allen, a liberal-minded Gladstonian and head of Cooper, Allen and Co. of Cawnpore. Sir George Allen was the owner of two other influential papers, *The Pioneer* of Allahabad (now of Lucknow) and *The Civil and Military Gazette* of Lahore, and it was at his instance that my father migrated to the Punjab.

Journalism neither retained nor maintained my father for long. In 1892 he married and with this the whole direction of his life was altered. My mother's father, Ishan Chunder Sirkar, belonged to a Christian family of Chandernagore, but at what stage the family adopted Christianity I do not know. Presumably the change took place before my maternal grand-

Indian Air Force in 1948 as a Wing Commander, entered the I.A.S. and is now a member of the Board of Revenue, Bengal.

father's time or during his boyhood, for he was never outcasted and according to his will retained his share of the ancestral house and property in Chandernagore. Ishan Chunder left his home early in life for the study of engineering at the recently established Thomason College at Roorkee in the then North-Western Provinces, a most unusual ambition for a young Indian at a time when the lack of even mechanics had forced British railway engineers to import them from England. On passing out from the College he was appointed to the Public Works Department in the Punjab, where he spent the whole of his official career, an expatriate Bengali never to return to his ancestral Chandernagore. His service life, however, was relatively short: for on reaching the rank of Executive Engineer he decided to retire and settle on the land.

The land itself was there for the asking. There were vast tracts of uninhabited forest and jungle in the wild areas of Oudh bordering on the still wilder lands of Nepal, particularly in the districts of Kheri, Bahraich and Gonda. After the suppression of the Mutiny and the confiscation of all land in Oudh to the Crown, the decision was taken to sell these waste lands in compact blocks, free of land revenue, to anyone willing to clear, settle and bring them under cultivation. In 1874 my maternal grandfather purchased three blocks in south Kheri totalling some 9000 acres. The buyers of such lands, legally termed Grantees, were not subject to the ordinary customary law governing the relations between landlord and tenant, since the Crown itself did not possess these customary rights. Once the Crown had taken over possession it automatically became the owner of the 'fee simple', the highest form of ownership in English law, and the title deeds of the sales transferred the 'fee simple' to the purchaser.

The work of pioneering oneself into the landed squirearchy, however, proved to be extremely onerous, and what was far worse, extremely expensive. The climate was very unhealthy, and cholera, malaria and a miscellaneous assortment of jungle fevers were endemic. Labour for the arduous tasks of clearance was hard to come by, and even after months of strenuous, un-ending work had succeeded in clearing a small patch of forest, tenants to take it up were as scarce as labour—an obstacle which actually forced my grandfather to pay out large sums from his own pocket in order to persuade men from Shahjahanpur, the neighbouring district, to come in and farm it. Communications were primitive. Even where they existed, they consisted of mere tracks through the tiger grass and the thick, deep forests, and only an unmetalled road connected the whole area with the district headquarters at Lakhimpur, thirty-five miles away. The railway was an unknown luxury, and until the metre-gauge line from Lucknow to Kathgodam in the Himalayan foothills was constructed through our Grants in the middle eighties, the nearest line was the broad-gauge at Shahjahanpur: and a journey to Shahjahanpur was in the nature of a major expedition, since it necessitated a trip lasting ten days or so in a *shikram.* This last, a light, two-wheeled cart drawn by specially bred trotting bullocks, is an excellent conveyance in the Indian countryside for a journey of ten or twelve miles, but for ten or twelve days is a slow mode of progress. A century ago it was not even sure: for on one occasion when my mother and her sister were returning home from school in Mussoorie, the whole party was held up by a gang of dacoits and looted of all its possessions, including the estate cash-box, the contents of which had fortunately already been deposited in the bank at Shahjahanpur.

Life in the wilds, a combination of the maximum of hazard with the minimum of profit, was thus neither easy nor comfortable in the last decades of the nineteenth century. It was not surprising, therefore, that long before his three Grants had been cleared and brought under the plough, my grandfather found that he was investing far more in the land than he was able to extract from it. To replenish the rapidly diminishing family coffers he decided to return for a time to his original profession. He was offered, and accepted, the post of Chief Engineer in Kashmir, which at that time was one of the serene, peaceful, happy countries of the world, combining natural beauty and charm with the added attraction of a healthy climate. It would have taken a very bold man, if not Cassandra herself, to have suggested that sixty years later its halcyon days would be over, and that Kashmir would be transformed not only into one of India's political and communal difficulties but also into a problem with uncomfortable international repercussions.

Here my grandfather remained for five years. But however
strong the pull of Srinagar may have been, the lure of Kheri
was far stronger, and as soon as he could my grandfather
returned to his land, to continue his work on it until his death
in 1893. Grants 3 and 11 with their headquarters at
Sirkarnagar were inherited by my aunt, while 18, Rampore,
devolved on my mother, whose marriage to my father had
taken place a short time before my grandfather's death.
Marriage brought my father also to the land, and he and my
mother settled down in their turn to develop their inheritance.
My brother was born in 1893, and my sister eighteen months
later; but I, a late comer on the stage, did not follow suit
until Sunday, March 10th, 1901 in Lucknow. For the eleven
years that intervened between the death of my grandfather
and our departure to England in 1904, my parents remained
out in the wilds, with no amenities and little companionship
but their own in conditions described by my father as being
almost the same as when the estate had been acquired some
twenty years earlier. 'They were still very primitive,' he wrote
later, 'with no social amenities outside the District Headquarters. Town servants shrank from the prospect of jungle
fevers. One at least of my orderlies was an ex-convict, and
incendiarism and violence made lurid patches in a countryside
of evil repute.'

Security of life and property was not enhanced by the
presence of some of the many gipsy tribes of the Province,
Nats, Kanjars, Sansiahs and others, whose menfolk lived by
petty theft and women by plying for hire in their wanderings
around the countryside. Left to their own devices by all previous
rulers, they forced themselves on the notice of the British
Government not only as an administrative but also a social
problem. Together with the passage of restrictive legislation the
Government encouraged religious and charitable organizations
to work for their reclamation. The Salvation Army were prominent in this throughout India; but in one such settlement
of Sansiahs a few miles from our Grant it was the local American
Methodist Mission that took up the work for some time.
It is noteworthy that the number of conversions was infini-
tesimal, there being only a total of 417 Christians in the whole
District in 1901. I mention this because, apart from the great

work done by Christian missionaries in the fields of education
and medical aid in the towns, their selfless and devoted labours
among the poor and downtrodden, the outcastes, the lepers,
all the flotsam and jetsam of the Hindu social system, have
seldom been given the appreciation they deserve. If some
few conversions resulted, what of it, when Hinduism itself had
thrown out these unfortunates from its fold for no fault of their
own save the metaphysical one of expiating the sins of their
past lives in the present, and had neglected them for millenia?
India has no doubt produced her rishis and her saints, in very
recent times even a maharishi of international notoriety, but
the Dr Schweitzers, if any, are few and far between.

Even after independence the fear of conversions to Christianity remains almost an obsession in some quarters, although the
actual number cannot be large. In the fifties an official
Committee roundly condemned the activities of foreign Missions
in Madhya Pradesh, and some years later there were reports
in the Press that seven missionaries, including four nursing
sisters, had been barred from working in the Tezpur Hospital
in Assam. It may be granted that Assam, with the Naga and
Mizo tribes (both largely Christian) in rebellion against the
Government, is a touchy area; but even so it is difficult to
see what harm nurses can do in a hospital, especially in a
country where there is a chronic shortage of nursing sisters
and where nursing is not considered a fit occupation for Hindu
girls of the higher castes. Then only recently there was the
interesting case of Father Ferrer, a Spanish missionary, whose
work in the villages of Maharashtra was highly praised by the
villagers themselves, but was equally strongly condemned by
the State Government as being 'undesirable' and 'anti-national'.
At the instance of the latter, Father Ferrer's residential permit
was cancelled. These orders were subsequently modified, but
the Father's position at the moment of writing is in doubt.

There are, I think, three important aspects of this apparent
obsession. First, it is an indication of a deep inferiority complex.
Secondly, its open expression is a denial of the concept of the
secular State, since the latter should not concern itself with
the religion of its citizens. Thirdly, it correlates nationalism
and desirable activities with a particular religion, the religion
of the majority. There is already a sizeable Christian population

of all varieties and sects in India which is a part of the so-called
Indian nation. Why, then, should it be classed as anti-national
to join it or to persuade others to do so? There is, in fact, a large
body of evidence in contemporary India to support Nirad
Chaudhuri's thesis that fundamentally the existing State is a
Hindu State. There is nothing wrong in this. What is wrong is
the refusal to face up to the fact.

I write this without any special feelings one way or the
other, for in 1928 I myself rejoined the Hindu fold. The term
'Hindu' resembles the term 'Jew' inasmuch as it connotes
both a people (or rather a conglomeration of peoples) and a
religion, and in saying that I rejoined the 'fold' I do not mean
the religion, although later on I became very interested in
watching the pull of the latter on Indian attitudes and performance. Since I had entered the I.C.S. by open competition
and not as a nominated representative of the Christian community, as, indeed, I could have done, the Government remained—and rightly so—completely indifferent to my religion
—or lack of it; and the only really interesting sidelight on this
event in my life was provided by the pandit who officiated over
the ceremony on the return of the prodigal. His theory was:
'Once a Brahmin, always a Brahmin, whatever may have been
the deviations of one's ancestors'—a truly comforting doctrine,
provided it was not applied, *mutatis mutandis*, if one had
started off as an outcaste.

Our closest neighbours were the Hearseys, who deserve
more than a passing reference. Their estates, legally designated
a *taluka* (of which more later), bordered on Rampore Grant,
and the Hearsey of the day lived at Mamri only a mile away.
The Hearseys were one of a small band of families of mixed
blood such as the Skinners, Wheelers and others which had
played a great part not only in building up British political
power but also in laying the foundations of what was afterwards to be transformed into the Indian Army. By the end
of the Great Rebellion of 1857 the head of the family had risen
to the rank of Major-General in the East India Company's
Bengal Army, and for their great services in 1857, the family
were rewarded with the grant of a large *taluka* in Oudh to
add to the vast estates already acquired elsewhere. It is a
discreditable reflection on the British that once they had

achieved political supremacy, they promptly kicked away
one of the ladders by which they had climbed to it. Their
contempt for these eminent families of mixed blood was
commonly expressed in such terms as 'a touch of the tar brush'
and the like, and one incident, somewhat akin to that of *The
Englishman* and my father was a good example of the manners
and modes of the age, before racial pride and prejudice,
'hubris' in short, had been toned down by a broadening of
intellectual and moral horizons.

After the Company's three Presidency Armies had been
consolidated into the Indian Army, the head of the Hearseys,
like the head of the Skinners, was always given by way of
hereditary right a Queen's commission in the General's old
regiment (later the 2nd Lancers). In one case this turned out
to be a dubious honour; for when in the nineties of the last
century the convention was duly followed, *The Pioneer* printed
a report from Rudyard Kipling which deeply deplored the
fact that 'a half-caste' had been given it. The latter in a fit
of righteous indignation picked up his riding whip, travelled
post-haste to Allahabad and burst into that holy of holies,
the editorial sanctum. Here, not content with a non-violent
verbal battering, he gave the surprised editor—a product of
Oxford—a sound horse-whipping in addition, and returned
in triumph to Kheri—a short-lived triumph, alas, since the
editor had the last word by successfully prosecuting him for
assault.[1]

Another incident some years later, on this occasion again
relating to my father, was equally illustrative of the inherent
feeling of racial superiority which permeated, with rare exceptions, Anglo-Indian society. In the course of his legal career
my father was once compelled to ask the permission of the
Court to declare one of his witnesses 'hostile'. Holding this to
be an unseemly, even impertinent, request, the witness, an
English bank manager of some social standing, lodged a
complaint with the District Magistrate. The latter in full
agreement sent off a peremptory order to my father demanding

[1] I first heard of this episode from my mother. It has been authenticated
by Dennis Holman in his recently published *Sikandar Sahib, the Life of Major General
James Skinner, C.B.* According to Holman (p. 213): '*The Pioneer* newspaper published an article by a reporter named Rudyard Kipling in which Andrew Hearsey
was described as a half-caste. . . .'

an explanation for the apparently unpardonable offence of calling an Englishman 'hostile' in a court of law, and thereby putting him in the unpleasant position of being proved a liar under cross-examination. Here, however, the District Magistrate reckoned without his host, as my father afterwards put it, for the latter was on the point of proceeding to England to see the family. On arrival in London he got into touch with *Truth*, a plain-spoken weekly journal always ready to campaign on behalf of justice for all irrespective of the pigmentation of the skin. *Truth*, having satisfied itself of the correctness of the complaint, took the matter into the House of Commons, where, on a question being put to the Secretary of State, an inquiry was ordered. On the outbreak of war in 1914, however, my father himself dropped the matter; but to round it off it is pleasant to be able to add that both parties having had their say became quite friendly. It was almost a *reductio ad absurdum* that the District Magistrate in question was at a later stage in his career moved into the Judicial branch of the I.C.S. and when I entered the Service was adorning the High Court, having presumably cast aside his former objections to the impropriety of witnesses being declared hostile.

Both my parents were very charitably inclined, especially my father, who gravitated that way by heredity. My mother with her education at the Convent of Jesus and Mary in Mussoorie and her subsequent experience as honorary secretary of the Indian Women's Education Association in London, was always a strong advocate of education for Indian girls, and in this hobby was aided and abetted by my father who subscribed to the view that to educate the mother was to educate the child. Taking up the cause of the Isabella Thoburn College at Lucknow, an American Mission foundation and the first college in India for the higher education of women, she founded and endowed a library and reading room there, both of which continue to flourish.[1] My father, too, developed similar tastes with special reference to the student community

[1] In founding this and other educational institutions in India the people of the U.S.A. were only repaying, no doubt unknowingly, a debt due. Of the two oldest universities in the U.S.A. one, Yale, owes its foundation to India. It was founded and endowed by Elihu Yale, an Englishman, who was Governor of Fort St. George at Madras from 1687 to 1691. He used the great wealth which he had amassed in India, not as might have been expected, for his native Oxford or Cambridge, but for the benefit of the American colonists.

Pitambar Bandyopadhay 1783-1855

Rev. Shib Chunder Bonarjee 1830-97

of Oudh, to which he now belonged by adoption. Having at various times helped many poor boys from the Grant and its neighbourhood, he conceived the idea of a library at Lucknow University which would combine the drabness of the textbook so beloved of the Indian student with a wider and more colourful education. To this end he provided his library with a large number of works on art and sculpture together with plaster casts and reproductions. This effort to broaden the cultural and intellectual outlook of the student, though laudable, was infructuous, and it was fortunate that my father died in 1941 before the student population in general were to prove that they had of their own accord broadened both in ways quite foreign to any known form of culture.

Activities of this kind served to illumine a facet of the Indian character which is all too often in evidence in every sphere of Indian life, the capacity to emphasize theory at the expense of practice and to combine an infinity of good intentions with a masterly inactivity in implementing them. It happened that in the thirties a philanthropist of Allahabad, Munshi Ishwar Saran, put forward a proposal for the establishment of a Home for Harijans (the new designation coined by the Mahatma for the depressed classes) and called for subscriptions. This was not only a deserving cause but was also one that was very much to the forefront at the time. The depressed and backward classes, the 'scheduled castes' of constitutional and legal documents, had been the subject of much acute controversy during the series of Round Table Conferences which had preceded the Government of India Act of 1935. Along with the Muslims they had been in the centre of the stage with much of the limelight on them. In answer to the call for donations my father sent his contribution to Munshi Ishwar Saran, and brought the scheme to the notice of others by circularizing his friends and a few strangers, too, who, in his opinion, would be sympathetic to a good cause. Although the Harijans were Hindus, albeit outcastes, and this was an opportunity of paying something more tangible towards a social purpose than lip-service, the only response my father received came from a *Muslim* nawab of generous and charitable nature, a leading figure in the political life of the Province whom I knew well but my father not at all. This trait in the

2

Indian character was exemplified on another occasion. My father had given an unsolicited donation to Rabindranath Tagore for the latter's cultural academy at Shantiniketan—a gift which marked the commencement of a friendship between the two. In expressing his thanks Tagore wrote in his somewhat mournful reply: 'It has deeply touched my heart by showing a genuine sympathy which I have so rarely met with for my cause, and thus been compelled to bear my burden unaided for these long, weary years. I have earned enough applause from my countrymen which has been of little use to me, and therefore whenever I received any suggestion of friendliness, I feel truly rewarded.'

The Hearseys were not the only *talukdars* (holders of *talukas*) in the vicinity. We were surrounded by *talukas*, Muhammdi, Mahewa, Oel and others, and the *talukdars* were of special importance both to Oudh as a whole and to the Government in particular. Many of their estates were vast in extent, covering in some cases about half of the district concerned, while the component villages often lay in two or more districts. The *talukdars*, as such, were the creation of the British after the Mutiny, but in fact were a revival of the old hereditary aristocracy which had acquired its rights and privileges generations earlier under previous rulers. Originally only farmers of the land revenue on behalf of the Mughal emperors, the *talukdars*, including all those in rebellion in 1857-58 but who laid down their arms by a fixed date, were granted *sanads* (title deeds) by the British Government, the first condition of which was absolute loyalty to the Crown. The *sanads* not only confirmed the original privileges—in so far as these did not conflict with the law—but also, with the confiscation of all land in Oudh to the Crown, granted the *talukdars* full proprietary rights in their specific areas. The former joint-ownership of land by co-sharing village owners was thus abolished at one stroke—for which the British came in for strong condemnation afterwards. In fairness, however, it must be said that the intention of the ruling Power, apart from the desire to build up an influential class of loyalists, was to raise a class of landed proprietors similar to the best Victorian landowners of the age—a body devoted to the development of agriculture and the general welfare of the tenantry. This was clear from the other essential clause of the *sanads* which laid down the promotion of the happiness, welfare and prosperity of the cultivator but which proved, as time passed by, to be only a vain and pious hope.

Like all aristocracies, the *talukdars* produced their oddities. More than one might have stepped straight out of the pages of Havelock Ellis or von Kraft-Ebbing. One tucked himself away in the recesses of his palace and seldom saw the street outside. Notorious as a miser, he kept his cash wealth in neat bundles of notes, securely locked away in wooden boxes. He counted the boxes at regular intervals, but never looked inside—an error which led to a great deal of wailing and gnashing of teeth on his death; for when a horde of claimants rushed *en masse* to lay their hands on whatever they could, they found, alas, that the white ants had long ago forestalled them. Then, too, there was the handsome Rajput, a member of the Provincial Legislative Council, who always wore his full regalia on his visits to the Deputy Commissioner. On arrival he would unbuckle the gold scabbard of his sword and lay it on the table for the Deputy Commissioner to touch lightly with his hand. It was not until this little ceremony was complete that ordinary conversation could proceed. Not that he followed this courtly procedure in all cases, according to a tale which went the rounds and which had a foundation in fact. It was said that he went one day to call on a newly-appointed sub-divisional magistrate. Accompanying him was a retainer carrying two gunny bags laden with silver rupees. The bags were dumped on the table in front of the surprised official, who waxed exceedingly indignant. The Raja, however, was in no way disturbed. 'Don't get excited,' said he, 'don't get excited. Some take it. Some don't. But I like to know at the start where I stand and with whom I have to deal. If you don't want it, I'll have it sent away'—which he did. An exceedingly tough character of the old Rajput school, he was fond of explaining that what he really understood was the sword and not the wordy wranglings of the Council House. He and I would occasionally fall out in our mutual dealings, for were there not rumours in circulation, dark hints, furtive whisperings, though no more, that some of the gang robberies in other areas were committed at his instigation? Yet he could often be helpful in difficult times, if he so wished: and although he could hardly win one's wholehearted approval, it was difficult not to like and appreciate his forthright, straightforward outlook and approach. It was said that on his death, long after I had left the District, tenants, shopkeepers and all turned out in a body to pay their last respects to the bier. As the procession wended its slow way along, the bystanders commiserated with one another. 'Ah,' they lamented, 'there goes a real man. He may have looted us himself, but he never allowed anyone else to do so.' And this, as I was to discover for myself, was not so surprising a reaction in the Indian context as might appear at first sight.

Not all the *talukdars* were oddities. Some were dignified, polished gentlemen, with cultivated tastes in music and art, and in Urdu and Persian poetry, delighting in living life to the full. These were the special protégés of Sir Harcourt Butler during his two terms as head of the Province. Sir Harcourt, an able and skilful administrator, who knew the art of managing men, limited his vision to the aristocracy of the Province, with particular reference to that of Lucknow, which he succeeded in converting into the *de facto* capital of the United Provinces in place of Allahabad. A genial extrovert, a *bon viveur*, and almost an honorary member of the *talukdari* clan, he was never happier than when he was in the company of a few *talukdars* of his choice.

Like all men, the *talukdars* had their good points. They were always ready—on official prompting, it is true—to subscribe to any cause sponsored by the Government, from the construction and to some extent, the maintenance of the Canning College at Lucknow to the provision of expensive decorations for a viceregal visit. Some maintained schools, colleges and hospitals in their estates, the best hospital in the Province being that of the largest *taluka* of all, Balrampur. Exceptions, too, here and there administered their estates efficiently, though with little thought for the interests of their tenants, who suffered considerably at the hands of extortionate subordinates in conditions where opportunities for graft of all kinds were endless.

As a class their faults greatly outweighed their virtues. Unnecessary pomp and ceremony, squandermania and an extraordinary adherence to the old proverb in the Oudh countryside that one could not be a real *rais* (country gentleman) without being in debt to the extent of one lakh of rupees at least, led to a heavy burden of encumbrances; so heavy, indeed, not merely in Oudh but throughout the whole Province, that the Government were compelled in the 1930s to come to the rescue of the landowners, big and small, with remedial legislation. While the *talukdars* scrupulously fulfilled the first condition of their *sanads*, loyalty to the Crown, the happiness, welfare and prosperity of their tenants sat very lightly on their souls. As an inevitable consequence the non-cooperation movement of the early 1920s and the civil disobedience campaigns that followed found fertile soil in the *talukas*.

My parents had nothing in common with the hereditary aristocracy, for whom they displayed a somewhat puritanical disapproval and from whom they were sharply differentiated by their simplicity, their lack of ostentation and, especially in the case of my father, their wholehearted devotion to the welfare of their tenantry. Here East and West had blended into an unusual amalgam. Both were well-educated, well-travelled and of cultivated tastes. Both had been abroad early in their lives—my mother quite possibly being the first Indian girl to see England—and were thus 'England-returned' at a time when this term carried with it something of the snob value of a peerage in Great Britain. On the surface neither appeared to be the type prepared to spend a large part of their lives in the Indian countryside. Indeed, my mother would certainly not have selected this way of life for herself had not the ownership of a few small hamlets placed on her the duties going with it. She was probably happiest during her stay of five years in the south of France. My father, on the contrary, enjoyed his life and work among the villagers, maintaining his contacts with the outer world through periodic visits to Europe and through his first love, journalism. This last he kept up till the end of his life. He collaborated with Sir Norcot Warren, the head of the (then) Imperial Bank of India, in an article on Central Banking in India for the London *Times Trade Supplement*, and wrote a number of pamphlets on various aspects of Indian village life and Indian agriculture. He also became very friendly with the late Sir Chiravoori Chintamani, the editor of the once influential newspaper of Allahabad, *The Leader*, who gave him the freedom of his columns at all times. Despite his anglicization, his rather serious Victorian liberalism, his admiration for the western humanism of his youth, he never entirely lost his inheritance from the past. Notwithstanding his criticisms too, of certain aspects of British rule, he retained his faith, even when it was badly mauled, in the British and the higher purpose of their empire in India. As he grew older the legacy of his heredity often came to the forefront in small ways. Nothing pleased and interested him more than to have long talks with the numerous sadhus who wandered into the Grant from time to time: and he won the hearts of his tenantry as much by bringing back from one of his many tours around India a large, long black stone smoothly polished by nature and picked up on the banks of the sacred river Narbada, as by looking after their material welfare. The villagers set up the stone under a peepul tree, built a platform round it, and duly garlanded it at intervals as the emblem of the deity Shiv. Judged by the conventional standards of the ordinary Indian provincial city or by those prevailing at a Delhi cocktail party, he was, I imagine, a mild but very pleasant and kindly eccentric, with no ambition whatsoever to be in the public eye. As he himself once put it: 'to every man his candle, as the French saying has it.'

If it was my paternal great-grandfather who first cast surreptitious glances towards the West, it was from my mother's side that we received an actual injection of the Occident. My maternal grandfather after his conversion to Christianity naturally sought a bride in the Christian community; and the one he found had Scots blood in her veins, her father being one Major Collins of the Bengal Native Infantry. Husband and wife parted company very early in their married lives, and Ishan Chunder Sirkar, having made provision for his wife, kept the custody of his two small daughters.

This was the family skeleton and as such was kept securely locked up in the family cupboard, never to be taken out and given a proper airing. My mother never treated herself as anything but an Indian, and the children were told little about their maternal great-grandfather—which I think was a pity.

It was not that he had an outstanding military career, since
whatever prospects he may have had, vanished early in his
service in a wound which incapacitated him and led to his
premature retirement from the Company's Army. Indeed,
his only claim to fame lay in the fact that he drew his pension
for the record period of fifty years (which must have made
him a great thorn in the flesh of the Government) before
death took him away at the ripe age of over ninety to be
buried in the cemetery at Mussoorie. Nevertheless, it would
have been of interest to have known more about him, his
antecedents in Scotland, the reasons that drew him into the
service of the East India Company (was there an Indian connexion or was he just turned out as the bad boy of the
family?) and the campaigns in which he had taken part.

The skeleton being there, there was nothing to be done
about it; and by a strange coincidence there chanced to be
another Bengali family in London with us with precisely the
same sort of one in *its* cupboard. We knew each other well,
but never peeped into each other's secrets. For myself I do
not regret this touch of Scotland. Indeed, I am inclined to
think that small infusions of outside blood at properly regulated
intervals might have done much to mitigate the generally
deleterious effects of an excessively long seclusion behind the
Himalayan barrier in the Gangetic plain, that 'vampire of
geography which sucks out all creative energy and leaves
its victims as listless shadows' in the telling phrase of Nirad
Chaudhuri.[1]

But the real personal importance of the infusion was that
it appeared to have worked itself out in me, with the novel
consequence that I was always the subject of much inquisitive
interest in Service circles. My confidential record contained
some highly speculative entries; but although the commentators

[1] 'There are many geographical regions in the world which are utterly
incapable of developing a high civilization, but there is perhaps not one other
which so irresistibly draws civilizations to it and strangles them so irresistibly as
does the Indo-Gangetic plain. It is the Vampire of geography which sucks out all
creative energy, and leaves its victims as listless shadows.' And again: 'So far no
foreigner in India—Aryan, Turk or Anglo-Saxon—has been able to escape
the consequences of living in the Indo-Gangetic plain. His energy has been
drained, his vitality sapped and his will and idealism enfeebled. Thus in the last
resort the perpetuation of the foreigner's rule and cultural function in India has
been dependent on continuous reinforcement from the home territory.' Nirad
Chaudhuri, *The Autobiography of an Unknown Indian* (Macmillan, 1951), pp. 502-3.

ranged over a fair selection of countries, no one got around
to Scotland, or even England for that matter. It was inevitable
that an heredity which included such diverse elements as
Bengal, the Punjab and Scotland would produce an unpredictable and explosive set of genes, one result of which was that
my westernization went deeper in many respects than a mere
veneer. An education, therefore, of twenty-one years in England
had a substantial foundation on which to build; and the actual
process of building was to commence in 1904, when the family
was taken across the seas to learn more about the distant
islanders, a handful of whom were ruling India, their achievements, and the qualities that had gone into them.

II

The Background

WHEN we arrived in London in October after a voyage of over one month from Calcutta, the great Queen who has given her name to an era in history had passed away only a few years before, at an advanced age and full of honour. A vivid word picture has been painted by Sir Winston Churchill of the period to follow, that short Edwardian and neo-Georgian interregnum between the nineteenth and twentieth centuries. 'Nations and Empires', he wrote in the first volume of his *World Crisis*, 'crowned with princes and potentates rose majestically on every side, accumulated treasures of the long peace. All were fitted, it seemed securely, into an immense cantilever. The two mighty European systems faced each other, glittering and clanking in their panoply, but with a tranquil gaze. A polite, discreet, and on the whole sincere diplomacy spread its web of connections over both. A sentence in a despatch, a cryptic phrase in Parliament, an observation by an ambassador seemed enough to adjust from day to day the balance of the prodigious structure.... The Old World in its sunset was fair to see.'

Despite the magic of Churchillian prose, however, history has clearly shown that the sunset was not as fair as its appearance from some angles. Tranquil though the gaze of the two mighty systems may have been on occasion, more often than not it was clouded over with hostility; and if the diplomacy of the Old World was generally more professional and decorous than that of the brave New World spawned by two World Wars, and was never directed to the market place, it was often neither sincere nor discreet. German diplomacy in particular during this period, and the years immediately preceding, was a classic example of indiscretion and toughness amounting almost to boorishness. The German Emperor had led the way with his notorious telegram of good wishes to President Kruger at the time of the Jameson Raid, and had pursued a similar course when he instructed the German contingent despatched to help in the suppression of the Boxer Rebellion in China to behave 'like Attila the Hun'—an infelicitous admonition which boomeranged with vigour on the Germans themselves in 1914. German diplomacy in general adopted much the same line and tone as that set by the Kaiser. At least twice in the decade before the outbreak of the first World War the iron hand was openly displayed for all to see: first when a thinly veiled threat of war was used to bring about the fall in 1905 of Delcassé, the French Foreign Minister, and again a few years later when the Kaiser in one of his periodic fits of histrionics ordered a small warship to Agadir as his contribution to the solution of the Moroccan crisis.

Nor, indeed, did German diplomacy stand alone. Germany's Austrian ally tended to take up similar postures from time to time, and the Government of the Austro-Hungarian Empire always adopted heavy-handed methods in the Balkans, with the hand more often than not rattling the sabre. Throughout the European continent, behind the rosy tints, were the deep rumblings of the national ambitions and animosities which heralded the storm of 1914, the rumblings which led to Lord Rosebery's gloomy foreboding in 1912 that 'this calm before the storm is terrifying'.

The decade from 1904 to 1914 seemed to many at the time to be the zenith of Great Britain's power and influence. Stability, security and Empire were the watchwords of the age. The recurrence of international crises and war scares, even actual outbreaks of war in Tripoli and the Balkans, did not shake the Englishman's firm belief until 1914 in reason as the governing factor in human actions, and in the essential virtue of the human race—or at any rate the fortunate European section of it. God was in His Heaven and, therefore, all was right with the world. God, moreover, was assumed to have a special affection for Great Britain; for how else would Britannia have risen from the azure main to rule the waves? The foolishness of war on a general scale was conclusively proved by two such serious writers as Norman Angell[1] and G. H. Perris[2] only a few years before the murders at Sarajevo actually precipitated one. Deplorable local conflicts might be inevitable in such rough and ready places as the Balkans;

---

[1] Norman Angell, *The Great Illusion*, (Heinemann, 1909).
[2] G. H. Perris, *History of War and Peace*, (Home University Library, 1911).

colonial and frontier expeditions might be necessary to 'teach the natives a lesson'; but few, even in high places, imagined that the 'two mighty European systems, glittering in their panoply' were soon to be at each other's throats.

This feeling of security had been greatly enhanced with the establishment of the *Entente Cordiale* with France in the year of our arrival. Lloyd George was to recall many years later a conversation with Lord Rosebery, who contrary to the prevailing opinion, viewed the arrangement with France with pessimism. 'I suppose,' said the latter, 'that you are as pleased as all the rest with this French arrangement;' and on Lloyd George's expression of delight added, 'You are all wrong. It means war with Germany in the end.'[1] But Lord Rosebery belonged to a very small and prescient minority, and to most English people in all strata of society the European continent, save for France, was a long distance away and could safely be left to itself and a few experts. In Parliament, and even in the Cabinet of which Lloyd George himself was a member, foreign affairs, like India, aroused little attention. On occasion, under the stress of German naval competition, there would be demands for an increase in Great Britain's power at sea, but for the most part public interest centred around domestic policy. In the Cabinet itself only a select few were kept in the picture where international affairs were concerned.[2] The troubles afflicting other countries were ignored as being irrelevant to the even tenor of British life. Monarchs were assassinated in Serbia and Portugal, and Russia could have its revolution in 1905, the portent of still greater upheavals twelve years later; but since such unpleasant things did not happen in wellordered, civilized Great Britain, the omens were disregarded.

This widespread euphoria was the product of a combination of many factors. The island had been free from foreign invasion for nearly one thousand years. The British navy was easily the most powerful in the world. It ruled the seven seas, and in the days before nuclear had been added to air power was a sure protection. A skilful policy in war and diplomacy, in commerce and finance, over a period of three hundred years had gained for the British a vast colonial empire. They had

[1] David Lloyd George, *War Memoirs*, vol. i, p. 1.
[2] David Lloyd George, *War Memoirs*, vol. i, pp. 46-7.

raced ahead in the commercial, financial and industrial revolutions of the eighteenth and nineteenth centuries, while potential rivals were still engaged in settling their own domestic problems. These achievements were crowned by a long period of peace and development, broken only by the Crimean war and minor wars for the consolidation or extension of the Empire. The combined result was a general feeling of security amidst prosperity, of stability, of permanence which was reflected in the intellectual and political life of the Victorian era and the years immediately following.

Humanism, the age of reason, permeated the educational system in which the ruling classes and the professions were nurtured. Science and technology, still far from supplanting the heritage of Greece and Rome, were held to be not only consistent with human progress but also essential for it. That they could be developed into a potential danger to human existence itself was inconceivable. The internal combustion engine was in its first youth. The aeroplane was still the 'flying machine' to many people, with the airship competing with it for supremacy. Few and far between were those who took seriously the prophetic scientific romances of H. G. Wells which were commonly regarded as the products of an overheated imagination suitable only as literature for boys.

Symbolic of this atmosphere of security and stability were the Monarchy and the Empire. Both had a real meaning and message for what would now be termed the Establishment, the duty of which was to honour the first and to ensure that the second remained one on which the sun never set. To the country as a whole the Monarchy meant much more than merely an exalted family whose function was limited to being present in glittering uniforms and bejewelled gowns on ceremonial occasions. To live for one's King and Country was no doubt good. To die for them was even better, and every public school boy, however little his Latin, had imbibed the meaning of the words 'dulce et decorum est pro patria mori', and knew where his duty lay if and when the need arose. Even for a small boy it was impossible not to sense the all-pervasive majesty and glamour of the Monarchy and the Empire and, in my case, not to be impressed with them.

In varying degrees all classes of society shared the aura of their country's greatness. Even the underdog felt pride in belonging to a ruling race with a far-flung empire, although he might not be the recipient of a fair share in the benefits accruing from its ownership. The call to arms in the summer of 1914 was voluntarily answered by rich and poor alike; for underpinning the euphoria and patriotic pride was the general attitude that, though the worst had come to the worst, the Englishman, and with him the Welshman, the Scotsman and even the Irishman, when he was not making a nuisance of himself with his perpetual and absurd demand for Home Rule, was far superior to anyone else. Everywhere, but especially in the public schools, this feeling was almost a component part of the atmosphere. 'The English as a whole are pleasure-loving and slack,' remarked one of the characters in Alec Waugh's semi-autobiographical novel of his school life at Sherborne a few years before 1914. 'They worship games, but after all the Englishman is a jolly sight better than the average Frenchman or German'.[1] Many years earlier W. S. Gilbert had expressed the same view in *H. M. S. Pinafore*. Was it not far better to be an Englishman than a Rooshan or a Prooshan?

Under the glitter of the gilt and tinsel, however, lay a harsher reality. Social and industrial unrest, the product of bad working conditions and constant unemployment, resulted in numerous strikes, one of which, the great railway strike of 1911, was brought home personally to me by the cutting short of my summer holiday. Processions of unemployed were a not uncommon feature, and even more common was the spectacle of a raggedly dressed man accompanied by an equally ragged wife and small children grinding away hopelessly at a barrel-organ, waiting for the charity of well-clad, prosperous shoppers. While such conditions drove some of the more sensitive of the upper classes into the ranks of the recently formed Labour Party[2] and began to arouse a new social conscience, they did not undermine the widespread sense of prosperity and well-being. After many a noisy political dog-

---

[1] *The Loom of Youth* was published in 1917. It dealt with the years 1911 to 1915.

[2] As for example a young man named Clement Attlee, who on coming down from Oxford saw poverty for himself when working with the Haileybury College Mission in the East End of London. Another was Hugh Dalton, the son of a Canon of Windsor, straight from Cambridge. A third, who forestalled both, was Beatrice Potter, afterwards Mrs Sidney Webb and Lady Passfield.

fight, a considerable body of ameliorative legislation was
enacted by the two Liberal Governments headed by
Asquith, whose Cabinets included basically Tory social reformers like the young Winston Churchill side by side with
ardent radicals such as Lloyd George. Inadequate though this
was from the standpoint of later generations, it was the small
seed from which the Welfare State of the mid-century developed. By keeping the discontents of the times within bounds
it helped to prolong, and perhaps even to accentuate, the
outward appearance of balance and stability.

That the country's great confidence in itself had a less
praiseworthy aspect was inevitable. A legitimate pride in the
national achievement tended to degenerate into an arrogance
akin to the *hubris* of the Greek drama. The popular national
poet of the day, the standard-bearer of Great Britain's mission
in the world, of the 'White Man's Burden' and of the
common belief in the innate superiority of the Anglo-Saxon,
was Rudyard Kipling, whose obeisance was made less to the
God of Peace and Understanding than to the Lord God of
Hosts, that great tribal God, whose power could humble those
who forgot Him. Kipling's full-throated imperialism was
always more in evidence than the 'humble and contrite heart'
advocated in his *Recessional*, and it was not surprising that
the mission which he eulogized, openly and by implication,
was readily accepted, while the warning was ignored. Even
so, both Gods existed in the Great Britain of my boyhood.
The British people remained at heart a civilized and kindly
people, possessed of an inherent tolerance which, though not
always appreciated at the time by Kipling's 'lesser breeds
without the law', was to prove noteworthy in the future.
The inner voice, the so-called nonconformist conscience of
Wales and the North, of the Scotts, the Massinghams, the
Gardiners, usually made itself heard in the long run, however
long the run might be. That I came to realize its strength
only after the passage of many years was the consequence of
a number of other factors which obscured it during my years
in England.

My father having entered Lincoln's Inn, we settled down
in Dulwich, a suburb in south-east London. The manor of
Dulwich (once in the county of Surrey) had been purchased

at the end of the sixteenth century by Edward Alleyn, the famous and wealthy Shakespearian actor of Elizabethan days, and the founder of the College there. Three centuries later the Governing Body of the modernized school made consistent and not unsuccessful efforts to prevent their inheritance from being ignominiously swallowed in the 'great wen' of London's expansion; for, despite the crowded areas on its borders, Dulwich in the decade before the first war retained something of its former rural character. It was still a small oasis in the midst of brick and mortar, with the genuine countryside fairly close by. A green belt and two small farms, together with a few country estates owned by City of London tycoons, helped to give an air of mild rusticity. The vast estates belonging to the College were largely free of buildings and had not been disfigured by a rash of suburban villas. The area round the College itself, with its unpaved roads, its carefully preserved Toll Gate, its park with a lake and a riding track, its woods, the relic of the forests which had once covered the North Downs, retained a picturesque touch of the countryside. The railway was certainly there, but was powered by steam only. Electricity was a very much later comer, and even the first motor bus, with its solid rubber tyres and its upper deck open to the four winds of heaven, did not come chugging along till three or four years before the war. The electric tram was two miles away and the horse, a daily sight in the shafts of the horse bus, was still in its element. A complacent dignity and formality were the hall-marks of the inhabitants. The professional gentlemen who sallied forth on week-days to the City or the Law Courts punctiliously wore their frock coats and silk hats, and the family doctor went on his rounds in the same dress and in a brougham. Their general demeanour matched their clothing, except on the frequent occasions when the City gentlemen were compelled to run the last hundred yards to the railway station on hearing the whistle of the incoming train.

In its social and political outlook, Dulwich, like all suburbs of its kind, was wholeheartedly conservative. Suburban class distinctions had a peculiar flavour of their own which was exemplified in the difference between the son of a gentleman and the daughter. There were still schools for 'the Daughters of Gentlemen'—we had at least one such in Dulwich—a gentleman for the purposes of the distinction being an adult male who did not soil his hands with retail trade and who preferably belonged to one of the Services or learned professions. On the other hand, so far as the education of boys was concerned, these meticulous differences did not exist, the sole criterion for entry into any school from Eton downwards being the capacity of the parents to pay the necessary fees. Here money and not the paternal occupation was the yardstick for measuring social status. When, after more than two centuries, Alleyn's College, which in origin was a charitable foundation, was remodelled in the middle of the nineteenth century, two schools were established, an upper with relatively high fees and a lower. As *The Public Schools Year Book* for 1907 somewhat quaintly put it: 'Parliament set up two schools, an upper to be called Dulwich College and a lower, Alleyn's School, the latter a middle class institution,'—which quite incorrectly implied that the former was an aristocratic kind of academy.

Feminine fashions were governed by Victorian conventions and Victorian concepts of morality. Hats were prodigious constructions, kept in their place by large ornamental hat pins, which apart from their legitimate use came in handy for sticking into policemen during the suffragette agitation in the years immediately preceding the outbreak of war. Skirts were unhygienically long and were daintily held up by their wearers as far as the ankle—but no more—to prevent them from sweeping the pavements. Nevertheless, the Edwardians and early Georgians had certainly begun to doubt the validity of Queen Victoria's alleged remark that in her young days 'young ladies used not to have legs'. Certainly by the time that I went up to Oxford in 1919 the 'young ladies', having been caught up in war lasting for four years, each of which knocked off a couple of inches or more from skirts, were clearly demonstrating its falsity for all to see—at any rate up to a modestly limited point. Convention notwithstanding, Dulwich had its young rebellious spirits. Among them was one of the older girls at my kindergarten school. Six or seven years later she attracted much virulently adverse comment from scandalized matrons for appearing in public in a new model garment, the hobble-

W. C. Bonnerjee
President of the Indian National Congress 1885 & 1892

A group at Cambridge 1906 or 1907
My father in centre of back row between the Godfrey brothers. My
mother seated, with Vithalbhai Patel on ground to her right

skirt. This was a very tight affair which caused its wearer to sway at the hips in a manner then considered most improper, but which in the present age of hurry, scurry, jeans, drainpipes, mini-skirts and legitimate waggling would not occasion a second glance from anyone, let alone an adverse comment.

Suburban social life centred round the 'At Home' day, whist and tennis parties, and, strangely enough, church-going. This last was a species of social as well as religious gathering, from which after the blessing had been given and the last 'Amen' duly intoned, friends would stroll off in groups for a walk and gossip in Dulwich Park, with well-behaved progeny following. This pleasantly innocuous ritual, rather than Christianity as such, helped us as Indians to be acceptable to the neighbourhood. Church-going apart, the focal point of social intercourse was the 'At Home' day—a day worth more than a passing reference.

When my mother in due course held her first 'At Home', its attainment signified that we had been vetted and had passed the test. The 'At Home' must have been quite an expensive pastime, as I look back on it, and could have existed only in the days of peace, prosperity and, above all, leisure. No invitations were issued since it was a case of 'open house' for any friends who chose to drop in either by themselves or as often as not accompanied by friends of their own. All were welcome to muffins, crumpets, cakes, gossip and 'Will you have China or Indian tea'. They were great days for me, too, for I was sometimes exhibited for the edification of the company. A pleasant custom existed whereby the ladies present would drop threepenny pieces into the pockets of a small boy's suit, if it happened to be a new one, and when I appeared at one of these functions in my first Eton suit, I earned money more easily and much faster than I was ever to earn it afterwards. But the 'At Home' was not destined to last. A relic of a past age, it perished for ever, along with many other leisured formalities, on August 4th, 1914.

It would be incorrect to assume that this short period between two centuries was a period of stagnation. It was very far from that. Despite the continued existence of irrational and outmoded conventions, the conservatism and narrowness

3

of outlook, the Edwardian and neo-Georgian era was steadily
moving away from the even more constricting attitudes of the
long Victorian age. Even in suburban London the stirrings of
a new and different life could be felt. New movements in art,
literature and drama were having a mildly antiseptic effect,
and political and social pressures of all kinds were on the
increase. Wells, Shaw, Lytton Strachey, of the Bloomsbury
Group, the evangels of the new dawn, were assiduously chipping
off bits and pieces from the heavy, solid Victorian edifice and
were replacing them with something more modern and more
in tune with the new age. The militant suffragettes under the
leadership of the Pankhursts, mother and daughters, took to
activities unheard of in the days when Queen Victoria's young
ladies were expected to faint at the slightest provocation. They
tied themselves to the railings of No. 10 Downing Street and
noisily interrupted proceedings in the House of Commons,
while one even committed suicide by throwing herself in front
of the King's horse as it rounded Tattenham Corner during
the Derby. Their activities were eagerly watched by my sister
and her generation of young women in College, and although
the suffragettes did not succeed in obtaining the vote in this
way (four years of war gave it them without the smallest
opposition from anyone), they did succeed in attracting a
great deal of uncomplimentary attention to themselves for their
undoubtedly unladylike activities. They were, I am inclined
to think, practising an early form of civil disobedience.

Even the thorny and eternal problem of sex was in the process of being brought into the open from the bedroom. Novelists
as far apart in style and theme as Elinor Glyn and Compton
Mackenzie were busily engaged in freeing it from its former
shackles, although both must have been surprised at the distance
and speed with which it was to travel not long after they had
assisted in its release. Compton Mackenzie's *Sinister Street* was
a new departure in novel writing, and Compton Mackenzie
himself is likely to find a place in future histories of the English
novel. Elinor Glyn, on the other hand, though she wrote what
were considered at the time very daring novels, would now be
considered merely lush and over-sentimental. She is probably
remembered today, if she is remembered at all, for the amusing
rhyme her *Three Weeks* provoked:

'Would you like to sin
With Elinor Glyn
On a tiger skin ?
Or would you prefer
To err with her
On some other skin ?'

In the sphere of entertainment, too, there were innovations and novelties which soon became popular with the youth of the time, notwithstanding the raised eyebrows and head shakings of their elders. A new form of light music, and with it a new style of ballroom dancing to match, was introduced from across the Atlantic. This was Ragtime, the precursor of the jazz of the twenties and thirties.

The winds of change were beginning to blow from all directions. They were mild, it is true, in comparison with the hurricanes which were to follow with the passage of time and which were in the not so distant future to sweep away the legacy of the Victorian age, virtues, vices and all, into the limbo of history. But in the decade before August 4th, 1914, few people speculated on what the future had in store, and certainly small boys did not do so. It was a powerful, dignified, imperial England to which I was introduced when just on four years of age: an England with a great belief in its purpose and destiny; an England of comfort, leisure, culture and prosperity for the moneyed, of a pluto-aristocracy and an upper class surbubia with its cooks, its housemaids and parlourmaids in their trim dresses and starched lace caps; an England which almost unknowingly went to its death, both literally and metaphorically, between the historic years 1914 and 1918 in the mud of France and Flanders, on the wind-swept cliffs of Gallipoli and in the desert sands of Mesopotamia and Palestine.

III

The Bending of a Twig

'WE are attempting to raise up a large class of enlightened natives. I hope that twenty years hence there will be hundreds, nay thousands, of natives familiar with the best models of composition and well acquainted with western science.' So wrote Macaulay in 1835. Seventy years later I was to wend my way along the path of enlightenment in its own homeland, to be enlightened in due course in ways perhaps not contemplated by Macaulay.

For our first three years my parents were with the family. W. C. Bonnerjee was one of the small Indian community in London who frequently visited us. He was at the time earnestly pressing on his English friends the great necessity for political reforms in India, but unhappily did not live to see even the small results embodied in the Act of 1909. He died unexpectedly at Dover on his way home to lead the agitation against the partition of Bengal. Another frequent visitor was Vithalbhai Patel, the elder brother of Sardar Vallabhbhai Patel under whom I was to serve forty years later in the States Ministry of an independent Indian Government. Vithalbhai was at Lincoln's Inn with my father, and at the time showed no leanings towards anything so serious as political life, being full of *joie-de-vivre* and much addicted to the singing of comic songs. He greatly endeared himself to me by always bringing with him a large bag of marshmallows which we would share until the bag was empty or, as more often happened, until my mother intervened in the interests of discipline. Entering politics at a later stage he finally succeeded Sir Frederic Whyte as President of the Central Legislative Assembly. Also reading for the English Bar were the two Godfrey brothers from South Africa, one of whom was subsequently to become President of the South African Indian National Congress. It was from them that my mother first heard the name 'Gandhi', though, as she afterwards used to say, his activities in South Africa conveyed nothing to her at the time and she paid little attention to them. Among the occasional visitors whom I recall was Rajkumari Amrit Kaur, who was studying, I think, at the Royal Holloway College for Women, and who was destined for high ministerial office in independent India.

In 1907 my father returned to India after his call to the Bar, leaving behind my mother with the family. Shortly before his departure he had been offered a newly created post at the India Office, that of Adviser for Indian students. For a variety of reasons, the main one being that he desired to keep a watchful eye on conditions in the Grant, he refused it; and in the event it was fortunate that he did so. A moderate nationalist of the early Congress school, he was no revolutionary, and strongly disapproved of the cult of the bomb and revolver which was rapidly growing in India and even spreading among Indians in Europe. The assassination at the Imperial Institute in London of Sir Curzon Wyllie by a young Indian student distressed him, and his distress would have been even greater had he been holding an official position at the India Office connected with students.

By this time my formal education had already been taken in hand. It began in the customary manner of the age at a Dame's School, one of those admirable institutions run by middle-aged ladies, whose sole qualification for teaching was the best one, a liking for and understanding of small children. At Miss Roberts's kindergarten there were twenty or so boys and girls, the former being prepared mainly for entry into the Dulwich Preparatory School. It must be conceded that in the present age of stress and competition, and with children vastly more sophisticated than we ever were, the Dames' Schools would not pass muster, since their basis and function were different from what is required now, and any idea of 'eleven plus' would have been anathema. Nevertheless, such schools suited the needs of a more simple and leisurely era, and the grounding given in them was sure, even though it may have been slow.

Prizes were freely awarded for almost every reasonable quality a child could display, not indeed for the inculcation of the competitive spirit but rather by way of encouragement. Intelligence naturally received its reward, but there were consolation prizes for good conduct — which always went to

the girls—for industry, for making an improvement over
past performance or for making special efforts. In fact, there
was no definite end to the subjects qualifying for a prize. My
first attempt at an English essay was given an award for originality. The topic selected was that hardy annual for children
of all periods, 'Your Favourite Animal', and whereas my contemporaries stood firm by their kittens, puppies or rabbits, I
struck a new note altogether by producing eleven words as
follows: "The pig is my favourite animal because it gives us
bacon." I diverged from convention on another occasion, too,
when I was billed at a Christmas play to take the part of
King Alfred the Great soliloquizing while he allegedly burnt
the cakes. Everything went according to schedule until I came
to the crucial words, 'I shall never give in, for I am a true-born
Englishman.' At this point I abandoned the main theme to
inform the audience, 'I'm not really, you know. I'm an Indian,'
an aside which brought down the house. Whether the explanation was to be found in incipient nationalism — which was
unlikely — or in incipient morality — afterwards I told my
mother that it was wicked to tell lies — or in some deep complex
which only Freud could have fathomed, I do not know.
Perhaps, too, this readiness to diverge from convention was
not a good omen for the future.

Six months after I had left Miss Roberts for the Dulwich
Preparatory School early in 1910 my father arrived from India,
and after a short stay returned, this time taking my mother
with him. Thereafter, the three of us, my brother, sister and
self, were left in the charge of guardians, the first of whom was
something of a character. A large Irishman with a shaggy
mane of white hair, he had practised at the Lucknow Bar for
many years before settling in England, and had made a fair
competence. This last he would have made much more had
it not been for a hot-headed habit, amusing to the onlookers in
Court, of telling the Bench, when the latter disagreed with
his arguments, what he would do to it later, alone in the
United Services Club. After his retirement he farmed for a few
years near Guildford, but when he became our guardian, he
had settled near Dulwich. I myself seldom saw him except
at meal times or when, as not infrequently happened, an
uncomplimentary remark in a fortnightly report from School

demanded his attention, and mine. His normal practice was to retire to his study after breakfast, accompanied by *The Times*, the monthly Reviews, a decanter of whiskey and a siphon of soda. His steady potations did not appear to have any damaging effect on him, except for the twinges of gout which afflicted him from time to time, during which periods I found it advisable to avoid adverse remarks from school. He was a very strong advocate of Home Rule for Ireland, but, on the principle that anything an Englishman could do in the matter of ruling an empire an Irishman could do far better, was an equally strong opponent of anything even vaguely resembling Home Rule for India. This, in fact, was a characteristic of other Irishmen of the older generation. Sir Michael O'Dwyer, for example, belonged to an old family of Irish rebels, and perhaps for that reason knew how rebels should be dealt with. Brigadier-General Dyer, too, was educated partly in Ireland. In fairness, however, it should be added that the younger generation of Irishmen were very different. One of the nicest, as well as most efficient, of the young I.C.S. magistrates to serve under me when I was a senior District Magistrate was a young Irishman from Cork whose father had been murdered by Sinn Feiners round about 1920.

The Headmaster of the Preparatory School, the Rev. W. R. M. Leake, was himself an Old Alleynian. To us he was a very Godlike creature, having played rugby football for Cambridge and England in the distant past. An Indian connection—his father had been a tea planter—had given him a special interest in India, and one of his brothers, after being Director of Agriculture in the United Provinces, became Agricultural Adviser to the Government of India. An impressive man, an imperialist of the old '*muscular Christian*' school, he had a fullblooded and sincere belief in Great Britain's predestined mission in the world, and his occasional talks to his boys were strongly tinged with it. In his private capacity he was a devout and very charitable man who did many a good turn to others without making a song and dance about it. As a master he was strict but not unduly so, and he understood the small boy of the period. I fell really foul of him only once, and received a sound caning in return—which I certainly deserved, though this aspect of the case did not impinge itself on my attention at the time; for when Leake used his cane he spared neither it nor his forearm.

Education in the Preparatory Schools of the day was based on English, Latin and from the age of twelve onwards on Greek in addition, together with the essentials of elementary mathematics, geography and history. Some French was thrown in as a concession to the modern spirit, but this was not taken seriously by most boys; and since it was generally considered only right and proper for the Frenchman to learn English, public school French remained a standard joke for many years. So far as English was concerned, we were put through the usual routine; but patriotic and what might be termed 'action' poetry was very much to the forefront in Leake's time at the Preparatory School. One consequence was that we automatically and unconsciously tended to become national-minded and patriotic (in the English sense of the term, of course). At least that was the effect on me for the time being. Out of the whole galaxy of English literature laid before me, Dickens, Scott, Stevenson, *Tales from Ancient Greece* and of course Shakespeare, it was G. A. Henty, an author not on the official list, who fascinated me most with his rousing tales of Empire building. I also drank in avidly a volume entitled *Deeds that Won the Empire* with the result that Lord Roberts became my hero until the more modern heroes of rugby football ousted him from first place. From my history book (S. R. Gardiner was, I think, our textbook) I learnt that the English had conquered India entirely for the benefit of its inhabitants and had built up an empire there almost against their own wishes. Clive's Indian sepoys, I gathered, had greatly contributed to this beneficence by giving up their rice rations at the siege of Arcot and living solely on the water, a hoary tale which if true only showed the good sense of the sepoys, since, as I was to learn long afterwards, it is the water alone that contains the vitamins. In general, my impression was that Indians on the whole were not nice people at all, being addicted to burning widows, to incarcerating men and women in Black Holes or murdering them and throwing the bodies into wells, excessive stress being laid on such themes—all the more so, indeed, when it is remembered that two centuries earlier the custom of burning martyrs at the stake was common enough in England, while the sophisticated tortures of the Spanish Inquisition received Papal approval throughout Europe. It was not suspected of course, that two decades or so later a Christain nation, a leader of European civilization, was to massacre six million men, women and children in gas chambers, after having first tortured most of them.

It was thus brought home to me at an early age that there was a clear distinction between my English companions and myself inasmuch as they had got something which I had not, namely an Empire. They possessed, while I only belonged. Mr Gardiner's verdict was that after the collapse of the 'Great Mogul' it was the British who set out to civilize Indians—which all fitted neatly into the doctrine of the 'mission' to which the Rev. W. R. M. Leake was so quietly dedicated. The totality of my historical impressions, therefore, was that the British were in India by divine ordinance. I accepted it all as being perfectly sound and reasonable, and I do not remember ever having had at this stage any feeling of resentment. Imbibing as I did the imperial ideas of the time with the air I was breathing, my only regret was that I was not a part owner of the Empire as the other boys appeared to be. Consequently, when shortly after their coronation, King George and Queen Mary drove slowly past the College grounds one day in May on their way to the Crystal Palace, I was present with a mass of boys of all ages, cheering and waving my cap with genuine feeling and enthusiasm.

This early imperialist period, as it might be called, was to vanish rapidly in the course of the next ten years as a result of the war and events in India, to revive, however, in a different form with the realization many years later that the history of the great cultural empires from the earliest times has been the history of human development. In the interval between 1920 and 1945 I disapproved of imperialism in general and the Empire in India in particular. That during this period I, like many others, served the maligned Empire by entering into the highest Service which it had to offer and that my intellectual opposition to it was based on the liberalism I had learnt in England, was conveniently, though not intelligently, blacked out from my mind.

Another early reaction was dead by the time that I came down from Oxford; and this was never to come to life again. In the era of Great Britain's imperial grandeur the greatness was reflected in the image of the national leaders presented to and accepted by the general public. Even small boys could not help being aware of the political agitations and excitement of the times, since the two general elections of 1910 were a combination of noise and truculence, and their aftermath generated far more heat than light. The newspapers published maps showing the various constituencies in circles, and children were encouraged to fill in the circles with the colours of the victorious party, orange or red for the Conservatives and blue for the Liberals. One learnt a certain amount of simple geography in this way, and additionally, from the wealth of photographs, the names and appearances of the individual contestants. The main, and really significant result, however, was the subtle, though probably unintentional, inculcation of the idea that all these quite ordinary men were endowed with qualities which in fact they did not possess, and that the leaders of the country at all events were men of destiny who were wiser than their fellows, who could control the results of their actions and foresee their consequences. The greatness of the nation as a whole was the yardstick for measuring the quality of its leading political figures, a somewhat dangerous superstition only possible in that pre-1914 age of innocence before the age of scepticism set in. In my case the consequences of an upbringing in this mythology were doubly unfortunate; for if for a few years I tended to attribute to England's leaders qualities which they did not possess, I also did not, when the age of innocence ended in the inevitable reaction, give them the credit for those which undoubtedly were theirs.

It was in these early years, too, that 'colour' was first brought within my range through an incident which has always remained fixed firmly in my mind, although it is most unlikely to have been remembered by any of my contemporaries. In 1909 or 1910 the negro boxer, Jack Johnson, won the heavyweight championship of the world by defeating, and heavily battering in the process, an Australian, Tommy (or perhaps Johnny) Burns. This by itself would occasion neither comment nor any great upsurge of racial feeling today. But far different was the case at the beginning of the century. The repercussions were widespread and resounding. Everywhere there was criticism and discussion, even the placid 'At Home' day not being exempt. Was it right? Was it proper that such things should be? Would not the prestige of the white man suffer? Suggestions were put forward for the prohibition of boxing matches between negro and white man; for it was held that although the latter was the cultural and mental superior he could not stand up to the former in the ring. A small episode, perhaps, unimportant in itself but of great significance in its wider implications. In this way it was rubbed into my immature mind that human pigmentation was a most important factor in human relationships, and that to be born white was a definite advantage.

A few years later, when I was in my teens, the existence of 'colour' was even more strongly emphasized; but this time the actual colour was different. I began to hear about the so-called 'Yellow Peril'. The peril was popularized by a writer of romantic mystery stories which achieved great success. Sax Rohmer is probably forgotten now, but in his day made a name for himself with a series of tales the central figure of which was a sinister Chinaman, Dr Fu-Manchu, an ingenious scientist who was perpetually plotting the downfall of the white race and always being foiled just in the nick of time. The learned doctor was, of course, the villain of the piece, but even at the age of fourteen or fifteen it struck me as odd that the powerful, imperial Europe, which was ruling the world and looked like ruling it in perpetuity should have been so perturbed at the alleged 'Yellow Peril', when to the Chinese who had been subjected to many humiliations over a long period of years the boot must have seemed to be on the other leg.[1]

Such matters were not of deep concern to me, but they had entered my unconscious, and in due course the natural

---

[1] After this passage had been written I came across a letter in *The Sunday Times* (London) in its issue of 28 January 1968 which is relevant to the point I have made. The correspondent wrote as follows: 'When, as a small boy at prep. school, compulsorily attending church, I heard the preacher announce that his sermon would be about the Yellow Peril, I settled back in the expectation of a thrilling story. But what we got was a dramatic warning that the heathen Chinese were about to overrun Christendom and that the only way to save ourselves was to convert them quick. . . . The difference between that preacher of *fifty years ago* and. . . .'

Fifty years ago—1918, or three years after the period of which I have written.

consequences followed. At the time, however, they signified
little against the really important things of life such as a place
in the football XV or the cricket XI : for despite periodical
lectures from the Rev. Leake on the paramount necessity for
hard endeavour in the classroom, there were very few small
boys who did not put in far harder effort on the field. The
happiest moments of my life were when I set out with the
teams in a commodious, horse-drawn waggonette to play other
schools in the neighbourhood. Conformity to the canons and
ethic of the English school came easily to me and it was not for
some years that a certain amount of deviationism became
apparent.

There was one other Indian boy with me at the Preparatory
School, a South Indian by the rather unlikely name of
Rangdam. He did not stay long, and I do not know what
happened to him. There were also some English boys whose
parents were in Service in India. Among them was a pair of
brothers, Tipple by name, whose father was a Professor in the
Indian Educational Service in the United Provinces. The
younger one and I became quite friendly, but on one occasion
he surprised me by pursuing me in the playground with shouts
of, 'Hi, you Bengali babu', and then bursting into loud laughter.
Being west of Suez and not having heard the phrase before, the
appellation together with its covert meaning was entirely
novel to me. Nevertheless it was clearly derogatory and signified
something which one ought not to be. Consequently young
Tipple and I came to blows, while an interested crowd looked
on with interest but in ignorance of what the commotion was
about. Young blood was shed, but before it had become too
copious, the master in charge appeared on the scene and
separated us. His demand for an explanation remained unsatis-
fied, since no one was in a position to give a reasonable one,
and the upshot was that being inured to small boys fighting
for no apparent reasons, he sent us off with a sound cuff each
to the lavatories to bathe our respective noses.

In April 1914 my parents came to England to see us after
an absence of four years, their original intention being to return
to India in the autumn. My father actually did so, but with
the uncertainties arising from the outbreak of war my mother
remained behind, at first on a temporary basis from month

to month and then finally settling down in Hampstead for the 'duration'. My brother and sister were now in their second year at the University of Wales (Aberystwyth), but I was in an intermediate and nondescript stage, having turned thirteen and being about due for entry into the College. In April 1914 no one in England was thinking in terms of war, except civil war in Ireland. The war clouds over the Balkans appeared to have lifted with the conclusion of the Balkan wars, and even many of those close to the international scene failed to sense the approach of the European storm. England turned happily to the exciting drama of domestic politics. Ireland was in the forefront of the stage in the full glare of the limelight. The suffragettes were in the background; and Mr. Lloyd George, that bogey man of the prosperous, the Cleon of his age and still quite a long way from his metamorphosis into the heroic role of the 'man who won the war', was merely hovering around in the wings for the time being.

My parents, thinking of their return to India, naturally wished to see me settled into my new school and acclimatized before their departure. Consequently I entered the College at an unusual time, the summer term of 1914, the last term of the school year. Having been in the top form of the Preparatory School for a year, I had been sent up as a matter of routine for scholarships, both at Dulwich and St Paul's. I duly failed, my standard not being high enough for either. On the other hand I did not entirely disgrace myself, since I managed to win as a sort of consolation prize an exhibition to Brighton at the next attempt. That I did not go there was due to the chance that when a cable was dispatched to India fixing a certain date for acceptance, my parents were already on the high seas, and the cable pursued them from place to place. For myself I cannot say that the misadventures of the cable were ever a source of any regret, and after four pleasant years at the Preparatory School, I entered Dulwich in May to stay there for five years until the time arrived for me to proceed to Oxford.

IV

A Little Learning

I HAVE tried in vain to bring myself into the frame of mind which would enable me to commence this chapter in the conventional modern manner with a strong attack on one's former school for the lamentable education dished up, for its being the source of much unnecessary misery and in general for being about the worst school in the kingdom. Abandoning the attempt, I must confess at the outset that my five years at Dulwich were in the main happy and that I enjoyed them. It is true that by the age of eighteen I was beginning to grow out of public school inhibitions and the general atmosphere; and by the time I left for Oxford I definitely *had* grown out of them. But the process of growing up is a natural one and one's school cannot do anything about it.

By the standards of today public school education at the commencement of the century was certainly below par; but by the same token the rating which a future generation may give to contemporary schools may well be equally low. The English school of my day was a combination of the complacence and massive solidity of the Victorian with the more critical Edwardian age. In the prevailing atmosphere of the period the education provided by so special a type of school as the Public naturally tended to become stereotyped. Nor should it be forgotten that the general development of present day youth everywhere is far more rapid than that of the youth of the day before yesterday. For a mixed bag of reasons, therefore, it is surely an error to use the standards and needs of the present as a correct measure for the past. Reflecting the image of its particular era the Edwardian school served its purpose and passed away.

For my part I was content to accept Dulwich as I found it, and Dulwich in turn accepted me. By 1917 I had reached the highest form, the Classical VIth, and before leaving two years later I had entered the ranks of the school's *élite*. In Dulwich parlance I had become a 'blood'—which for the ordinary boy was always a pleasant goal to reach. I had been awarded my

Ist XV colours and a Prefect's quartered cap. At cricket I represented the school in two or three matches, but so unsuccessfully, it must be confessed, that I had to be content with remaining in the 2nd XI for two consecutive years. On the academic plane, if my classical scholarship did not reach the standard necessary for an open award at Oxford, the fault was mine and not that of the school. By all the tokens of the time, however, my school career was successful without being outstanding. In my last year, it was true, signs of nonconformity with my environment were coming into conflict with my regard for tradition, but save in one instance Dulwich paid small attention to them. In many respects, indeed, and more specifically from the Indian angle, it was a remarkable school.

Like Westminster and St Paul's, the two other leading London schools, Dulwich was only partially a boarding school. The boarders, however, numbering about 130 or a fifth of the total and divided into four Houses, played a greater role in the life of the school than their mere numbers would suggest. The general life was much the same as elsewhere, a somewhat Spartan simplicity being the keynote. By a custom which never commended itself to me we commenced the day, winter as well as summer, with a cold plunge—an exercise in the toughening process in which I did not indulge when left to my own devices in the holidays. Bullying in the tradition of *Tom Brown's Schooldays* had died out everywhere long before 1914. New boys were not tossed in blankets or roasted before fires—the latter in any case being quite unfitted for the purpose since they used to be damped down at regular intervals with coal dust. A certain amount of horseplay sometimes took place in the chilly, gas-lit dormitories before the arrival of the prefect in charge. A custom, too, known as sheep-washing, existed under which the new arrival shivering on the brink of his first cold plunge was not given any option in the matter. Eager hands seized him, cast him in and after turning him over once or twice like a catherine wheel hauled him out. A childish custom, certainly, but one which never actually damaged anyone, and which had died out before I left the school.

In one respect there was a sharp distinction between Dulwich and the purely boarding school. The rigidly monastic seclusion which was one of the hall-marks of the latter was impossible. No official authority could prevent a boarder from becoming friendly with the sister of a day boy contemporary, and the meetings were not necessarily surreptitious. Prefects by virtue of their position were exempt from local 'bounds', and the latter were not inviolable by anyone else ready to take the small risks involved in breaking them. Since mild heterosexuality could be open and above board, homosexuality was rare, though perhaps not entirely non-existent. The normal adolescent misdemeanours were common coin; and an occasional minor scandal occurred. One such according to school gossip, resulted in the expulsion, quite unjustified, of two girls from one of the local Schools 'for the Daughters of Gentlemen' for what would now pass off as a little escapade in petting. Their partners in sin remained on at the College, unscathed save for a slight tarnishing of their reputations in official circles, a matter of very small account during the war which was shortly to swallow them. Here was proof, if any were needed, that life at that time was more onerous for the daughter of a gentleman than for the son, of whom nothing superhuman was expected.

Although ancient in point of time, the ancestry of Dulwich, a charitable foundation, was not prepossessing. The seventeenth-century registers of Alleyn's College contain a very mixed selection of items ranging from orphans who were given clothes and boots to poor scholars who were awarded stipends to proceed to Oxford. As a public school Dulwich dated only from its reconstruction by Act of Parliament in the middle of the nineteenth century; and like all the many new foundations of the time its traditions had been copied from those of the original seven schools designated 'public' in the Public Schools Act. By the end of the century it had risen to high rank in the hierarchy of schools, being one of the three or four day schools to be accepted as a public school in general estimation. Its prestige in both the academic and athletic spheres had been greatly enhanced by the work of the third of its Masters (as the Heads were called). This was Arthur Herman Gilkes, who was in the line of those great headmasters of the nineteenth century, Arnold of Rugby and Thring of Uppingham. Six feet six inches tall, and broad to match, with a large Victorian beard, his outstanding personality kept parents, staff and boys

Preparatory school 1913

On arrival in England in 1904 with
my elder brother and sister

The author's parents' house in Rampore Hamlet

in considerable awe. He was an inseparable part of the Dulwich landscape for many years. Perhaps the most memorable tribute ever paid to him was that from a contemporary at his own former school, H. W. Nevinson, who described him as the nearest approach to Socrates that one could imagine. He was, however, far more puritanical than Socrates was ever likely to have been, for even the mildest profanity was anathema, and smoking even worse. On one occasion during a House football match he heard a loud, violent expletive emerge from the depths of a scrum, as, of course, such expletives do from time to time. He announced later to the assembled school that during the game he had heard a great oath, and that unless the culprit surrendered himself forthwith very serious consequences would ensue for everyone. At the end of a long, gloomy silence a sporting youth decided to sacrifice himself for the benefit of society and confessed to having used a good hearty 'damn' in the heat of the moment. Gilkes's reply was, 'Well, you lose your prefect's cap, but that wasn't the word I heard!'

Gilkes took over the mastership in 1885 from Welldon, who after a short spell at Harrow was later to become Bishop of Calcutta. A liberal humanist of the school of Benjamin Jowett, he built up during his régime of nearly thirty years a great tradition of liberalism in its widest sense, and individual talent was encouraged far more than in most schools of the age, a point which has been touched on by Sir Roy Harrod in his biography of the late Lord Keynes.[1] Like many schools of the same class, Dulwich tended to specialize in sending men into the various Imperial and Colonial Services, with particular emphasis, I think, on the Indian Civil and the Indian Army. In reverse, Gilkes welcomed boys from all parts of the globe, of all colours and creeds. My own contemporaries, apart from several Indians, covered China, Malaya, Burma, Ceylon, Iran, the Gold Coast, and the West Indies, as comprehensive a list as could be imagined. With India, a close link had been forged

---

[1] Macmillan (1951). 'Dulwich at this time seems to have been remarkably fertile in the production of men of strongly individual genius' (p. 66). The four men selected by Sir Roy Harrod were Mr P. G. Wodehouse, Mr T. T. Sheppard, (Provost of King's College, Cambridge), Mr A. H. Smith (Warden of New College, Oxford), and Mr G. E. Moore of Cambridge, the founder of a new school of Ethics. Another leading philosopher was G. D. Broad, fellow of Trinity College, Cambridge.

from the time when the two grandsons of the last Nawab Nazim of Bengal, Bihar and Orissa entered the school in the last decade of the nineteenth century. From that time to this a steady stream of Indians has been educated at Dulwich. Best known to independent India for the prominent part he has played in the judicial and public life of the country would doubtless be Vivian Bose, a contemporary of my elder brother and till recently a Judge of the Supreme Court. Of the dozen or so with me, three passed into the Indian Civil Service, one ended a long official career as Chief Commissioner of Railways, the first Indian and last holder of the post before it was abolished; one entered the Indian Army when the King's Commission was opened to Indians in 1918, dying prematurely as a Brigadier; another was commissioned into the Indian Medical Service; a seventh who was in my House and a contemporary at Oxford is still practising successfully at the Bombay Bar.[1]

Gilkes was not merely international in the breadth of his intellectual outlook. Even more significant was the tradition of equality which he laid down, and which permeated the school for many years after his retirement. At Dulwich 'colour' was not a handicap. Indians (and other coloureds), for example, were not only made prefects, if considered suitable, but were also given all the rights and privileges that went with a prefect's cap. These included the right of corporal punishment—which was usually inflicted on the delinquent with an O.T.C. swagger stick. Having lived in England for a decade before entering the school I had grown accustomed to taking for granted much that was of real note and for which I did not give the British their due credit for many years. This was a case in point: for here in this small, conservative community of a school with the tradition of Empire behind it, in the heart of the Empire's

---

[1] The I.C.S. men were S. S. Bajpai, the younger brother of the better-known Sir Girja Shankar Bajpai; M. D. Bhausali, a Wrangler at Cambridge and later Chief Secretary, Bombay; and lastly N. C. Bakhle, who after a brilliant career, both academic and athletic, at school and Oxford, died prematurely, of typhoid fever, in 1935. Of Bakhle's elder brothers, one was commissioned into the I.M.S., while another become Chief Commissioner for Railways in 1947. Visheshwar Nath Singh was commissioned into the Indian Army in 1919 and died as a Brigadier. K. S. Shavaksha of my House captained the Boxing team and later won a half-blue at Oxford. He was a successful barrister in Bombay and for some years was Registrar of Trade Marks. Mention should also be made of Tin Tut of Burma. After resigning from the I.C.S. in 1945 or '46 he entered politics and was a member of the ill-fated Burmese Cabinet which was collectively assassinated shortly after Independence.

capital and at the zenith of British imperial power, potential ruler and potential subject received the same treatment and lived on the same level.

This was all the more remarkable for being contrary to the generally prevalent attitudes, which, I think, have been correctly summed up by Shane Leslie. 'The experiment,' he has written, 'of bringing Rhodes scholars from all over the world to Oxford, or Indian *babus* to Cambridge is doubtful. The colonials are better for their own colleges instead of learning to imitate English sportsmen. The Indians are the worse for being educated as an equal race in England by way of prelude to *being ruled as an inferior one in India*'[1] (my italics). A deplorable sentiment, doubtless, from the standpoint of the sixties, but one worth more than a passing thought, nonetheless. Whether the tradition laid down at the school sank deep enough in all, or even most, cases, is perhaps doubtful; for in a volume entitled *Must England Lose India* there is a pointed reference to 'the supercilious and icy disdain of young Mr Snooks of Dulwich and the Indian Civil Service, or the more bombastic dislike of Lt. Smith of Charterhouse and the Indian Army.'[2] The school magazine, too, printed many letters from young officers on active service which indicated the very temporary nature and tenuous effects of the intellectual attitude which Gilkes sought to inculcate.

Since the humanities were still rated high in the Great Britain of the day, the Classical side took precedence in some respects over the others, even boys destined for the Army proceeding a short way up the classical ladder before transferring to the specialized Army Class. Certainly up to the end of my schooldays the prestige of the classics tended to remain higher than that of modern languages or science, and it was the prerogative of the senior prefect

[1] *The End of a Chapter*, pp. 50-51. This was written in 1916 when the author was convalescing in hospital from wounds received in action.

[2] By Lt. Col. Osburn, D.S.O. (Alfred A. Knopf, 1928), p. 31. I am not sure that the author's thesis that the only breeding ground for racial prejudice was the public school was wholly true. In my experience I have found it equally prevalent among men who had never been inside one.

Again on p. 30: 'What can the English boy or girl who has been brought up in some select suburb and put to school at Cheltenham, Dulwich or Charterhouse possibly know of the degradation, the drink, the overcrowding, the cruelty, the incest, and even the bestiality that may, and often does exist within a few thousand yards or a few miles of their homes in England.'

of the Classical Sixth form to be the Captain of the School.
Classics apart, perhaps one of the greatest differences between the schools of yesterday and those of today lies in the
change in the tempo of school life and the wide diversity of
interests now catered for. Dulwich now possesses a host of
societies with a range of subjects far beyond the scope of
ordinary work and games, societies devoted to the arts, the
drama, history, archaeology, even those two subjects which
were taboo fifty years ago, religion and international affairs.
This is a far cry from the restricted intellectual horizon of
1914, when except for a Science and Photographic Society
which held an annual exhibition, nothing of the kind existed.
One's spare time was one's own, but literature, poetry, the
arts in general and anything beyond the immediate range
of school work received no official encouragement.

At least in so far as art was concerned this should not have
been the case, since Dulwich was unique among the schools
of Great Britain in its possession of an Art Gallery of international repute which contained many treasures by Rembrandt,
Rubens, Velasquez, Gainsborough and others. The school's
artistic tradition was of fairly long standing, and a number of
leading R.A.s of the early years of the century began their art
careers at the school, and the gallery itself came into prominence in 1968 as the victim of the record art burglary
involving pictures worth £1½m. sterling. My parents, whenever
the occasion offered itself, had always tried to foster whatever
there was of a cultural side to my nature, but this I displayed
pianissimo during term, relying more on conformity to house
and school custom. In the holidays, however, I deviated into
byways not normally trodden by my contemporaries. I paid
many a quiet visit to the College Gallery and other galleries;
and having discovered through Aristotle that man was a political animal voraciously read all the serious Reviews on which
I could lay hands in the Hampstead Public Library in order to
try to find out for myself what the war was really being
fought for.

Since Gilkes resigned the Mastership at the end of my first
term, I was not fortunate enough to be under his direct
influence; and of the assistant masters only two—each for a
different reason—left any lasting impression. One, Hubert

Doulton, a scion of the Royal Doulton Pottery family, a sardonic disciplinarian with a forceful personality, would commence each term with the warning: 'If you boys do not work while you are here with me, I'll make your lives a misery to you'—which he could and did do, as and when he thought fit. The other, Henry Hose, the master of the Form immediately below the VIth, had a close connexion with India. His brother in the I.C.S. was Chief Secretary of the United Provinces at the time, and his sister was married to another member of the I.C.S., Benjamin (afterwards Sir Benjamin) Lindsay of the Allahabad High Court who was friendly with my father and whom I was to meet in the years to come. Hose was the best classical scholar on the staff, deeply imbued with the spirit of the classics. Although he never succeeded in turning me into a replica of himself, he did arouse in me an abiding interest in the importance of Greece and Rome to the western world before the age of science and technology transformed its life and thought.

It was the war, however, rather than my school life as such that had the strongest influence on me during my formative years. Since my school days covered the five years from 1914 to 1919, I belonged in a way to the war generation, without, however, being one of those who came to be called 'The Lost Generation', that particular generation born in the 1890s for the preordained purpose, it seemed, of fighting and largely dying or being maimed in the Great War. But both generations overlapped inasmuch as many of the battle-scarred survivors of the 'lost generation' and those like myself who grew up during those years unscathed found ourselves together at Oxford after the war.

The immediate reaction of the public schools to August 4th 1914 was automatic—a reflex action. Some who might have stayed on another term or two at once volunteered for active service, perhaps adding a few months to their ages for official purposes. The remainder stayed on, impatiently looking forward to the time when they, too, could join the forces. It was impossible for any boy who grew to adulthood during those historic years not to be deeply influenced by the impact of the war, when term after term once familiar faces became mere names in casualty lists which expanded in volume as the months passed. Indeed, this was so much the case with me that to this day mention of 'the war' means first and foremost the war of 1914 to 1918.

For me the war fell into two parts, the line of demarcation being somewhere between my 16th and 17th birthdays. The first period was remarkable for the early excitement and enthusiasm which engulfed all, young and old. This was the period of Tipperary; of gusts of anger at Germany, and in particular at the German Emperor, for their treatment of 'gallant little Belgium' and for tearing up solemn treaties as being 'scraps of paper'; of the retreat from Mons with its apocalyptic angels; of rumours for the credulous, the most popular being the disembarkation of Russian soldiers at Liverpool together with realistic accounts of alleged eye-witnesses who had seen the snow falling from Cossack boots; of amateur concerts and pageants for the benefit of the Red Cross and other war-time organizations. One of these last, in which I took part, was a Pageant of Empire depicting how Britannia's children rallied round the mother in her time of need. Together with a few other selected fourteen-year-olds, I was chosen to represent Black Africa. In black swimming costumes, with all visible parts smeared with burnt cork, in mini-skirts of plaited straw, and carrying massive clubs, we sang *Swanee River* in cracked voices, our efforts receiving an encore from an enthusiastic audience which did not appear to notice the indisputable fact that the Swanee River was a very long way from Basutoland.

As time passed, with muddy stalemates in France and Flanders, thinly disguised defeats in Gallipoli and Mesopotamia, and a dangerous increase in submarine warfare from the side of the German navy, the optimistic and boundless enthusiasm that had heralded the outbreak of war died. War ceased to be a 'big picnic' after the long drawn out battles of 1915 and 1916 had resulted in casualties running into hundreds of thousands for no more gain than a mile or two of mud. The propaganda of the time which was directed to the inculcation of a belief that these great battles of attrition, as they were called, were real victories and that the generals perpetrating them were among the great captains of history, now began to be suspect. But the first and most important victim of public suspicion, of widespread disillusionment and even of some discontent, was not a general or admiral. The axe fell on the Prime Minister, Mr Asquith, whose place was taken by Mr Lloyd George, a political transposition which would have seemed inconceivable only a few years earlier.

Nor was the propaganda always for purely military ends. Often it was crude, and turned to even cruder purposes such as the fomenting of mass hysteria on the basis of fictitious atrocities, like the story—denied later—that the Germans were by some mysterious process utilising corpses from the battle-field for the manufacture of glycerine.[1] It even took the bizarre form of attacks on prominent national leaders. In the early days of the war the Prime Minister himself, Mr Asquith, was not exempt. He was accused of being sympathetic to Germany because his wife had visited German prisoners of war in their internment camp. The man responsible for the remodelling of the British Army into the *élite*, professional force which helped to stem the German advance, Lord Haldane, was driven from office for being a student of German philosophy, and, what was far worse, for having rashly committed himself to this statement one year before the war. The First Sea Lord, Prince Louis of Battenberg, one of England's leading sailors and grandfather of the Duke of Edinburgh, was forced to resign, his German ancestry being sufficient to condemn him, and the Royal House of Saxe-Coburg-Gotha was transformed into the House of Windsor. Lower down the scale, pacifists and con-scientious objectors (known generically as 'conchies'), came in for rough handling before the storm of public feeling abated, a number being sent to prison. Trinity College, Cambridge, of which better might have been expected, led the way and distinguished itself by depriving of his Fellowship one of the most brilliant men of his age, Bertrand Russell, who exchanged his rooms in the College for a term in prison for preaching pacifism.

Propaganda notwithstanding, however, it is doubtful if public hysteria ever reached the commanding heights attained in Germany with its perpetual Hymn of Hate against England. There were episodes, too, which showed not only restraint but

---

[1] It must be confessed that the Germans with their experiments on human 'guinea pigs' in the next war were to prove that such things were not beyond their ingenuity.

also a noteworthy sense of fair play and justice. One of these concerned the school, on the staff of which were two German brothers. Neither was a naturalized British subject when war broke out, and one, paradoxically enough, was not only a Housemaster but was also in charge of the Army Class. There were patriotic demands for the removal of both, but the Governing Body of the school stood out firmly, the only consequence being that the elder of the two relinquished the Army Class and his House. Then, too, there was the case of the German owner of a small engineering works who was systematically swindled by a member of the House of Commons and who sued in the Courts for redress. That a British jury, at the height of the war, with anti-German feeling running strong, awarded the plaintiff substantial damages was an outstanding example of justice which, as the plaintiff himself admitted, would certainly not have been displayed in his own country.

Within two years we, in the safety of England, had slipped into the routine of war. Air raids had become a common feature, the Zeppelin, a clumsy engine of aerial warfare, having soon been superseded by the aeroplane. They were, it is true, chicken feed compared with what the next war had in store, but gave us a taste of what H. G. Wells had foreshadowed. They drove us out of bed many a time, while the solitary anti-aircraft gun half a mile off pattered away cheerfully, without ever hitting anything seriously. A school concert was once brought to an untimely end with the wail of the warning sirens; and there was real excitement when a flight of Taubes passed over the school buildings at midday during the summer of 1918, jettisoning their bomb loads in the vicinity, smashing a row of cottages, severely damaging the covered tennis courts, where up to 1914 the European championships had been played, and causing many casualties. Loss of life, however, was relatively small, even if casualties from all air raids throughout the war were combined in one total, since aerial warfare was very much in its infancy. The scientific marvel of the splitting of the atom was still more than two decades away, and even such refinements as napalm and the fragmentation bomb had not been developed by western science. When I look back to the years of the Great War, it seems curious that the comparatively insignificant loss of life and damage to property should have caused so much indignation. That they did was due to two simple reasons. Aerial warfare was a novel form of attack, and to its novelty was added the fact of its indiscriminate nature. The civil population, which was to become merely a hypothetical entity thirty years later, still existed as something apart from the fighting forces. The bombing of civilians, men, women and children was held to be not merely against the recognized canons of war as it should be waged, but worse. It was evil. One had to wait another thirty years before western politicians and scientists were to demonstrate in the eastern hemisphere that it was a civilized and conventional form of warfare.

Food shortages resulted from the German submarine campaign, another form of waging war that was a fruitful source of public indignation. Labour, too, owing to the heavy drain on the country's man-power, was in short supply, and to overcome the scarcity of farm hands during the harvesting season parties of schoolboys were recruited to work in the fields or the orchards during the summer holidays. I joined two such parties, working on a farm one year at Bluntisham in Huntingdonshire, and for a change the next year as a fruit picker on a mixed farm at Melbourne cum Meldreth, a village near Royston in Cambridgeshire. Basically the work was voluntary, but since under the law at least a nominal wage was necessary, we received 5s. per week as pocket money—which regrettably we spent on Black Cat cigarettes and the odd pint of beer, this last being a very innocuous brew, watered down out of all recognition under a special wartime order.

Many years later, when I was out on tour in the Indian countryside with its mud huts and general untidiness, I was to recall these pleasant little English villages, now no more in the petrol age, with their life centred round the ivy-covered Norman tower of the church at one end and the village inns at the other. The thatched cottages were fragrant with the scent of the honeysuckle and rambler roses climbing in profusion over the walls. The larger and more pretentious houses, the Rectory and the village Doctor's, of brick or stone, had been mellowed with age and were largely hidden in masses of dark ivy or covered over with the russet of virginia creeper. Taken as a whole they diffused an air of compactness, neatness and order; and the good, solid qualities rooted in the English soil.

By this time a fairly intensive study of the classics, together
with the events of the day, was leading to a rapid erosion of
some of my traditional beliefs. Although this was certainly not
its intention at Dulwich, the Socratic teaching of not accepting
one's environment uncritically was seeping deep down. I now
began to ask myself what the war was really being fought for,
what its causes had been and what were the basic aims of the
belligerents in general and of Great Britain in particular.
These were not matters of moment to my English contemporaries, since the root of public school ethic was acceptance
of a specific situation as a fact and not its critical examination.
Theirs not to reason why, and certainly not during a war.
For the youth of Great Britain the causes of the war had been
reduced to very simple terms, German imperial ambition,
German aggression, German militarism. British aims were
equally simple, the destruction of all three. But the commencement of 1918 saw the promulgation of other more high-toned,
though at the same time more nebulous, ideas. Themes such
as freedom and self-determination, a war to end all war, a
war to make the world safe for democracy, began to be bandied
around. H. G. Wells was arguing strongly in favour of a League
of Nations; while early in 1918 the President of the U.S.A.,
which was a late and very reluctant combatant, had put out
Fourteen Points and Four General Principles as his blueprint
for a rosy future for mankind. I still have in my possession a
selection of the literature which we were not only encouraged
to read but also to believe. Such books as Norman Angell's
Prussianism and its Destruction and H. G. Wells' *In the Fourth Year*
make very odd reading in the sixties.

For the first time, too, India came to loom large in my
eyes. It was not that nationalist ideas were consciously pushed
into my mind by any particular person. But external influences,
the circumstances of the day, had begun to impinge on and
arouse my curiosity. For some time past my mother had been
the London Honorary Secretary of the Indian Women's
Education Association, a staunch supporter of which was
Henry S. L. Polak, a solicitor at the Privy Council Bar and
well known in Indian circles for his work in India's cause.
In addition to his other activities Polak edited a weekly (or
fortnightly) entitled *Free India*, so far as I remember, and during

the holidays I met him occasionally. Then there were other
mildly radical influences. My sister, who had added an LL.B.
degree from London University to her B.A. from Wales, mixed
in minor artistic and literary circles, considered 'advanced'
for the period. Their members, I hasten to add, far from being
conscientious objectors, were mostly clad in khaki, and either
off to, or back from, active service. Their talk was free, and
their opinions were uninhibited.

Strong doubts soon clouded my mind regarding the much-
publicized war aims of the Allies. These were not applicable,
it seemed, to Ireland, that unhappy country having been almost
pushed into rebellion only eighteen months earlier. Would
President Wilson's Fourteen Points be relevant to India after
the war?   And if there were to be no annexations, what would
be the position of Egypt, which in fact *had* been annexed on
the outbreak of war, or of the Ottoman Empire? The division
of Turkey and its possessions had already been made clear, although the details of the secret treaties between Great Britain,
France, Russia and Italy—each of which contradicted the
other—were to be known only after the war. Zionism, too,
had been recognized in 1917 with the promulgation of the
Balfour Declaration, which promised the Jews a national
home in Palestine without clarifying the effects of this on the
lavish assurances already given to the Arabs as the price of
their rebellion.

The consequences of this unconventional kind of cerebra-
tion were to make themselves apparent in an essay set to the
VIth Form on the capacity of a democracy to govern an
empire successfully. The underlying intention, suggested in
the first instance by the fact that we were engaged at the time
in studying the Pelopponesian war, was that a comparison
should be made between Great Britain in the role of Athens
as the defender of freedom and democracy and the militarism
of a neo-Spartan Germany, to the disadvantage, of course,
of the latter. I gave the expected answer that the Germans were
totally unfitted to govern subject peoples, and that they should
be deprived of whatever small portions of the globe they had,
as very late-comers into the race for empires and markets,
been able to garner. Unfortunately I then abandoned my
safe position and deviated considerably from the accepted

canons of public school ethic. I went on to argue that even a
democracy could not be successful in the governance of an
empire without granting Home Rule to its component parts.

This, a novel and certainly not popular thesis, caused a
furore worthy of a better essay. In the VIth Form, official
reports in printed forms were not customary, their place being
taken at the end of each term by informal, personal letters
to one's parents on the subject's work and general demeanour.
The consequences of my adolescent effort were somewhat
alarming. My Form master, Philip Hope, was a kindly, well-
meaning soul, given to nervous breakdowns from time to
time, and my essay perturbed him a great deal. So much
so that he wrote to my mother to warn her that a continuance
on these lines would see me end not in the Indian Civil Service
as hoped for but in prison as a 'seditious editor'. This was an
unnecessarily alarmist view, but my mother with visions
before her of Madan Lal Dhingra—the student who had
assassinated Sir Curzon Wyllie some years earlier—was seriously
distressed. It was not until she read the offending document
(thoughtfully sent by the next post) that her fears for my
future evaporated, for she herself was in full agreement with
most of the views expressed in it. The episode was brought
to my notice again nearly fifty years later in a less serious
manner. The other Indian boy in my House at the time,
Shavaksha, was a year senior to me. When I happened to be
his guest in Bombay in 1964, he mentioned the incident, adding
that Philip Hope in real distress had asked him to do something about it, and to lead me back to the path of political
righteousness. Shavaksha, it seems, passed the matter off in
an elder-brotherly kind of manner with a 'boys will be boys'
attitude. He certainly never spoke to me on the subject at the
time, and I did not know that he had ever been approached
at all until he told my wife and myself in Bombay.

By the standards of the time, however, Hope certainly had
reason on his side. Although Plato's Dialogues were a regular
feature of the VIth Form menu, authority did not expect
their application to the problems of the day by beardless
striplings. If there had to be doubt or criticism, went the
theory, let it come later; but at school even the mildest ques-
tioning of the alleged values of the Empire or a critical exami-

nation of its structure was thought to be in bad taste—one
of the things a gentleman did not do. In the course of time,
afterthoughts, long-after thoughts—brought home to me the
fact that it was neither the originality nor the lack of convention shown in my essay that was praiseworthy. It was the
official reaction that was creditable. It was not difficult to
criticize. It was less easy for the opposite party with political
and patriotic feeling running high to be tolerant of the criticism. In this case Dulwich, beyond writing more in sorrow than
in anger to my mother, took no further action. I was not
reprimanded. My prefect's cap was not taken away, and I was
not reported to the India Office as an undesirable Indian or
as a potential revolutionary. I did not speculate at the time,
as, indeed, I could well have done, on the consequences that
would have ensued in a French *Lycée* or a German Gymnasium
had I written in the same strain in the middle of a war for
national existence. Forty years later the wheel had turned full
circle, and the smallest good word for the British Empire was
classed as an indication of oddity, if not of downright perversity.
It was only with the lapse of the years that I came to realize
that the essential problem in the expression of opinions is the
selection of the right time and the proper location. Tolerance
on the other hand is in a different category. It should take
heed neither of time nor place.

Religion, too, as a consequence of the war, had entered my
mental picture, and my former beliefs, though not yet a complete casualty, were being severely mauled. My parents,
officially Nonconformists by creed, were not by nature narrow.
They regarded the various sects of institutional Christianity as
fundamentally one, a surprisingly unorthodox outlook when
they were all at loggerheads over the smallest matters affecting
doctrine and ritual. On his visits to England my father would
take me to a selection of services, presumably to give me
experience. They varied from Brompton Oratory at the Roman
Catholic end of the scale—which greatly impressed me with
its solemn music, its ritual and processions—to the queerest
little chapels with unimpressive exteriors and even duller
interiors. For the rest I was brought up as an Anglican. The
process culminated early in 1917 with my premature confir-
mation, premature because the impulse behind it was the herd

instinct rather than true belief. Since it was the 'done thing' to be confirmed, why not do it and conform?

This easy-going, simple attitude was short-lived, and was soon clouded over with doubt. Our prayers in Chapel were devoted largely to victory for the Allied cause, to the safety of the King and the Royal Family, to the preservation of His Majesty's Dominions overseas and of the Empire, which included Ireland, then in a state of suppressed rebellion, Egypt, annexed only four years before, India, shortly to receive the rough end of the stick, and similar parochial matters. Since it seemed to me to be only reasonable to assume that all the other belligerents were acting in the same manner with their prayers directed solely to their own tribal ends, while simultaneously claiming a monopoly of virtue, it was not long before the faith which had been so carefully and assiduously inculcated was considerably weakened.

Three months after the armistice of November 11, 1918 and six months before I left school there took place in India the disturbances which were described in the British newspapers as rebellion. The full details were not revealed publicly until the Report of the Hunter Commission was published in 1920. But sufficient information had leaked out long before to weaken in my adolescent estimation most of the ideas in which I had been reared. I was no longer prepared to believe in the civilizing mission of the Empire which was still, an article of faith, axiomatic and unquestioned, in all British circles. I was no longer able to accept the theory that the long war had been fought in order to initiate the reign of justice and freedom for all. The specious and tendentious propaganda with which we had been deluged for four years had the reverse effect on me of what had been intended, and I had now definitely outgrown the restricted intellectual confines of Dulwich. With a great deal of political and religious scepticism combined into one fermenting mass, it was a very doubting young Thomas who proceeded to Oxford in October 1919 for three years, three years which far from removing my existing doubts added a great many more to them.

V

More Learning

'IT WAS bliss' was the verdict of Desmond Young in his Autobiography, 'to have been alive and young and at Oxford in those halcyon days before the war'; and blissful they certainly must have been if one could live as pleasurably as he did on a modest £200 per annum. Sandwiched in between the halcyon days of 1910 and the middle and late twenties— an era which was to become almost legendary and which ended with the great depression of the 1930s—was a short period of three years, the like of which the University had never seen before and was never to see again. These three years formed a transitional stage, a kind of bridge, between the England of my boyhood and the new England born of the Great War.

It was not that the University had altered in its externals. Oxford remained the city of dreaming spires, the first sight of which was so entrancing. The buildings mellowed with age, the Clarendon, the Sheldonian, the Bodleian, the Colleges with their well-trimmed lawns in the quadrangles were there as before, unchanged. The High Street, undisfigured with traffic lights, was still the most beautiful of all the beautiful streets in the British Isles, and the Thames continued to be the Isis. Yet if all these seemed immemorial and unchanging the times were not, and with the change in the latter went a change in the type of undergraduate. That one could not step twice into the same river, even the Isis, soon became abundantly clear.

By October 1919 the University had returned to normalcy in point of numbers, after having been almost denuded for four years; but the undergraduates were now undergraduates with a difference. There were the remnants of the halcyon days, men who had been in their first and second years in 1914 and who returned as seniors, to become my contemporaries in point of time though not of age and experience. At the other end of the ladder was the customary contingent of young men like myself straight from school. This was small in numbers and of the freshmen in my own college not more than a round dozen were of my kind. But the great majority formed a category of their own—ex-servicemen who lacked the necessary means in 1914, but were now able to enter the University on grants from the Government and on their war gratuities, men who had fought their war in many parts of the world, who had been wounded or taken prisoner, who, in brief, had seen life at its most raw. Maturity and experience now confronted complete immaturity. Yet such was the unconscious influence of Oxford, its atmosphere, that all types fused into a surprisingly harmonious whole in a surprisingly short time. For this small period of three years, the era of the ex-serviceman as it might be called, Oxford ceased to be merely an extension of the public school in which the schoolboy grew to maturity. It was a more mature University, set in a more serious atmosphere than that which had prevailed up to 1914. Gilded youth, the Bertie Woosters, were certainly there, but their presence was at a temporary discount, overshadowed, and was not to come into full bloom again until the age of the ex-serviceman had ended.

Perhaps one of the most unusual features of the immediate post-war period was the general attitude of the ex-servicemen to politics and politicians. It was not that they were uninterested in the world around them. The traditional Conservative and Liberal Clubs continued as before. The debates at the Union were well-attended; and the post-war spirit produced a new political infant in the shape of the Labour Club. But there was an air of unreality about such matters. The ex-serviceman was suspicious of politicians as a class, taking their speeches and appeals with a large grain of salt and appearing to be little interested in politics as a career.

I can recall only three undergraduates of my time who were to scale the heights of political office, and of these only two belonged to the 'lost generation', Anthony Eden (Lord Avon) of Christchurch and Hore-Belisha (Lord Belisha) of Balliol. The third of the trio, Malcolm Macdonald, like myself, was a freshman from school. His father was under a cloud at the time for his alleged pacifism during the war, and had lost his seat in the House of Commons in Lloyd George's notorious Coupon Election of 1918. Six years later, when the fog of war had lifted, and the war itself had passed into history, Ramsay Macdonald was to stage a dramatic comeback as the first Labour Prime Minister of Great Britain. Malcolm Macdonald was one of the progenitors of the new Labour Club, which I joined for a term or so out of curiosity. I was rewarded at the first Club dinner, when Ernest Barker, a don of New College, presided and with great ingenuity combined loyalty to the Crown with liberty, equality and fraternity in a toast to 'The King and the People', the only occasion in my life when I have raised a glass to this combination.

Politics, indeed, were down for the time being, although not completely out. Literature and the arts were probably rated higher, with Evelyn Waugh, who entered the University towards the end of the period, destined for future eminence. A new undergraduate magazine, *The Cherwell*, came to life in 1921 as a rival to the older *Isis*, with a different cover and devoted to wider interests. The O.U.D.S., too, had its attractions for many, and flourished. Politics, it seems, did not fully revive for some years after the exit of the ex-servicemen, until in fact, the commencement of the thirties, and of this period Osbert Lancaster has recently recorded: 'Oxford had undergone some profound and, to me, depressing changes. Aesthetics were out, and politics were in, and sensibility was replaced by social consciousness.' Oxford, the intellectual foster-mother of Asquith and Curzon, of Simon and Birkenhead, and of four Viceroys of India in my lifetime, the alleged home of lost causes, was soon to nurse the future leaders of social and political progress. It became the spiritual home of the Crossmans, the Gaitskells and the Wilsons.

Differences notwithstanding, the Oxford I knew was closer in many respects to the Oxford of 1880 than of 1960. Industrialization had touched only the fringes of the city, which still revolved round its University. There were living links with a past generation. The legendary figure of Dr Phelps (the Phelper), Provost of Oriel, and the doyen of the Old Alleynian dons, was often to be seen walking rapidly up or down the High, slightly bent, certainly, but full of surprising vigour. Dr Spooner, former Warden of New College, most of whose Spoonerisms, and certainly the dubious ones, were the product of ribald undergraduate wit and ingenuity, was not always in monastic seclusion. Most venerable of all was Dr Boyd, the

Principal of my own college, who however was seldom to be
seen outside his Lodge; for he was over ninety years of age
and was to die while I was in residence. The race of Life
Fellows, too, lingered on in the person of its last representative,
F. H. Bradley, the philosopher, who was still in residence at
Merton. Shane Leslie has remarked of the Cambridge of his
time—fifteen years earlier—that the education at Oxford and
Cambridge was 'more intelligent than scientific'. This verdict
remained true for the period immediately succeeding the
first war. At Oxford the education and general training were
directed more at making one think for oneself than at the mere
accumulation of uncorrelated facts, it being rightly held that
the amount of factual information to be gathered in the small
space of three years could neither be large nor in itself of great
importance. Three elements, however, certainly differentiated
Oxford from Cambridge, two academic and one very pleasantly
earthy and material: All Souls, the School of Literae Huma-
niores, and, as a rapid descent from the sublime, the custom of
sconcing in Hall.[1] To these three there were no equivalents at
Cambridge. The humanities and the legacy of Hellenism
lived on, and had not yet been completely ousted from pride
of place in Great Britain's intellectual life. Oxford's unique
School, Greats, remained for the time being a strong factor
in the essential Oxford atmosphere, with its high prestige
undimmed. Another forty years were to elapse before it was
to be transformed under the corrosive effects of a second World
War into the mere relic of an antiquated past and its intelligent
training to give way to technology.

The College I joined was Hertford, a small, friendly, soci-
able, in one short word, homely college. The drab exterior of
its old buildings, all the more unpretentious for being adjacent
to the grandeur of the twin towers of All Souls, was relieved

---

[1] Sconcing. A pleasant penalty levied at dinner in Hall for a breach of
conventions such as talking 'shop' or mentioning a lady's name. The offender
supplied free drinks to the whole table. He could select anything he liked, but
naturally beer was the normal. It came in a three pint silver tankard which
would be placed before him. He would start the ball rolling by raising the lid,
taking a few sips, wiping the rim with the table napkin provided and then pass
the sconce on to the man on his left who would repeat the process. A sconce could
be 'floored' if the culprit was able to drink it himself within two minutes without
taking his lips from it. In that case the whole table was 'sconced' in return—free
beer for quite a time. I saw a sconce 'floored' only once, and then a short time
later it got its own back and 'floored' the drinker.

somewhat by the Bridge of Sighs which connected the old quadrangle with the new; and the old quadrangle itself contained a curious mixture of medieval and modern architecture. The college had had a chequered career. It had originated in the thirteenth century as a Hall of Residence and was not given its charter as a College until the early part of the eighteenth century. After going bankrupt later on, it was refounded through the munificence of the Baring family in the middle of the Victorian age. As a Hall of Residence it had produced its quota of eminent men—Tyndale, the translator of the Bible, Hobbes, the philosopher, and Charles James Fox among them, but in this respect the modern foundation still has to catch up with its predecessors. With neither the social prestige of Magdalen and Christ Church nor the halo of intellectual superiority with which Benjamin Jowett had endowed Balliol, it never attempted to arrogate to itself airs and graces to which it was not entitled. When I went up it ranked half way up or down in the hierarchy of colleges. Ten years later it was still a 'middling' college according to Stephen Spender; and that, it seems, was its position in the middle of the century[1]—an apparent lack of dynamism representing according to individual taste either mere sluggish conservatism or the more solid qualities which do not alter with the passage of time. Housing neither hearty heavyweights who delighted to burst into one's rooms to burn the furniture out of sheer exuberance nor gentle aesthetes who burnt incense in privacy behind their 'oaks' it was the embodiment of the Aristotelian golden mean, and what was good enough for Aristotle was good enough for me.

My three years were in no way spectacular. The routine of college life came naturally to me. I enjoyed being a member of the college Rugby XV, despite the fact that this pursuit was an ill-chosen one in view of my slight physique and the heavyweights who consistently opposed me. I was pleased, too, when one year I coxed the college boat in the Torpids, even though I was so unsuccessful that I was never invited to do so again. Best of all were the long discussions in the privacy of

---

[1] *World within World*, p. 33. And according to Evelyn Waugh who went up to Hertford a term before I came down, the position of the College in 1960 was exactly where it was in 1920. *A Little Learning*, (Chapman and Hall, 1964), p. 160.

one's rooms when the circulation of coffee and port would assist deep thought, and grave conversation with friends on abstruse matters would be prolonged into the small hours. Not the least of the College's good points was the possession of an excellent kitchen and a cellar that was by no means to be despised. The beer, too, was as good as both, and, what was of equal importance, was cheap, since the custom of sconcing in Hall during dinner was a frequent indulgence. It was a good life.

It could have been even better had not my allowance been about the minimum on which to support existence. But my father had assumed, without good evidence, that my failure to win an open scholarship was more an indication of lack of industry than of classical capacity, and was not disposed to be generous—a defect which, I should add, he made up five years later on my passing into the I.C.S. In my undergraduate days, however, I was unable to appreciate to the full the delights of the college cellar, my depredations being limited to an occasional bottle of sherry and port. This was all the more unfortunate because as a result of frequent visits to my sister's small vineyard in France I soon learnt to distinguish between what might be termed the rough from the smooth (my sister's produce belonging exclusively to the first category). It was equally unfortunate, too, that when in later life I was able to indulge more freely in the second category I had succeeded in ruining whatever palate I had once possessed by the free smoking of Indian cheroots and a fair consumption of the 'chhota peg', that real blessing of British rule which, I fancy, will outlast parliamentary democracy and similar ephemeral political mechanisms.

Fortunately for my purse, my confrontations with the Proctors were not numerous, and would have been even less had it not been for my desire to indulge in ballroom dancing, a social accomplishment which I had acquired during my visits to the Riviera and which I saw no reason to forgo even in term time. The authorities, on the other hand, did not see eye to eye with me, and looked with great disfavour on the Masonic Hall where public dances were held every Friday. This prohibited, albeit highly respectable, haunt, along with the local pubs, was the subject of the attention of the Proctor and his two bowler-hatted Ganymedes once each half. Their glances were sometimes merely of a routine nature, but were less perfunctory when, as often seemed to be the case, the University needed funds. An enforced appearance before Authority next morning cost one two guineas for a first offence. This, however, was cheap when compared with the penalties exacted some three hundred years earlier during the chancellorship of Archbishop Laud, a stern and uncompromising moralist who not only prohibited undergraduates from visiting places where there were 'wine, women or the nicotian herb on pain of being publicly flogged' but also debarred them from 'proceeding to a degree.if they played at football'.

The University coffers did not benefit greatly from my few misdemeanours, the most costly of which took place during my first Eights Week. During the previous vacation I had met a girl who was at Reading University, and I now invited her for a day to see the summer Eights. Owing to the Reading authorities taking the view that the safety of their girl students lay in numbers, she arrived with two unexpected friends, thus compelling me to call on two friends of mine from New College for assistance. This was readily given, and a pleasant (and respectable) time was had by all; so much so, indeed, that when the time arrived for the girls to leave, we found that the last suitable train for Reading had left long before them. We therefore hired a car for the journey of twenty-five miles, and my guests were safely back in their Hostel within the time limits allowed by the rules. We, on the other hand, arrived back in the small hours—which, so far as I was concerned, entailed either risking my neck on an unknown way into the college over walls or ringing up the night porter. Taking the simpler and, I fear, less adventurous course, I was duly mulcted next day of £5 in addition to expenses already incurred to which was added a fatherly warning that the proctorial successors of Archbishop Laud did not really regard such things with favour, even during Eights Week.

On going up to Oxford I gave up classics in favour of the History Honours School. One reason for the switch-over was that my English prose was less bad than my Greek and Latin, but the main one was that under the revised regulations for the I.C.S. examination, classics had been reduced in importance in the marking and history had been upgraded. From the start I was fortunate in my Tutor, C. R. M. F. Cruttwell, who was also Dean of the College. Cruttwell, a colourful and unusual personality, had a different effect on different people. Evelyn Waugh, for example, unduly sensitive to Cruttwell's disconcerting little idiosyncracies and strongly disapproving, it seems, of his bias against the presence of women undergraduates at his lectures, has devoted a disproportionate number of pages in his *A Little Learning* to a surprisingly savage and, to my mind, quite unjustified attack on him.[1] Cruttwell certainly had the reputation of being a misogynist (but when was misogyny a crime?), but whether he ever drove any girl misguided enough to present herself at his lectures out of the room by his obscenities, I do not know, since I attended very few lectures. He once described the literary output of Mme de Stael as being that of a 'woman of rapid conception and easy delivery', but this verdict, apt and possibly not original, could scarcely have hurt the virgin susceptibilities of any girl, even in 1920. Cruttwell, moreover, was not alone in his dislike of having girl undergraduates in the lecture hall. Osbert Lancaster, with a lighter and more human touch, tells of one Professor Dawkins of the School of English Literature who suffered from precisely the same lack of cordiality.

Cruttwell, an admirable tutor for anyone who took the smallest interest in his subject, had the great virtue of taking as much trouble with his commoners as with his scholars. He impressed me as wanting to find out what interested his man, and on occasion even took the opportunity of telling the latter what *ought* to interest him. He once mildly suggested to me that I should read more Indian history than I was doing at the time, informing me frankly that there was no reason for me to imitate his ignorance of it. The criticism sank in, and in due course I did my best to remedy the defect. A very able man himself, a Fellow of All Souls, Cruttwell did not expect everyone to reach his level, but for his scholars he naturally set a high standard, since he himself had been largely instrumental in selecting them. He tried to get the best out of his material and was free with his praise when his men did well. He certainly wrote me a very nice letter on my obtaining a high second.

[1] Ibid., pp. 173-5.

His conspectus of history was narrow, as Evelyn Waugh has remarked, but within his chosen field, Franco-German relations, he was an acknowledged expert. The same criticism, moreover, could have been directed against the History faculties of all the British Universities of the time, including the Oxford School. Everywhere the scope given to the subject was very limited, being confined to the growth and development of the British Isles, the Empire, and the European continent. Asia and Africa were merely colonial playgrounds for the European powers. The Eastern Question had nothing to do with the East proper, but concerned itself with the decline of the Ottoman Empire and its final liquidation in a fit manner. Japan, which had risen to the status of a First Class power by the end of the nineteenth century, consisted of only a group of islands on the map; and the possibility of China, Napoleon's 'sleeping giant', ever arousing itself to claim the status of a Great Power and to give a sudden jolt to historical evolution, was never given even a perfunctory thought. Toynbees there doubtless were. They were the products of Oxford, and had received their intellectual stimulus and training there; but they did not hold professorial chairs. This complacent, parochial approach, the product partly of the (incorrect) view that history should be written not less than fifty years after the event and partly of the deep-rooted idea that Europe was destined to perpetual supremacy, resulted in the continuance of a dangerous optimism which was still heavily coloured with that pre-1914 'White Man's Burden' complex in which I had spent my preparatory school days. To all British Universities the world continued to mean Europe, with possibly the U.S.A. in addition, under the leadership and guidance of Westminster and Whitehall.

I think I was the first Indian to be a member of Hertford, but I was soon to be joined by two more, S. K. Ghose, who had been nominated into the I.C.S., and the Hon. Tarun Sinha, a younger son of the first Baron Sinha of Raipur, the only Indian to have been raised (incongruously perhaps) to the British peerage. Of my contemporaries a number were to make their mark later, some in the I.C.S., some in other walks of life, the most outstanding of the former being K. P. S. Menon, and of the latter, Liaquat Ali Khan. Menon took a brilliant first in History, narrowly missed a Fellowship at All Souls and headed the combined list for the Civil Services in 1921. Liaquat Ali Khan, whom I came to know well later in the United Provinces, was always more distinguished in the political than the intellectual sphere. The right-hand man of Mr Jinnah, the leader of the Muslim League, he was destined not only to be one of the makers of Pakistan but also its first Prime Minister.

Indians in general, it must be said, along with other coloured races, were not popular in the University. The position of the average Indian was inevitably difficult. Confronted suddenly with different values and standards from those prevailing in India and also a way of life which in most cases he knew only from hearsay, he did not find it easy to get his bearings. In India the English had so far kept very much to themselves, forming a close corporation which did not welcome the intrusion of Indians. They were, so to speak, in a tank looking out, with Indians outside inquisitively peering in. In England, if Indians were diffident and sometimes displayed the aggressiveness that often accompanies diffidence, the Englishman remained parochial, with the insularity for which he was notorious throughout Europe preventing him from being an easy mixer with those of a different colour.

Oxford, moreover, was in 1920 still a living part of the old traditional England, with all its faults as well as its dignity, its charm, its solid virtues. Along with Cambridge it was unique among the Universities of the world, with a specifically English texture, the good points of which an Indian could appreciate after long residence in the country, the texture which S. P. B. Mais has feelingly summed up as 'The old England which the Old Lady of the last century preferred to Heaven'.[1] Oxford knew in her heart that on the basis of her own Hellenistic tradition and teaching she ought to be more international in outlook, more aware of the rights of others, apart from the peoples of Europe; but it was her nature to move step by step, with caution, until the time came a generation later when the whole country, its old values uprooted in the storm of a second

---

[1] Preface to *The Loom of Youth* (1917).

World War, was pushed rapidly into what has been termed 'the shadowy vale of cosmopolitanism'.[1]

'The shadowy vale', however, was a long distance away in my time. Oxford then was the Oxford which Evelyn Waugh has described with commendable frankness as a place where 'Asiatics abounded, and these were usually referred to as black men whether they were pale Egyptians [something radically wrong with Waugh's geography here] or dusky Tamils. There was no rancour in the appellation, no hint of deliberate personal contempt, still less of hostility. It struck us as being whimsical to impute cannibalism to these earnest vegetarians. We may have caused offence.'[2]

Although I knew all aspects of English life intimately, this particular one always irritated me. On the other hand identification with the ordinary life of his college and an interest in its daily affairs were normally sufficient to enable an Indian to surmount the attitude that he was a rather unpleasant element in the basically English cyster. I did not realize for many years that Indians themselves showed little of that broadmindedness, tolerance and friendliness towards one another, and still less to foreigners such as Africans, which they expected from others, especially Europeans. The efflux of time was to demonstrate clearly to me that Indians were by no means always on the side of the angels, and certainly not as often as they have deluded themselves into believing.

The traditional British habit of sweeping unpleasant things under the carpet and hoping for the best has now been abandoned, but it was very prevalent at the time of which I am speaking. The most important factor determining the relations between Englishmen and Indians was the one that was kept well out of view—race. Race, like other four-letter words, is no longer considered a matter unfit for discussion. Projecting itself into the forefront as the most important of all the problems confronting the modern world, it is now argued about in the House of Commons, legislated for, discussed in the daily newspapers, on the B.B.C. and at the U.N. with a freedom undreamt

[1] Shane Leslie, *The End of a Chapter*, p. 57. 'A few more sentimental mistakes, and Oxford and Cambridge, like old English boxing and London Society itself, will pass into the shadowy vale of cosmopolitanism'.
[2] *A Little Learning*, p. 184.

of in the era of British and European supremacy. The racial factor, though under the carpet at Oxford for the most part, often pushed its way through. Events exacerbated it.

It existed on both sides of the fence with equally baneful consequences. In the case of the British it was enhanced by their victory in the war. They were clearly the dominant power politically, though not financially, with their Empire not merely unscathed but even expanded. To the normal Anglo-Saxon antipathy to colour was added the consciousness of physical superiority. The white man ruled the globe as before, and he intended to push his domination home. The less commendable and more strident aspects of the imperialism of the pre-war age were enhanced and brought into sharper focus by the magnitude of the victory. On the Indian side there was a strong undercurrent of resentment, with the former uninhibited respect for England and all things English wearing thin. All coloured undergraduates were conveniently lumped together in the composite category of 'wogs' or 'niggers', derogatory terms both, carrying with them the stigma of inferiority. There could be good 'wogs' and bad 'wogs', acceptable 'wogs' and the reverse; but 'wogs' all Indians were by virtue of their nature and colour. Similar attitudes existed as much in Anglo-India as in Great Britain. 'Victory brought about a certain racial arrogance', was the verdict of *The Rise and Fulfilment of British Rule in India*. 'No European showed any recognition of the political and social changes of the war period. It was treated merely as an interlude, and the chief anxiety was to resuscitate the old Anglo-Indian life'.[1] The consequences in both countries were deplorable.

Contemporary events in India were abrasive to feelings on both sides and caused an immediate rise in racial temperatures. During my first year at the University, the Commission headed by Lord Hunter to examine and report on the suppression of the disturbances in the Punjab in the early months of 1919 issued its Report. A mild and colourless document, it contented itself with passing a few gentle reprimands on Sir Michael O'Dwyer, the then Lieutenant-Governor of the Punjab and on Brigadier-General Dyer, the officer charged with the martial

[1] p. 605.

law administration, and in due course received the imprimatur of the House of Commons. But whatever may have been the result in the division lobbies, both O'Dwyer and Dyer were the recipients of much sympathy, and even eulogy, outside the House. The House of Lords, not unexpectedly, was almost wholly in their favour. Some of the newspapers, headed by the notorious *Morning Post*, followed the example set by their lordships; and public acclamation took the generously tangible form of a subscription of £20,000 (which was a large sum at the time) not for the relief of the 379 Indians massacred and the 1200 wounded, but solely for the alleviation of the inconvenience caused to the unfortunate General by his enforced retirement.

In a Minority Report the four Indian members of the Hunter Commission—all of the very moderate school of politics—differed sharply from the studied mildness of their British colleagues. Racial passions were inflamed on both sides, giving rise to imperial complacence on the one hand and deep resentment on the other. To most people in England, within my experience, General Dyer was the saviour of the Empire in India. To the Indian, Amritsar with its Jallianwala Bagh was simply a 'ghastly massacre'.[1] It was clear that there could be no common meeting ground between two such divergent standpoints. With exceptions, of course, Oxford subscribed to the general British attitude, taking the line which I myself heard that 'it served the niggers right'. The depth and prevalence of the view that the Empire was saved through the exertions of O'Dwyer and Dyer was again apparent a few years later. A libel case, a *cause célèbre*, was brought by Sir Michael O'Dwyer against Sir Sankaran Nair, a former member of the Viceroy's Executive Council, in which the events of 1919 were the main feature. The jury, with the honourable exception of Harold Laski of the London School of Economics, were wholly in favour of the plaintiff, while the presiding judge availed himself of the opportunity of passing unnecessary *obiter dicta* which were a clear reflection of the strength of popular British opinion.

The reason for Indian resentment was not merely the

---

[1] K.P.S. Menon, *Many Worlds*, p. 53.

excessive amount of firing at Amritsar on an unarmed crowd. Far more excoriating to feelings, certainly mine, were the callousness of the methods used and the deliberate infliction of humiliation for the purpose, in the frank and almost proud words of General Dyer himself, of creating a moral effect. The trapping of a large crowd, many of those present being villagers, in an area with only one small exit (rapid dispersal thus being impossible); the firing of 1600 rounds *without warning*—an illegal act in itself; the refusal of the General to render any assistance to the wounded who were left either to die or to look after themselves; the bombing of crowds from the air and machine-gunning at other places in the Province; the notorious Crawling Orders; the public floggings for minor breaches of the martial law orders such as the failure to salaam a commissioned officer, for showing disrespect to a European, for refusal to sell milk or to hand over a car, jointly and severally appeared to me, rightly or wrongly, to be examples of that 'frightfulness' which according to the highly moral and elevated propaganda on which I had been so carefully spoon-fed at school was the exclusive attribute of the Germans. 'I fired', said the General in his evidence, 'and continued to fire till my ammunition ran out and the crowd dispersed, and I consider this to have been the least amount of firing which would produce the necessary moral and widespread effect it was my duty to produce. If more troops had been at hand the casualties would have been greater in proportion. It was no longer a question of dispersing the crowd, but one of *producing a sufficient moral effect from a military point of view not only on those present, but more especially throughout the Punjab.*'[1]

Amritsar and the so-called rebellion of 1919 have long ago passed into history along with British rule, 'old, forgotten, far-off things', and history will not judge that rule by a single episode, black though it was, at least in Indian eyes. Its results at the time however were a calamity, and one rendered all the worse from the Indian angle because events in the Punjab followed close on the Rowlatt Report which only one year earlier had recommended strong measures to curb political agitation. This Report not only coincided with war-time propa-

[1] My memory of these events has been checked with the details given in *The Rise and Fulfilment of British Rule in India* pp. 608-11. The italics are mine.

ganda on the subject of freedom but also with what was more important to India, the Montagu-Chelmsford Report on political reforms. 'The two were read together and educated Indians can hardly be blamed for the conclusions they drew. Indians who had confidently been expecting a complete change in their status at the end of the war now saw the Government of India taking new powers for repressive action, and found little comfort in Mr Montagu's experimental reforms after they had been whittled down by an unsympathetic and hostile Parliament'.[1]

What to even a thoughtful Englishman was merely an episode, of no great significance, was to an Indian a repudiation of the high sentiments of Queen Victoria's Proclamation of 1858, and of the supposedly higher purposes of British rule. To a complete negation of the aims for which the war, as I had been led to believe, had been fought, was added an assertion of physical might based on racialism which seemed to me to be positive proof of political insincerity. Memories of my days at my Preparatory School came flooding back, of the emphasis the English had always laid on the Black Hole and the Well at Cawnpore. Not only did I feel that Sir Michael O'Dwyer and General Dyer between them had more than avenged both. Also the fact was driven home that race and colour were of significance and real importance in the governance of the Empire. My mind travelled back to the episode of Jack Johnson ten or twelve years before. I recalled the fact that the Irish rebellion of 1916 had been suppressed in six weeks without either floggings or Crawling Orders or any of the methods adopted in the case of a coloured people. Indeed, the Irish were once again carrying on a kind of guerilla warfare against the British when the Report of the Hunter Commission was made public. In the case of Ireland, too, the Nonconformist conscience of England was beginning to rebel against the relatively minor atrocities alleged against the Black and Tans (The Royal Irish Constabulary) and was soon to force a reluctant Westminster into a settlement with the rebels. But if the Scotts, Massinghams and Gardiners worried themselves over the wrongs of Ireland, they had little influence in matters relating to India.

[1] Ibid., p. 604.

The happy memories of my boyhood were thus pushed into the background, and the great mission of the Empire, which I had been taught to regard as a moral and civilizing force, now appeared to me to be a complete myth. The earlier doubts engendered in my mind during the war now crystallized into a distrust of the British and their intentions which was to harden even more as one by one, much-publicized war aims were thrown on to the scrap heap, and as British policy gradually unfolded itself between the two wars. This distrust remained unchanged until the end of 1945.

This metamorphosis in the Indian attitude towards Great Britain and the creation of disbelief in British sincerity were general in India. In my own case I mention them only as facts. I do not justify them; nor do I claim that they were correct— indeed, honesty compels the admission that my assessment was limited in its perspective. But such was the effect of the events in the Punjab, of the Hunter Commission and of the general British reaction that I know of no Indian of my generation who did not lose in a greater or lesser degree whatever faith he may have had in Great Britain and the British people. O'Dwyer and Dyer had completely superseded Mountstuart Elphinstone and Allen Octavian Hume.

A subject people, however, are ill-equipped psychologically to broaden their angle of vision into a wider and more balanced view until the cessation of foreign domination. As independence was to make evident, Indians were too prone during the British era to exalt their own virtues, to depress those of the British and to see only the faults of their rulers. Understanding of the bitter reaction against the British is perhaps difficult for the modern generation in the British Isles in an age inured to the massacre of millions in gas chambers for the sin of their race, to the wholesale destruction of large cities by atomic power— also without full and due warning—and to regular outbursts of racial violence in the U.S.A. and elsewhere. Let it be conceded, too, that within thirty years Indians themselves were to massacre one another on a far more generous scale on religious grounds than General Dyer had ever contemplated on imperial and racial. But in my last five years in England the veil had still to be lifted from the future. So far as Indians were concerned in 1920 the Martial Law Administration of 1919 formed an even more important turning point in Indo-British relations than the suppression of the Mutiny of 1857.[1]

On the British side of the hill, too, there was a certain lack of sensitivity, which is probably natural to all colonizing and imperial nations. James Baldwin has recently pointed out the unbridgeable gap between the white American and the negro in 1960, and the difficulty confronting even the most sympathetic superior in trying to place himself in the position of the inferior. 'Americans', he says, 'evade so far as is possible all genuine experience, and, therefore, have no way of assessing the experience of others, and no way of establishing themselves in relation to any way of life not their own.'[2] He is correct: for imagination can never be the equivalent of actual experience, and certainly can never supersede it. His dictum, with small changes can, not unfairly, be applied to the England of 1920. Within my experience it was not possible for the Englishman, even if he desired to do so, to enter into the mind of the Indian over the Punjab. He had imposed the Crawling Orders on Indians, but had never himself been subjected to their imposition. He had ordered public floggings for trivial offences, but these had never been inflicted on him; and he had not been machine-gunned from the air merely for gathering into a crowd with his fellows in order to protest against foreign rule. For Great Britain as a whole wider experience and with it less complacence, less glorification of its own righteousness and less belief in the innate superiority of the white man was not to mature until the widespread suffering and hardship of the Second World War.

The story of the Punjab in 1919 is of historical importance, apart from the emotional reactions evoked in India at the time. How, I have often wondered, is history taught in the schools of contemporary Great Britain ? Are the Punjab, O'Dwyer, Dyer and the other British actors on the stage given the same prominence in history textbooks as the Black Hole, the Cawnpore Well, Siraj-ud-Daula and Nana Sahib were given in my

---

[1] 'The Mutinies have produced too much ill-feeling between the races to render any mere change of name of the rulers a remedy for the ills which afflict India . . . . . . Perhaps confidence will never be restored, and if so our reign in India will be maintained at the cost of suffering which is fearful to contemplate.' Russell, Correspondent of *The Times* (London), after the suppression of the Mutiny
[2] *Notes of a Native Son.*

schooldays? Or are they glossed over as trivialities of no significance? If the teaching of history is to have any value at all,
unpleasant or discreditable facts, whether Indian or English,
should be given their correct place in assessments of the impact
of one race on another.

As I look back on these years and the years to follow, two
points of some interest have occurred to me. The first was the
existence of a feeling, not always expressed in words, the
suspicion that the action taken was 'un-English', in Sir Winston
Churchill's phrase, and was a real matter for regret. It is probable that this attitude was more widespread than I imagined it
to be, especially in the case of the next generation of young
Englishmen who entered the Indian Services. Embodied in it
was the typical public school reaction, 'Let it all be buried in
a handshake, and let's start off afresh on the right foot.'
Unhappily the scars left behind by General Dyer were not
susceptible to this simple treatment; and if I with my long
years of residence in England and my understanding of the
English people failed to place Amritsar in its correct historical
setting, how much more difficult was it for others to do so who
had not had that experience?

Lastly, the conclusions which I drew at the time as an angry
young man were an interesting postscript to the views of Shane
Leslie which I have quoted earlier inasmuch as they were to
some extent the consequence of the equality of treatment I had
received in England, and were all the stronger for that reason.
In India itself Indians were more attuned to accepting their
inferior status as a subject people with a certain degree of
fatalism. Not having been subjected to the full blast of insincere
war-time propaganda, even Indians of my generation educated
in European schools in India accepted the actions and outlook
of Anglo-India with far less surprise than I did. The notice, for
example, placed outside the semi-public library in the hill
station of Mussoorie with the information 'dogs and Indians
not admitted' was regarded with a mixture of resentment and
resignation; but, of course, there was nothing to be done about
it. Yet, as I shall mention later, the patent incongruity between
my new, and deep, distrust of the British and my intention to
sit for the I.C.S. examination in the hope of joining them in
their Administration did not impinge itself on my mind any

more than it occurred to the other young Indians who were addressing themselves to the same task.

As events turned out, however, the prospects of my ever entering the I.C.S. were very doubtful by the time I had taken my Schools in 1922. It was not rumbustious nationalism on my part that dimmed them. It was the depressingly large number of unsettled bills which descended on me at the last moment like an avalanche. A rapid calculation disclosed debts amounting to something over £200, my college battels being among them. Since the Bursar could hardly be expected to accommodate me in regard to the latter, I was reluctantly compelled to make a formal report to my father, the upshot of which was that I was now instructed to go out into the wide world for a space to earn my own living. Realizing that I had received my deserts I did not complain, and being just over twenty-one years of age was possessed of the robust optimism of youth. As the days passed by, however, and the remnants of my bank balance grew thinner and thinner, my optimism, too, followed suit until it nearly vanished altogether.

The value of a degree in History in the employment market was, and probably still is, limited to the teaching profession, but, so far as I was concerned, it soon became clear, after I had answered dozens of advertisements from the Educational Agents, that the schools of England were not clamouring for my services. There were large numbers in the market; for 1922 saw the exodus of ex-servicemen from the universities and preference was inevitably given to them. My nationality, too, was a handicap in an England still far from internationalism.[1] Having exhausted my importunity on a number of public, private and grammar schools, I eventually found myself in the study of the Headmaster of my preparatory school, the Rev. W. R. M. Leake. Here I was in luck, for Leake was willing to employ me, as an old boy of the School, in a temporary vacancy carrying with it the unprincely salary of £235 per annum, to be paid in instalments each half-term. Hastily borrowing £20

---

[1] The Headmaster of Birkenhead School in 1922 was Kennard-Davis. In 1923 R. C. Bonnerjee, one of the sons of W. C. Bonnerjee, met Kennard-Davis, who had been a friend of his from his Rugby and Oxford days. Kennard-Davis recalled my application for a post at Birkenhead because of the name, and told R. C. Bonnerjee that he would certainly have called me for an interview had I been an Englishman.

from my mother, who, unlike my father, had been inclined to forgive and forget, in order to open a new bank account, I found the cheapest lodgings available and consistent with the status of schoolmastering, and within a week was present at morning prayers appropriately clad in a graduate's gown.

It was now brought home to me that for millions of others life was rougher than it had so far been for me. My bed-sitting room, with board, cost 30s. per week, and was naturally not to be compared with the accommodation in an Oxford college. Though comfortable in its own way, its decor was disconcerting, since the artistic tastes of my landlady, like those of many landladies, were restricted to prints of Landseer in the general sitting room, and to the Bible as inspiration for the bedroom. An oleograph of the infant Samuel at prayer hung above my bed, and over the wash-stand was a large card with forget-me-nots in the corners and the inscription 'God is Love' in the middle. Chary of hurting the feelings of my landlady, who was good to me, I refrained from removing these formidable decorations, and left them intact for my successor.

My fellow lodgers were of different types. One, a girl, chanced to be a temporary mistress at the Preparatory School. After school hours she attended University College, London, from where she took her degree in Modern Languages and then migrated to a better post in a large school for girls. Of the men one was so eccentric that he ended in a mental home. Then there was the young man straight from school who was perpetually falling in love and telling us of his troubles in the hope of obtaining advice on how to free himself from each successive entanglement. At the commencement of his adventures he had purchased a ring which did the rounds until one stony-hearted girl took a fancy to it, put her foot down and refused to return it.

An ex-serviceman, named Preece, and I became friendly, and on our small earnings managed to enjoy what for me was an entirely new life. If London was an expensive city, it could also be a cheap and pleasant one for the impecunious. Any of the little restaurants in Soho would provide a good dinner, cosy surroundings and an atmosphere undisturbed by an orchestra of dubious quality for a matter of 4s., and very reasonable wines and cigars were sold at what would now be regarded as give-away prices. Nor had other forms of entertainment to be expensive, since it was not essential always to sit in the stalls of a West End theatre. The Alhambra (soon to follow the way of the Empire, that landmark of the naughty nineties, and convert itself into a cinema), the Hippodrome and the Coliseum all functioned well as variety theatres. One could also go slightly farther afield to the Victoria Palace, near Victoria Station, close to which was one of the best little Italian restaurants in London. With the Lyric and King's theatres in Hammersmith and the Old Vic in Waterloo Road—at all of which the quality of the productions was in inverse ratio to the low prices—to cater to one's higher tastes, life was not unpleasant, though it was not in any way dramatic.

The grimmer side, while not affecting me personally, was also present. There was economic chaos in Europe, the direct result of the failure of Great Britain's democracy to face squarely the facts of post-war life as presented by Keynes in his *Economic Consequences of the Peace*. The leaders of both component parts of the Coalition Government were hamstrung by their election promises of making Germany pay in full for the war and of 'squeezing the German orange till the pips squeaked'—a policy which produced much bitterness and no juice whatsoever. Trade and business languished. Employment became irregular and unemployment frequent. Large firms retrenched their staff, and small ones closed their doors. It was in this difficult period that my friend Preece lost his job for the time being, and was forced to put himself on the dole, or, as the official euphemism had it, Unemployment Relief. Unlike the unemployment relief of forty years later the dole of 1923 was barely sufficient to keep the wolf from the door. It was an end to be avoided rather than sought. The unfortunate Preece was thus in real distress for some weeks, during which our landlady, who held all ex-servicemen in great regard, kept him free of charge and the rest of us did our best to maintain his spirits until he was able to find another position. When I was on leave in 1933, I chanced to meet him again, and was glad to find him prospering.

The routine of schoolmastering, which I never regarded as anything more than a stopgap, was not burdensome. Work and games filled in the day, and the evenings belonged entirely to oneself. My subjects were History, English and Mathematics. The first two were simple enough, but the last was in a different category, since my own knowledge was not very much higher than that of my charges, and I was usually compelled to mug up each lesson before passing on the results. At the age of twenty-one or twenty-two one has the great advantage of not having forgotten one's actions and reactions at the age of twelve, memories which stood me in good stead in the maintenance of discipline. Bearing in mind my own demeanours some ten years before, I named some luckless child for Punishment Drill on the second day of term for prodding his neighbour in the ribs for no valid reason. Since I did not give the customary preliminary warning I immediately established a reputation for unprecedented ferocity which remained with me throughout my teaching career. This was in strong contrast to one of my older colleagues, whose form room was divided from mine by a wooden partition. Queer things went on on his side, often punctuated with loud laughter, and sometimes with mild cheering. On one occasion the door of the partition flew open and a small boy, red in the face, hair on end, burst in, going strong for the exit. Close behind him was my colleague, his gown flying in the air, a blackboard pointer in his hand and going even stronger. They passed out of sight and down the main staircase into the playground, where chastisement was no doubt (illegally) administered. The institution of Punishment Drill, too, had its amusing aspect. There was one bright youngster who made it a point of being selected for P.D. every Friday. This I discovered by chance on receiving a letter from his mother, a lady with a pleasant sense of humour. She knew, she said, from her own experience that her Peter could be a very great nuisance; but he always set out to be a particularly unmitigated one on Fridays. Friday, it transpired, was the day for his music lesson, and this he regarded as a far worse evil than mere punishment drill. Would I, requested his mother, please select any other day for disciplining him?

During my year at the Preparatory School I made two efforts to find a suitable position in India. I was interviewed by Sir Norcot Warren who was willing to take me into the Imperial Bank of India at any time, but who strongly advised me to wait and see if my father would relent in time for me to make an attempt to pass into the I.C.S. before I exceeded the age limit. 'There is no Service in the world to equal the I.C.S.,' said Sir Norcot. The same advice was given to me by Mr Mackenzie, the then Director of Public Instruction in the United Provinces, who added the caution that he did not think that the atmosphere of the Educational Service after its provincialization under the reformed Constitution would be congenial to me. Many years later, when I was safely in the I.C.S., he met my wife and myself at a dinner party in Delhi, and greeted my wife with the remark, 'You see what excellent advice I gave your husband long ago, Mrs Bonarjee.'

By the end of the summer of 1923 I had completed three terms of teaching, and in September my father paid an unexpected visit to see for himself what improvements, if any, time had effected in me. Unaware, fortunately for me, that my tailor's account continued to run on placidly, he appeared to be satisfied, and after an amicable talk, the decision was that I should be given another chance of working for the I.C.S. examination. It was, of course, made clear that this would be my last opportunity, and that my future, though no doubt in the lap of the Gods, was, in fact, entirely in my own hands. The short interlude in my academic career had closed.

I now joined the London School of Economics, selecting for myself those courses which suited the examination. Here, as was natural, the general atmosphere was the antithesis of that at Oxford: for Oxford was its University, and the University was Oxford. But in Houghton Street in the middle of London we were swallowed up in the impersonal vastness of the great, sprawling, bustling, throbbing city. The buildings, a solid block of modern masonry, were architecturally unprepossessing and bore a striking resemblance to the externals of any business house in the City close by. The impression was heightened by the lack of academic dress on the part of both students and staff. The men in their bowler hats and carrying attaché cases and the women in their sober costumes could have belonged to any Bank or Insurance Office in Threadneedle Street. Then, too, the London Colleges, save for one or two exclusively for women, were non-residential. There was no close-knit life as at Oxford, and at 10 p.m., when an Oxford College would be a blaze of light preparatory to its inmates starting out to unravel the mysteries of the Universe, the L.S.E. would be in darkness, the home of the night porter alone.

The four Inns of Court, not far off, had been careful to seclude themselves from the main stream of London's busy life. In a backwater of their own they retained much of their ancient grace and charm, with their panelled Halls, their traditions, their Chapels and their old custom of a fixed number of dinners in Hall as a prerequisite for the final call to the Bar. All this was absent from Houghton Street; for the L.S.E. was strictly practical and very modern, as befitted its designation. To keep in touch with commerce and industry, a Faculty of Commerce had recently been established, and special evening classes were held for young business men who sought to add theory to practice after their offices had closed. There were thus wholetime and part-time students, both being entitled to all the privileges of the School. Lectures were duplicated so that the benefit was equally distributed. It was the high quality of the staff and the lectures that gave the School its name and standing in the academic world. The buildings may have been undistinguished, but the Staff included many of the most brilliant men of the time. Names like Hobhouse, Graham Wallas, Laski, Tawney, Gregory (later to be Economic Adviser to the Government of India), Seligman and Malinowski would have lent lustre to any institution in the world, and the L.S.E. was well aware of the fact. The Director, too, Sir William (later Lord) Beveridge, was an economist of repute in his own right who came into great prominence twenty years later as one of the progenitors of Great Britain's Welfare State. He had spent his early life in India, with which his connexion was close; for his father had been in the I.C.S. and was the author of a standard History of India, written from the standpoint of a Gladstonian liberal.

Having wasted a complete year I was now left with only one chance for the open competition. I adhered to my own fixed programme, the authorities leaving me to my own devices, since I was not working for a degree. Having joined the School for the strictly practical purpose of working for a particular examination, I used it mainly as a moderately priced Club with a good library and some useful lectures. Its social side was pleasant. There were the usual clubs, two of which I joined,

the Rugby Football and the Rowing. The Students Union
(a very different body from the Oxford Union) looked after
all activities other than sporting, from the organization of
weekly dances to the issue of invitations to prominent persons
to come and address the School. Among these last was Lala
Lajpat Rai who spoke with deep feeling on the poverty, illiter-
acy and general ills of India under British rule. As a counter-
blast there arrived soon afterwards Lord Meston, a former
Lieutenant-Governor of the United Provinces, who assured
us that the position was not really as bad as was often alleged.
In between the two extremes was Bertrand Russell who, taking
as his theme the need for political scepticism, sensibly warned
us, though the advice was unnecessary in my case, not to
accept uncritically all that the professional politician was
accustomed to dish up for our youthful edification.

The I.C.S. examination took place in August 1924, the
written papers being preceded by an interview, the memory
of which remained with me to good purpose. The interview
lasted for perhaps thirty or forty minutes, but despite its length
was in no sense an inquisition. The Civil Service Commissioners
did their best to put the candidate at his ease, and my first
ten minutes were devoted to games and similar extraneous
topics before more serious matters were taken in hand. Many
years later I was to recall their friendly methods, and attempted
to emulate them to the best of my ability when it fell to me to
be a member of Selection Boards for the selection of officers
for emergency commissions during the war, and still later
when in 1950 I was appointed Chairman of the Public Service
Commission, Hyderabad.

Some three hundred and fifty candidates sat for the examination, the number of vacancies being limited to ten. The
reasons for the restricted quota were, first, that a certain
number of places continued to be filled by nomination, and,
secondly, that the system of concurrent examinations in India
for which the Indian National Congress had been pressing
since its first session in 1885, had been in vogue for three or
four years. I passed in seventh, three places higher than I had
ever hoped for even in my most optimistic moments. Out of
the ten successful candidates, seven were Indians, and of the
remaining three, one was an Englishman, one a Welshman

and one an Irishman. After the open competition the passing-
out examination at the end of the probationary year was
merely a formal anti-climax. I cannot say that I overstrained
my mental capacity in any way during my last year in England.
Instead, I made the most of what was to be the close of a
chapter in my life. The only subject, if that is the correct word,
which I took seriously for the passing-out examination was
riding. Here I headed the list, but somewhat like Charles
Lamb, who always left office early to make up for coming late,
tempered this mild success by being last in everything else.
I hasten to add, however, that the standard of horsemanship
required of us was no higher than the jumps over which we
were put. Cross-country riding in India brought me up against
obstacles, not always surmounted with success, far worse than
anything the pleasant young subaltern made us negotiate
in the Artillery Barracks Riding School at Woolwich.

October arrived, and with it the time for us to proceed to
the India Office to sign our Covenants with the Crown. In
looking back at this small ceremony I can see that it was no
mere formality on my part when I pledged myself to serve
His Majesty the King, his heirs and successors, loyally and
faithfully, to carry out all orders, to follow all service rules
and regulations, and not to engage in private trade of any
kind. I might (and normally did!) disapprove of His Majesty's
ministers, particularly his Secretaries of State for India, though
I had never met any of them in person; but the King himself
remained above his ministers, on a pedestal by himself, above
criticism. If we had our grievances, I did not hold the King
responsible for them. A few years later I lived as an honorary
member in the Mess of the 10/7 Rajput Regiment at Fatehgarh.
Every night after dinner the decanters would make their
conventional round and glasses would be replenished. The
Mess President would rise with the words 'Mr Vice, the King';
and Mr Vice would duly respond with 'Gentlemen, the King-
Emperor', on which the regimental band would commence
the anthem. It was with perfect sincerity that I would raise
my glass and empty it to the toast, a natural Royalist, never
a Roundhead. This was an attitude which was to come to the
forefront quite unconsciously seventeen years later in 1942,
a curious hangover, perhaps, from the early training of my

first decade in England, from my unconscious absorption of the idea of the Monarchy as the summit of the Establishment but apart from it, a relic of the small boy who waved his cap at the King and Queen as they drove past the school grounds in 1911. Here was another example of one Indian's schizo-phrenia, but in this case of a pleasantly harmless description.

Three weeks after signing my Covenant I set sail for India, to arrive at Bombay in the first week of December, a stranger to my own country after an absence of just over twenty-one years.

VI

The Indian Civil Service

FIFTY years ago it was difficult to assess correctly what the British had in mind as regards India. Prefectly sound cases can now be made out both for and against their ultimate intention to hand over power to Indians. Warren Hastings himself at the dawn of British dominion had envisaged its end when he inscribed in a translation of the *Bhagavad Gita* the words: 'These writings will survive when British dominion in India shall have long ceased to exist and the sources which it once yielded of wealth and power are lost to remembrance.' Thirty or forty years later another Governor General of the same name but no connexion, the Marquis of Hastings, was even more specific in his private journal. 'A time not very remote will arrive', he recorded on May 17th 1818, 'when England will on sound principles of policy wish to relinquish the domination which she has gradually and unintentionally assumed over this country and from which at present she cannot recede. In that hour it would be the proudest boast and most delightful reflection that she had used her sovereignty towards enlightening her temporary subjects, so as to enable the native communities to walk alone in the paths of justice, and to maintain with probity towards their benefactor that commercial interest in which we should then find a solid satisfaction.'[1]

Warren Hastings, the Marquis of Hastings, Elphinstone, Munro, Macaulay, Hume and many others of lesser eminence were all agreed that when the time came for the renunciation of power, it would be a matter of real pride for England. In support of these and similar pronouncements were packets of political reforms from time to time designed to implement them; and the final proof lay in the graceful demission of power in 1947. This is the *ex post facto* view put forward and argued with fluency and charm in Philip Woodruff's second volume of 'The Men Who Ruled India', *The Guardians*. The

---

[1] Quoted from an article by Admiral of the Fleet Earl Mountbatten of Burma in the *Times of India* Independence Day Supplement, August 15th, 1967.

Guardianship theory is not merely tenable. It is also to some extent irrefutable in the light of the final act. On the other hand, rightly or wrongly, this is not how the position appeared to Indians of my generation; for on the other side of the medal was engraved a series of declarations and actions, the cumulative effect of which went to prove to Indian minds that the British granted their reforms only as concessions to political agitation and with great reluctance, and that they then sought to nullify with the left hand what they had given with the right. 'Ever since 1917,' wrote one of the architects of independent India, 'I had been dealing with constitutional reforms. I had never expected that I would see freedom for India in my lifetime.'[1] And so, I am sure, would have said all of us.

Seen in retrospect the period between my entering the I.C.S. and the outbreak of war in 1939 was inchoate and indeterminate, with neither Indian nor Englishman thinking, at least for the first ten years of my service, in terms of a second war and its possible consequences. To Indians it always appeared that British policy was equivocal, and that Britannia intended to outwit her political petitioners in much the same manner in which Penelope had once dealt with her matrimonial suitors. A little skilful diplomacy here, a little suitably realistic action there, would be enough, we thought, to negative the high-toned declarations of policy which were made from time to time, and to side-step their consequences. It was, of course, accepted as axiomatic on the Indian side that Indians would administer the country as well as, if not better than, the British, but this was of small moment, since the idea of their ever being put to the test was held to be too remote for serious consideration.

Although this line of thought was proved by events to be incorrect, there was much evidence at the time to justify Indian scepticism. If the Marquis of Hastings set off with the ball in the direction of one goal, it was another Governor-General, Lord Curzon, whose goal nearly a century later was the exact opposite. As early as 1900 Lord Curzon informed Westminster of his 'firm belief that the Congress was tottering

[1] 'I had never expected that I would see freedom in my lifetime, and since it had materialised, my life's ambition had been fulfilled.' V. P. Menon, *The Integration of the Indian States* (Orient Longmans, 1956), p. 92.

to its fall, and that one of his great ambitions was to assist it to a peaceful demise'. This he followed up soon afterwards with the unambiguous declaration that 'it will be well for England, better for India, and best for all progressive civilization in general, if it be clearly understood from the outset that we have not the slightest intention of abandoning our Indian prossessions, and that it is highly improbable that any such intention will be entertained by our posterity.' Oddly enough it was Lord Curzon who redrafted the preamble of the India Act of 1919 in such a way as to include the words 'Responsible Government'. A few years after Lord Curzon's Viceregal dictum, no less a person than Lord Morley, the Secretary of State for India at the time, unequivocally stated that if the Act associated with his name (the so-called Morley-Minto Reforms) was to be treated as being the road to full representative government, then he for one would have nothing to do with it. Some thirty years more were to elapse before Mr (as he was at the time) Churchill, as Prime Minister, made his famous statement that he had not become His Majesty's First Minister in order to preside over the liquidation of the Empire. But Mr Churchill had already burnt his boats as regards India: for his declaration of 1942 had already been preceded by a series of equally robust speeches over a long period of years. 'Sooner or later,' he announced early in 1930, 'you will have to crush Gandhi and all they [Congressmen] stand for', clarifying his meaning beyond all doubt a short time later with the addition that 'the British have no intention of relinquishing control of Indian life and progress'. Nor was this all. Dominion Status, he explained in January 1931, in order to take the gilt off the earlier pronouncements of the Prime Minister and the Viceroy, had no meaning in relation to India. 'We have always contemplated it as the ultimate goal,' he said, 'but no one has ever supposed, except in the purely ceremonious sense in the way in which representatives attended conferences during the war of 1914-1918, that the principle and policy would be carried into effect in any time which is reasonable or useful for us to foresee.' These sentiments he buttressed further at the end of the year with a speech in which a definition of Dominion Status was given wholly at variance with the Statute of Westminster and the official Declaration preceding the Statute. It was during this period, too, that under the aegis of Mr Churchill and others of the same school of thought the Defence of India League was formed. The Secretary of the League was a retired member of the I.C.S. from the United Provinces. This was Douglas Dewar, whose activities in the defence of India, it must be said, were in a large measure redeemed by his two admirable volumes on Indian birds, and who had been friendly with my wife's father when he was District Magistrate, Ghazipur, and the latter was District Judge. When my wife and I were on leave in 1933, Dewar hospitably entertained us in his pleasant house in Camberley, and explained the aims and objects of the League, the expenses of which, ironically enough, were borne by the feudatory Princes of India. When it is remembered that many others in all walks of life in England, including Lord Birkenhead, the Secretary of State for India in 1925, held equally strong views, it can hardly be denied that there was much justification for Indian doubts and distrust. To us, during this period, contemporary statements of this kind emanating from the corridors of power were of far more significance than the ideas, apparently lost in oblivion, of Elphinstone, Macaulay and the idealists of the past. Many years later Sir Liddell Hart tells of an incident which has a bearing on Indian suspicions in the twenties. 'Indian resentment', he has recorded, 'was increased by a profound suspicion that British promises of giving them self-government by graduated stages masked an imperial-minded determination to advance them merely from the nursery to the schoolroom, and keep them in perpetual pupilage. The sentiments expressed by British officials in India or parliamentary speakers in Westminster too often had a ring which in sharp ears and minds fostered such a suspicion. Moreover, it was in some cases too well-founded. The first jolt to my admiration for Winston Churchill came in the course of a luncheon at "No. Eleven", where his old friend, General Sir Bindon Blood, a famous veteran of Indian frontier wars, deplored the new policy of "Indianisation" which the Government had announced—and Churchill explained with a cynicism that shocked me how this well-sounding declaration of policy might be nullified in practice.'[1]

[1] *The Liddell Hart Memoirs* (Cassell, 1965), vol. i; pp. 204-5. The

It thus seemed to have been made clear that political agitation was to be the deciding factor in the issue of political advancement, and from that time onwards all the emphasis on the British side was laid on the obstacles standing in its way, the problem of the feudatory Princes at one end of the social ladder and that of the Depressed Classes at the other, and the perennial antagonism between Hindus and Muslims. That the difficulties were present must certainly be conceded, although Indians brushed them aside as being largely the creation of the British and only capable of solution through political freedom. It cannot reasonably be denied that during the last twenty years of British rule conditions in India gave ample excuse for the arguments of the realists who contended that Indians must settle their own problems before any large step forward towards the attainment of full freedom could be taken.

When, therefore, I signed my Covenant with the Crown, I had no idea that I was entering the Indian Civil Service in its twilight. A few weeks after taking over charge as Assistant Commissioner in my first District, I went to Lucknow to attend the annual Service dinner. By convention the first of the after-dinner speeches was made by the President of the I.C.S. Association, and the second by way of reply by the juniormost member present. It so happened that I found myself in the unenviable position of the latter. In the course of my five-minute oration—my Deputy Commissioner's parting admonition had been 'Don't talk for more than five minutes, and whatever you do, don't get tight'—I took the opportunity of mentioning that the President had kept me on pins and needles for an unconscionable time dilating on the losses the Service had suffered during the year, but that at the end of it he had quite forgotten to mention the gains—which I thought rather unfair of him. I added, however, that perhaps in thirty or thirty-five years time some more kind-hearted President might yet give a glowing account of 1925 as having been a vintage year. Laughter and applause greeted this effort; but as I look back I wonder how many of those present had the slightest suspicion that the great

reference to 'No. Eleven' shows that Mr Churchill was Chancellor of the Exchequer at the time.

Service in whose honour we had just drunk a toast would cease to exist in less than twenty-two years.

It was only after the Crown had taken over the reins of government from the hands of the East India Company that the I.C.S. assumed its modern form and became Her Majesty's Indian Civil Service under the control of a Secretary of State. Less than a century later it terminated on the grant of independence. It did not die; but like the Old Soldiers of 1914 simply faded away. The process commenced, although few of us realized it, with the Government of India Act of 1919 and the inauguration of the new constitution.

With the passage of the Act the I.C.S. fell from pride of place in the estimation of young Englishmen seeking careers overseas. So much so that stimulants had to be supplied continually during the interval between the two wars. The principle of nomination had been revived in 1919 for a year or two in order to fill the gaps caused by the stoppage of British recruitment during the war, and no doubt to sidestep the racial issue Indians were also nominated for this short period. But from 1922 to the middle thirties recruitment by nomination was retained only to help Indians of the minority communities, a kind of back door entry for Muslims and Christians who were not able to cope with the open competition. Round about 1935, however, the principle of nomination was re-adopted for British candidates in addition to selection by open competitive examination. In the course of my probationary year I chanced to meet Sir Benjamin Lindsay of the Allahabad High Court while he was on leave. He had spent a great portion of his time in touring all the British universities in order to encourage the continuance of British recruitment to the Service. Fifteen years later Sir Maurice Hallett, the Governor of the United Provinces, told me that he had done the same thing in the late thirties. Indeed, considerable effort was put into the maintenance of a steady supply of British recruits for all the basic Indian Services, the I.C.S., the Indian Army, and the Indian Police, right up to the year 1939. The fact that these efforts had continued unabated and were largely successful is a strong indication that during the interval between the two wars the British themselves were not thinking in terms of an early end of the I.C.S.

As was only natural, political changes produced a few Cassandras who foresaw in the Montagu-Chelmsford Reforms an early end to British dominion, but on the whole little credence was given to such catastrophic forebodings. Among the few was a member of the I.C.S., Calcraft-Kennedy, an Old Alleynian who had entered the Service in 1895 or thereabouts. No admirer of democratic processes for the Orient, he wrote one or two books under the pseudonym of 'Al Carthill', one of which, entitled *The Lost Dominion*, created a considerable stir in imperial and Service circles.[1] 'Al Carthill's' skilfully argued and lucid thesis was that the hatching up of any scheme for responsible government would produce within itself the seeds of the rapid end of the British Raj. Power, it was maintained, would soon slip into the wily hands of the Brahmin and the small minority of educated and discontented dissidents (all lumped together under the generic term 'panditji'), and since these were fundamentally anti-western in general and anti-British in particular, the fall of the Raj was imminent.[2] Others, however, reached a somewhat similar conclusion by a completely different route. These held that the British, far from abandoning their destiny in India, had now fulfilled it. The end of the Raj, as they envisaged it, would not be a fall, not a sacrificial act for the propitiation of a band of malcontents, but one of wisdom and in full accord with its true purpose. This formed the basis of one of the best and most impartial histories of modern India, *The Rise and Fulfilment of British Rule in India*.[3] Notwithstanding differences in outlook and treatment of the subject, both extremes regarded the liquidation of British rule as the common end.

But the 'Al Carthills' on one side of the circle and the Garratts and Thompsons on the other were, I think, exceptional in their respective attitudes, and as I look back to the night when I made the junior member's speech at my first I.C.S.

[1] *The Lost Dominion* was published by Blackwood in 1924.
[2] This, of course, was not entirely correct. The early leaders of the Congress, many of whom were Brahmins, were sincere admirers of the English people as a whole and of what the latter stood for.
[3] Of the two authors, Edward Thompson and G. T. Garratt, the latter was a member of the I.C.S. from 1913 to 1923, when he resigned. A strong radical, he stood thrice for election to the House of Commons. His brother was a senior Major in the 10/7 Rajput Regiment and he and I knew each other well at Fatehgarh in 1927-28.

dinner, I cannot find any evidence that an early end of the Service, the embodiment as well as the instrument of British rule, was ever contemplated. Some time, perhaps; but not this year; nor next year; and never, let it be hoped, in our lifetime. So sensible, so practical a people as the British would hardly be expected to continue encouraging their able young men up to the end of the 1930s to take up careers in India with the knowledge or even suspicion that the Indian Civil Service was destined to be wound up within a decade or less.[1] Nor, I am sure, did any of us, Indian or English, realize, when we signed our Covenants at the India Office in 1925, that the recording angel could have written under our signatures not merely 'ave' but 'atque vale' in addition.

It was Warren Hastings, that outstanding, albeit much maligned, Governor-General, who took the first step to build up a sound administrative Service out of the traders and factors of the East India Company, and his early work was continued by Cornwallis and others. The next important milestone, however, was not reached until the middle of the nineteenth century. In 1854, on the recommendation of the Committee presided over by Macaulay, the Company's College at Haileybury was abolished (to become one of England's leading public schools) and the old system of recruitment by nomination was replaced by open competition. 'It is on the virtue of its servants and not on their ability that the Company must rely' was the principle laid down by Warren Hastings. Macaulay went farther; for his Committee made it clear in sonorous, Victorian language, expressing ideas which would probably draw a smile from later generations, that they would insist on both. 'The probationers,' said the Report, 'will be young men superior to their fellows in science and literature, and it is not among young men superior in science and literature that scandalous immorality is found to prevail. Indeed, early superiority in science and literature generally indicates the existence of some qualities which are securities against vice, namely industry, self-denial. . . . We, therefore, believe that the intellectual test which is about to be established will be found in practice to be the best moral test that could be

[1] Among others, two sons of former Governors of Indian Provinces entered the United Provinces cadre of the I.C.S. in the early thirties.

devised.'[1] From then onwards both virtue and ability were to be the hall-mark of the altered Service from which the Indian Civil Service stemmed a few years later, although it need hardly be added that 'virtue' in its excessively narrow sense had struggled out of its Victorian strait-jacket long before the end of the first World War.

Up to the end of 1920 the Service remained almost entirely a social and racial oligarchy, recruited wholly by open competition in London and mainly from the prosperous upper-middle, professional class, with a dash of the county here and there. Its educational background was for the most part public school, and heavily weighted in favour of Oxford and Cambridge. Representatives of other universities were few, save for the Irishmen who patriotically adhered to Trinity College, Dublin: and the number of Indians was so small as to be negligible. In 1909 out of a total cadre of 1142 for the whole of India, only 60 were Indians, with less than a dozen in the United Provinces, the largest and most populous of the Provinces. In the special conditions and circumstances in which it worked the Service was not unnaturally influenced by its environment, and the environment was restrictive. Living in a country where the caste system had been stretched to its extreme limits, it inevitably tended to assume some of the system's attributes—for which Indians have always thrown the blame on the British rather than on themselves, the system's inventors, developers and upholders. As the authors of *The Rise and Fulfilment of British Rule in India* have expressed it: 'The Mutiny, the growth of the Services, and the Government's reluctance to admit Indians into the higher posts, all helped to turn Europeans into a separate caste, the white Brahmins, with the usual features of the caste system, endogamy, commensability and control by members.'[2]

Big changes, however, were not far off. In Great Britain even before 1914 the extension of the scholarship system had already eroded to a large extent the exclusiveness of Oxford and Cambridge. With the fermentation of new ideas generated during the war a great metamorphosis in attitudes began to take

---

[1] Sir George Trevelyan, *The Life and Letters of Lord Macaulay* (Longmans Green, 1890), p. 611. It is also of interest to see that the English reformed the Civil Service in India before putting their own in order.
[2] p. 533.

shape in 1919, and social democracy ceased to be as fruitful a cause of bourgeois alarm as it had been in the first decade of the century. So far as India was concerned, the first effect on the British in their own homeland of political reform in India, coupled with the policy of Indianization, was a decrease in the number of recruits for the I.C.S., which had to be countered by the propaganda to which reference has been made. Since these efforts were widespread and covered *all* universities in the British Isles, it was not long before Oxford and Cambridge, not to mention the public schools, ceased to be the breeding grounds for the future administrators of the Indian Empire. That young Englishmen had to be encouraged in this manner to enter the I.C.S. was in itself a change of considerable significance; but the policy of Indianization produced an even greater one in India.

Ever since its first session in 1885 the National Congress had continued to press that the open competition for the I.C.S. should be held concurrently in India. Thirty-five years later, when the demand had become a fact, young Indians with the inheritance and background of the true Indian middle classes began to compete on level terms with their counterparts in Great Britain. This was clearly the most important change in the fabric of the Service since the taking over the government of the country by the Crown after the Mutiny, a change not merely of administrative but also of political and social significance for the future, whether near or distant, for it ensured that at some time India, quite rightly from the general Indian angle, would be governed on Indian principles and practices.

Up to 1947 the portents did not come into the open, because Indianization had just reached the half-way stage. The I.C.S. remained essentially British in its basic nature, its traditions, its principles, its core. It continued to be an expression of the British national character, an impersonal ruling corporation, which reflected, despite its racial undertone, the high standards of the era in which its great quality had been built up. It remained one of the many institutions to which the Englishman gives—or perhaps I should say used to give—his loyalty, the school, the college, the regiment, the Service, even possibly the trade union, all with the supreme institution of the monarchy at the summit. Although its impersonal nature tended to produce an aloofness which became an easy target for its critics, let it be said in answer that it was from this very quality of being impersonal that the Service drew much of its strength; for at its best the institution produced a body of administrators distinguished for conscientiousness as well as ability who did not allow themselves to be deflected from their duty by extraneous considerations or by their personal likes, dislikes or idiosyncracies. 'It must be said', is the assessment of Naresh Chandra Roy, 'that for about one hundred years the Civil Service discharged its responsibilities both with efficiency and impartiality.' And again: 'But there is no denying the fact that it built up excellent traditions of efficiency and integrity. It is true that in some cases where white men were concerned there were lapses, but generally speaking they held the scales even between man and man. As for their equipment for their duties, there could be no question after the inauguration of the competitive system in 1853 (sic). Even before this method of recruitment many of the civilians proved themselves as vigorous and informed as Plato's philosopher kings were expected to be.'[1] My personal experience, too, was that the I.C.S. as a Service judged every man by the quality of his work—the yardstick being British, of course—and not by his race or minor eccentricities. As for the latter considerable latitude was allowed, for it was a creditable attribute of the British, at least in the evening of their power, to regard mild deviations or non-conformity with tolerance, provided they did not bear adversely on one's work, and even with interest, as something to be examined, and to be laughed away, if need be, but not necessarily to be extirpated.

Most important from the standpoint of independent India

[1] Naresh Chandra Roy, *The Indian Civil Service* (Book Company, Calcutta, 1935), pp. 289-90.

In connexion with the question of justice, it is worth noting that Lord Curzon, for all his habit of telling Indians what he thought of their national character—which was very little—always stood out firmly for justice as between man and man. When a mess cook was severely beaten by some English Army Officers, Lord Curzon came down heavily on the whole regiment, and compelled the C.O. and the Second in Command to go on leave.

There are three or four histories of the I.C.S. by Englishmen. N. C. Roy's is the only full one by an Indian. K. L. Panjabi's *Civil Servant in India* (Bharatiya Vidya Bhavan, Bombay, 1965) contains a short sketch of the Service at the end, but is actually not so much a history of the I.C.S. as a collection of interesting and useful reminiscences of their service days by twenty Indians, covering the period from 1918.

was the fact that the Service embodied the British concept of duty, public as well as personal. If its primary function was to govern, its duty was to perform that function in accordance with British standards of justice, with the rule of law, and with the great liberal traditions for which the British themselves had fought, and from which had been developed freedom of speech and freedom of the individual and of association. In the administrative sphere the concept of duty imposed on itself by the Service involved, amongst much else, the free exchange of opinion. No courtier himself, the Englishman had little admiration for the species, and the 'yes-man' was not given the high status later accorded him by independent India's leading politicians. Independence of thought and action was encouraged, and willingness to accept responsibility was essential. An honest reply to an honest question was expected. It could be for or against a proposal of the Government. There was no resentment in the second case, and no special encomium in the first. On more than one occasion I myself expressed, as District Magistrate, views which ran counter to those of my British colleagues. They were not by any means always accepted; but they were always heard, provided, and this was an important proviso, they were founded on observation and solid fact and not on personal prejudices. In circles higher than those of the District full and free expression of opinion was common. Once when I was Secretary to the Government in 1945, the Financial Adviser to the Governor strongly opposed in writing a proposal to which the Governor was equally attached, and continued with his opposition until the Governor regretfully overruled him, also in writing. On another occasion no less a person than the Finance Member of that august body, the Viceroy's Executive Council, stoutly protested against certain financial propositions put out by Westminster as being against the true interests of India. When it is remembered that the Home Government in point was under the leadership of the redoubtable Winston Churchill, it requires no more to show how cardinal to the Englishman was the duty of expressing opinion fearlessly and without favour.[1]

---

[1] The case has been mentioned by H. V. R. Iengar, a former member of the I.C.S., in a series of articles in a Bombay weekly, *Commerce*, in its issue of 10th April 1964. In *The Second World War* (Cassell), vol. iv, p. 181, Sir Winston

All the way up and down the Service ladder there was steadfast adherence to what the Englishman deemed to be his public duty as opposed to his personal preferences; and where institutional duty, duty to the public, duty to India, as the Service conceived it, came into conflict with personal preferences, it was the former which prevailed. This apart, three other attributes added to the high and distinctive quality of the I.C.S; a great sense of responsibility, a capacity for taking it regardless of personal consequences, and complete integrity. The sum total comprised the factors which gave it its unique character in Indian history, its inner power and its outward prestige. Many harsh and adverse criticisms have been levelled against it by Indians both before and after independence. Some of these are considered and evaluated later; but here it is enough for me to say that if the British Empire in India generated a great deal of heat in its time, the light should also be remembered. This is not to say that the I.C.S. as an institution, its principles, its ethic as an instrument of governance, were fundamentally suited to India or in tune with the Indian character. Twenty years of freedom, and the rapidity with which Indian standards have replaced British are proof of the reverse. But now that the Raj has passed into history, and with it its instrument of government, it should be possible for both to be regarded objectively and in the right focus. Although there appears to be small prospect of this at the present time, perhaps one may hope that when the intoxicating effects of freedom have worn off, the high general quality and the special qualities of the I.C.S., foreign though they were to the Indian way of life inherited from the distant past, will be recalled and better appreciated; for up to the end of British rule there were men in the I.C.S. who were conscientiously dedicated to India's service. Their ideal of service may have been different from that of modern, independent India; but for myself I regret that that ideal has passed away for ever.

In 1939 there were 1299 members of the Service of whom 759 were British. On August 15th 1947 not all the 540 Indians remained, since the majority of Muslim officers had opted for

---

Churchill has recorded that 'British Government officials in India were wont to consider it a point of honour to champion the particular interests of India against those of Great Britain whenever a divergence occurred.'

Pakistan, but it could have been said that India was left with a sound nucleus for her new and independent Administration. Unhappily, it was not long before the appearance proved illusory, and the reality, if measured by former standards, turned out to be different. The replacement of the Union Jack by the Indian tricolour signified a far deeper change than the mere substitution of one flag for another. Indian ethic in general and Indian administrative ideas and practices in particular came into their own again after the lapse of more than a century. When the creators of the Indian Civil Service left India, their administrative traditions, indeed the whole corpus of their administrative precept and practice, left with them.

Much light on this aspect of the I.C.S. as an essentially British Service has recently been shed in a series of articles in a monthly journal, *Seminar*, and in three lectures on Jawaharlal Nehru by P. H. Patwardhan.[1] 'Unfortunately', said the latter, 'even [*sic*] the British tradition has been debased under Congress Ministers. I.C.S. men lost their spirit of fearless independence. The Mundhra case and other similar incidents have exposed the *spineless subservience* [my italics] of the top bureaucracy. The corruption, confusion, inefficiency and irresponsibility that have spread in the Administration and in society deep down are the result of lack of purpose.' More specific still is Niranjan Majumdar in *Seminar* with his assessment that 'the British element was the core of the I.C.S. When it disappeared in 1947, the steel of the steel frame was gone. Left was a rusty frame. . . . The traditions they [the Indians] will have left behind are not the traditions they inherited. . . . Perhaps the truth is that the I.C.S. never made much sense without the British element. India will now get the Administration she deserves.' To which verdict one might not unreasonably add 'and also the Administration which basically Indians have desired for the last fifty years and which for the most part is more in line with the

---

[1] *Seminar* published a special issue, no. 84, in August 1966, entirely devoted to the I.C.S., which is of great importance. Out of the seven articles three are pseudonymous, while the remainder are from the pens of Niranjan Majumdar, Assistant Editor of *The Statesman*, Frank Moraes, Editor-in-Chief of *The Indian Express*, D. K. Rangnekar. Resident Chief Representative of *The Economic Times*, Delhi, and H. K. Paranjape, Project Director of the Indian Institute of Public Administration. The seven constitute a representative and influential cross-section of the Indian intelligentsia.

Mr Patwardhan's lectures were reprinted in *The Financial Express* in 1966 and the reference here is from the third, in the issue of September 26th.

Indian way of life than the foreign ethic introduced by the British.'

These and many similar opinions are worth more than a passing thought; for although much of the blame for India's inadequate performance after independence has been laid at the door of the Indian members of the former I.C.S., it would be more correct for the critics to place the burden on Indian (more strictly Hindu) society as a whole. It is in Hindu ethos, Hindu dharma, call it what you will, that the key to an understanding of free India will be found. Why should it not be frankly conceded that Hindu administrative ethos must differ fundamentally from British, since it is deeply rooted in India's past? A public Service as an institution with a duty to the people in general is not an Indian creation. The Hindu way of life, the Hindu concept of duty, and Hindu values as a whole have always centred round the joint family, the caste, and the geographical community—fundamentals which a series of Islamic conquests did not alter. In India before the advent of British power public administration in the higher grades was a purely personal affair, with the ruler, Hindu or Muslim, the fulcrum. The feudal system had remained more or less unchanged since the time of the *Ramayana*.

The strength of the three factors mentioned has doubtless been weakened as a result of the impact of the West, but it has not been obliterated. Throughout the ages two significant features have distinguished Hindu ethos, the instinct for survival and an equally outstanding adaptability to changing circumstances. Modern politicians have thus been very successful in redirecting its fundamental characteristics into economic and political channels through the medium of universal adult suffrage and the full panoply of western democracy. All three elements in their modern forms flourish freely in independent India; and in the light of the fact that out of India's millenia of history effective British rule lasted for a little more than a century, for a third of which it was the subject of resentment and bitter opposition, the recrudescence of the ancient administrative ethic was inevitable.

It is, I think, worth notice in this connexion that India today is not merely India. The framers of the Constitution of 1950 recognised this when they designated the new State 'India that is Bharat', a designation which seems to me to have a special significance. Bharat is an ancient legacy with deep roots in the past, and the conflict between India and Bharat, though never admitted in theory, is conducted very noisily in practice without being recognised for what it actually is. Was it not Pandit Jawaharlal Nehru who said that the temple of the new India was the Bhakra-Nangal dam? It has yet to be seen how the new and the old fit together, how the still living ideas born of the ancient temples at Khajuraho, Puri and Madurai can successfully blend with the western technology underlying the new ones. Although Pandit Jawaharlal Nehru perceived the dangers of seeking 'to cover truth by the creatures of our imagination and endeavour to escape from reality to a world of dreams',[1] he was essentially a romantic himself, and admitted the strength of the concept of Bharat Mata. 'It is curious', he has written, 'how one cannot resist the tendency to give an anthropomorphic form to a country. Such is the force of habit and early associations. India becomes Bharat Mata, Mother India, a beautiful lady, very old, but ever youthful in appearance, sad-eyed and forlorn, cruelly treated by aliens and outsiders and calling upon her children to protect her.'[2]

It was not surprising, therefore, that the Indian members of the I.C.S.—with a few exceptions—sought to break away from the canons of a foreign system, and that public services in the British sense have not been built up in two decades of independence. In the I.C.S. the Indian residue retained the three letters as suffixes to their names, but disintegrated into a collection of individual units with neither the cohesion nor *esprit-de-corps* of the former British Service. During the British régime the great majority of Indians covered over their basic, inner Indianness in administrative matters so far as was possible. They accepted outwardly and discreetly, through lack of choice, a foreign system with its foreign disciplines, while inwardly rejecting the corporate feeling, the orderliness, the impartiality, the deep sense of public duty as opposed to personal preferences, which were the essentials, and to my mind the virtues of the British system. British administrative ethos, in short, was accepted merely as an expedient, to be cast aside as soon as

[1] Jawaharlal Nehru, *Autobiography*, (John Lane, 1936), p. 431.
[2] Ibid.

independence and the resurgence of the Indian way of life made this possible. Indians, therefore, could in reality only be *in* the Service, but never *of* it. Even a year before independence became an accomplished fact, I myself witnessed as Chief Secretary of my own Province the rapid rise to the surface of an entirely different set of administrative canons, to show with their emergence after their temporary submersion under British rule how small and superficial was the dent made by the British administrator in the traditional armour of India that is Bharat.

The distinction which I have drawn between British administrative ethos and Hindu administrative dharma did not force itself on my attention for many years—a slow awakening with the passage of time. Although it was a distinction which the majority of Indians would perhaps not readily admit, it was, I think, always present in the calculations of the British. The British administrator regarded the art of public administration, including public finance (one of free India's many blind spots), strictly from the British angle and through British spectacles. Indeed, how else could he look at it? Consequently he accepted the fundamental difference in outlook, and on his side differentiated between the two wings of the I.C.S., the British and the Indian. This distinction, sometimes open, sometimes subtle, was, I confess, from a detached and objective standpoint, reasonable; but it was always irksome and unjustified in Indian eyes. It had been openly expressed in 1914 five years before the policy of Indianization had been officially launched.

When in 1913 a Royal Commission under the chairmanship of Lord Islington was set up 'to examine the limitations which still exist in the employment of non-Europeans in the Superior Civil Service', there was complete official agreement on the British side that Indians were unfitted for the higher and more responsible executive positions in the I.C.S. Mr H. L. Stephenson (afterwards Sir Hugh Stephenson, Governor of Bihar) summed up the consensus of opinion in the words: 'The natives of India who belong to the Indian Civil Service are on the average distinctly inferior to the European officers of the Service in force of character and initiative. Their national character would prove a great disadvantage to them in administrative charges where they would come into contact with a large non-official European community or where there is widespread racial tension or unrest. For these reasons it is not usual to employ natives of India, even though members of the Indian Civil Service, in the heaviest district charges, where personality and power of control count for very much.'[1]

While on the evidence of twenty years of independence it can hardly be claimed that Indians have disproved such assessments, uncomplimentary though they may be, they got under the skin of all Indians at the time. It would certainly not have been correct to have accused the British of deliberately giving Indians unfair treatment. In my experience Service *esprit-de-corps* was strong in official matters, and there were instances of Indians in difficulties being treated more leniently than the actual circumstances warranted. On the other hand serious failures on the part of British officers were never condoned. During my own period of service no less than six District Magistrates in the United Provinces alone were permanently passed over for further promotion for a variety of inadequacies, and at least two more would probably have suffered a like fate had the war not intervened. There was also the case of the Governor of one of the Provinces who was requested to resign his post 'for reasons of health' before the expiry of his term of office. The official British attitude, however, continued in general to be that Indians on the whole did not make as strong, efficient and impartial district officers, judged by British standards, as their British colleagues. The simple general principle appeared to be that while the young Englishman was by virtue of his birth and national character a potentially sound administrator, the Indian was expected to prove his worth first, the presumption being that he was unlikely to be in that category until the contrary was clearly shown.

Two examples from my own service indicate how the distinction worked in practice. In the United Provinces large and important civil and military districts such as Lucknow, Allahabad, Meerut, Jhansi, Cawnpore and the like were normally reserved for British members of the Service until almost the close of British rule. In 1931 I was due for my first independent charge as district magistrate, and this would ordinarily have been Jhansi, since I had been in independent

[1] N. C. Roy, op. cit., p. 107.

charge for two years of its most important Sub-Division,
Lalitpur. Jhansi, however, with its fort on the hills overlooking
the city, its memories of the Mutiny only slightly less evocative
in English minds than those haunting the battered walls of the
Residency at Lucknow, the headquarters of a Civil Division,
a Military Brigade and a Railway, was classified as an important
charge, a Class I District. The presumption was accordingly
made that I should not be able adequately to fill the bill.
Instead, the young English City Magistrate from Cawnpore,
a neighbouring, but not adjacent District, was posted there,
although junior to me in service, while I was moved to the
other end of the Province as Deputy Commissioner, Gonda.
In itself Gonda, despite its being of far less importance than
Jhansi, was one of the best districts in the Province—in addition
to official experience it gave me a tiger and panther and a
great deal else—and I spent two very happy years there. But
its prestige was not the same, and for a long time I felt that in
a better ordered world Jhansi would have been my portion.
Only with the lapse of the years was it brought home to me
that what I had wrongly assumed to be unfair discrimination
was neither inherently unfair nor administratively unsound.
Long residence in England by itself was not a correct premise
for the logical conclusion that I must possess those qualities
deemed necessary by the British for high executive office. Time
was also to demonstrate to me the fact that the British and
Indian approach and attitude to the business of government
are so antithetic that what in the eyes of the former constitutes
the essence of good administration is looked on with positive
disfavour by the latter in actual practice, however much
lip-service is paid to British theory.

The second episode was somewhat bizarre both in its origins
and effects. My appointment early in 1940 to the very important
charge of Meerut sparked off an abnormal stir in some official
quarters. It was certainly an appointment of great significance.
Meerut had never before been in the hands of an Indian. The
work was heavy, and for a variety of reasons was in arrears at
the time. To crown all, the District was a key one from every
angle, civil as well as military, being the headquarters of a Civil
Division and of a Military District. Both town and countryside
had achieved fame (or notoriety) in 1857, for it was from

Meerut Cantonments that the first of the mutinous regiments, after murdering its European officers, had marched off to Delhi to try to restore to his former glory the unhappy, titular, shadowy Mughal Emperor, whose authority did not extend beyond the walls of his own palace. It was in the villages, too, that the rebels gathered to their side large contingents of Hindu Gujars and Jats, all sympathetic to the cause and ready to fight for it.

In the circumstances, therefore, it was perhaps not surprising that my appointment was productive of raised eyebrows in some quarters. How would an Indian Magistrate fit into a society in which even after the lapse of eighty years discordant memories were easily conjured up on both sides? The Commissioner of the Division, a man whom up to that time I had never met, had no doubts whatsoever. His name is not material. A Senior Wrangler in his time at Cambridge, he combined great ability with force of character and physical courage. He had won a Military Cross during the first war, and was a very close friend of Jim Corbett. All in all he was a man to win one's respect, and, what was quite as important, was an admirable Commissioner under whom to work. These, however, were not the first points which brought themselves to my attention. As a result of his failure to take into account the caution with which the Government had acted—the British never lifted the lid of Pandora's box merely to ascertain what would happen— he took strong exception to my appointment, and embodied his views in a letter to a leading member of the Government at Lucknow. A duplicate of the letter was retained in the official papers, attached to my personal record, and when I myself took over charge temporarily as Commissioner some months later there was the letter awaiting my interested perusal. I had, of course, been aware in a general way of the Commissioner's opposition to my appointment, but it was not until I had read the terms in which it was expressed that I knew how strong his feelings had been. I quote the letter here, not because of the importance of the personalities concerned— which was small—but because the episode taken as a whole and given its proper setting was a good example of three of the cardinal principles of British administration which I have mentioned earlier.

'My dear Percy,

Can you tell me what is the great idea behind this posting of a man with a Hindu Bengalee name to Meerut in the present circumstances? I believe he is an Anglo-Indian, but whatever his complexion may be, and however able he is, every hairy Muhammadan is not to know that, and would not alter his views very much, if he did.

You know, and so does Tennant, and so does Frank, that these four districts are the frontier for the Hindu-Muhammadan civil war when it comes. Does someone want to bring it on? If not, why put a man with a name like that in charge of the centre district of the frontier?[1] How can I meet these magnificent ex-soldiers who showed such loyalty last month and pretend that this is the way we look after them as we promised?

Then there are the British officers in Meerut. It is friendship, joint games and so forth that puts a District Magistrate in position to meet trouble with the strong arm.

The first reaction I notice both among them and the local big Muhammadans is that they think it just a damned insult, and I'm not sure that I don't think the same myself for its being done without consulting me.

Cannot this dreadful thing be altered before it is too late? Will you show this to Tennant?

Yours Sincerely,

This Kiplingesque letter I read nearly eighteen months after it had been written, and that I should have allowed it to rankle was unfortunate, since there was no rational as opposed to emotional justification for righteous indignation beyond the fact that righteous indignation came very easily to all Indians in 1940. The fact was that from the commencement of the imbroglio I had failed to observe its really illuminating and important features. In the first place the Governor of the Province and his Advisers, only one of whom was an Indian, and the Chief Secretary, stood by their decision and refused to alter the original orders of appointment. I failed to give them the

---

[1] The four Districts from south to north are Bulandshahr, Meerut, Muzaffarnagar, and Saharanpur. The great importance attached by the writer to the four was quite correct.

credit which was certainly their due; for here was an example of the implementation of the policy of giving Indians a share in the more important executive charges. The objections of a third party, highly placed though he was, were overruled. Secondly I was equally at fault in not giving the Commissioner himself his share of credit. He took the rebuff in good part, and, what was very significant in the light of Indian ethos, never permitted any personal antipathy to cloud his assessment of my official work. At the end of the year, by which time the arrears had been cleared, the whole District, Muslims, Jats, Uncle Tom Cobley and all were well under control, and the aftermath of a communal riot had been speedily dealt with, he commended my work in generous terms. The commendatory report was on my personal file along with the uncomplimentary letter. That I should have emphasized the latter at the expense of the former showed a lack of discrimination which unfortunately did not bear out that portion of the commendation referring to my possession of a logical mind and sound judgement!

Lastly, the Commissioner's remarks on my work were a good example of the British characteristic of keeping strictly to the matter in hand, of not allowing the personal equation to enter into an assessment of official work. This is the complete reverse of the Indian way of life and thought according to which family relationships, personal friendships and very often caste affiliations are made the yardstick for measuring efficiency rather than the quality of the work itself. The consequences of this attitude have been far-reaching, with nepotism and favouritism of all kinds seeping into every nook and cranny of the Administration and an inevitable weakening in the strength of the country as a whole.

One miscellaneous but significant point also emerged from the episode. Although the Commissioner and I started off on the wrong foot, the District was never allowed to gather the impression that advantage could be taken of the bad beginning. We sometimes went out hacking together, played tennis together and had our chhota peg together after it; all of which went for close-knit and impersonal administration. In free India, by contrast, on the many occasions when the heads of district administrations fail to keep in step, awareness of the fact is publicized, to the detriment of good administration. It is now a common practice for each of the officials concerned to establish a local faction centred on himself and under the protective umbrella of one or other of the many local politicians anxious to gain influence in the District. Party faction and party politics in every sphere are the breath of life in independent India.

As I look back on the last period of British rule I no longer resent as unjustifiable the Englishman's insistence on Indians in the I.C.S. working their passage, as it were, in British administrative ethos and on their proving their worth in its practice as well as in mere theory. But it was unfortunate that Indian self-esteem was hurt in the testing process, and that the eternally thorny problem of race relations, always a cause of an immediate rise in racial temperatures, was opened up. In his letter to the Government my Commissioner overtly touched on them, at least in their superficial aspect.

An examination of race and colour in their deeper manifestations is not my object here. Both have been implanted in the human race by Nature, and may well be insoluble except by Nature herself by her own methods. But the impact of Englishman on Indian and vice versa was of importance in day-to-day relations and in normal administration. By the time I entered the I.C.S. the Englishman's conviction of forty years before that 'he belongs to a race whom God has destined to govern and subdue'[1] had given place to less exalted ideas. Nevertheless, India was still British India, and although there were the beginnings of a partnership between Briton and Indian, the former remained the senior partner, with official life based on the British way of life, on British manners, modes and conventions. The Commissioner's fears that an Indian District Magistrate would be a misfit were not entirely without justification. His error lay only in his allowing his innate racial prejudices to outrun his discretion and in his failure to realize that his own Government never acted precipitately in the business of administration.

---

[1] 'The Bill [Ilbert Bill] outraged the conviction shared by every Englishman in India from the highest to the lowest, by the planter's assistant in his lowly bungalow and by the editor in the full light of a Presidency town, from those to the Chief Commissioner in charge of an important Province and the Viceroy on his throne, the conviction in every man that he belongs to a race whom God has destined to govern and subdue.'—Seton Kerr, I.C.S., once Foreign Secretary in the Government of India, in a speech in London in 1884 against the Ilbert Bill.

In fact, Meerut presented no special difficulties to me. To the Muslims I was merely another District Magistrate. The leading Muslim zamindar of the District became a personal friend and was always most helpful, while except for a young Irish magistrate of the I.C.S. my best subordinate magistrates from the standpoint of efficiency were Muslim. The British military officers, though a little wary at first, were not unfriendly, and in the ordinary course I was made a member of one or two of the Regimental Messes. Having shared a bungalow in my bachelor days with three Indian Army officers, all Englishmen, and having lived in their Mess, the ways of the Army were no novelty. My experience was that horsemanship was always an asset, and provided politics, art and literature, in that order, as subjects verging on conduct unbecoming an officer and a gentleman, if not positively prejudicial to good order and discipline, were avoided as topics of conversation in the Ante-Room in favour of duck and snipe, one could not come to any harm. At Meerut, moreover, I had an advantage denied to anyone else in the Province, British or Indian, Civilian or military officer. This was that my wife was a tennis player of some repute, having won several open tournaments and having capped this on one occasion by reaching the quarter-finals of the All-India championships at Allahabad. She had thus put herself into a class of her own among Service wives. The glory, of course, was hers, but for myself I did the next best thing and took the reflection!

Riding, tennis, shooting, the Club—relatively trivial in themselves, certainly had their value and made for a pleasant life. But two criticisms seem to me to be valid. The first is that the British laid excessive stress on them in the case of the Indian, some reporting officers tending to lose both their sense of humour and proportion in dealing with the latter. In 1944, for example, when I myself was soon to be promoted to a Commissionership, my last Commissioner penned a very full character sketch of myself in my confidential record, leaving nothing at all to chance or the imagination. Amongst other things, he recorded that his subject 'keeps a good house and dresses well'—this last statement hardly being correct as a general proposition, though it probably was relevant in relation to himself. He included in his small essay praise for my horsemanship—he was no horseman himself—but as a first-class shot came down heavily on my performances with a twelve-bore: 'An enthusiastic but poor shot' was his comment, the most unkindest cut of all after my twenty years of consistent trying. I mention this small instance as an indication of the great emphasis laid not only on the importance of outdoor life in the work of a District Officer, but also as an example of the emphasis given to trivialities such as food and dress. In my particular case, too, almost everything beyond a tribute to efficiency written by this Commissioner was of no relevance whatsoever to a man who himself was shortly to join him in the same rank.

Yet India is so productive of incongruities that to almost every statement made about it there is the inevitable 'but', and the opinion of the British on the Indian official was no exception to the rule. In a slightly different form the feudatory Princes adopted a somewhat similar racial view in their strong objection to the appointment of Indians to the Political Department of the Government of India.[1] The Princes constituted a class of ruler not to be found in any other part of the modern world, and, in fact, could have existed only in so paradoxical a land as India. The Political Department was a Janus-faced organization staffed by officers drawn partly from the I.C.S. and partly from the Indian Army. Its function was to keep a maternal eye on the vagaries of the Princes, for whom *sauviter in modo* was the outward motto, and an equally paternal one on the North-West Frontier, where for the tough and volatile Pathan *fortiter in re* was usually more in evidence.

To implement the assurance of a rapid Indianization of all Services, a few Indians were seconded from the I.C.S. to the Political Department in the twenties. Standing as it did over the Princes as the watchdog of the Crown, the Department worked directly under the Viceroy as the Crown Representative. The Residents and Political Agents constituted the link between the Princes and the Crown, and the Princes insisted that it should be British, taking a dim view of the appointment of Indians from the I.C.S. to posts in which the latter would be

[1] K. P. S. Menon has referred to this paradox. See *Many Worlds*, p. 169.

in positions of potential authority over semi-independent rulers. The Princes had no objections to Indians as Ministers, even as *Dewans* or Chief Ministers, since in such capacities the officers concerned were the servants, at least in theory, of the Prince and not of the Crown; but they did not approve of Indians in the position of independent supervisors. It was not until the unilateral abandonment of the doctrine of paramountcy in 1947 and the collapse of the protective walls the British had erected around them, that the Princes switched over to accepting all comers freely as Regional and Chief Commissioners with an acquiescence previously unimaginable. Thus it was that the few Indians who were seconded to the Political Department in accordance with the British promise to Indianize the Services returned, with one exception, to their parent Service within five years of their appointment; and the one exception was given a Political Agency only for a short-term vacancy.

No account of India in the first half of the century would be complete or accurate without a reference to the schizophrenia which afflicted the Indian intelligentsia of the period, and which remains as a hangover, independence notwithstanding, of the British era. It was one of the many consequences of the impact of Great Britain on India. A compound of covert admiration and the 'emasculation of Indian culture' theory, an odd love-hate complex based on a regression to the legendary glories of an ancient past, spiced with antithetic urges to every form of modernity, its manifestations are as prevalent today as ever before.

From the time when the genuine admiration of the early Congress leaders for Great Britain gave way to the idea that India, far from being conquered by the West because she was weak, had been rendered weak and submissive only through that conquest, there was certainly an impressive inconsistency in the ambition of all young Indians to enter a Service like the I.C.S. which was both the embodiment and the mainstay of that very imperial rule which had allegedly been the ruin of the country; and the inconsistency was made even more prominent by the manner in which we all made the best of both worlds when once in it. As Pandit Jawaharlal Nehru himself has remarked, 'the I.C.S. became the Elysium of the English-educated classes',[1] an odd situation, the incongruity of which has been noted by other Indians. Writing of his Oxford days, K. P. S. Menon, for example, has dryly commented that 'we made vehement speeches which we thought patriotic and which the British thought seditious. At the same time, we went on studiously preparing for the I.C.S. The inconsistency between the making of anti-British speeches and the attempt to enter the I.C.S. . . . did not strike us.'[2]

So far as I was concerned, I cannot give any satisfactory answer to the question why I should have sought to enter the Service after my reactions to the activities of Sir Michael O'Dwyer and Brigadier-General Dyer. Certainly it was not with any idea of ever supplanting the British, since in 1924 the latter showed no indication whatsoever of being supplanted. Deep down in my unconscious there was doubtless the feeling that I owed it to my parents to make the attempt after they had educated me for the purpose at great expense and sacrifice. At a higher level of consciousness there must also have been the youthfully egotistical desire to prove to all that I was as good as the next man (English, of course !). But probably the only sensible explanation to cover the cases of all Indians, including myself, would be similar to George Mallory's reason for essaying the ascent of Mt Everest. The I.C.S., like the mountain, was there.

Looking back to the days when I read some of the comedies of Aristophanes, I cannot help thinking how greatly that master of amusing satire would have enjoyed the anomaly, making fun of Indians, with their ambition to rise high in the service of those who were 'exploiting' India, as was the political currency of the time, and no doubt reserving his unstinted praise for the liberal and creditable tolerance of the British who took a barrage of criticism in the legislatures and the Press in good part. Bernard Shaw, of course, could have been a modern Aristophanes, had he so wished; but at the time— the early twenties—that genial sexagenerian was still engaged

[1] *The Discovery of India*, p. 395. Oddly enough, although Pandit Jawaharlal Nehru himself was very critical of the I.C.S., which he greatly disliked, more members of the Nehru family in general entered it than of any other known family in India.

[2] *Many Worlds*, p. 54. and again on p. 63 the author observes: 'Despite the glamour, was I not going to serve a foreign Government?' Much the same point has been noted by some of the contributors to *The Civil Servant in India*.

in making Irish wisecracks, mostly at the expense of the English, their traditions, their imperial attitudes and conventions from his pleasant English home in the English countryside. 'Everywhere in India,' wrote Louis Fischer in June 1942, 'whenever an Indian criticized the British I would insist that he explain to me why he was anti-British. I said to an Indian Moslem who is a high civil servant in the British government, "Why are so many Indians anti-British ?" "Why shouldn't we be ?" he exclaimed. "That is the more appropriate question; no nation likes the foreign nation which rules it," he added.'[1] As the author of *Many Worlds* has rightly pointed out, the Government of India knew that all Indians with any spirit were nationalist in outlook; 'only some Indians flaunted their patriotism; others cherished it discreetly and some others concealed it carefully.'[2] That the British knew it was certainly true, but they are still not given the credit due to them for a tolerance and understanding which few, if any, other imperial powers would have shown in similar circumstances.

In my case, so far as opinions went, the Government had no doubts. 'Although he has been in England from an early age, he sometimes expresses strong nationalist feelings, but gets on quite well in Station society.' So wrote the Collector of Fatehgarh under whom I served in my early years. 'He is, I believe, a man of strong opinions,' reported a Commissioner soon afterwards. Even as late as 1944 my last Commissioner (the essayist) could speak of my 'anti-British kink', although by this time the kink, if it was one, was no longer what it had been in the 'good old days'. If I had lowered my guard and committed myself at an early stage, I hasten to add that this was not out of any desire to make a display of patriotism, but partly because my effervescent ideas were largely the consequence of my long residence in England (a point missed by the Collector of Fatehgarh). In addition, I was slow to realize that the free and easy attitudes of the British in England stiffened somewhat imperially east of Suez. A casually adverse remark against a Secretary of State for India, for example, which would

[1] *A Week with Gandhi*, (International Book House, Bombay) p. 120. As a sidelight it is of some interest to see that the reply was given by a Muslim official. To anyone cognisant of the period it is easy to identify him, since the number of highly placed Muslims in the Government of India in 1942 was very small.
[2] Op. cit. p. 111.

have met with approval in the National Liberal Club under
Gladstone's life-size portrait, could be the cause of pained looks
and an embarrassed silence in the lounge of any Club in India.

While I certainly do not attempt to justify my youthful
absurdities, I must confess that the social life of Anglo-India
was very narrow in its outlook and restricted in its scope, and
I often used to wonder what the English talked about amongst
themselves, apart from shooting and the ordinary 'shop' of
Service life. On the surface there appeared to be no intellectual
life whatsoever. It was certainly present in the case of many
men in the I.C.S.,[1] but between Englishman and Indian it was
never in evidence. The taboos of the Officers' Mess at Fatehgarh
were equally strongly maintained in the I.C.S.—which, I think,
was a pity, since a little more of general intellectual (or perhaps
I should say intelligent) life, an occasional free and open discussion on what was going on in the world around one, *might*
have brought about a greater understanding between the two
races, or at any rate reduced the area of misunderstanding.
Yet in the twenty-two years during which I mixed freely with
the English I never discussed a book of any kind, except
Katherine Mayo's notorious *Mother India*, and still less any
subject so esoteric as art, Indian or Western. Indeed, in the
matter of literature I was soon put in my place; for when as a
young Joint Magistrate I somewhat thoughtlessly (as was
proved later) proposed a book by H. G. Wells for the Fatehgarh
Club Library, my Collector's wife, more possibly in sorrow
than in anger, gave me a little lecture on suitable literature.
'Wells,' she said in conclusion, 'is such a terrible iconoclast'!
East of Suez again, that great dividing line! It had never
occurred to me that anyone, anywhere, could regard so harmless
a Fabian as Wells in that light three years after the first Labour
Government at Westminster and only two before the next.

[1] During my period of service at least one Governor of the U.P. was a
noted classical scholar. This was Sir William Marris, who had translations of
Homer and Horace to his credit. Indeed, the cynics used to say that he was a
better classical scholar than Governor! Hutton of Assam and Grigson of the C.P.
and Hyderabad were anthropologists of repute. One or two, Penderel Moon
and Philip Mason, wrote novels (or near novels), dealing with Indian life; and
Calcraft-Kennedy (Al Carthill) has already been mentioned. There must have
been many others unknown to me. Nor should the I.C.S. men who have written
on wild life and sport be omitted. Edye's *The Angler and the Trout* (though it deals
with his native chalk streams) is a classic of its kind. Before my time, of course,
the Service had produced scholars cum administrators of all kinds, and even
a minor poet or two.

Fifteen years later a Commissioner—another Wrangler, the I.C.S. seemed to specialize in the species—one of the nicest of men, with whom I was on the best of terms, asked me what all the books in my bookcases were about. After I had given a summary, and he had satisfied his curiosity with a rapid look around, he took no further interest beyond wondering whether I really had read Lloyd George's *War Memoirs* ! That Englishman and Indian had closed their minds to each other was perhaps inevitable in the circumstances of the time, but was, I feel, one of the minor tragedies of the last days of the British Raj.

Katherine Mayo's *Mother India* (Jonathan Cape, 1927) requires more than a passing reference, because of the ill feeling it aroused on both sides. Purporting to be a sociological study of India's social evils—child-marriage, rape, seduction, the pardah system, untouchability, and bristling with facts and figures from the law courts, official reports etc, it was stigmatized in India as a 'drain inspector's report'—which in fact it was. It would probably not have attracted much attention (its sequels, *Slaves of the Gods* (1929) and *Volume Two* (1931) were a relative flop as a result of the Civil Disobedience movement) had it not coincided with the Simon Commission on Constitutional Reforms. From the start the Commission never had the smallest chance of success in any case: first because it contained no Indian members, and secondly, as a guarantee of failure, its Chairman was Sir John Simon, never a lovable character in Indian eyes. *Mother India* was forthwith pounced on by the British Press, lily-white, yellow and extreme pink, as a powerful argument against any form of swaraj for India. This strange assortment of bedfellows included *The Times* and *The New Statesman*, and many other examples of lions lying down with lambs. Said the *New Statesman* in a long review, after describing the book as 'by implication one of the most powerful defences of the British Raj that has ever been written': 'she [Miss Mayo] makes the claim for swaraj seem nonsense and the will to grant it almost a crime.' The argument itself was nonsense on the face of it; for if after a century of British rule such general conditions prevailed, clearly that rule had been a complete failure, and might well liquidate itself. Moreover, if social conditions were to be taken as a criterion for independence, how many nations would qualify?

Certainly not Katherine Mayo's, whether in 1927 or 1967.
English opinion in India took the *New Statesman's* line, and I
recall Col. Strong, the Officer Commanding the 10/7 Rajputs
quite seriously saying to me with soldierly (and rather engaging)
simplicity: 'India cannot expect to get anything till she puts
her own house in order.'

As a piece of political skullduggery the book was a complete
failure and overshot the mark. It put up the backs of all Indians.
It killed what little belief Indians may have retained in British
good faith. It was regarded as the velvet glove of diplomatic
skill after the iron hand of Sir Michael O'Dwyer and despite
vigorous denials to the contrary, all the evidence pointed to
official blessing, and probably official inspiration in addition.
No denials could in Indian minds override the timing, the great
publicity given in the British Press, the fact that *The Times*
(which was regarded in India as the reflection of opinion in
Whitehall) refused to publish a letter signed, among others,
by Sir Atul Chatterjee, the then High Commissioner for India,
and Sir Tej Bahadur Sapru, an ex-Member of the Viceroy's
Council shortly to be elevated to the honour of a Privy
Counsellorship, and lastly the book's free distribution both in
England and the U.S.A.

In general, however, Indians took the book and the English
newspapers too seriously. Only a few years later *The Times*
under the editorship of Geoffrey Dawson distinguished itself
by becoming an ardent apostle of appeasement and presumably
of a new type of social reform: and the *New Statesman* merely
created a distrust in many Indian minds of both the good faith
and the intelligence of left-wing intellectualism in Great Britain.
Indian replies to *Mother India* (such as *Unhappy India* by Lajpat
Rai and *Father India* by C. Rajagopalachari) were too long and
lacked snap. The best was *Uncle Sham* (1929) by K. L. Gauba
which was short and to the point, a kind of 'look to the beam
in thine own eye, brother,' a '*tu quoque*' based on a precise
examination of all the malodorous social drains of the U.S.A.
with which Miss Mayo as a good American did not concern
herself—murders, rapes, lynchings, kidnappings, the 'untouch-
able' position of the negroes—the whole gamut of hidden
American failings in fact. None of the replies was given publicity
abroad. But even if *Uncle Sham* had been published in the U.S.A.

and had found any readers, the U.S.A. as a messianic, powerful *and independent nation* would certainly have laughed it off in 1929.

That as a result of my long residence and training in England I developed a few specifically individual paradoxes over and above those common to all Indians was only natural. The most important from the standpoint of my usefulness to an independent India was that while my mental reactions were superficially Indian inasmuch as I disapproved of the British position in India (on the best English, liberal principles, it need hardly be said), my physical reactions to problems on the spot normally conformed to the British and not Indian pattern. This last was a characteristic which remained unchanged after 1947, a kind of irremoveable hangover, and which was not in consonance with the re-emergence of Hindu administrative ethic. For example, I still do not approve of displays of disorder and indiscipline in official circles. Both of these, however, have different meanings, according to whether the spectacles are British or Indian, and what to the Englishman appears to be plain disorder to the Indian is merely freedom of expression. Conformity to British administrative principles in practice has not been a notable feature of any Indian Government or Administration, Central or State, since independence. It is in the anomalous combination of opposites—government according to abstract British theory mixed with action, or as often as not with inaction, according to the Indian temperament and Indian ideas—that the vast hiatus between ambition and performance is to be found.

For similar reasons, the difference in meaning attached to the same word, assessments of the general standard of ability in the I.C.S. vary very considerably, and not all Indians agree with the verdict of N. C. Roy which I have quoted earlier. Pandit Jawaharlal Nehru, for example, admits that 'it would be idle to deny the good qualities of the I.C.S.' and in one place in his *Autobiography* even uses the words 'with all my admiration for the Service,'[1] but despite this had a low opinion of it both from the intellectual and administrative standpoints. 'It is true,' he wrote, 'that the Service has kept up a certain standard, though that standard is necessarily one of mediocrity. . . .

[1] *Autobiography*, p. 441.

They were, on the whole, reliable officers in their limited way, doing their day-to-day work fairly competently'.[1] Some of his more astringent and damning estimates I shall have occasion to mention and comment on at a later stage.

It does no Service any harm to see itself as others do. Nevertheless, when I look back on the I.C.S. solely as the British Service it was, my personal estimate is that up to 1914 its general intellectual level was very high indeed, and although there was some drop after 1920, that level remained high until the end. Up to 1914 the Service certainly took the cream of Oxford and Cambridge, and even thereafter there were many men with first-class degrees, men who would have been classed as of high calibre in any country, men who judged by intellectual standards could not have been classified as mediocre. Success later on in Service life was, of course, another matter. But here again, what constitutes ability? To most Indians it is the material position achieved, and a man is adjudged able or clever if he obtains a high position irrespective of his intellectual merit or the methods employed. Yet I have known Wranglers who never progressed higher than the ordinary rungs of the I.C.S. ladder. Temperament and intellect may or may not run together in harness, and in saying that the intellectual level of the Service was generally high, I am limiting the statement to intellectual attainments alone.

As I look back at the past, not with nostalgia for an ethic which is now a part of history, and which in any case was foreign to India, but unblinkered and with objectivity, I have no regrets whatsoever at having passed into the I.C.S. I may not have been of the Service; but I consider it a great privilege to have been *in* it.[2] It was a great Service. Indeed, it can justifiably claim to have been the greatest of the Imperial Services of the modern imperial age: great not for its power and authority—the French, the Dutch, the Japanese, the Italians, the Belgians, the Portuguese, all held dominion over palm, though not over pine as well—but for the manner in which that power was exercised: for its virtues, its rectitude, its sense of justice, its tolerance, its sense of public duty, and despite the critics,

---

[1] Ibid., p. 442.
[2] Some of the contributors to *The Civil Servant in India* have also written in high praise of the quality of the I.C.S.

its high administrative ability. Possibly in its near century of history one or two may have slipped from its high standards and fallen by the wayside; but the Service went on untainted.

VII

The District

THE I.C.S. was an all-pervasive Service. From the Viceroy's Executive Council downwards it spread into every nook and cranny of the Government and the Administration, the Judiciary as well as the Executive. While, as has been seen, its Political Department dealt with the Princes and the North-West Frontier, its foreign branch looked after His Britannic Majesty's diplomatic interests in Aden, the Persian Gulf and Nepal. Its members found their way into the Customs and Postal Departments; the Auditor-General of India and the Accountants-General in the Provinces were taken from the Service; and even the mysterious post of Northern-India Salt Commissioner was included in its cadre. In fact, short of being a Bishop or a Field-Marshal there was scarcely a post which an Indian Civil Servant could not aspire to hold. This notwithstanding, the District was the basic unit of the British administrative system and the District Officer was its pivot. For anyone seeking to understand the difference between the administration of independent India and that of the British, a preliminary sketch of the District Officer's role under imperial rule is a necessity.

If the District was the basic unit of the British system, its essential human element was the village or group of villages, and since from the early days of British rule special stress had always been laid on the village, the District Officer held a place of special importance in British eyes. For even the highest posts in a Province, long apprenticeship in the District was normally (there were exceptions) a necessity. The links between the District, the Division—in the United Provinces this was a combination of five or six districts under the general coordinating control of a Commissioner—and the Provincial Government's headquarters were close and strong, and save in exceptional circumstances the rule was that a period in the Secretariat should be limited to three years. There was a constant interchange between the District and the Secretariat with a constant influx of district experience into the latter. Fresh blood thus kept coursing through the veins of the Secretariat, while on the other hand close experience of affairs at the Governmental end reduced to some extent the confirmed District Officer's somewhat contemptuous attitude towards a group of men who tended to become so immersed in their files that they lost sight of the human beings down under for whose benefit their voluminous noting was intended.

As a designation the term 'District Officer' existed only in fact and not in law. It was in common use officially as a composite, generic description to cover the dual nature of the Government's representative in the Districts. As the head of the criminal administration the District Officer was the District Magistrate; as the Chief Revenue Officer, the Collector; and his full legal designation was Magistrate and Collector. Even this did not cover the whole of the United Provinces; for in Oudh as a result of historical accident the term 'Deputy Commissioner' was in vogue. On its annexation by Dalhousie in 1856 Oudh had been placed under a Commission for administrative purposes similar to the Commissions established in the Punjab, Central Provinces and elsewhere. These Commissions were manned by personnel drawn from both the Company's Bengal Civil Service and the Company's armed forces. The Bengal laws and regulations were applied by the Commissions where found suitable, but the latter were empowered to enact special legislation for their own particular jurisdictions and conditions. For the sake of simplicity I have used throughout the synthetic designation 'District Officer'.

The District Officer retained his great importance right up to the end of British rule. It is true that from 1920 onwards the popularly elected political leader began to replace him to some extent as the 'true representative' of the people and their aspirations; but the District Officer remained the great co-ordinator. He was the Government's main and most important representative on the spot in regard to *all* aspects of the Administration, the man on whom every local department was likely to fall back at some time and in some degree; the Forest Officer, for example, when adjacent villages illicitly grazed their cattle in his reserves and damaged his saplings; the Irrigation Engineers when their canal banks were cut; the Inspector of Schools when he wanted sympathy and indirect assistance

for the new school he proposed to open; the Health Officer
when the village wells required to be disinfected during an
epidemic or when mass inoculations were the order of the day.
The British administrative edifice in fact rested on four columns,
stability, order, security of life and property, and a sound treas-
sury, and it was only if these essential columns remained firm
that the Administration could function effectively. It was
the function of the District Officer to see that the columns
were kept in good order, so that within the edifice itself social
and political progress could be ensured.

A little more than one year before independence a Congress
Government was returned to power in the United Provinces,
and immediately set in motion the process—to be rapidly
accelerated over the years—of altering the whole concept
of what a District Officer should be and simultaneously
reducing the importance attached by the British to the District
as the basic administrative unit. These rapid changes were
to be expected, since only the British could manage successfully a system constructed by themselves from British material
and on British precept and practice. The new concepts of
administration born of the Indian way of life necessarily involved a complete break from British tradition and method. The
shadow was retained, while the substance was removed, and
the retention of the former designations and terms, District,
District Officer, Magistrate and Collector, Superintendent
of Police and so on, should not be allowed to obscure the
fact that the fundamentals underwent a complete metamorphosis. Only if this is understood is an understanding of modern
India possible.

Out of my twenty-two years serive in the I.C.S. from 1925
until its winding up in 1947, sixteen were spent in Districts,
one as Commissioner of a Division, and only the balance in
either the Government of India or the Provincial Secretariat.
This was a long period for anyone, British or Indian, and
especially the latter. I think it would be generally correct
to say that Indians preferred posts in the Secretariat at the
headquarters of the Government for a variety of reasons,
such as amentities of life and the possibilities of promotion
inherent in being at the headquarters of the Government,
escape from the nuisance of the perpetual friction between

Hindu and Muslim, freedom from the odium attaching to the suppression of political disturbances and from similar inconveniences attaching to the duties of a District Magistrate. From the early years of my apprenticeship in the Districts, however, the fact was brought home to me that the real life of India lay in its seven hundred thousand or so villages, and time, the influence of my father and my personal experiences in our own Grant combined to strengthen this conviction.

Uttar Pradesh (the United Provinces of old) is divided by nature into four distinct areas, the Himalayan Hill tracts, the Terai or foothills, the Districts of the Indo-Gangetic plain, a thickly populated area watered by the river Ganges and its great tributaries, and lastly Bundelkhand together with the Mirzapur District, a large tract traversed by the Vindhyan hills and with more affinities with Central India than with the remainder of the Province. During my years as a District Officer and Commissioner, my experience covered the last three areas, and it was not long before I realized that in addition to Nature's geographically horizontal divisions there were vertical ones, man-made, ingrained in history and of even greater political and social importance. Thus the western Districts with a large proportion of Jats had, and still have, more in common with the Jat areas of the Punjab than with the rest of the people of the United Provinces whom they lump together under the slightly contemptuous term 'purbiyas' (easterners);[1] and the real purbiyas of the eastern side display little brotherly love for their western fellows, preferring to turn to neighbouring Bihar with its similarity of language and customs. In Bundelkhand the Bundela Rajputs have been an entity of their own for many centuries, with their roots elsewhere than in the Province. Caste, too, which I was often optimistically told was in the process of disintegration and complete disappearance, played a great role in the life of the people everywhere. In one District to which I was posted the Kayasthas—an urban caste—were at perpetual loggerheads with the Kshatriya (Rajput) landowners; in another the Jats with the Jains; in

---

[1] In 1966 the Jat districts of the Punjab were separated in order to form the Jat State of Haryana, and I have not the least doubt that in the course of time the Jat areas of Uttar Pradesh will be joined to it. The present State of Haryana is only half a State.

yet a third the Brahmins were ready to take on all comers. Indeed, even within the same caste, some sub-castes were held in greater esteem than others. The Taga Brahmins of the west, for example, and the Bhumihars of the east have never been considered to be in the same category as other U.P. Brahmins— not quite out of the top Brahminical drawer. To crown everything else, was the perpetual religious conflict between Hindu and Muslim. These, jointly and severally, were antipathies the roots of which were buried deep in India's long history. They were not the creation of the British, not even the communal antagonism between the Hindu and Muslim communities. They were kept in check under a powerful Government, to come to the surface when weakness and indecision took the place of a strong Administration.

Although I was brought into early contact not merely with different geographical areas but also with a variety of peoples of different histories and with different customs, it was only with the passage of time that I eventually, through the compulsion of events, realized the basic truth of the British theory that India was not, as all Indians liked to believe, a nation in the full, scientific sense of the term, but only a conglomeration, not completely syncretized, of races, communities, castes, languages and endless distinctions. I use the word 'eventually' because for many years I refused to draw the correct logical conclusions from what I saw around me. Clothing myself in that cloak of euphoria which was popular with the intelligentsia of the day, I was very like Sherlock Holmes's friend Dr Watson, who saw but never observed. It was not until I became Chief Secretary just before the end of British rule that I discarded the rose-tinted spectacles through which I had been accustomed to survey the Indian scene and began to face the facts of Indian life squarely.

My first posting was to Hardoi District in Oudh, the headquarters of which was more a large village than a town, its population of some 15,000, however, entitling it to the privilege of a Municipal Board. Undistinguished though the town was, the same could not be said for the District as a whole; for it was famous as being one of the best small-game areas in the Province, and its numerous *jheels* (lakes), varying in size from small to very large, were a winter haven for every kind of waterfowl. By way of a counterweight to the fame, however, Hardoi was also notorious for crime, dacoity being quite a normal activity with some sections of the rural population. From the dual standpoint of business and pleasure it was an excellent District in which to begin one's apprenticeship. The system of proprietary and tenancy rights, as well as the rent and revenue laws of Oudh, differed radically from those of the Agra portion of the United Provinces, and in many respects were far more complex. So complex, indeed, that some of the military members of the early Oudh Commissions—a simple and straightforward breed, with an acute distaste for legal complexities and arguments—adopted the direct method of dealing with them. Col. Harrison, for instance, one of the early Deputy Commissioners of Kheri, was said to have perfected a swift procedure for disposing of the revenue appeals in his Court. Dividing them into three roughly equal batches, he would tap the first with the words 'Appeals dismissed', the second with 'Appeals allowed', and the third would be retained 'For argument'. His system, oddly enough, appeared to work satisfactorily at the time. But by 1925 the Oudh litigant was by no means so easygoing, and it was incumbent on me to learn my way around the intricacies of the land system and the law connected with it as soon as possible.

My Deputy Commissioner, A. B. Reid, one of the kindest and most conscientious of men, hospitably gave me a roof over my head for as long as he remained in the District. Although he had completed thirteen years' service, the exigencies of the war had cut short his district experience, and Hardoi was his first independent charge. Considerably embarrassed at the idea of having anyone inflicted on him for training, he wrote to the Chief Secretary with the suggestion that, since he himself was ignorant of the work, and was hardly in a position to instruct anyone else in it, I should be sent to a more suitable person. The Chief Secretary, a humorist by the name of Lambert (afterwards Sir George Lambert), merely replied that such being the case, Reid and I could not do better than learn the work together! And so we did, although it must be said that Reid had underrated his capabilities as a trainer of the young.

One incident within a fortnight of my arrival in the District

9

deserves mention for its moral. Almost my first act was the purchase of a horse. Since the prospective seller was one of the local *talukdars*, the transaction fell within the ambit of private trade, and was thus strictly forbidden, without the prior sanction of the Government, both under the ordinary rules applicable to all government officials and more specifically under the I.C.S. Covenant. The mare was accordingly carefully inspected by various authorities with the object of obviating the possibility of the price being too low. In fact the boot turned out to be on the other leg. The most noteworthy feature of my purchase was the possession of a mouth so hard that it required almost everything from a regulation bit to the iron-mongery in the Hardoi bazaar; and on the whole the sum I paid was generous. The importance of the incident lay in the strictness with which the rules relating to private trade were enforced. Nor was this an isolated example, for the scope of the rules was wide. It was even incumbent on an I.C.S. officer to obtain the sanction of the Government if he desired to purchase the shares of a public limited company which functioned within his jurisdiction. The Government made sure that there would be no suspicion of a return to the palmy days of the East India Company. Different times have brought in their train different ideas, for after independence the ban was lifted, and officials of all services have been encouraged to augment their salaries in various manners. Loans are given for the purchase of land and for building purposes, and the houses so constructed are often leased out at fantastic rents. Many officials are able to raise funds for the construction of two or three houses for business purposes. Others run small agricultural or poultry farms, either themselves or through the agency of their wives. While the new system is of great help to all officials in counteracting the drop in the value of money with its lowering of actual salaries, it can, and often does, lead to a number of abuses. Allegations— by no means unfounded—are common that government servants acquire land or other properties at low rates through official influence, and that governmental agencies are used both for building houses and for the easy and cheap purchase of materials. Official influence, too, is brought to bear on government Departments for miscellaneous assistance, and this is given more readily to those in high positions than to the ordinary mortal, whose need may be greater. I have always considered the British tradition and practice to be better in every way from the administrative angle. The likelihood of the present system degenerating into the conditions prevailing in the days when the East India Company was a mainly trading concern and when the Company's servants were allowed to indulge freely in private trade with all its attendant corruption and favouritism is always there. Present day trends would indicate that perhaps this time may not be far off; for the pagoda tree has not withered in India, and there are always plenty of hands ready to shake it in the absence of a strong check. This, of course, is an individual view only, based, moreover, not on moral grounds, with which I am not concerned, but on the need for good and impartial administration.

The British reposed great trust in even the junior officers of their Civil Service who were given responsibility from the start. Men learnt by their own mistakes, and there was always the father-figure of the District Officer to correct and guide. But any attempt to shift responsibility onto subordinates was strongly condemned. An error made in good faith, provided it was not too foolish, would be condoned with a warning; the evasion of responsibility never. The British theory of administration as distinct from practice was contained in a number of massive volumes of regulations and rules, the most formidable of which was entitled the *Manual of Government Orders*. This comprehensive compilation dealt with every conceivable subject from Christian burials and the correct way for I.C.S. officers to wear civil officers' uniform (in case one should ever rise to such heights) to such esoteric matters as how to deal with eunuchs—though in this last case I never heard of anyone applying the rules to them. But theory and practice were not necessarily the same. The British knew how to apply rules from the practical, commonsense angle, when to apply them strictly and when and how to stretch them. It was in its practice that the British Administration differed materially from that established by independent India. Close-knit, with the chain of responsibility running down from the Provincial Government through the Division to the District Officer, the system depended on discipline, order, method and regularity at all levels. Rules and regulations were enforced from the

standpoint of their effects, since with the British officer it was
the spirit and not the letter of the rule which counted. Two
small examples will illustrate this. Every I.C.S. officer had to
pass a series of departmental examinations at the end of his
first year of service. The subjects were not of equal importance
from the practical angle. One, indeed, 'Treasury and Accounts',
had little bearing on the day-to-day work of a District Officer's
life, although failure to pass in it entailed the postponement of
one's annual increment in salary. One young assistant magistrate, whom I shall call 'G.', habitually failed in his Accounts
paper, despite every possible leniency. His third attempt coincided with my being the examiner in this along with other
subjects, and the letter of appointment from the Chief Secretary
included the following delightful suggestion:—'With reference
to G.'s persistent and consistent inability to pass the Depart-
mentals in Treasury and Accounts, I am now directed to ask
you to set him a paper which he *can* pass.' And this even after
prior consultation with G. proved no simple matter. By way of
contrast the normal Indian method of following a rule—where
it is followed at all—is its application without thought for its
real content and purpose. The pension rules lay down that an
annual life certificate must be given on the 1st of April each
year. The rule is a salutary, and, indeed, necessary one to
prevent pensions being fictitiously drawn in the names of persons
who may have died. But clearly there need not be anything
sacrosanct in the particular date, the intention of the rule
merely being that there should be proof that the pensioner
was actually alive during the previous twelve months. My
pension was once held up through weeks of argument with the
Treasury Officer concerned on the ground that the life certificate was given on the 1st of June and not the 1st of April,
and it was a long time before the Treasury Officer, a high
official, could be persuaded to believe that the fact of being
alive in June was perfectly good proof of life two months earlier.
Much of the maladministration in India is the product of
too-literal application of rules by men unwilling to risk a
commonsense interpretation of them, even when no personal
considerations are involved, combined with a readiness to break
or ignore rules to oblige friends, relations or powerful politicians.

The District Offices at district headquarters dealt with all matters relating to the daily life of the citizen. In addition there was a large staff of magistrates and revenue officers whose judicial work required supervision if delay in the disposal of cases were to be avoided. The British I.C.S. officer's methods of dealing with his work were largely indirect. There were meticulous rules for the inspection of work, but if every such direction had been followed to the end, the wood would never have been visible for the trees. Subordinates were experts at putting up charts and statements which were impeccable on the surface, but which were not so innocuous underneath. Offices were scheduled to open at 10 a.m. daily. In India, where time has never been an object of worship nor punctuality considered a special virtue, an office could be made to function more effectively by the simple method of the District Officer's making it a habit of visiting it himself on time. Example meant a great deal, and as a result even the most sluggish soul would be at his post a few minutes before the arrival of the head of the District. If the latter had no judicial work fixed for the day, he could spend an easy, but salutary hour merely in looking over the various branches of his Office. In this way he could see that the judicial Courts had commenced their work, that the clerks were not perusing the daily newspapers and that routine had started. A quick look at the charts of files pending with three or four clerks together with a check of the actual files on the filing racks would enable the District Officer to see at a glance whether the charts were correctly maintained or not, and where delays, if any, had occurred. A short round of the Copying Department, the duty of which was to issue on payment of the regulation fees, copies of judicial orders and other official documents, would put the whole branch on the alert. The fees for urgent copies were higher than those for ordinary, the normal time for the issue of the latter being a fortnight to three weeks. If the proportion of urgent copies asked for was abnormally high, the inference was that excessive delays were occurring, since no one would wish to pay a higher fee than was necessary. Five minutes would suffice to trace the causes and to deal with those concerned.

Indirect methods of this kind not only halved the District Officer's work, but also kept the whole staff on its toes for fear of having them trodden on. Surprise rounds every ten days or so could work wonders in the disposal of work without hurting anyone unduly; and a word of praise here and there for good disposal of files was never out of place. The District Officer thus gained a reputation for alertness, if nothing else, and if at the same time one was able to dig out some obscure rule, which meant nothing and of which no one had ever heard, for an omniscience which was certainly spurious but none the less valuable.

Similar indirect procedures could be used in the case of the subordinate magistracy and the police. A short note at the end of the day from each magistrate added a mere five minutes to his work, but would enable the District Officer in his capacity of District Magistrate to see at a glance how many witnesses a Court had handled during the day, whether adjournments were being too freely given either at the behest of the police or out of kindness to the defence, or whether the prosecution were asking for too many remands—which might be an indication of slackness in the production of evidence or of poor investigation on the part of the police at the outset. The monthly inspections, too, of the District Jail provided another rapid means of testing the work of the magistrates, since each prisoner under trial carried with him a card showing the date of his arrest, of his appearance in Court and the number of remands allowed. A word later with the magistrate concerned usually had the desired effect of speeding up disposals of case-work. If it did not, words could give place to indirect action, there being many ways, unorthodox but well within the letter of the law, by which a District Magistrate could make the life of a sluggish subordinate uncomfortable without troubling those higher up.

One of the cardinal points in the British system was the need for harmony between the District Officer and the Superintendent of Police, and in military stations between both and the military administration. The District Magistrate, as head of the criminal administration, had a close connexion with the work of the police as a whole, and liaison went all the way down the ladder in respect of all district and police officials. This link between the magistracy and the police was the target of much adverse criticism in political circles, and there could be no doubt that the system was open to abuse. The idea, however, that the District Officer and the Superintendent of Police were interested in hatching conspiracies to put innocent men into jail was quite erroneous. It arose mainly from the political situation and the political agitation that erupted from time to time, both of which involved a close watch on the Congress. A strong movement for the separation of executive from judicial functions, spearheaded by the political intelligentsia of the urban areas, was its consequence. This, as with so much else in India, was the product of the inculcation of English legal and political theories, since the union of Executive and Judicial powers in one person was in no way contrary to either Hindu or Muslim precepts before the advent of British rule, and in my experience was not the object of any special opposition from the side of the villager. During India's two decades of freedom allegations of political interference and of political pressures being brought to bear both on the police and the Courts have been constantly made— and not without good reason in many cases, without the public conscience being unduly disturbed. Many such cases were brought to my notice officially during my tenure as Chief Secretary; but in a country where political power is worshipped for its own sake, even the separation of the two functions, executive and judicial, is no safeguard against the misuse of political influence.

Every system of government is dependent in the last resort on the men who work the administration. The British criminal administration on balance, apart from the political movement, did not lead to injustice. Even in political cases it was not as bad as it was often made out to be. In general the dual system, indeed, had certain advantages, although it was inevitable that personalities played an important role. Where the District Officer was weak and allowed himself to become the rubber-stamp of his Superintendent of Police the system was at its worst; and the same held good when the latter fell into the hands of his subordinate deputies or inspectors. But within my experience such cases were few, and the system suited the conditions of the period. For this due credit should be given to the British Police Officer, who had a certain inherent sense of legal procedures and natural justice derived from the course of British history. The best type of British Police Officer made genuine efforts to keep the subordinate police within measurable distance of the path of rectitude; and no one with knowledge of India requires to be told how difficult a task this can be. Nor did he indulge in palpable injustice merely for its own sake. Nevertheless, it must be admitted that the system in its modern form was essentially British. It could only be worked successfully under British supervision, and became a definitely harmful anachronism after 1947.

Discipline and efficiency were maintained at a far higher level than was to be the case after independence. The magistracy saw the actual work of the police not only within the four walls of the Court room, but also outside, and they had the opportunity of testing its worth on the spot during the cold-weather touring. In the course of my service I worked with more British Superintendents of Police and Deputy Inspectors-General than Indian. Although there were occasions when we would agree to differ, informal discussions usually settled any difficult matters in issue. Most often we found ourselves in complete agreement. No Superintendent of Police ever asked me to interfere with a magistrate's discretion once a case was in Court, and I often disagreed with police suggestions to lodge appeals in the case of acquittals without the Superintendent taking this amiss. Except in the matter of the actual quantum of sentences awarded I never interfered with a subordinate's handling of a case in Court. But here the laying down of guidelines was not only justifiable but essential, both in the interests of abstract justice and of good administration. It was neither logical nor just that one Sub-Divisional Magistrate should award a completely different sentence from that given by a colleague in the adjacent Court room for a similar offence committed in identical circumstances. While allowances were rightly made for major differences in the background to a crime, there always remained a large area where uniformity was desirable. If, for example, cattle theft began to show an abnormal increase—in the Indian village the ownership of cattle is still a measure of wealth—it was both reasonable and necessary for the District Officer as District Magistrate to exercise his responsibility by the issue of strict orders that sentences should be deterrent and not less than a fixed minimum. In independent India the adulteration not merely of foodstuffs but also of medicines and drugs has reached such alarming proportions as to be a menace to public health. Various Governments have repeatedly complained of the inadequacy of the sentences given—usually a small fine which can soon be made good by the delinquent—but unless the District Magistrate as the Government's representative on the spot is allowed to supervise, guide, and in the last resort to take action against, subordinate magistrates, the position is hardly likely to improve. On the other hand, there were many cases where leniency was desirable as a normal practice, as with juvenile or first offenders, and in such cases I saw no reasons why instructions should not be issued to subordinate Courts for the coordination of sentences as far as was possible and for the use of the First Offenders Act and the Probation Laws.

Of equal importance to his magisterial duties were the functions of the District Officer as Collector of the District, the Chief Revenue Officer. The designation 'Collector' was a somewhat unfortunate one, with a repellent odour attaching to it, which gave rise to much misconception as to the work actually involved. Contemporary critics of the British in their perpetual search for scapegoats to account for the many inadequacies in Indian performance since 1947 have strongly and roundly condemned the whole British system as being nothing but a tax-collecting machine and an instrument for the suppression of political advancement. These and similar adverse judgements are not correct, and are largely the results of appraisals made on a different set of values and without any solid basis in fact. The work of the District Officer as Collector went far beyond the mere collection of land revenue. It involved a knowledge of village life, the deeper the better, of the various land tenures and customs and of the general outlook of the rural areas. Here the knowledgeable Collector came into direct contact with the many and varied problems relating to agriculture and allied subjects like irrigation and forestry. He learnt, too, to distinguish the feasible from the impracticable, between the dream and the reality. The vast amount of beneficial legislation in the United Provinces dealing with tenancy rights, agricultural debt, land alienation and the co-operative system was the product of the detailed knowledge of Collectors, the actual laws being drafted in the first instance by the Secretary of the Revenue Department, himself a Collector of long standing. Nor was this the case in the United Provinces alone. One of the most beneficial of all the works undertaken in the Punjab, one that led to an immediate increase in prosperity, the colonisation and settlement of the Lyallpur and Montgomery Districts, resulted from the combined efforts of a series of District Officers, one of whom was afterwards to become Lord Hailey. The Co-operative movement in the same Province owed much of whatever success it was able to achieve to the enthusiasm of another District Officer, Malcolm (later Sir Malcolm) Darling, while yet a third, F. L. Brayne, undertook a new series of experiments in rural uplift while Deputy Commissioner, Gurgaon. The British District Officer of the old régime certainly did not stop at merely the collection of taxes by the due date. Not everyone was a Lawrence, a Hume or a Hailey, but certainly the best type up to the end of the Raj possessed considerable understanding of the Indian villager and viewed the latter's problems with far more detailed knowledge and sympathy than did the political intelligentsia of the cities and towns.

The Revenue Officer, indeed, could be useful even in the rarefied atmosphere of the heights of the Government of India, an establishment which was cut off from the daily life of the people in the thousands of villages and small country townships. My own temporary elevation to New Delhi was in this capacity. In 1935 the Government of India entangled itself in a Cost of Agricultural Production Enquiry, which had been triggered off in the first instance by a constant verbal barrage of criticism from the Swaraj Party in the Central Legislature. That the poverty of the Indian peasant was to be found in the alleged iniquities of British rule was the conventional ammunition of the Congress armoury, and the world-wide depression of the thirties with its calamitous fall in commodity prices provided a golden opportunity for using it. The Enquiry was designed to prove that after all necessary expenditure had been met the cultivator still had a reasonable surplus in hand. Unfortunately for the Government the tabulated results showed the exact reverse. They proved mathematically that the rural population should have been dead of starvation long before, and thus supported the stand taken by the Swarajists.

The investigation had started off on the wrong foot from its inception. It was too limited in its geographical scope, only a handful of villages having been selected as representative of the whole country. The collaboration of the Provincial Governments did not appear to have been sought, so that the tabulators appointed by New Delhi descended on the villages from above and laboured in a vacuum. Most unfortunate of all was the appointment as head of the operation of an expert who had just returned from the U.S.A. after training in American rural economics and the latest American statistical methods and practices. The application of American methods designed for the large-scale, sophisticated farmer of the Mid-West to the small-scale, subsistence farming of the illiterate Indian cultivator, with, in the United Provinces at all events, an average holding of less than two acres, and that, too, in scattered fields, produced a crop of anomalies. The Government of India were now placed in a serious quandary, since the draft Report could not be made public as it stood, and, no longer enamoured of their statistician, they decided to summon a District Officer to their assistance. The Executive Counsellor concerned was Sir Jagdish Prasad, a former member of the I.C.S. in the United Provinces, who not unnaturally turned to his own Province; and the Chief Secretary at the time, Sir Hugh Bomford, under whom I had served when he was a Commissioner, sent me up to New Delhi to see what could be done to unravel the knots which the Government of India had so successfully and quite unnecessarily tied round themselves.

Straightening out the figures so carefully collected took much time and effort, but eventually I was able to produce some order out of chaos; sufficient at least to keep the rural body and soul together. The misapplication of a highly scientific statistical system which had no relevance to Indian conditions had understandably led to astonishing results. Expenditure had been inflated on one side of the account, while on the other many items of income which are normal in village life had been rigorously excluded. Marketing expenses included notional wages to the cultivator's wife, for example, for taking a cart-load of vegetables to the local market town; and even the cart itself would be charged eight annas for hire. The whole family came under the head *Labour Charges*, even down to the ten-year-old who grazed the village cattle instead of going to the village school. On the income side many not inconsiderable items such as the proceeds from the sale of thatching grass or of ropes locally made from sunn hemp were omitted. In addition to an abundance of incongruities, it was evident that many of the entries were based on fictitious information which clearly indicated that the informant was more interested in ridding himself of the questioner than in giving the correct information. City 'snoopers' have never been welcome in an Indian village.

My labours actually turned out to be unnecessary. By the middle of 1937, thanks to the unremitting activities of Hitler and Mussolini, the attention of the Swaraj Party was deflected towards international affairs, so that greatly to the satisfaction, indeed, relief, of the Government the final results of the investigation, as edited and corrected, were quietly filed without the slightest flutter in the political dovecote. From being a mere Officer on Special Duty, I was now promoted to a regular vacancy in the Education, Health and Lands Department as an Additional Deputy Secretary. In this capacity I dealt with the Indian Medical Service (Civil), the Archaeological Survey of India, the Zoological Survey and Delhi Local Self-Government. I found nothing of interest in any of these subjects. Even in respect of the Archaeological Department what would have been of real interest to me, the touring, with its visits to places of historical importance, was dealt with on a higher level. My work was limited to the checking of departmental budgets, the preparation of progress reports, the postings, transfers and leave of officials and similar dull routine. Although I was definitely on the lower slopes of Olympus and Service ambition might have pushed me into an attempt to climb higher, I could not bring myself to make the effort. My heart was in the Districts and I was never able to rid myself of the belief that New Delhi and Simla were not, and were never likely to be, the real India. I was not in the least sorry, therefore, when at the end of my two years' term the Secretary of the Department, Girja Shankar Bajpai (afterwards Sir Girja Shankar with a record collection of letters after his name), who was to the Government of India bred, having been there since his third or fourth year of service, returned me to my parent Province. His parting certificate—a kind of obituary notice—was open to a variety of interpretations according to one's service education. 'Mr Bonarjee', wrote Bajpai, 'has ability, but is more the type required in the Districts.' The first portion of this dubious eulogy could be discounted, because Bajpai was far too good a trade-unionist to suggest that any I.C.S. officer who had ascended to the Government of India and who, more specifically, had been precipitated into his Department was not possessed of ability. As regards the second, which I took as a compliment, Bajpai belonged to the school of thought which looked on District Officers as a somewhat uncouth species, addicted to riding and shooting and generally lacking in spit and polish. I had gained some valuable experience in New Delhi, but there were no broken hearts on either side when the Government of India and I parted company.

After my return from the artificial and rather hot-house atmosphere of the Government of India, I spent the next five years without a break in the Districts. No account of the life of a District Officer would be complete without mention of his touring in the cold weather. As soon as the heat and stickiness of the rainy season had given way to the clear blue skies and pleasant cold of the northern India winter, I would be under canvas along with my wife and family, including the baby and the ayah. It was during these four months, from November to the end of February, that District Officers would see their districts at the grass roots. The touring was leisurely, the District Officer riding and his family travelling from stage to stage in bullock-carts comfortably padded up with pillows and cushions. The tents—four in all—were comfortable and in size compared not unfavourably with many a modern flat. And for warmth in the chill of the evenings there was the Moradabad stove to add to one's comfort. Our cold-weather touring, it must be confessed, did not include the hardships of a military campaign.

It was now the function of the District Officer to keep his fingers on the pulse of the countryside, and for official purposes the pulse consisted of the men of importance and influence in their small world, the landowners, big and small, the headmen, the *lambardars*,[1] the *patwari*, or village accountant (of whom more later) and the numerous small men whose importance has since been immeasurably enhanced with the extension of full adult franchise to the villages. This, however, was not all. Everywhere the inquisitive District Officer—and much of his business consisted of being avidly inquisitive—would examine the working of the governmental machine in all its aspects. One of his many duties was to keep a general eye on all the departments of the Government in their dealings with the countryside in addition to his own such as Agriculture, Public Health, Forest, Irrigation, Education, and he was entitled to make inspections as, when and where he thought fit.

Not the least of his duties as head of the District and the sole representative of the Government was to be approachable, to hear local grievances and, wherever possible, to redress them on the spot. All touring officers had in any case collected a number of petitions handed in at headquarters during the previous months for personal investigation in the village in point. To which would usually be added another batch as soon as he arrived there. Not that the contents of every petition presented to him would turn out to be correct on inquiry, since petty, personal and even family quarrels were often inflated far beyond their intrinsic merits or importance. Nevertheless, it was the business of the District Officer to listen. He was the eyes and ears of the Government, and, if he spoke no evil, he certainly saw and heard a great deal.

In his own specific sphere, he would make discreet inquiries into the general reputation for (reasonable) integrity and efficiency in the case of subordinate officials—and in doubtful cases of even higher ones. How were the local police, the revenue staff and all the little cogs in the official machine working? Correct evaluation of general reputation came only with experience, and even then mistakes were easy to make. Vague complaints, the result of personal enmity, were never in short supply, but where local opinion in a number of

---

[1] In the United Provinces, in villages where there was a large number of co-sharers, one of the latter was appointed under the revenue law to collect the land revenue on behalf of the Government. He was called the *lambardar*, and was given a commission of 4 per cent on his collections.

villages was unanimous it could reasonably be accepted as essentially correct.

General inquiries apart, there were detailed inspections to be made of Police Stations and Revenue Offices, and rather more cursory ones of dispensaries and schools. The amount of crime in his District, and the relations between Hindus and Muslims in difficult villages, were of special importance to the District Officer as District Magistrate. Every village was well aware of the persons in the neighbourhood who made a profession of crime, and if a touring officer made local inquiries as he wandered through the villages and jotted down the names, he was in a good position to check them later with the registers and charts maintained in the Police Stations. If the names did not tally or if crime continued in a particular area where preventive action had been taken by the police, it was clear that evidence was being faked for the edification of the Courts, and that the wrong men were being prosecuted. Sub-Inspectors of Police were never above falsifying their records on occasion for the sake of an easy life, and it was pleasant to be able to catch them out in the game.

A frequent delinquent in his own sphere, and one whose failures to keep to the path of rectitude only too often evaded detection, was the *patwari*, the smallest cog in the revenue machine and at the same time the most important. The *patwari* maintained half-a-dozen records which were the basis of the Land Records system. Often the only literate man in the village, he would in addition write petitions and even private letters for the inhabitants for a small fee. For his official work he received an average wage of Rs. 18 per month and was permitted to have a few acres of land for his personal cultivation. The system, though cheap and reasonably efficient, as efficiency goes in India, had many obvious defects. The *patwari* had almost unlimited powers in his hand, or rather his pen, since he was in a position to manipulate the records, despite constant inspections, in favour of anyone willing to pay him. This he was only too prone to do under pressures from a powerful landowner or influential tenant to the detriment of those unable to grease his palm. Much avoidable litigation was the direct consequence of the *patwari's* all-too-human inability to resist temptation. Not that every *patwari* was unpopular, for some combined unscrupulousness with a considerable degree of skill in keeping in the good books of the village. In one of the districts where I was a Sub-Divisional Officer a *patwari* died worth, according to reliable reports, Rs. 20,000 in jewellery and ornaments—no mean sum for a man, who, if he had saved his complete salary every month, would have taken a century to achieve it. Yet there had never been any serious complaint against him. I never discovered into what status he was reborn.

There was a long line of inspecting officials over the *patwari*, headed by the Sub-Divisional Officer, and the District Officer could join in the game himself on occasion, if he wished, listening to the inspecting officer droning out selected entries in the records, and asking the assembled villagers to verify their correctness or otherwise. Errors were often found on the spot, and, where serious, suitable action would be taken.

Indeed, there was neither beginning nor end to the miscellaneous jobs a District Officer could find to do during his touring. Everything depended on the individual and the individual's own inclinations. Even on his shooting trips he could, apart from seeing the precise condition of the crops he passed through and picking up much local gossip which might prove useful at some future time, learn a great deal about the bird life and the flora and fauna of his district. There was no District, too, that did not contain much of real interest, historical, archaeological, ethnological, which had no connexion with the figures of crime and the collection of the land revenue.

In the Lalitpur Sub-Division of Jhansi District, a sparsely populated, hilly tract, belonging more to Central India than to the United Provinces and where the transport of one's camp equipage was by camel and not by bullock-cart, there lived a humble caste, the Saheriyas. Aboriginal and tribal in their origins, and at one time only forest-dwellers, their conditions had not been investigated since the reports of Atkinson (1874) and Crooke (1898) in the second half of the nineteenth century. Becoming interested in them from the time when they acted as beaters (the rate was As. 4 for an ordinary and As. 8 for a tiger beat) I made a detailed inquiry into their origins and development for the Census Report of 1931. As was to be expected, I found that great changes had taken place in their conditions in the course of forty or fifty years.

The origins of the Saheriyas were obscure, and with neither folklore nor legends they were quite unable to account for themselves. Allied to the ancient Gonds of Central India in appearance, they were certainly of Dravidian origin, but classed themselves as below the Gonds in status. By 1930 they had entirely lost their former tribal characteristics and had ceased even to be a collected tribe. Scattered over three or four hundred villages all over the Sub-Division, they were to be found also as labourers in the small townships. One significant fact emerged from my inquiry. The Saheriyas by a process of gradual but steady evolution had finally emerged as a Hindu caste. They had been fortunate in not having been excessively exploited by unscrupulous townsmen. The Government had not interfered unduly with their lives, and their contacts with Hinduism having been slow and unforced they had adapted themselves to it without undergoing great stresses. They claimed to be Hindus, and were accepted as such by the higher castes, their position in the Hindu social scale being higher than that of the Bhangi (sweeper) and Chamar (leather-worker) and just below that of the Dhimar or waterman. They had, in short, been allowed to 'civilize' themselves in their own way and in their own time. Never having been forced into any form of modernity—Lalitpur town itself was not ostentatiously modern even in the late twenties—they had in the absence of undue external pressures grown into Hinduism of their own free-will, and Hinduism with its sponge-like capacity for absorption had taken them into its substance as a humble, backward, low caste.

I have given this account of the District Officer during the last twenty years of the British Raj not out of a desire to indulge in nostalgia, but for a very different reason. The District Officer has passed into history along with British rule, and in due course history will pass judgement on him as an element—in my view the most important element—of that rule. In this context it seems to me, writing twenty years after he made it, that Lord Wavell's assessment is not correct. 'The English in India,' he said in 1947, 'would not be remembered for this institution or that, but by the ideal they left behind of what a District Officer should be.'[1] I could wish that this view were

---

[1] Quoted in *The Guardians* (Oxford University Press), p. 360.

10

borne out by the facts of twenty years of independence; but the facts are very different.

A new generation has come to maturity in India which had neither experience nor knowledge of the British District Officer of the past. Born in the early thirties or later, it never saw a District Officer in the flesh, except perhaps when he was dealing with political agitation on the part of students in the schools and colleges. The political leaders of free India set out from the start to rid the country not only of such externals as statues and the names of roads but also of the essence of the British tradition. In this they have been remarkably successful. The members of the new Indian Administrative Service are not to be blamed for the consequences of the killing of the old ideals and their replacement by a new set of precepts. But the District Officer of today (in some cases he is a she, for women are now appointed to the post) is no longer the sole head of his District and the only representative of the Government, save in name and theory. The local heads of other District Departments are treated as being on a par with him, and the District Officer is merely first among equals. He no longer tours for three or four months on end, and such touring as is done is spasmodic and by jeep. He is compelled to share authority with party politicians of all shades of opinion on the one hand and with panchayats and a host of local organizations on the other, without having real power over them. So much so that everywhere at various times he has become a cog in the machinery not of the Government as such but of the Party organization and the local faction.

The new generation of administrators naturally follows its leaders—no blame can be attached to them for this—and the leaders have given unmistakable evidence by their actions that they do not desire to keep alive the ideals and the image of the old-time District Officer. To me one of the symbols of the change from the British concept of what was required of the District Officer is the appointment of women as heads of Districts. There have been several such, and only recently the City Magistrate of the town in which I live was a girl. To the old-timer it seems somewhat out of place for a girl to march around clad in a sari and with a tin hat on her head wondering whether to order the police at her command to use batons, tear-gas or rifles to disperse mobs smashing shop windows in the main shopping centre—as actually happened—or damaging cars with number plates in English. Incongruous or not, this is a definite break from the British system; and a definite and clean-cut break was the goal free India desired. It was only a short time ago that a highly placed officer of the former I.C.S., with little experience of District work but a great deal of the Secretariat, told me that in his view the importance of the District Officer in the new India was small. He appeared to regard the old-style officer as one of the worst products of British imperialism—which he still greatly disliked. Criticism of the new age and of the new type of leader, whether political or Service, would be foolish, and only one comment is necessary. The District Officer of the British period of Indian history is no longer remembered. He died in 1947 and was buried—I fear without any honours—almost immediately. May he rest in peace! If his work as a whole is judged over the period of a century, he had nothing of which to be ashamed. He did his duty conscientiously and well.

VIII

Rural Interlude

DURING his touring the District Officer would pitch his tents in a convenient mango grove near a village, but never actually in it. He became a part of the countryside in general, but not of the village itself. A certain indefinable aloofness, in fact, was essential to enable him to deal impartially and effectively with the variety of problems that cropped up. When I visited my parents in Rampore Grant, however, I was not the visible emblem of an invisible, white *badshah* in England of whom our villagers had vaguely heard but whom they had never seen; and if I was looked up to at all, it was as the son of my parents and not as the District Officer of the neighbouring district, Shahjahanpur or Bahraich. 'Ah,' remarked a grey-beard on my first visit in 1930, 'I saw the chhota sahib when he was a babe in arms, and now look at him. He's getting Rs. 3000/- a month.' That the sum mentioned was about three times that of my salary at the time was a small matter. He made his remark casually, and certainly without rancour. He was merely interested, and intended to convey that this was the way of an inscrutable Providence. If he himself lived virtuously in his present status, he might well be born into mine next time. Who could say? That was his belief, and no doubt his hope as well.

I was, indeed, almost literally a part of the village; for my father, after the collapse of the original bungalow outside Rampore, did not trouble to rebuild it. He simply converted the upper storey of the estate office in the village itself into a residence. This was no palace of stone outside and marble within, but an unpretentious affair of sun-dried brick, plastered over; comfortably, though certainly not luxuriously furnished and in no way an excuse for the Congress to point the finger of scorn at my parents as being despoilers of the poor and humble. Electric light and modern plumbing were, of course, not on the list of amenities, but their absence mattered little to me, since even the commodious residences of District Officers and Commissioners lacked the second and only a few large towns possessed the first.

My visits were usually short, being limited to ten days at Christmas, but in the cold weather of 1938-39 I spent about three months of my leave in the Grant. There was now no wide panorama before me to be inspected as a high official; for although their son was in the glamour of official life, my parents were regarded with affection by their tenantry for their simplicity. The ten hamlets of the estate housed the usual conglomeration of castes, including many Kurmis, a cultivating caste second only to the Jats of the western districts for good farming. There were no Christians, it having been a fixed principle from the time of my grandfather that there should never be any attempts at conversion; but we had a Muslim hamlet, Sirkargarh, while tucked away on the far side of the Sarda canal was Bijokha for the Chamars and other untouchables such as the Pasis. The Pasis were a reformed, or semi-reformed, erstwhile criminal tribe, many of whom were recruited into the police as village watchmen, doubtless on the principle that reformed poachers make the best gamekeepers. Somewhat surprisingly, unless this was an hereditary relic of their past when they were accustomed to organise themselves into gangs, they could throw up excellent organisers, and it was a Pasi who organised the first peasant upheaval in Oudh at the end of the first World War. Our Chamars, on the other hand, had no such title to fame, being mostly notorious for the rigour—far surpassing that of the Brahmins—with which they enforced their caste rules in the case of offenders against caste customs. From what I heard from my father, an investigation into their methods would have startled the most enthusiastic village 'uplifter'. Few Chamars were able to survive unscathed even the financial troubles involved in being compelled to provide an expiatory feast to their caste fellows, unless my father was ready to help the delinquent—which he occasionally did in a deserving case. The modes of trial too, which were summary, to say the least, and sometimes by ordeal, often shocked my father, inured though he was to the surprises of rural life.

Although legally it was my mother who was the landowner, our villagers not unnaturally regarded my father as their zamindar, and being surrounded by the *talukas* of rajas often from force of habit addressed him as such. Almost every morning they would approach him to solicit his blessing and to prefer their requests. They would stand in silence with folded hands until he spoke, when many would touch his feet. The usual recital of village affairs would follow, much in the style of the complaints at the camp of the District Officer. Kishori's bullock had died, and how was Kishori to finish his ploughing unless my father gave him a loan to buy another, which often actually meant that my father should pay half the cost. Or Lekhraj had allowed his cattle intentionally to trespass into the fields of Pheman *dhobi*, and would my father do something about it? Sometimes a woman would be among those with a prayer. Advancing shyly with her *chaddar* drawn closely over her head and face, she would settle herself comfortably at my father's feet, and touch first them and then her own forehead seven times, thereby hoping to acquire merit. My father would mildly shrug his shoulders, and ask me whether these things should be in the twentieth century: and to that I could only give the stock (and totally incorrect) answer of a half-baked nationalist who in 1938 still had much to learn, that they were the result of a slave mentality, which in turn was the consequence of foreign domination. Politeness in our area ordained that my father should not ask the woman's name, and still less that of her husband, for such questions were reserved for the Law Courts, where politeness of this kind was at a discount. Instead he would ask the woman whose mother she was and what he could do for her. Sometimes my mother, too, would be present on these occasions and the feet-touching process would be repeated. All of which took up much time before the real matter in hand was brought to light.

I was beginning to learn an early lesson, that at least in our area the Indian villager was fundamentally feudal at heart, and time has shown me that everywhere he is still far more so than the westernized urban intelligentsia are prepared to admit. Only a few years ago when the Queen as Head of the Commonwealth visited New Delhi crowds of villagers from even quite distant places trooped into the city to have 'darshan'[1] of the

[1] There is no precise equivalent for 'darshan', in English, and the philosophical meaning is different from the ordinary. In the ordinary sense it conveys the meaning of seeing or viewing a superior being, human as well as divine, with the intention of soliciting a blessing from the superior in addition to obtaining for oneself the merit inherent (or supposedly inherent) in the former. It is more than the mere paying of respect.

In Hindu philosophy 'darshan' means philosophical insight, the deeper view, and the six schools of Hindu philosophy are the Sad (six) Darshanas.

gracious young Maharani who, they knew, might have become their Empress. An Indian lady who was present throughout the visit, and who was in close touch with the Queen's entourage, told me that they stood quietly with their hands folded in the customary, and true, Indian mode of respect. Had these simple people had their way, they would have touched the Queen's feet, too. Indeed, some actually attempted to do so—all of which greatly mystified the Queen, who, it seems, had been imperfectly briefed, and had expected cheering. Nor did politics enter their picture: for, according to my informant, many in real wonder asked, 'But why is the great Maharani from England not wearing her crown?'

One can make what one likes, according to individual taste, of such episodes. For myself I would only add that the essence of the gesture of touching feet lies in the sincerity with which it is made, and the thought behind it. That it has been turned into political channels since independence for the purpose of gaining favours by means of empty flattery is very far from its true meaning, and that this does happen was brought home to me some years ago when I more than once saw two I.C.S. colleagues of mine touch the feet of the then Chief Minister of the United Provinces.

Since the Grants were in compact blocks, the owner could, if he so desired, keep in personal contact with his tenantry, and could thus be in a position to combine efficient with sympathetic management. From the outset, when they were still completing the clearance of the land and its settlement, my parents confined themselves to a single fixed rent from their tenants, without any of the side exactions and levies taken by the hereditary aristocracy of Oudh and their underlings, even the customary *nazars* (ceremonial gifts) of the important festivals being strictly taboo. Apart from these last, the list was very varied and included payments both in kind and cash, wheat and rice straw, one twentieth part of the sugar cane, cash *nazars* on such occasions as the marriage of the *talukdar's* son or daughter, and odd contributions towards payment of the subordinate staff. In fact, the list could be endless, and I heard of cases where, if a new car was required, *motorana* would be levied on all and sundry! Altogether it was not in the least surprising that Congressmen working in the rural areas during their agrarian campaigns took advantage of the existence of such impositions to stress the immediate need for the abolition of the prevailing system of land ownership. Nor were these the only extra burdens on the tenantry. *Begar* or forced labour was equally common in almost all estates; but here again Grant No. 18 was an exception to the general rule, and everything was meticulously entered in the Estate account books, with payments duly made for work done on the basis of the rates for labour in the neighbourhood.[1]

Linked to the time-hallowed exactions of the hereditary landowner were the customary levies taken by the subordinate official. These were of infinite variety, and they certainly never withered through age. In the Courts, for example, litigants were always expected to give in addition to the fees payable under the rules, a tip to the Court clerks who produced documents for inspection by the parties. Records from the Record Rooms, copies of documents from the Copying Department, could both be obtained more speedily by the tactful greasing of the palm here and there. In fact, the whole subordinate establishment had a variety of ingenious methods of extracting illicit pocket-money which could be kept within limits, but certainly never abolished. The police with their greater power were the most notorious, and the most disliked as a consequence. But episodes tinged with humour resulted from time to time. One such occurred in a District to which I was once posted. Sub-Inspectors were accustomed to maintain a very secret little diary in which customary payments were entered. The diary was expected never to leave the keeper's personal possession; but in this case the Sub-Inspector, on going out to the scene of a *dacoity*, handed it over to his second officer for safe custody. Communal enmity between the two—one being a Muslim and the other a Hindu—led to a local politi-

[1] Although the responsibility for the existence of forced labour was always cast on the British at this period—it being customary for Indians to blame the British for their own faults—it is of melancholy interest to see that the position in 1969 remains much the same as it was thirty years ago. 'Forced labour is prohibited under Article 23 of the Constitution, but every year the Commissioner for Schedules Castes and Scheduled Tribes discovers new areas where this inhuman custom prevails without let or hindrance. His latest report adds Kerala and Tamil Nadu to a list which already includes Rajasthan, Bihar, Orissa and Mysore...........Can the Tribals be blamed then for believing that forced labour has the blessings of the Administration?' (Leading Article in *The Times of India*, dated June 2nd 1969).

cian's being allowed to have a glimpse of the sacred document. The sequel provided some excellent comedy.

According to tradition in the countryside, Revenue Inspectors, *patwaris*, canal *amins* and the like expected to receive what was termed *faslana* from the cultivators and landowners at the end of each crop season. In our own Estate my father paid these and other extras from his own pocket in order to save his tenantry from possible, indeed very probable, harassment, and the recipients, secure in the knowledge that they would be given this fixed biannual addition to their salaries without let or hindrance, went their ways satisfied. That my father was thus condoning a felony was doubtless true; but since this saved his tenants from extortion, what of it? To my father the contentment of the latter was an end that justified the means. All in all, however, it was fortunate that he died in 1941 and did not live to see India in 1960.

The histology, as it might be termed, of corruption in India, varying from the relatively harmless tip to the downright bribe given and accepted for an illegal or illicit purpose, its many ramifications in Indian life, would provide an excellent subject for a sociological study. In its basic form corruption can be limited to the taking of money, but in its wider aspect might more purposefully include intellectual dishonesty, the deliberate glossing over or twisting of facts to suit a particular objective, as well as nepotism and general favouritism to benefit particular persons possessed of no special merit. What has been the effect of corruption in this wide sense on the development of the Indian peoples in the past, and what, in particular, have been the consequences on the political and economic administration of the country since independence? An examination of this subject would be out of place here, and I mention it only because of the disconcerting contrast between British India of the past and free India of the present. In the former the Administration at the higher levels was entirely free from corruption. But since 1947 there has been a steady deterioration in all spheres. Ministers, political leaders, big and small, industrialists and civil servants have led the way, and a consequent fall in the standards of both governance at the top and general administration lower down has been inevitable. It may well be that corruption is endemic in India's soil, a part of the Indian way of life, in a greater or lesser degree, and must be accepted as such. Given a genuine desire and effort on the part of India's leaders and intelligensia, it could be controlled, curbed and kept within reasonable limits, but its complete eradication is hardly possible. It is of long standing, with an ancient pedigree. Over two thousand years ago Kautilya, Chandragupta Maurya's Chief Minister, had a great deal to say on the subject,[1] and it continues to be a subject of interest to contemporary writers, who spend much time and paper in commenting severely on the modern attitude of 'cynicism blended with complacency'. One of Kautilya's twentieth century successors, in fact, has gone farther. Said the late Dr K. N. Katju, once Home Minister and subsequently Chief Minister of an important State, 'there is no condemnation of corruption, and bribe-takers are looked upon as worthy, respectable and even honoured members of the community'.[2] To meet this situation a new term has been coined which has rapidly reached the status of a cliché. There is, it is said, 'a crisis of character'; and here the matter may safely be left, since an historical inquiry into the development of this crisis of character from Kautilya's era to modern times is not relevant to my present purpose.

The Oudh, known so well to my father and for which he felt a deep inner sympathy, was the Oudh neither of the Government nor of the itinerant political agitator. In his own words it was the 'Oudh of attenuated stomachs and scanty clothing, where one anna laid at the village temple or shrine would ensure *darshan* of the deity, and where every festival was an occasion for merrymaking'. My parents were catholic in their support of all village festivals, contributing from their own pockets towards the expenses of the *tazias* constructed for Muharram by the inhabitants of Sirkargarh as well as of the dramas staged by the Hindus at Dussehrah. And at Christmas there would be footballs for the boys, glass bangles for the girls, and for the babies in their plenty, little painted mud toys made by the village potter's wife. In the evening, *gur* and sweets would be handed round freely, while the highly popular *katputli nautch* (puppet show) was in progress with its good little

---

[1] *Arthasastra*, Book 2, chapters VIII and IX. Translation by R. Shamasastry (Wesleyan Mission Press, Mysore, 1929).
[2] *The Pioneer*, December 11th 1965.

badshahs (emperors) to the delight of all cutting off the heads
of the bad little *kotwals* (police-magistrates) for oppressing
the poor.

I have no doubt now that so far as I was concerned my father
was indulging in a little brain-washing; and the results were
certainly beneficial, since the idea seeped in that here
was an India about which I should learn and in which I should
interest myself. Often my father would covertly suggest that I
should not allow myself to be over-impressed with the glamour
of my official position, where life was usually rosy, and often
superficial. Now I saw another India. It was not the official
India of Anglo-India; and it was not the India of the upper
class Indian who had achieved a crust of westernization
and who looked down on the villager. It was an India where
my father could say to me: 'It is possible to make too much of
the new Indian spirit. Do I not know it who have been told a
hundred times that a gift to a Brahmin ensures greater merit
than the feeding of a multitude of *acchut* [outcaste] children!'
And to this dictum I would certainly not say 'no' now that I
have seen many a religious festival, many a religious ceremony
and the daily rituals at Benares.

Quite apart from the big Hindu festivals, religion plays a
great part in the life of the Indian village, as I was beginning
to see for myself at closer quarters than before. Our villagers
did not have to go far, to Hardwar or Benares, for the purifica-
tion of their souls. A few miles away was the small town of
Golagokarannath with its ancient and hallowed temple and
tank. The origin of the lingam in the temple, a symbol of the
Deity Mahadeo, is shrouded in mythology. One legend tells
of its having been brought there from Shri Lanka (Ceylon)
by Ravana, the King of that country and a non-Aryan, who
stoutly resisted the Aryan invasions from the north, while
according to another the Mughal Emperor, Aurangzeb, tried
millenia later to remove it by the use of chains and elephants.
The lingam, however, refused to give way to such sacrilegious
onslaughts and finally burst into flames, thereby inducing the
astonished Emperor to endow the temple with extensive rent-
free lands, which, though a most unlikely action for that zealous
iconoclast, added greatly to the lingam's symbolic divinity in
the eyes of the countryside.

Of great antiquity, the whole area was once a centre of
Buddhism, traces of which remain. Later the Goshains, a
Hindu monastic sect, celibate in theory but certainly not
always in practice, became all-influential. There are numerous
tombs of the latter in the vicinity of the main temple. These
are on the pattern of Buddhist *stupas*, but the only special
point about the temple itself is that it stands below ground
level with the *lingam* in a kind of well.[1]

Not infrequently we were visited by a venerable old sadhu
who lived in seclusion in a lonely grove belonging to a neighbouring *taluka*. He was much respected throughout the area, and
on his rounds would visit our hamlets to meet my father and to
pay his respects at the little shrines dotted about under the
peepul and burgad trees. The tinkle of his bell would herald
his arrival in the evening, as he approached with his *lota* of holy
water and a leaf platter containing *batasa* (small meringues)
and cardamoms as *prasad* for the deity. My father would greet
the old man and ask him to convey salutations to Shri Thakurji
Maharaj;[2] and in return the Babaji would commend my father
to Him as 'being one of us, albeit apart from us'. Villagers
would soon gather in large numbers to solicit the Babaji's
darshan and to obtain the Deity's blessings through him. The
regulation programme of worship would follow, with my father
solicitously watching the proceedings. The sacred *tulsi* would
be placed on one side of the masonry platform built round the
pepul, suffusing the still air with its aromatic scent. The religious
ablutions would be carefully and punctiliously performed
before the bell would again tinkle, and the Babaji would repeat
a number of sacred *shlokas* from the Puranas. Again the tinkle:
some ghee would be dropped on the fire crackling on one side;

[1] *Imperial Gazetteer of India*, vol. ii, Kheri District, p. 373. The tradition
could perhaps have its origin in Valmiki's *Ramayana*. Ravana, King of Shri
Lanka, after resisting the Aryans, is said to have invaded India in return. He
attacked the kingdom of Kosala, which included modern Kheri. The lingam
was probably not an Aryan symbol at that time and was of Dravidian origin.
It is possible that if there is any historical basis for the legend, and indeed for
the poem itself, Ravana may have left behind lingams elsewhere as a mark of
his temporary conquests. On the other hand, the Gazetteer of the U.P. Government (1909), vol. xlii, Kheri, pp 184-6 goes into the history of Golagokarannath
in greater detail and asserts that the lingam is probably a portion of a Buddhist
pillar.

[2] Another designation for the Almighty, Lord of the material world. Many
of the *maths* or religious foundations in the U.P. owned vast properties, and,
as the owner, Shri Thakurji Maharaj could sue, and very often did do so, in
the Revenue Courts for his rents and to eject tenants and the like.

the holy water would be sprinkled; *prasad* would be offered, and the emblem of the deity would be garlanded with *gaindas* (marigolds) first by the Babaji himself, and then by the villagers who till then had stood by with folded hands and in silent contemplation. No sound would be heard as they stood, since dusk had deepened and the birds had long since gone to roost in the trees, save for the silvery tinkle of the bell, the crackling of the fire and the voice intoning the *shlokas*. Then the bamboo clumps would rustle suddenly in the background as the evening breeze caught them, and the old man, murmuring the refrain 'Hari, Hari, Narayan', would wend his way slowly back to his solitary little hutment in the grove, leaving behind an aura if not of happiness, most certainly of peace, an atmosphere far removed from the hurlyburly of daily life and of the Law Courts.

Not all sadhus were, or are, as deserving of respect as our unknown, unworldly local Babaji. The abduction of young girls, the kidnapping of children and other criminal offences are not infrequently to be laid at the door of the religious man, and it is notorious that temples are not always used solely as shrines dedicated to the worship of God in his various manifestations. Temples have been, and still are, used as centres of political agitation, as secret armouries for the collection of weapons and for other very secular purposes; and I know of one recent case where a temple became a granary for the storage of food grains for later dispatch to the local black market. Nevertheless, the influence of the priest and the sadhu not only on the rustic mind but also on nearly all classes of Hindu society is as pervasive today as it was yesterday. It was through my experience in Rampore Grant that this facet of Hindu life first began to be impressed on me. Twenty five years after I had watched our own villagers contemplating with rapt attention the religious ceremonial of our own local holy man, Pandit Jawaharlal Nehru's Home Minister, Gulzari Lal Nanda, one of the most prestigious actors on the Congress stage, gave official recognition and blessing to the association of sadhus, the Sadhu Samaj, and called upon its members to use their undoubted influence on behalf of the Government in the implementation of the official political and economic plans, and even for the eradication of corruption. So widespread, too, is

the power of the sadhu and the popular belief in the efficacy of
expensive ritual that on more than one occasion the Government of India have permitted, despite a shortage of food and
other necessities, the performance of religious *yagnas* on the
banks of the Yamuna (Jumna) river at Delhi itself for the
purpose of warding off from the world the evil effects of a
supposedly deleterious conjunction of planets. Hundreds of
sadhus participate in these methodical ceremonies, at which
large quantities of rice, milk and ghee are utilized to propitiate
and influence the human manifestations of that cosmic power
which is held to govern the sensual, material human world.
Whether these beliefs and rituals are scientifically sound is
neither relevant nor important. The faith is present, and in its
strength lies its significance. Ancient Mother India of the
twentieth century B.C. is as much a part of India of the twentieth
century A.D. as the Atomic Energy Plant and the Oil Refineries
at Trombay. When I read of rioting outside Parliament House
in New Delhi over the preservation of the sacred cow—of which
species there are in fact far too many useless and half-starved
ones—and of heated debates inside on the interesting but
scientifically unimportant question whether the Vedic Aryans
did or did not eat beef, I am always reminded of my father's
dictum of thirty or more years ago. Even in 1968 it is still
possible to make too much of the modern Indian spirit.

The somewhat idyllic side of rural life which impressed me
during my all too brief visits to my parents was certainly not
always uppermost. Nor was it what my father in his personal
capacity and I as an official always saw. Along with the simplicity and devoutness went all the vices inseparable from ignorance, superstition and the interminable jealousies and factions
engendered by caste. Chicanery of all kinds and an uninhibited delight in the gamble of litigation, accompanied by perjury
on a monumental scale, were endemic in the countryside of
my experience. Gambling on the law's uncertainties was, in
fact, a common form of sport, it being quite customary for a
wealthy landowner to finance a neighbour's litigation on
condition that he would be given a share of the latter's property
in the event of success. Personal enmities and quarrels were
the source of one of the most common of rural crimes, arson,
and many a riot ending fatally for one or more of the partici-

pants could arise over fights for water-supplies or over the boundaries of a field. Cruelty to animals, including as the sublime paradox the venerated cow, together with a general indifference to the suffering of others, was as normal in the villages as in the towns, both being held to be merely a part of the ordinary hardships of this material life, final release from which through a series of rebirths was the truly desirable objective. My father once helped to extinguish a fire in a neighbour's village, and the only thanks he received was the astonished query why he should have gone out of his way to have done so when it was not his village and he stood to lose nothing.

In such conditions rural improvement and the development of agriculture were not as easy in practice as they might appear in theory. Greatly interested in both, my father was forced to the conclusion that his efforts yielded small results. 'The problem of Indian agriculture,' he wrote in the early thirties, 'is a big one, which, I fear, will prove insurmountable. Leaving aside such stupendous obstacles as the alarming increase of population, the time is not inopportune for asking why so much good rent legislation, with its large admixture of rights and obligations, has failed to respond to expectations. Why is the cultivator less well-off today than he should be? The reason mainly is that too much is expected of rent legislation. We cannot expect to make men prosperous by law any more than we can make them good by law, if the other factors making for goodness and prosperity are absent.'

This, however, was not the opinion of urban Congressmen as a class, the official Congress theory being that the ills of the Indian countryside were the product of British misrule and lack of sympathy. Yet even at that time I had begun to realize that this criticism was untrue. By the time I entered the I.C.S. there was in force a large corpus of excellent legislation for the protection of the rights of the tenant, and this was greatly expanded during my service. The Oudh Rent Act, the Agra Tenancy Act, the Bundelkhand Land Alienation Act, the Usurious Loans Act and much else will always remain as historical proof of the importance attached by the British to the village as something more than a mere pawn on the political chessboard. Under the Agra Tenancy Act twelve years of continuous occupation of land earned for the tenant *occupancy rights*, the legal title to a heritable, though not transferable, right in the tenancy. Real efforts were made to curb excessive enhancements of rent and ejectments from land without due, legal cause. That much of this good legislation was nullified by the actions of landowners and their underlings, of the kulak class of tenant, the Permanent Tenure Holders, the Fixed Rate Tenants and the more prosperous tenants as a whole, and by the fatalistic lethargy of the smaller cultivators themselves, cannot justly be laid at the door of the foreign administrator. Even today after the passage of still more allegedly protective legislation, there are regular complaints that save for political purposes the interests of the vast majority of small-holders are neglected. In order to obtain votes commodity prices are maintained at a high level, but the benefits go mainly to the kulak and the moneylender. Illegal ejectments, illegal grabbing of land by the more powerful men in the village and similar evils have everywhere become progressively more prevalent as the State Administrations grow weaker and more urban-oriented. Then, too, it was not the British who approved of the fragmentation of holdings into microscopic units under Hindu customary law. It was not a British theory of agricultural economics that the landowner, petty official and superior class tenant should exploit the weaker elements in the village. These difficulties and problems were and still are inherent in the Indian way of life to a surprising extent. '*Riayat ko dayiat, to sukh payiat*', a proverb of the Oudh countryside which I first heard from my father, who in his turn had been told it by a cultivator of the kulak class, expressed a common attitude.[1] Its general acceptance reminded me strangely of the public reaction to the death of the Rajput *talukdar* mentioned earlier.[2] The more prosperous tenant often displayed, in the words of my father, 'an appalling lack of feeling and kindness towards his less fortunate neighbours'—a somewhat grim aberration, by any criterion, on the part of those who themselves suffered at the hands of others and one which I had already often seen for myself in my official career.

---

[1] A rough translation would be: 'Grind the underdog, if you want ease and comfort.'

[2] See p. 201 above.

So far as village uplift was concerned the praiseworthy efforts made by my father over a long period of years were not lit up with the brilliant light of success, but in their failure they provided lessons for the present. Two experiments were note-worthy for being a long way ahead of their time. My father had always considered it axiomatic that there could be no lasting improvement in the agriculture at least of Oudh, unless an improvement could be made in the physique and health of the cultivator. This idea he had reached after often seeing the peasantry of France and Switzerland whose sturdy physique and capacity for hard work he attributed, rightly or wrongly, to good cooking on the part of their womenfolk. There were many ordinary little articles which remained unutilized by the Oudh village wife, in his eyes a notoriously bad cook, either through ignorance or pure conservatism. He told me, for instance, that the pith and pod of the ordinary banana, much valued by the Bengali village woman in her kitchen, were entirely wasted in Oudh. Enthusiastically he set out to teach his village wives a little real cookery three decades before the delivery of speeches in the legislatures on the need for changes in the dietary habits of the people. He persuaded the Health Department of the Government to print at his own expense five thousand pamphlets in Hindi and Urdu containing simple but novel recipes for building up what he hoped would be the sturdy new generation together with much other useful information for his village mothers. What he actually received in return proved to be very different from his optimistic plan. The pamphlets when produced contained a mass of secretariat jargon couched in highly technical terms detailing the precise amount of foodstuffs, with their chemical components, required by an able-bodied farmer for good husbandry. A meeting was summoned of men, women and, of course, children all eager to hear what experiment was being tried on them. The contents of a pamphlet were duly intoned. The audience listened as the beautifully balanced schedule of daily rations, vitamins, pro-teins, carbo-hydrates and all, was passed on for information, comprehending but dimly what it was all about. At the end of the reading the deep silence continued, to be broken at last by one mystified but courageous old man. 'Does our *malik*,' he asked, 'mean to remit our rents?'

11

The problem of how to bring the beneficial results of science home to a simple villager was never successfully tackled by an urban Secretariat even in the British days, and it is still with us after two decades of independence. The reactions of an Oudh villager to the often incomprehensible actions and directives of a distant bureaucracy in Lucknow were usually unpredictable. Once the Deputy Director of Agriculture, whom we had known well since his student days at Edinburgh, chanced to pay us a visit. I was away at the time, but my car was standing under a tree. By the time I returned the Director had departed to another area in search of partridge and quail; but during my absence he had delivered an address of one hour in length to all our tenants who had been specially collected to hear him. The address was full of the highest scientific agronomy, spiced up with information on the best uses of tractors—which were non-existent for miles around—and might have gone down well had our tenants been a Science Congress. I asked my father what the results of this discourse had been and his reply was: 'The only reaction I heard was the remark that "Director Sahib has a better car than our Chhota Sahib"—which everybody seemed to take as a personal affront to the whole estate.'

Here were two good examples, though not the only ones, of the necessity for the administrator to approach the village not from a superior level but from the angle of the villager himself. On another occasion my father, on the principle that practice is better in the Indian village than scientific precept by itself, sought to demonstrate in his own small world that better farming would produce higher profits. To this end he tried to persuade a diploma holder in Agriculture to take up a tenancy on the estate. He offered ten acres of good land, rent-free—about ten times the provincial average—plus a stipend of Rs. 20/- per month, plus one-third of the profits, or as an alternative, two-thirds without the stipend. No such young man was forthcoming. The diploma-holders churned out by the Agricultural Colleges preferred subordinate Government Service where, although the actual pay was low, the opportunities for increasing it on the side were large, where the work-load was light and where the amenities of town life were to be had.

Similar difficulties faced my father in other fields of good intentions. In the early thirties the Government established a Rural Development Department with the purpose of developing and improving all facets of rural life. My father joined in what to the tenantry appeared to be merely another odd game on the part of the Government. He made as little headway in this direction as in any other. A very good *dai* (midwife), trained at a Dufferin Hospital for Women, was engaged to look after the welfare of our village women. She was given free accommodation and good pay; but she soon pined for the relaxation of the cinema and for her friends in her home town, and eventually fled to them. Leaving aside nurses and midwives, twenty years after independence it is still impossible to persuade young doctors to work in the countryside. The popular general practitioner of the English village I knew in the early years of the century has always been non-existent in India, and amid much talk in official circles of social service there is little of it in practice. The only doctors and nurses who work far out in the villages of rural India, apart from those of the Ramakrishna Mission, are members of foreign Missions, while even in the towns, big and small, much of the 'social service' soon converts itself into social and political climbing.

A school for girls opened in one of the hamlets came to grief when one of the girls was seduced. It was re-opened later through the efforts of my mother, who was able to persuade the people that seduction was an unfortunate occurrence that might happen to anyone, and was not an essential element of girls' education. Of the two primary schools for boys opened and maintained by my parents, the most that could be said for them, according to my father himself, was that the education provided was not as bad as that given in the schools operated by the District Board. On the health side, the Red Cross Medicine Boxes which had been purchased from the Health Department and put in charge of selected headmen for the contents to be distributed from time to time to villagers with head and stomach aches soon found their way back to the Estate office, mostly unopened. It seemed that our villagers preferred to accept pills from the hands of my mother.

My father's assessment that his efforts at village development had been in vain was perhaps not entirely correct, for he had certainly planted a few seeds which matured with the passage of time. To generalize on the conditions of rural India as a whole after one has seen only a part is a notoriously dangerous exercise, which lays one open to easy criticism. Nevertheless, a combination of personal and official experiences certainly impressed on me some general propositions, the validity of which in my judgment has not been weakened by time and change.

The first relates to the conservatism of the Indian farmers. It is often supposed that the backwardness of Indian agriculture is entirely the product of this attitude. But to me this is only partially true. The Indian cultivator moves slowly in his own good time, and as often as not under pressure of circumstances rather than of propaganda. But eventually he does move. Far more significant than his hereditary conservatism—rendered all the more conservative because of the fatalistic outlook engendered by his religion—is the complete absence of civic sense, duty to his fellows outside the immediate circle of his family and caste, and the cooperative spirit. The lack of these qualities is a distinctive feature of the townsman also; but their non-existence in the village is of far greater importance to the country, since about 70 per cent of the people of India are living in the rural areas, and the remainder are dependent on them for their daily food. Having seen village life from two angles in northern and central India, the relative failure of the cooperative movement (now over sixty years old), and of such well-intentioned modern projects as the Community Development and Extension schemes, Panchayati Raj and the like, does not surprise me. Yet, since rural life in general and agriculture in particular are based on the small man and the small holding, their improvement is very largely dependent on cooperation in all spheres of village life. Unless factionalism can be eradicated, or at least curbed, unless it gives way to a more cooperative spirit, the main consequence of the money pumped into the countryside is likely to be the creation of a new kulak class. The powerful, individual farmer, who is the beneficiary and the protégé of the politician, will certainly improve his own status and conditions, but only at the expense of the weaker. The general body of agriculturists will continue to remain depressed.

My second conclusion was that differences of climate, geography and historical development have combined to produce different types of farmers and different methods of farming. The Punjab, for example, where climate has evolved a vigorous and sturdy physical type and where the *ryotwari,* or peasant proprietary system, has always been in vogue, produces the best farmers in India. Next door in my own Province rural life differed with different conditions. Some castes, the Jats and Kurmis as an instance, were ahead of others in their agriculture. Some, like the Kachis and Muraos, specialized in market gardening; but taken as a whole the Province lagged far behind the Punjab. That there has never been a single category of agriculturists which could be taken as being representative of the whole body may appear to be a truism. Yet in contemporary India there is an entity known to the Legislatures, the political platform, the professional economist, and the Press as 'the Indian farmer'. To me 'the Indian farmer' has always been a convenient figure of speech and no more. He does not exist in fact.

The third lesson was the need for good, simple and reasonably honest administration on the spot. Seed and Fertilizer Depots which provide inferior articles, or where the working principle is 'tip first, service afterwards' do not encourage the small man, the lesser lights of the village, to patronize improved techniques. Irrigation works from which water is denied at crucial times unless an illicit payment is made do not stimulate belief in the good faith of the Government. A Cooperative Credit Society in which the powerful first help themselves to loans and then embezzle the balance, without action being taken against them, is not a good advertisement for the co-operative movement. If the Government's propaganda is to achieve anything more than interested scepticism from the side of the millions of small-holders and landless labourers, a more personal, a more disinterested and above all a more honest approach to the village is essential. How this is to be achieved is a problem that deserves more serious attention than it has so far received.

IX

Hindu versus Muslim

THE communal antagonism culminating in the partition
of the sub-continent twenty two years later was well under
way by the time of my return to India. In the meantime
British policy towards the defeated Turks after the First
World War had produced a temporary accord between Hindus
and Muslims which was based, however, not on any real community of interest but solely on a common anti-British sentiment. A short-lived marriage of convenience, it collapsed as
soon as Kemal Pasha (Ataturk), after having restored the
waning fortunes of Turkey through a successful war of resistance,
proceeded on his own account to abolish both the Sultanate
and the Caliphate. Deprived in this unexpected manner of
their joint platform, both Hindus and Muslims reverted to
their positions of mutual hostility.

For the greater part of my service I came into contact with
the communal problem at the grass roots in the districts and
villages, and since the District Magistrate's sole duty here
was the maintenance of the peace, my first reactions were
that the issue between the two sides was more religious than
political. Several years were to elapse before I realised that
in fact it was the reverse. My early attitude was natural enough
in the conditions in which I found myself, since it was the
religious aspect that was first strongly impressed on me.
Communal peace, always in the balance, became particularly
precarious during the four great religious festivals, two Hindu
and two Muslim, which spanned the year. It was then that
local élites (if they could be called this) competed for influence
and power by the simple process of working on, and working
up, religious differences as such—never very difficult between
two such opposites as Hindusim and Islam.

My personal experiences of the explosive possibilities
inherent in the respective attitudes of the two communities were
no different from those of other District Officers. The same
difficulties, the same dangers, were present everywhere. Routes
and times had to be carefully fixed beforehand, so that a

Hindu procession—India is a land of processions at the least opportunity—would not arrive in front of a mosque with its band in full action just when prayers were being intoned; for the playing of music before their mosques at such times was so serious an offence in Muslim eyes that a riot could usually be taken for granted, and certainly always if, as was common enough, the worshippers had taken the preliminary precaution of laying in a stock of brickbats for just such a contingency. Areas had to be set aside where at the Muslim festival of Id cow sacrifice would be permitted according to local custom; and although I had, of course, always known of the reverence surrounding the cow, it was not until my return to India that I began fully to comprehend the almost totemistic sanctity with which the Hindu had invested an animal which he normally maltreats, and which to the Muslim is merely very useful for mundane purposes. Just as *Ganga Mai* (Mother Ganges) was nature's symbol of *Bharat Mata* (Mother India), so also was *Gow Mata* (Mother Cow) the living symbol. Then, again, I was to learn that in a country where numerous objects, animate and inanimate, are regarded with special reverence for mythological or symbolic reasons trouble could crop up over anything. The ubiquitous peepul tree, for example, was, and still is, of great religious significance to Hindus, because it has been singled out in the *Bhagavad Gita* not merely as the tree of Shri Krishna, but also as the symbol of both *samsara* (the course of worldly existence) and of eternity.[1] How were its sacred branches to be lopped in order to allow for the un-impeded passage of *tazias* during the ten days of the Muslim festival of Muharram? There was always the danger, too, that at the Hindu festival of Holi, when it is customary for light-hearted revellers to spray all and sundry with coloured water of various hues, a Muslim who had received a good sousing from a garden syringe would call upon his friends to avenge the affront.

The mere passing of necessary orders for the control of processions, for the fixing of routes, for the posting of extra police at vital spots and similar arrangements presented no

[1] 10th Discourse, shloka 26. And 15th Discourse, shlokas 1, 2, and 3. Metrical English Translation by Vedantacharya Swami Tulsi Ram Misra Vidyanidhi (Newul Kishore Press, Lucknow, 1924).

difficulty, since these had become stereotyped over a long period
of years, and only a few variations had to be made to suit
the particular occasion. Even the peepul tree would submit to
its branches being surreptitiously cut at dead of night, for
what the Hindu eye did not see the heart did not grieve for.
But the actual implementation of the orders on the spot was
often more complicated. Carelessness on the part of the
magistrate in charge and the police might lead to a procession
starting on its long route just those few minutes ahead of
time which would enable it to arrive in front of a mosque
precisely at the moment of prayers. Or the processionists, if
going according to schedule, might in the absence of tactful
prodding take it into their heads to dawdle on the way.
There were usually long-winded arguments, too, before the
District or Sub-Divisional Magistrate from disputatious deputa-
tions as to what was and what was not the local custom regula-
ting cow slaughter. It was impossible to satisfy both parties
simultaneously when an order in favour of one side was the
cause of immediate resentment on the other; and the alteration
of orders once passed was fatal—as was shown to be the case
in 1934 or 1935 when a last-minute change led to a big riot
at Ajodhya in Fyzabad District during the Id-uz-Zoha festival.
The District Magistrate, an Englishman, was immediately
transferred, and shortly afterwards resigned the I.C.S. when
his further promotion was in question.

Even with the best will in the world coupled with the best
arrangements it was impossible to foresee all the snags that
could arise in a country so adept at producing the unexpected
at any time and where even the shooting of the antelope miscalled
the *nilgai* (blue cow/blue bull) could provoke a village riot
anywhere. Mischief makers too, were always at hand to stir
up a rumpus almost for fun. Cases were reported of beef
being flung into temples and pork into mosques, the suspected
culprits in the first instance being Hindus themselves and in
the second Muslims. The Cawnpore riots in the early part of
1931 in which the deaths alone totalled four hundred were
political in origin, local Congressmen insisting on the closure
of Muslim shops in honour of Bhagat Singh, who had been
executed for the assassination of a young English Police Officer
in the Punjab. At Lalitpur on one occasion during the early

days of my service a wrathful deputation of Muslims arrived
at my house to protest against the embryonic conversion overnight of a small Hindu shrine on a piece of waste land into
a fully-fledged temple, although there was no reason at all for
adding to the already adequate number of Hindu places of
worship. The new construction, if completed, would automatically have been followed by the installation of an idol,
the appointment of a *pujari* (priest), the inevitabilty of more
processions and the certain demand from the Muslims for a
mosque next door by way of compensation. With such a combination of fruitful sources of future trouble, sanction for the proposed temple could not have been given in any circumstances,
but fortunately refusal was a simple matter here and could not
be disputed, because the land happened to belong to the
Government. If on this occasion the Hindus took the initiative,
it was the Muslims in another District who set the ball rolling
by claiming as a burial ground a patch of waste, which, according to the Hindus, had never seen a grave. By a stroke of good
luck a surprise visit enabled us to catch half-a-dozen earnest
workers busily engaged in throwing up mounds of earth to
represent graves, without, unfortunately for them, having
safeguarded their position by the elementary precaution of
bringing the first essential of a funeral—a corpse!

At the end of a decade or so of experience in various districts
I had not only come to the conclusion that Aldous Huxley was
correct in his appraisal that religion was a luxury that India
could not afford,[1] but also that the communal problem had
lost its purely religious content and had been transformed into
a political issue between the two communities. Religion, it
seemed to me, had been converted into an instrument of
political policies at the higher levels, and although the
communal fanaticism which burst out at regular intervals
lower down might have the outward appearance of religious
madness, deeper down there was method in the madness rather
than madness in the method.

Baldly stated in this manner this proposition requires
clarification. The standard nationalist, indeed general Hindu
position rested on three assumptions. The first was the alleged

---

[1] *Jesting Pilate* (Chatto and Windus, 1928), p. 130.

existence of a composite Hindu-Muslim culture, a Hindustani
way of life.[1] The second was the idea of the deliberate *creation*
of the communal rift by the British,[2] who for fifty years after
the Indian Mutiny had favoured the Hindus, the Muslims
being classed as the repositories of Mughal imperial tradition,[3]
but who had switched their affections to the Muslim side
when the Congress dropped its moderation to take over the
more revolutionary policies of Bal Gangadhar Tilak. The
third was the allegation that by adopting the principle of
separate electorates for Muslims in 1909 and extending it
from time to time, the British worked on the doctrine of *divide
and rule* for the perpetuation of their domination.

Certainly by the outbreak of war in 1939 I had commenced
to have serious doubts about the validity of these comforting
ideas. So far I had not seen any special signs of a composite
culture, certainly not of a true culture founded on an inherent
sense of common nationality and common interest, beyond,
so far as concerned the latter, a common desire to oust the
western foreigner. No such culture seemed to me to have
evolved out of the numerous Islamic conquests, Arab, Afghan,
Turk, Mughal, from the time of Muhammad-bin-Kasim in
the eighth century to the incursions following the decay
of the Mughal Empire. Indeed, had it existed in fact and not
in the imagination only of later generations, the British would
not have been able to install themselves so easily in the first

---

[1] Rajendra Prasad, *India Divided*, p. 175 (Hind Kitabs, Bombay, 1946).
'We have considered at some length the thesis that Hindus and Muslims constitute
two separate nations and we have seen how during the long period of Muslim
rule in India a culture which was neither exclusively Hindu nor exclusively
Muslim, but a Hindu-Muslim culture—a Hindustani way—was developing
as a result of conscious effort on the part of both Muslims and Hindus and of
the reaction of economic, political, social, and religious factors which were operating all through the period.'
[2] Asoka Mehta and Achyut Patwardhan, *The Communal Triangle in India*
(Kitabistan, Allahabad, 1942), p. 222. 'We have pointed out that the problem
as it confronts us to-day, is largely the creation of the British.'
    Pandit Jawaharlal Nehru was a strong advocate of the composite culture
theory and an equally strong critic of the separate electorate for Muslims. This
last has been dealt with at length in *The Communal Triangle in India*, chapter IV
and in *India Divided*, pp. 109-115.
[3] *The Rise and Fulfilment of British Rule in India*, p. 540. Also Surendra Nath
Sen, *1857* (Publications Division, 1957), p. 67. 'There was a King at Delhi.
He had no kingdom, but the memory of his ancestral empire still lingered. His
authority did not extend outside his palace fort and inside it was narrowly
circumscribed by British supervision. Convention conceded him all the forms
and etiquettes of the past, and popular reverence invested his office with a majesty
not sanctioned by the facts.'

place, and certainly no amount of Machiavellian devilment on their part would have succeeded in eroding it later even after the complete establishment of their supremacy. For evidence of the fact that firmly established cultures can be very resistant to physical conquest one need not go beyond the example of Hinduism itself.

Neither of the two revivalist movements arising in the eighteenth century was motivated by the concept of nationality and nationhood, or even of an Indian nation-state. The Maharatta Confederacy under the leadership of Brahmin Peshwas was conceived mainly in terms of Hindu nationalism, was far too loose in organisation to form a nation-state, and stood for Hindu supremacy. The Sikhs of the Punjab who round about the same time consolidated themselves into the Khalsa considered themselves a nation in their own right, and the Khalsa a nation-state of their own.[1] In both cases the significant feature was that the old roles of Hindu and Muslim were now reversed, the former regaining for a short period much of the dominance lost for centuries and the Muslims accepting the position—save in such areas as Hyderabad—until British power impartially overthrew both. Thereafter, the sole bond between the two, a fragile one always, was the joint ambition already mentioned, the eviction of the intruder.

Nor had efforts to evolve an eclectic religion through a fusion of Hinduism and Islam been any more successful than the growth of the concept of nationhood. The Sufis, with their mysticism, the early Sikh Gurus, the Emperor Akbar with his ambition of establishing an imperial State religion of his own fashioning, all failed; and the failure was finally under-scored when Prince Dara Shikoh, who was inclined towards Sufiism and who was generally latitudinarian in his opinions, was executed by order of his brother, the iconoclastic Aurangzeb. With the acquisition of the imperial throne by the latter all hopes that may have been entertained by fringe groups of a combination of the two religions into a single national faith were killed for ever.

It was only natural, indeed inevitable, that over the centuries

---

[1] Khushwant Singh, the modern historian of the Sikhs, refers to this in *The Fall of the Kingdom of the Punjab*, (Orient Longmans, 1962). On p. 146 he writes 'the nation began to rise in arms' and again on p. 147, 'thus did a local rebellion become a national war of independence.'

a *modus vivendi* had developed between Hindu and Muslim,
especially in the villages which were self-contained entities,
where the Muslim population consisted of converts and where
general conditions were propitious. At the other end of the
social ladder, in the Imperial Court and amongst the aristocracy, at least in northern India, Persian influences had their
effect on language, music, the arts as a whole and even on dress
and manners. But the totality hardly added up to a national,
composite culture. At the lower levels it was little more than
abstention, in the interest of good neighbourliness, on the
part of both communities from persistently attacking each other;
a species of co-existence with neither solid foundations nor solid
superstructure. For the rest, Indian culture centred round the
Court and took its tone from it. The idea of a composite
Hindustani culture, a joint national ethos, certainly appeared
to me by 1939 to be quixotic in theory and, within my own
experience, ineffective in practice—nothing more than a myth;
a noble myth no doubt, but a myth nonetheless. I had now
come to the view that it was only the feudal concept of over-
lordship and not of nationhood which had put some life into
such cultural co-existence as there may have been in an age
when the right of the ruler, Muslim or Hindu, to rule was
never questioned on grounds of religion or political ideology
so long as actual power was present and visible.

The British were not responsible for the presence of Islam
in India, nor did they work on the principle of *divide and rule*
as was the popular modern superstition. They merely took
advantage of an existing split which was ready to hand and
ruled by virtue of it as, indeed, any realistic power would
have done. It is true that they did not attempt to create a
psychological sense of nationality, nor until the last two years
of their rule did they attempt any real bridge-building. But
there was no good reason for them to have done either. When
any endeavour on their part to weld together a miscellaneous
assortment of Hindu castes and communities would have
been resented as an unwarranted interference with the Hindu
way of life, there was certainly no logical ground for criticism
of the British attitude to the Hindu-Muslim imbroglio.[1] There

[1] Hindu fear on this account was the main underlying cause of the upheaval

was nothing immoral in the policy followed by the Imperial Power, and one can be quite certain that Kautilya, if one may judge from his very practical treatise on Government, far from objecting, would have strongly endorsed it.[1]

With the gradual tempering of the generally liberal bureaucracy in India by successive extensions of the elective principle from 1909 on, the communal problem boiled down to what it had been at the time of the decay of the Mughal Empire, a simple one of power politics. The one-time ruling religious minority was now up against the clear fact that it could never recover its former dominance in the face of the ballot-box, the new divinity imported from the West to which all had to make political obeisance; and in these circumstances considered it both necessary and justifiable to demand special protection through political mechanisms for its own interests. That the British accepted and even encouraged the demand for separate electorates was immaterial, for had a real sense of common nationhood existed no amount of encouragement or even of persuasion could have been successful. In a parliamentary democracy—and this was nationalist India's objective —a political minority with its own political ideology must by virtue of its adherence to the democratic principle accept the political policies of its opponents until such time as it can persuade the electorate to give it its turn of power. The position of a religious minority in the absence of national feeling is not comparable. Not only will political power always be denied to it, but additionally in India the situation was complicated by the fact that the permanent minority, now apprehensive of being in a position of permanent inferiority, had once been the rulers of the sub-continent.

The minority's demand for effective safeguards was underlined significantly in the Report of the Committee set up in 1928 by the All-Parties Conference in its short, factual elucidation of the points in issue. In the first place the Report contained

---

of 1857. As a consequence, interference with Hindu social and religious customs was expressly forbidden in the Queen's Proclamation of 1858.

[1] *Arthasastra*, Book 2, chapter 12 (The Institution of Spies). Again, chapter 13, para. 24: 'Honours and rewards shall be conferred upon those that are contented, while those that are disaffected shall be brought round by *conciliation, by gifts, or by sowing dissension; or by punishment*.' R. Shamasastry's translation, my italics.

the frank admission that 'the communal problem is primarily the Hindu-Muslim problem, though other communities have lately taken up an aggressive attitude.' The Sikhs and Non-Brahmins of the south were singled out among the latter, but within a few years Mahatma Gandhi's Harijans and the tribal areas also put forward their claims to special protection. Secondly, the Report, while recommending the replacement of the separate by the joint electorate, made the further most significant proposal that the Muslims should be given safeguards through the medium of the reservation of a fixed number of electoral seats on the basis of population. To this was added the concurrent right to contest the general constituencies.[1] These remedial suggestions pointed to two conclusions; first, that composite culture or not, protection of some kind was necessary for the Muslim community; and secondly, that the essence of the problem centred round the machinery of democracy and not round an imaginary Hindustani way of life.

When in 1946 the British made it clear that they intended to leave India at the earliest possible moment, the communal impasse was embittered by the insistence of the Congress with its handful of Muslim members on the tall and unsustainable claim to represent the whole Muslim community in the face of the Muslim League. The idea of Pakistan or the Partition of India now took on real importance. Originally expounded by one Rahmat Ali in 1933[2] it was only one of the many schemes put out for a communal solution—a confederation of six States with common defence, cultural zones within one unit, a zonal federation and the like[3]—and was not adopted by the Muslim League until 1940, and then only in part, mainly as a bargaining counter.

[1] The Committee consisted of Pandit Motilal Nehru, Chairman, leader of the Swaraj Party in the Legislative Assembly, Sir Tej Bahadur Sapru, Sir Ali Imam (both ex-members of the Viceroy's Council), Mr Shoaib Qureshi, Mr G. R. Pradhan, Mr Subhas Chandra Bose, Mr Madho Rao Aney, Mr M. R. Jayakar, Mr N. M. Joshi and Sardar Mangal Singh. The secretary was Pandit Jawaharlal Nehru, who was also General Secretary of the Congress at the time. All were leading men, whose influence on events, except in the cases of Pandit Jawaharlal Nehru and Subhas Bose, turned out to be negligible.
The important sections dealing with Muslim representation are contained in chapter 3 of the Report.
[2] In a pamphlet entitled *The Millat of Islam and The Menace of Indianism.*
[3] These and other proposals are considered in detail in Part 3 of *India Divided,* and in Dr B. R. Ambedkar's *Pakistan or The Partition of India.*

That the British Government and people were sincere in their desire to hand over power as soon as possible was obvious to any observer not afflicted with complete political myopia, and in fact has received the imprimatur of no less a person than Maulana Abul Kalam Azad, the leading Muslim in the Congress Party and its President until his replacement by Pandit Jawaharlal Nehru in April 1946. 'Anyone with the slightest imperialist tendencies,' he has written, 'could easily have exploited India's weakness.... In spite of our opposition the British could have governed this country for another decade. We must, therefore, give due credit to the motives of the Labour Government. They did not wish to exploit Indian weakness for their own advantage. *History will honour them for this judgement, and we must also without any mental reserva-tion acknowledge this fact*'[1] (my italics).

The British Cabinet Mission of 1946 rejected outright Mr Jinnah's demand for Pakistan, and instead plumped for a three-tier zonal scheme with a federal centre for Communica-tions, Defence and Foreign Affairs. Included in the scheme were provisions for the establishment of a Constituent Assembly to work out details and for the immediate formation of a provisional government in New Delhi. In the face of the Delegation's flat refusal to countenance an independent Pakistan, the Muslim League accepted the plan immediately without reservations or conditions, Mr Jinnah, however, making it clear at the same time that the acceptance was dictated by the British decision and only as a result of his inability to extract any more out of the Cabinet Mission. The Congress, on the other hand, procrastinated, discussed and hemmed and hawed for several days, despite the efforts of Maulana Azad, who realistically had always sought a compromise with the Muslim League as the real representative of Muslim opinion.[2] When finally on June 26th 1946 the Working

---

[1] *India Wins Freedom*, (Orient Longmans, 1959), p. 178. I have quoted only the relevant portions of the passage.

[2] It is of historical importance to note in this connection that the U.P.C.I.D. Report for February 1946 stated: 'There are signs that the Congress President, Maulana Azad, is becoming increasingly anxious over the need for a solution of the communal tangle. He now regrets the action taken in 1937 when the Congress refused to have coalition ministries, and has definitely made up his mind that such action will not be repeated. This is not palatable to Patel, who expressed his anxiety as to Azad's ideas. *It is learnt that Azad will make a definite step after the elections to come to terms with organised "Muslim opinion"* (italics mine).

Committee accepted the Mission's proposals, approval was hedged round with reservations relating to the formation of the provisional government. It was not until July 7th that the All-India Congress Committee overruled the Working Committee and took over the whole scheme. That the first rejection had not been welcomed by the public, of the United Provinces at least, was reflected in that Government's report to the Government of India which stated that 'the non-acceptance of the proposals by the Working Committee, though conditional, has come as a great disappointment, and there is a general feeling of depression and apprehension.'[1] The decision of July 7th came as a welcome relief to public opinion.

The Mission's plan, however, had never appealed to the rigid view of Pandit Jawaharlal Nehru, who was not only Congress President at the time but who was also the obvious choice as head of the provisional government envisaged by the Mission. In the first week of July he had voiced his doubts in a public speech at Jhansi[2] in which he had emphasised the determination of the Congress to apply its own interpretation to the Mission's scheme. Three days *after* the final decision of the Congress to withdraw the original objections he held the important, even historic, Press Conference of July 10th. Here, in reply to questions 'whether with the passing of the resolution of July 7th the Congress had accepted the plan *in toto*, including the composition of the Interim Government', he said that the Congress would enter the Constituent Assembly 'completely unfettered by agreements, and free to meet all situations as they arise'. Pressed further, he emphatically clarified the position with the unambiguous declaration that 'The Congress had agreed only to participate in the Constituent Assembly, and regarded itself free to change or modify the Cabinet Mission's plan as it thought fit.'[3]

These were novel propositions which certainly had not

[1] C.I.D. Report for week ending July 5th 1946, and the U.P. Government's letter to the Government of India of June 24th. There is some confusion in the precise dates. Maulana Azad gives the date of the Working Committee's decision as June 26th, and that of the All-India Congress Committee as July 7th. On the other hand, the official C.I.D. Report refers to the first as being in the first fortnight of June. As regards the final decision the C.I.D. refer to this in their issue for the week ending July 5th. From the standpoint of consequences the actual dates are not material.

[2] C.I.D. Report for week ending July 5th.

[3] *India Wins Freedom*, p. 155.

been envisaged by the Cabinet Mission on its departure from India. Maulana Azad has made it clear that in his view Pandit Jawaharlal Nehru was wrong, since 'it was not correct to say that the Congress was free to modify the plan:'[1] and he ascribes the statements at the Press Conference to Pandit Jawaharlal Nehru's fondness for abstract theory. Whatever may have been the cause, however, (and it is difficult even to guess at the 'abstract theory' which could lead to the misinterpretation of the whole scheme in such concrete and unequivocal terms), the position was now radically transformed for the worse. The Congress Working Committee, in a serious dilemma, hastily met, and tactfully avoiding any reference to the Press Conference, reiterated the decision of July in clear language; but by then the damage had been done. Mr Jinnah, always the cold, practical, precise lawyer, with no romanticism in his make-up, argued, as might have been foreseen, that, despite protestations to the contrary, clearly no reliance whatsoever could be placed on the good faith of an organisation which had first put forward objections, had then withdrawn them, had seen its President publicly negative the withdrawal, and had finally returned to square number two. Unfortunately, too, Muslim suspicions were increased by memories of an incident in 1937 when an agreement with the Muslim League on the composition of the Ministry in the United Provinces had been negotiated by Maulana Azad on behalf of the Congress and promptly vetoed by Pandit Jawaharlal Nehru—a decision which was followed, possibly by chance only—by the Muslim League's partial acceptance of an independent Pakistan at the Lahore Session three years later.[2] Now once again the whole issue was pushed into the foreground, with the stress laid on the utmost need for an independent Pakistan as the only salvation for the Muslims.

Future historians alone will be in a position to assess these events with detachment. Only when the Congress archives are thrown open for inspection will an objective account be possible of the course of negotiations with the Cabinet Mission, the discussions in the Congress itself, and the grounds, if any, apart from abstract theory, of Pandit

---

[1] *India Wins Freedom*, pp. 160-61.
[2] Ibid.

12

Jawaharlal Nehru's strong but obviously erroneous view that
the Mission's plan was not final. No doubt, too, the latter's
private papers will throw light on his reasons for repudiating
a decision to which he had already agreed on July 7th. This
is the essential point which is likely to give the historian many
a headache; for in the last analysis it is not the wickedness of
Mr. Jinnah in disbelieving Congress good faith that is material
—neither side had ever trusted the other—but the ground
for giving him the option of imputing or not imputing bad
faith.

Maulana Azad has remarked that while 'Jawaharlal's
mistake of 1937 was bad enough, the mistake of 1946 proved
even more costly',[1] an assessment which is entirely correct
in terms of human life alone. The Muslim League at once
declared *Direct Action*, primarily against the Congress, but
also with an eye to forcing the British Government to accept
Pakistan in the changed circumstances. The Congress—in
power in the Hindu majority Provinces after the general
elections in the early part of the year—was consequently
hoist with its own petard, for it was now faced with a mass
uprising of Muslims which differed from its own against the
British in 1942 only in the fact that Mr. Jinnah made no
pretence whatsoever of non-violence.

Commencing on August 16th (designated Action Day)
in Calcutta where the casualties amounted to those of a major
battle—6000 dead and 20,000 injured—with arson, looting
and rape on an unprecedented scale, the upheaval rapidly
spread, to cover the whole of northern India from Bengal to
the farthest tip of the north-west. I had by this time been
appointed Chief Secretary of the United Provinces, where in
the three months prior to my arrival in Lucknow there had
already been riots in a dozen places. Widespread disturbances
continued for the next eighteen months, the worst being at
Garhmukhtesar in Meerut District where a small-scale version
of Calcutta was re-enacted, with 374 deaths and 161 injured,
a very large total for the rural areas. During 1946 the United
Provinces alone accounted for 3176 riots of all kinds of which
374 were classified as communal, in addition to which 148

[1]Ibid., p. 162.

separate and individual murders were reported as having been communal in origin.[1] These figures are of importance inasmuch as they constituted the high water mark for a very abnormal period. Actually they were greatly exceeded later in the normal course of independence. On October 9th, 1968, twenty two years afterwards, the Home Secretary of Uttar Pradesh at a Press Conference reported in *The Times of India* gave the following details in respect of riots in the State: 1965—4106; 1966—4120; 1967—4317; 1968, to the end of August —4484. The increases are noteworthy despite a good deal of complacency in political and service circles. The mass disorders of the period were never actually suppressed, for as soon as the fires were extinguished in one area they blazed up in another. They simply burnt themselves out six months after the inevitable partition in 1947 with its consequential two-way migration of fifteen million persons half a million of whom were said to have died of disease and privation during their trek from one Dominion to the other. One of the most disturbing features of the period, an ill-omen for the future of independent India, was the rapid formation of private armies in the United Provinces which totalled in January 1947 no less than 102,000 men. Various Congress organizations accounted for 25,000: Muslim National Guards for 37,000; the R.S.S. Sangh (a militant Hindu body) for 25,000; Khaksars (militant Muslim) for 6,700; while miscellaneous bodies belonging to both communities covered the balance. These were never forcibly disbanded, as they should have been, but simply faded away with the passage of time, to re-emerge twenty years later in the form of Senas and the like with regional, linguistic and other purely parochial objectives. On May 31st it was officially reported from New Delhi, according to the *Times of India* of June 1st, that these Senas numbered no less that sixty, though it was only in the states of Maharashtra, Assam, Mysore, Gujarat, Madras and Kerala that they were functioning effectively. In the Punjab an extreme group of Sikhs was reported to have established an Akal Sena for the defence of the Sikh religion, although, so far as

---

[1]Figures taken from the U.P. Police Administration Report for 1946. For the Garhmukhtesar riot, figures are from the Chief Secretary's Report dated 25th November 1946.

I am aware, no one has shown any desire to attack it, while in Uttar Pradesh the Communists, not to be outdone, are trying their hand with a Hal (plough) Sena for the defence not, of course, of religion, but of the small farmer.

With a kind of civil war going on in the Districts, another war, fortunately bloodless, was being waged simultaneously with pens, paper and words in the Provisional Government in New Delhi. Here the Muslim Finance Minister, Liaquat Ali Khan, whose political acumen and common sense the Hindu leaders of the Congress consistently underrated, proved himself to be a continuous thorn in the flesh of his Hindu rivals by the unerring skill with which he and his advisers made use of finance as a weapon against the Congress. It was notorious that the Hindu capitalist had been the financial pillar of the Congress temple for at least two decades, notwithstanding Pandit Jawaharlal Nehru's denials,[1] and the Finance Minister set about the task of pulling down the pillar by taking advantage of the Prime Minister's well-known devotion to socialism in order to soak the capitalist. In addition he kept a tight hold on the purse strings. By these methods—unexceptionable in theory —he was able to bring about a political and administrative impasse at the highest level which, combined with the turmoil in the districts, eventually convinced Sardar Patel, a realist not given to gossamer dreams, that so dangerous a situation could no longer be allowed to continue. As Home Minister responsible for the general maintenance of internal security and stability he now realised that the establishment of an independent Pakistan was the only way out of the trouble. 'He was now convinced,' wrote Maulana Azad, 'that Muslims and Hindus could not be united in one nation. There was no alternative except to recognise the fact. In this way alone could we end the quarrel between Hindus and Muslims.'[2] Within a short

---

[1] In *The Discovery of India*, note on pp. 589-90, the accusation that the Congress depended on the Hindu trader and big capitalist for its funds has been strongly denied by Pandit Jawaharlal Nehru. But according to Louis Fischer, Mahatma Gandhi confirmed it. 'What truth is there in these assertions?' asked the former, referring in particular to the Bombay Millowners. 'Unfortunately, they are true,' was the Mahatma's reply. 'The Congress hasn't enough money to conduct its work.' To a further query as to the proportion of the Congress budget covered by rich Indians, the reply was, 'practically all of it. In this Ashram, for instance, we could live much more poorly than we do and spend less money. But we do not, and the money comes from our rich friends.' *A Week with Gandhi*, p. 51.

[2] *India Wins Freedom*, p. 185.

time the Congress, compelled at last to face the facts of the situation, followed Sardar Patel's lead.

Thus ended my personal experiences of the communal struggle as I had seen it for the twenty two years of my service up to the partition. Once again the historians will enter the picture, since they alone will be in a position to deal objectively not only with the events of this period but also with the relations between the two independent States of the sub-continent, bedevilled as they have been from the start by the quarrel over Kashmir. In the process of their examination they will be faced with a large number of interesting problems, the answers to which are certain to differ according to the outlook of the individual concerned. Whether a zonal scheme on the lines of the plan proposed by the Cabinet Mission or any other scheme for a united India such as that of the Congress Muslims under the leadership of Maulana Azad would have had any chance of success is, of course, purely hypothetical; but it would have been interesting to see how Congress ideas would have worked in practice. In a united, democratic India, the North-West Frontier, the Punjab, Kashmir, Sind and Baluchistan would have formed a solid Muslim majority block on one side. In the north-east there was a small Muslim majority in Bengal and a portion of Assam; and sandwiched in between lay Uttar Pradesh and Bihar where the Muslims for a variety of historical reasons wielded far greater influence than their actual numbers warranted. There would thus have been Muslim blocks at both the north-western and north-eastern sides of the peninsula and an intervening area where Muslim political and cultural influence would have been very powerful. It is more than possible that the Hindu majority in the Congress would have found this solution distasteful in practice, and whether the formation of a composite Indian nation would have been fostered in this way is very problematical. It can reasonably be said that in India, with its genius for producing a crop of difficulties at any time for any solution to any problem, no plan for keeping Hindus and Muslims together in one unit would have had any chance of real political or administrative success; and, indeed, this had already been fully demonstrated by the fate of the ill-omened Interim Government.

In his *Between Oxus and Jumna* Arnold Toynbee has examined

in some detail this particular area, of which West Pakistan is an important section, and has brought out its historical significance. If it is difficult to foresee the precise nature of the future relations between India and Pakistan, it is impossible to assess the international consequences—not yet really felt—of Pakistan's westward turn towards the vast, influential Islamic bloc stretching from Kabul to Constantinople, with a long arm in North Africa. The historical process has still to show itself and to work itself out. But so far as the immediate consequences of the partition of the Indian subcontinent are concerned, one positive gain for India certainly appears to have accrued from the events of 1946-47. The establishment of two independent States at least solved the two-nation theory; for the forty or fifty million Muslims who elected to remain in India automatically abandoned it of their own volition, and by exercising their option became citizens of the constitutionally secular Indian Republic. Henceforth their problems were those of a minority community (though the largest) among other communities and not those of a community claiming a national entity of its own.

A few words may be said by way of postscript. The British did not desire the partition of their Empire in India, for this would have negatived their justifiable claim to have given political and administrative unity to at least two thirds of the sub-continent and the idea, erroneous in my view, that it must of necessity form one geopolitical unit. The uncompromising denial of Pakistan in the first instance together with the framing of a zonal scheme which scrupulously avoided it is clear proof of this. What they seemed to be searching for was some suitable formula acceptable to both Hindus and Muslims, in order rapidly to hand over, in accordance with their oft-repeated policy, an Empire, which in any case had been transformed from being the brightest jewel of the British crown into a plain encumbrance.[1] It was the religious and political civil war which finally killed and buried the Mission's plan, so that the British were left with no

---

[1] This was beginning to be realised even before the Second War. Sir Basil Liddell Hart records in his Memoirs, vol i, p. 292, a conversation with General Dill (afterwards C.I.G.S & Field-Marshal): 'He (General Dill) raised the question where could we let Germany expand? Half seriously, he suggested India, *which was becoming a burden*' (my italics).

choice but partition; but in the last analysis both Congress and Muslim League triggered off the rapid descent downhill, the former by its original vacillation over the zonal plan and the latter by its inveterate distrust of the Congress as a purely Hindu body. For Indians to absolve themselves from responsibility and to cast the entire blame for the partition onto the British is not only disingenuous but also clear evidence of their consistent efforts always to find scapegoats for their own inadequacies. The frequent assertion, in different words, that it was the British who 'true to their genius divided the country they were forced to leave',[1] does not square with the facts as they appear to me. It would be more correct, on the contrary, to say that it was the divisive genius of Indians themselves that produced the partition of the sub-continent— that ever-present divisive genius which manifests itself daily in free India.

Twenty years after the demission of power by the British, the abolition of the old system of separate electorates and the establishment of a secular State in an essentially religious and ritualistic land, the Hindu-Muslim problem remains. It may perhaps be somewhat milder than before, but it appears to be no less intractable and may be of international importance in the future. Concurrently a new batch of communal, regional and linguistic divisions between Hindus themselves has been added to it. Sporadic riots between Hindus and Muslims had been common enough after the inauguration of the Republic in 1950—Pandit Jawaharlal Nehru commenced the era of 'stern warnings' as early as 1949—but in the later sixties there took place throughout the country a concerted series, in Assam, Calcutta, Ranchi, Allahabad, Meerut, Ratlam and elsewhere, the most significant feature of which was the mixed bag of reasons which sparked them off: here the language question, Urdu versus Hindi: there a religious festival; somewhere else a petty quarrel. In Kashmir, political sympathies with the Arabs against the Israelis in June 1967 took an anti-Hindu turn later, as so often happens in this State, and finally exploded over the marriage of a Muslim youth to a Hindu girl, the latter allegedly having been abducted as a preliminary.

[1]These words were used by Acharya J. B. Kripalani, a veteran Congressman, in an article on Independence Day in *The Times of India* dated 13th August 1967.

Kashmir, the only predominantly Muslim State in the Republic, is in a privileged and happy position, with a special status under Article 370 of the Indian Constitution. Its leading politicians are rightly contented with their position, and a great deal of the general taxpayer's money (that is Hindu) is spent on the State. Almost the whole of the State's Third Plan was financed by the Centre and the *per capita* expenditure, Rs 172, was the highest in India. It is expected that the *whole* of the Fourth Plan will be financed in the same way. Food prices, too, are kept down by heavy subsidies, and in the year 1967-68 amounted to eight crores of rupees. There is little doubt that Kashmir has captured the imagination of India as an outstanding example of the secular principle. Here, however, this particular manifestation of the communal problem has gone into reverse; for it is not a Hindu-Muslim but a Muslim-Hindu question with the Hindu minority in the position of plaintiffs and with a recently established association the object of which is autonomy for those areas in which Hindus predominate.

Writing on the subject of the general relations between Hindus and Muslims after independence, excluding presumably the special position of Kashmir, Mr P. H. Patwardhan, a Gandhian in outlook, has frankly stated 'the Indian Muslim remains unreconciled. He is an outsider in Indian society.'[1] Nor is Mr Patwardhan alone; for at the meeting in October 1967 of the All-India Congress Committee more than one speaker admitted the gravity of the existing situation. A Muslim Minister of the Union Government referred to Muslim loyalty to India being under suspicion on the one hand, and to Muslim fears for their lives and property on the other. Mr Rajbojh, a Hindu, deplored the growth of inter-caste and inter-community conflicts after twenty years of freedom; and Mr Banarsi Das, another Hindu, roundly accused Congress workers of having a hand in many of the disturbances.[2] All of which merely provides ample proof that the former euphoric theories, now apparently in abeyance, of a composite Hindu-Muslim, Hindustani culture, and of Anglo-Saxon sinfulness getting the better of Hindu-Muslim virtue by the crooked

---

[1] In the second of two articles in the Financial Express of Oct. 1st 1966, entitled *Homage to Mahatma Gandhi. His Impact on Posterity.*
[2] From the proceedings of the Jabalpur meeting as reported in *The Times of India* of 30th October 1967.

device of the separate electorate, have failed the test of independence not only in Hindu majority areas, but also in Muslim Kashmir; and when an official Congress Committee was set up at the end of 1967 to examine Muslim grievances, implicit in its appointment was their public, though unostentatious, burial.

'Emotional Integration' has now become a fashionable cliché in a cliché-loving land; integration not merely between Hindus and Muslims, but between one Hindu caste and another, between Hindu and Sikh, region and region, linguistic group and linguistic group, Aryan and Dravidian, Aryan and aboriginal; every possible form of integration. Over eighty years ago in his presidential address at the first session of the Indian National Congress in 1885, W. C. Bonnerjee enunciated the second objective of the Congress in the following words: 'The eradication by direct, friendly and personal intercourse, of all possible race, creed or provincial prejudices amongst all lovers of our country, and the fuller development of those sentiments of national unity *that had their origin in our beloved Lord Ripon's memorable reign*' (my italics). Forty years later another great Congress leader of the early days, Surendranath Banerjea, entitled his autobiography *A Nation in Making*. Another forty years and more have elapsed and the nation, it seems, is still in making, with all the problems of 1885 and 1925 as acute as before. It was, I think, an observant Frenchman who at the conclusion of a visit to India a few years ago produced the epigram, 'Other countries *have* problems. India *is* problems': to which one can only reply that, if the Indian peoples have not displayed any capacity to solve their great variety of problems, they are at least learning, through the media of conventions, committees, discussions and resolutions, to live with them, and even it would appear, to enjoy them for the dialectics involved.

X

Rebellion

ON COMPLETION of my term in the Government of India I
proceeded on long leave, to be posted on my return shortly
before the outbreak of war to Fatehpur as District Magistrate,
and then after eight months to Meerut in the same capacity.
For the three years of my absence from the United Provinces
the course of events throughout India, while of political and
constitutional importance, had been remarkably placid—
indeed this was probably the most placid period in my service.
General elections had been held under the new Constitution
of 1935, and in 1937 Congress Ministries were installed in
all the provinces except the Punjab, Sind and Bengal. It was
the stormy international sky that over-shadowed the world
in general, and India was no exception. But here the internal
calm was soon to be shattered by the explosion of war, and
from September onwards political relations between the
Congress Party on the one side and the Governments in both
New Delhi and London steadily deteriorated until the inflammable situation burst into flames in 1942.

Like its two predecessors of 1919-22 and 1930-32 the upheaval was widespread, but, this apart, differed from them in
two respects. It was, in the first place, more concerted and far
better organised; and secondly, though not an armed uprising,
many of the cadres directing it clearly belonged to the revolutionary wing of the Congress Party. The prolix and platitudinous resolution of August 8th (the Quit India resolution)
which followed two months after the failure of the negotiations
with Sir Stafford Cripps, sanctioned 'the starting of a mass
struggle on *non-violent lines* on the widest possible scale' (my
italics), but the mass struggle turned out to be violent enough
in my experience to merit the simple term rebellion without any
qualifications, and this was the term applied to it afterwards by
many of its leaders. Much had taken place since the second
session of the Indian National Congress had expressed both
gratitude and loyalty to the British and the goal of the infant
nationalist movement had been similar to the mild form of

Home Rule demanded by the Irish of the period. Twenty years later, between 1905 and 1910, the Congress had moved into active opposition (termed sedition), and three decades after that into undisguised rebellion against British dominion—a very far cry indeed from the presidential speech of Dadabhai Naoroji in 1886. 'It is our good fortune,' said the latter, 'that we are under a rule which makes it possible for us to meet in this manner.... Such a thing is possible under British rule, and British rule only. Then I put the question. Is this Congress a nursery for sedition and rebellion against the British Government (cries of "No ! No" !), or is it another stone in the foundation of the stability of that Government (cries of "Yes ! Yes !")?'

Although the Quit India resolution had probably been passed as a device for further negotiations with the British and its implementation was not intended for another month, the Government of India could scarcely be blamed for viewing the language in which it was couched as a serious threat and for taking immediate action to forestall its likely consequences. The war situation was critical everywhere. The fate of Malta hung in the balance. The 8th Army was recovering from the shock of a severe defeat in North Africa. The Japanese advance continued and the danger to India's North-Eastern frontiers grew more ominous daily. In such circumstances it is difficult to understand how any Government heavily engaged in the business of trying to win a war could have sat by idly, waiting for a mass struggle apparently designed to prevent it from doing so.

The Government of India and the Provincial Governments had made preparations well beforehand to deal with possible disturbances. The C.I.D. possessed detailed reports, and even precise transcripts, of the discussions at the various secret sessions of the Working Committee of the Congress. In Meerut there had arrived well in advance a special organisation under the pleasantly innocuous designation of *Ministry of Economic Warfare*. This had no connection with either economics or warfare as such, but was a high powered Secret Service body under the expert guidance of an officer from Scotland Yard, Mackenzie by name, the function of which was to keep a watchful eye on subversive activities in general. I was never able to

discover more exactly on whom or what it was directing its
economics, because, although as District Magistrate I was
responsible for the administration of the district, I was never
officially informed of its existence. Attached to this interesting
set-up was one of the outstanding personalities of the I.C.S.
of my time, Micky Nethersole (afterwards Sir Michael
Nethersole K.B.E.). Micky had been a good friend of mine for
some years and was staying with me when the rebellion broke
out on the morning of August 9th with the arrests of the All-
India and local leaders. A man of strong character and of
equally strong likes and dislikes he would fight for any cause
that appealed to him (he once took me up as a suitable one
when I became involved in a small contretemps with the
Government!), and he greatly disliked make-belief, a quality
not present in everyone and one which was greatly to my liking.

The original *Twelve Point Programme* of the Congress, like the
Quit India resolution, envisaged only non-violent revolt, but
later instructions from local Committees were often the
direct opposite. Indeed, there were many contradictions in the
orders issued by the Congress Working Committee and the
various Provincial organisations.[1] The Andhra Pradesh
Provincial Committee, for example, followed the non-violent
line, specifically laying down on July 29th: 'The whole movement is based on non-violence. No act which contravenes this
instruction should ever be undertaken.' On the other hand
the secret orders sent from Bombay to the Kerala Congress
Committee included the following: 'Burn important offices,

[1] In February 1943 the Government of India issued a booklet for the public
entitled *Congress Responsibility for the Disturbances*, which together with its fifteen
appendices gives a picture of the background of the rebellion as well as of
the rebellion itself. The U.P. Government also produced a pamphlet entitled
The Congress Rebellion in the United Provinces. Both are a mine of information from
the side of the Government.
   The story of Meerut District is within my own knowledge and experience.
   The Congress case awaits full and objective examination, and no doubt this
will be done in the third volume of the *History of the Freedom Movement in India*
now under preparation. Meanwhile, *The Discovery of India* and *India Wins Freedom*
contain references to and opinions on the events of 1942; and newspaper articles
appear from time to time. Of these last the Independence Day Supplement of
The Times of India, August 1967, may be specially noted. One of the best publications is *India Unreconciled* (Hindustan Times Press, December 1943). This is a purely
factual publication of nearly 500 pages, containing only actual documents,
extracts from speeches made in the Legislature at Delhi and in the House of
Commons, articles culled from the British Press both in England and in India
as well as the views of American officials and publicists. Numerous articles in the
Mahatma's own weekly, *Harijan*, have yet to be elucidated from the historical
angle.

buildings, post offices, Government buildings, railways, pull down (*sic*), issue (*sic*) notices, derail by putting stones, remove all roadside posts, remove all lights from the roads, close all shops, offices etc., cut off communications. These are some of the things going on here daily.' Again, the United Provinces Government officially reported that 'the cutting of communications and the attacks on outlying Government buildings are in accordance with the instructions given by Congress leaders who returned to the Province after the Wardha meeting of the Working Committee. According to the instructions of the United Provinces Congress Committee issued immediately after the arrest of the leaders in Bombay, "the students are the vanguard of our struggle. It is their solemn and sacred task to arouse and awaken the dumb millions from one end of the country to the other".' It is also true that local speakers often incited the people to rise in violent rebellion. The Congress were to contend afterwards that the movement took a violent turn solely as the result of the arrests of so many prominent leaders. Whether this was so, or whether from the commencement the intention was a mass upheaval which in any case could not fail to become violent, will be a problem for the historians who deal with these events in the future, but how difficult it can be to pin down non-violence to a precise definition is clear from many other interesting and instructive circulars issued at this time and shortly afterwards. According to the Home Member in the Central Assembly on September 15th 1942, Mahatma Gandhi declared at a Press Conference on July 19th of the same year: 'I do not want rioting as a direct result. If in spite of precautions, rioting does take place, it cannot be helped.' Writing in *Harijan* in its issue of August 23rd 1942 he was more specific. To the question, 'What may be permitted for disorganising Government within the limit of non-violence ?' his answer was: 'I can give my personal opinion only. In my opinion looting or burning of offices, banks, granaries etc. is *not* permissible. *Dislocation of traffic communications in a non-violent manner without endangering life* . . .*Cutting wires, removing rails, destroying small bridges cannot be objected to in a struggle like this provided ample precautions are taken to safeguard life*' (my italics). The precautions to be taken have not been specified, but it is difficult to envisage the steps which can be successfully undertaken in such cases for the safety of human life. Then, too, a number of Congress bulletins were issued at later stages. Instruction six of *Inquilab Bulletin One* included the direction: 'Completely paralyse communications, and transport, dislocate tram and bus services, uproot telegraphic and telephone posts, dig up roads, cut railways, tear out motor and bus tyres and dislocate government machinery in every possible way.' *Bulletin Six* reminded its readers of Mahatma Gandhi's statement on May 25th 1942: 'I am convinced that we are living today in a state of ordered anarchy. This ordered, disciplined anarchy should go, and if as a result, there is complete lawlessness in India, I would risk it, and people will evolve real popular order out of chaos.' Instructions on the above lines continued to be sent out secretly even after the close of the outbreaks. One of the circulars from the Central Directorate of the All-India Congress Committee dated January 26th 1943, appealed to 'peasants to form guerilla bands, workers to form guerilla bands and to sabotage, and students to form guerilla bands.'[1]

In Madras sabotage commenced on August 12th with organised attacks on railway stations and everywhere the story unfolded on the same lines, the worst affected Provinces being Bombay, the Central Provinces, Bihar, the United Provinces and parts of Bengal. In a large portion of Bihar and in the eastern Districts of the United Provinces the District Administration actually collapsed for about three weeks; in the words that I often heard later these Districts 'had to be reconquered'. Ballia, one of the eastern border Districts of the United Profinces, 'rather resembled a country that had been fought over and conquered. Not only were there numerous signs of material destruction, but the attitude of the people changed almost overnight from rebellious truculence to abject fawning'.[2] The whole area east of Allahabad in the United Provinces was very seriously affected. Railway lines and bridges were sabotaged, and both the broad-gauge and metre-gauge railways running eastwards to Calcutta were put out of action in parts for some weeks. 'These incessant attacks,' in the words of the official

---

[1]Extracts taken from appendix XIV, appendix XV and appendix VIII of the Government of India's booklet.
[2]*The Guardians*, p. 312. The speaker was a young I.C.S. officer, Hugh Lane, who was sent to Ballia to assist in clearing up operations.

Report on the disturbances, 'achieved remarkable, though temporary success, and communications were not permanently restored until the end of August.' The number of goods trains transporting war material and military stores derailed and looted in this area was exceptionally large, only tins of corned beef being thrown aside, the odd tin to be recovered and enjoyed at leisure by the unregenerate.

Communications were not the only target. The Administration itself came under heavy assault. The Courts and District Offices at Benares and Allahabad,[1] two examples out of many, were attacked by large mobs, with women and girls sometimes in the van; and at least in three other Districts fighting for the possession of Police Stations took place, especially those lying in the not easily accessible triangle between the confluence of the rivers Ghagra and Ganges. The defence of the Madhuban Police Station—a remote place in Azamgarh District—was one of the instances of the courage with which these symbols of authority were defended. Here the District Magistrate, who had left his headquarters to deal with trouble at another outlying township and who had been forced to divert his attention to Madhuban, was besieged for two days. His effective force consisted of four or five subordinate Police Officers and seventeen constables with a miscellaneous armament of 10 muskets (single-barrel smooth bores with a lethal range of about fifty yards), a few revolvers with the officers, two confiscated 12-bore shot-guns and four spears. Two mobs totalling some 5,000 men, armed largely with spears, converged after having burnt down and looted the Post Office, and then made a concerted attack on the Police Station with the assistance of two elephants. The District Magistrate beat off all attacks for three hours, in the course of which 118 rounds of miscellaneous ammunition were fired. When the attacking force retreated with a loss of some 30 dead and 50 wounded, it cut off the escape of the besieged by digging trenches across the road. The blockade continued the whole of the succeeding night, but on the next day the District Magistrate managed to extricate himself and his small force and return to his headquarters, where he met a relief force

---

[1]'While Cawnpore, Agra, Lucknow and Meerut cities were considerably quieter than formerly, the situation at Benares deteriorated, and Allahabad city was quite out of hand.' Provincial Government's summary for August 12th.

under the personal command of the District Magistrate of Fyzabad, an adjacent District.

In other eastern areas the same pattern was followed. In Mirzapur a mob of 2,000 surrounded the Police Station and tried to set it on fire with kerosene oil, several constables being injured in the ensuing fight. In Ghazipur District the staffs of all outlying Police Stations were withdrawn after some of the latter, in the words of the official Report, 'had fallen into the hands of the rebels'. In many cases the Police, both officers and men, came in for treatment which by no stretch of the imagination could be brought within the ambit of non-violence. At Dhanapur the Sub-Inspector in charge was killed while negotiating with local Congress leaders. At Sadat the Sub-Inspector with the help of a solitary constable put up a stout resistance. They were captured and beaten to death, and their bodies were cremated on a pile of looted furniture. In another District another Sub-Inspector with a lone constable retreated to a cattle-pound in the vicinity where they fought alone against heavy odds. They were finally captured by the mob and speared to death.

The worst of the Districts in this portion of the Province was Ballia, where the rebellion was astonishingly successful. The local Administration had collapsed, with the District Magistrate and the Superintendent of Police besieged in their own Police Lines. In the rural areas all but three Police Stations had been lost and some Government offices had been surrendered to the Congress. The District Magistrate had made a well-meant effort to negotiate with local leaders and had released them from jail on condition that they would restrain the mobs from violence. Unfortunately this had the reverse effect, as indeed might have been expected, for the released leaders, now in undisputed control of the Headquarters of the District, immediately issued proclamations that the British Raj was dead. The usual outburst of looting on a lavish scale, which is a common feature of Indian life once the restraining hand of authority is removed, then began with vigour.[1] Relieving

---

[1] Twenty five years later Master Tara Singh, the Akali Sikh Leader, in dealing with Indian conditions is reported to have said: 'Anarchy of the type we see in China today may soon be India's fate, too. Only there will be far less killing *and more loot*' (my italics)—*The Statesman*, February 18th, 1967.

columns of troops and police did not push their way through until August 23rd, arriving by the only means of communication open, the river Ganges. It was not until the expiry of some weeks more that the position was fully restored. In the eastern portion of the Province military assistance, Indian as well as British, was called in on a large scale for the suppression of the rebellion, and on August 17th Nethersole left Meerut to take charge of operations there with almost unlimited powers to restore order. Two transport platoons of the R.I.A.S.C. were dispatched to reinforce the police and military already operating in Azamgarh and Ghazipur Districts. They arrived in time to prevent an outbreak of large-scale looting. One detachment under the District Magistrate, Ghazipur, came unexpectedly on a gang dismantling a road bridge, which was only saved by the Magistrate's opening fire and driving off the mob. A determined attack on the *Tahsilder*-Magistrate's Office at an outlying town, Mohammadabad, 'was repulsed with a loss of six killed to the enemy', as the official Report succinctly put it. What could be described as almost pitched battles took place in East United Provinces and neighbouring Bihar. In one such operation in the United Provinces '200 rebels were shot', according to a telephonic message received by the Superintendent of Police and myself early in the afternoon of August 20th, and three days later aircraft were used for the dispersal of mobs gathering for further attacks in Ghazipur District. The last real battle for the control of the eastern portion of the Province took place at Said Raja Railway Station on the border of Bihar. Here a determined mob of about 1,000 men collected together in a fairly disciplined formation. They came up in small sections of about twenty men each, racing over open ground and joining up when cover was reached. They had also brought up a train of bullock carts. The small Police Guard—a *naik* (corporal) and nine constables—repeatedly resisted sorties from all directions until reinforcements arrived from farther up the line. These consisted only of seven men in a patrol train, but with their help the attack was beaten off, the mob finally retreating and leaving behind fourteen badly wounded men as prisoners. In the meantime a subsidiary assault on the Police Station had also been defeated, and as the attacking force dispersed, it ran into a magistrate returning from a protective patrol from the

13

direction of Patna, and received a further dose of punishment. 'This', said the official Report, 'was the last attack by an organised mob, for as soon as the rebels saw that the Administration commanded adequate force to deal with them they lost heart even more quickly than they had taken it.'

The rebellion never obtained so strong a hold in the western districts, not indeed through lack of organization and energy, but mainly because communications were better, and control was far more easy to maintain. The outbreaks soon became isolated and sporadic, and provided the District Magistrate kept in constant touch with his outlying areas by frequent reconnaisances it was not difficult to keep mobile columns moving out to whatever particular area demanded attention. Meerut was representative of the disturbances in this portion of the Province, and here luck was on my side in dealing with them. In the first place I had been in the District for over two years, and having toured its nooks and corners was well acquainted with its people and its turbulent parts. Then, too, the District Police had been brought to a state of high efficiency through the ability and energy of one of the best Police Officers in the Province. This was Bill Colville, who was with me until six months before the outbreak, and with whom I had worked in complete harmony. Lastly, the Division as a whole was strongly garrisoned, Meerut Cantonment alone originally housing a cavalry brigade, two infantry regiments and some miscellaneous arms. That by 1942 the exigencies of war had altered the composite formation into a collection of heterogeneous units did not affect me as District Magistrate.

My personal part, therefore, was in no way dramatic, however exciting it may have appeared to me at the time. Beyond throwing stones and bricks at me, no one attempted anything unpleasant. I was never besieged in a Police Station, nor was it my fortune to lead a column of constabulary for the relief of an outlying office. Early in the morning of the outbreak I summoned my Indian subordinate magistrates, and explained to them where we stood. The position as I saw it was simple. We were Government Officers, cogs in the imperial machine, and it was our first duty to suppress the upheaval. I explained that I intended to do so. This was first and foremost an administrative matter, a question of the maintenance of law and order.

Magistrates must, therefore, take every measure to ensure this end, including firing, if they deemed this necessary for the protection of life and government property. They were in no case to allow a situation to go out of control. The force used must be kept to the minimum, but it must be used where and when necessary. The responsibility was mine, and they would be fully supported. There was to be no hesitation in dispersing mobs, making arrests, and doing whatever else they considered necessary. As Government Officers, we could not allow political or any considerations outside the purely administrative to enter the picture. I added that if anyone considered this to be anti-national or unpatriotic, he should resign forthwith from the service of the Government which was paying him. Rightly or wrongly, but not unexpectedly, this last proposition found no takers, and magistrates left for their Sub-Divisional Head-quarters knowing precisely where they stood, and what was expected of them.

For the first two days, the trouble was confined to Meerut city. Here crowds of students from the local colleges, numbering about 2,000 each, made concerted attempts to take possession of the Revenue and Civil Courts, and the Government offices. On August 9th and 10th these attacks continued at regular intervals from ten o'clock in the morning until late in the evening, the attackers receiving regular reinforcements and giving us little respite. They were broken up consistently through baton charges and the use of mounted police. One such mob succeeded in manhandling the Additional District Magistrate and the City Magistrate before it was dispersed, and the young Assistant Superintendent of Police, an Englishman, received a brick in his ribs and was thrown from his horse. For the most part the crowds were unarmed, although a certain number of hockey-sticks were in evidence, and bricks and stones were flying around freely. As an amusing sidelight, I found that small stature and a relatively insignificant presence were a definite asset; for the bulky frame of the City Magistrate in my vicinity attracted far more hostile attention than I did. In these brawls I could certainly have ordered the police to fire on more than one occasion, but I preferred to keep this in the background as a last resort, to be used only if there were real fear of the Courts and offices being invaded. If mobs could be broken up by less drastic methods and by mass arrests, there did not seem to me to be any justification for adding fuel to the anti-British feelings that had already flared up. This Fabian policy succeeded, but only just. On the third or fourth day student violence abated considerably. When one of the last of the batches from the Meerut College across the road was chased away from the main collectorate buildings, those who escaped arrest burst back into their own College grounds and completely wrecked their own science laboratories, apparently forgetting in their exuberance that the Meerut College was not a Government institution. This was, I think, a good example of mob psychology. It showed that a crowd setting out in some kind of order and formation to invade, capture or destroy a particular type of property is quite likely under emotional stresses, if its original purpose is frustrated, to divert its attention to any property which comes to hand. In this case damage to the College did not cause me any headaches, for it was not my duty to protect it from the depredations of its own students. Nor, in fact, did the College authorities ask for assistance.

Similar attacks on government property occurred in the outlying towns of Ghaziabad and Hapur and elsewhere; but here in both places the magistrates were compelled to order firing. They and other officials were injured by brickbats. The forces under their command were small, they had no reserves at their back as we had at Headquarters, and the threat from the mobs was imminently dangerous and showed no signs of abating. At Hapur three persons were killed and four injured. On the 14th the magistrate at Sardhana on the other side of the District sent an urgent call for assistance—which arrived just in time to drive off an organized mob from surrounding villages before it launched a concerted attack on the Police Station and local Courts. Five were killed in this operation.

Organized attempts to take possession of government property continued throughout the first ten or twelve days of the rebellion. There were more unsuccessful assaults on the Post Office at Ghaziabad, many cases of attempted arson in Meerut City, and much damage was done to the main railway station at the latter place before the gangs were broken up. Although no District Magistrate liked to call on the military authorities for assistance, since this implied a slur on the capacity of the civil

power to maintain its authority, this had already become
essential. A company of 10/2 Punjab Regiment had been quartered in the Meerut Town Hall, and their presence and patrol-
ling had a stabilizing effect. The Armed Police Reserve could
now be relieved from their work in the City for duty in the
rural areas. Mobile police and military patrols were sent out
in various directions, basing their operations on the five *Tahsil*
headquarters. They were followed at a later stage by more
mobile military columns, so that within a few days the whole
District was covered.

Attacks on government buildings having failed, the movement was now directed to the sabotaging of communications,
railway signal wires, telephone cables and telegraph wires. Small
bodies of students from Meerut, evading arrest, dispersed themselves into the countryside, where special efforts were made to
arouse the villages, the inhabitants of which had so far been
content to wait on events and to see what the official reaction
to the Congress campaign would be. Canal banks were cut in
order to flood and consequently render useless the canal roads
which formed a useful auxiliary line of communications running
vertically through the west, centre and east of the District.
These roads linked up at various points with the metalled
roads maintained by the Government and the District Board.
Railway stations, too, came in for several attacks, the first of
which was at Muradnagar, some twenty miles from Meerut on
the main line to Delhi. As early as August 12th a large mob
had burst into the station, completely destroyed the signalling
apparatus, cut the signal and telephone wires, burnt the records
and looted the cash in the safe. In the course of the next week
or ten days, stations at three places on the light railway running
from Shahdara, a Delhi suburb, to Saharanpur in the north
were destroyed, and the line damaged at various places throughout the length of the railway, despite the running of special
patrol trains as a protective measure. The inhabitants of the
villages adjacent to the line merely waited for the patrol trains
to pass and then tampered with the rails and sleepers at their
leisure.

The second half of the month was crucial for the District.
News from the distant areas was spasmodic owing to the
sabotage of communications. The Jat and Gujar villages, the

potential sources of danger together with a few Chauhan
Rajput areas on the far side of the District near the river Ganges,
were all showing signs of restiveness. The collection of land
revenue, which I had not halted, provided an additional source
of friction. Despite the difficulties, however, police and military
columns were able to cover the District adequately, and were
equal to the situation. Once Meerut city had settled down, I
took the opportunity of making several expeditions into the
interior. These were long-distance reconnaisances not only
for the purpose of gaining first-hand information but also, and
more particularly, to put heart into subordinate officials in the
depths of the countryside. It required little courage to remain
cool, calm and collected at one's Headquarters, with a brigade
at one's beck and call, and an Armed Police Reserve adjacent to
one's house. A Sub-Inspector of Police at a Police Station forty
miles away, with only a handful of men and a few antiquated
weapons, was not in so happy a position. Police and Revenue
officials in India have never been popular, especially the former.
During the last twenty years of British rule they had been the
constant targets of bitter criticism and hostility from the side of
the Congress as being the symbols and instruments of an
unpopular foreign rule. Surrounded by hostile and potentially
hostile villages, most of which must have had at some period
a deep grudge against them, and subjected to daily taunts and
threats, a Sub-Inspector and his men might have been forgiven
for having second thoughts as to where their own interests lay.
My particular purpose, therefore, in showing myself to my subordinates out in lonely areas was to give a tangible indication
that they had not been forgotten. If I could reach them, so
also could assistance as and when required.

If these all-round rapid tours were not especially hazardous,
they were equally no picnics. I spent many hours out at a
stretch, usually arriving back at Meerut in the small hours of
the morning; and the month of August is not the season one
would normally select for taking joy-rides in police trucks and
jeeps. On the first occasion, after receiving information of the
looting of the Muradnagar railway station, the Assistant
Superintendent of Police, now happily recovered from his
bruises, and I went out together with a platoon of extra police.
As we neared the station, or its remnants, a train passed us. It

was crawling along towards Meerut Junction, its driver doubt-less under compulsion, since the signal wires had been cut and neither driver nor fireman knew whether or not the points had been tampered with. With cheering passengers even on the roofs of the carriages it resembled a slow-moving but very noisy ant heap. One could only hope that the police on duty at the Junction would be able to deal with it effectively. At Murad-nagar, after a few rapid inquiries, a detachment of police was left behind to live on, and off, the delinquent countryside, to patrol the villages on the railway, and to protect the Modi Sugar Mills. The mills had recently been forcibly closed by rioters, and had to be reopened in more or less the same manner by the police. We then made a complete tour of the south-eastern portion of the District, looking in at both Ghaziabad and Hapur to review the situation after the firing. We also visited numerous villages and all the Police Stations on the way. The two towns were quiet and under control. The rural population appeared to be sullen and waiting on events, but apart from the occasional brickbat flung at our truck no overt movement was made against us. At the same time we were not received anywhere by a welcoming committee except perhaps at one village where all the village damsels turned out and waved their hands. Whether this was in derision or by way of greeting we did not stop to inquire. Waving cheerfully back we proceeded on our way. Odysseus-like, I instructed our driver, who displayed much interest and showed signs of coming to a halt, to stop his ears to all such sirens with their blandishments and to drive on. We arrived back at Meerut at about 1 a.m., having covered in our round trip close on 100 miles. After badly needed refreshment I sat down to digest a batch of reports from other areas preparatory to getting down to my own for the Government; for 'sitreps' (Situation Reports) were now the order of the day.

My expedition two or three days later, on the 15th, turned out to be far more arduous. Early Sunday afternoon I set out with a young I.C.S. magistrate, Treanor, who had been sent to me some months earlier for training. By chance I decided to look around the north-eastern side, with its headquarters at Mowana. The Superintendent of Police had not informed me of impending trouble there and of the previous dispatch of

police reinforcements. In ignorance of this we went in my
private car, though I had taken the precaution of taking with
me two of the constables from the guard at my bungalow. In
this way we went into the unknown without leaving behind
information of our destination.

We ran into difficulties. Mowana township consisted of two
large villages separated by some two miles. Between the two
we were confronted with the remnants of a road block and
this, along with the fact that the sole telegraph wire connecting
the *Tahsil* office with Meerut was lying out by the roadside, was
the first indication that events were moving to a climax in this
area. With difficulty and after much delay we arrived for the
aftermath of a riot. The cheerfully ubiquitous Assistant
Superintendent of Police had again come in for rough treatment. He had been manhandled, his service revolver had
been stolen, and his orderly's wrist and the arm of another
constable had been fractured. In the circumstances no reasonable person could claim that the firing which had been ordered
in self-defence was either excessive or unnecessary. Three men
including the leader of the mob had been killed and a few others
injured.

The attack on the *Tahsil* here had been organized not from
Mowana proper, but from neighbouring villages, populated
mainly by Gujars, a caste (or more properly a clan in origin)
not notable for their generally pacific or non-violent outlook
on life. We visited the adjacent villages, had a large number of
arrests made and clamped down punitive fines on those villages
we thought responsible. It was late in the evening when we
left for Meerut, making a long detour along a branch of the
Ganges Canal and, as usual, visiting all the important villages
and the two Police Stations on the way. Apart from sporadic
incidents such as the one at Mowana, there did not seem to me
to be any likelihood of a concerted uprising, since mobile patrols
were operating everywhere. At Kithore, a large, mainly Muslim
village, the Sub-Inspector was on the alert, although it was
midnight. He informed us that all was well in his circle, but
appeared to be glad to see us nevertheless. After instructing
him to inform his colleague at Garhmukhtesar, ten miles away
in the lonely Ganges Khadir, that we had him in mind, we
left for Meerut. Arriving there at 2 a.m. I found that my good

friend Nethersole had been worrying about us for some hours, no one knowing in which direction we had gone. Nethersole had finally contacted the Deputy-Inspector General of Police with the intention of having a search party sent out and our return was just in time to prevent this. We had scarcely settled down to a welcome and refreshing drink when a telephone call came through from the District jail with the information that the outer wall had collapsed through heavy rain. The jail guard having been reinforced, I left the matter at that for the time being, but at 7 a.m. I visited the jail to find the non-political prisoners busily engaged in rebuilding their own prison wall! I wonder whether there is any other country where such a thing could happen. The normal population of 400 had more than trebled with the arrests and detention of political offenders, and a combined and concerted attack on the jail staff could have produced a very serious situation. Yet here were the ordinary prisoners working on their own wall, while the 'politicals' confined themselves to shouting 'Mahatma Gandhi ki jai' at intervals—which released their surplus energies without harm to anyone.

Bhamori is an obscure village in an obscure corner in the north-west of the District. Here the local police had been compelled to open fire on a crowd threatening the Police Station, killing seven men. Police reinforcements were dispatched to augment the slender resources at the command of the Sub-Inspector. Accompanied by the Superintendent of Police I went out to the spot with them. We never arrived at Bhamori. A few miles short of our destination our jeep came to an abrupt halt in the mud and slush, and the trucks with the reinforcements were completely bogged down, blocking such tracks as there were. The men marched off on foot, but by the time we had unravelled ourselves, the trucks and the jeep, the shades of night were falling fast upon us. The Sub-Inspector himself had come to meet us, and informed us that all was now well, and that with the extra police his circle would be under control. Our main object was thus accomplished, since every village in the vicinity realized that we *could* manage to get somewhere at all times. By this time there were so many mobile columns of Armed Police and military moving round the District that no village

wanted the addition of the District Magistrate and the
Superintendent of Police together with two more platoons in
its vicinity, even if they were all unheroically stuck in the
mud.

The only remaining area requiring personal attention
contained the Jat villages in the west bordering on the river
Jumna and traversed by the S. S. Light Railway. These villages
had strong personal links with the Jat Districts across the
river in the Punjab, and memories of 1857 had never completely
died out, especially in the eighty four which were collectively
designated 'the Desh'. In 1942 local reactions were very
different from those of ninety years earlier when the initiative
had been taken by the Jats. Now the latter contented themselves with sporadic sabotage, while sitting on the fence to see
how authority would act before setting in motion any violent
reaction from their own side. It was clear that if preventive
action were taken first from the side of the Government there
was no likelihood of any real uprising.

A detachment of the 2nd Punjab Regiment had already
been dispatched to the area, and had established its headquarters at Baraut. Baraut, a flourishing town in the sixties
with a considerable trade in grain and other commodities, was
merely a large village in 1942. The road link was unmetalled and
often under water during the rainy season, and Baraut's only
permanent connexion with the outer world at that time was
the Light Railway. Its great importance to me lay in its being
one of the focal points for the supply of recruits for the Indian
Army. Along with the surrounding villages it formed a compact
Jat bloc, and the leading men were all retired Army pensioners,
Risaldar Majors, Subedars and lower ranks. The officers of
the 2nd Punjab Regiment had very creditably established
cordial relations with the ex-servicemen, who at the commencement of the disturbances had done little to assist in
keeping the area under control. The presence of two platoons of
the 2nd Punjab Regiment soon produced a change, and it was
enough for me to tie up the loose ends of what had been started
by others. Village defence bodies were formed for the supervision
of groups of villages and were placed in charge of pensioned
officers. It was made clear at the same time that any further
sabotage or any act in furtherance of the rebellion would be

met not only with the levy of collective fines on the village concerned but also with the complete stoppage of pensions. The
Jat, a practical man, admitted the illogicality between expecting the Government to pay him a pension and simultaneously
trying to subvert it. Collective fines had already been levied
on a number of villages throughout the District, but this was
not a punishment that commended itself to me, since it presented
subordinate officials with extensive opportunities for lining
their own pockets. The stoppage of pensions was simpler and
in this particular part of the District quite as effective. I had
no official authority to order this, but official orders were
hardly necessary. All that was required was a suggestion to
the Treasury Officer to find himself too busy with other work
owing to the general dislocation caused by the rebellion
when the pensioners arrived at his office. In the alternative
I could have closed the Treasury on the pretext of a possible
attack on it. To these methods no objection could have been
made, and no sensible person wishes to travel forty or fifty
miles in the heat of August merely to find the Treasury closed,
and to be told to come again. In addition to other unofficial
pressures, it was publicly announced in every village that no
civil employment under the Government would be given to
the young men of any village which joined in the movement,
a threat which carried great weight in a country where a safe
official position has always been the ambition of all young
men. To add a touch of real colour to the threat I put a few
subordinate officials on the task of preparing lists of all potential
candidates for future employment. Perhaps I should add that
I never saw the lists; nor do I know what happened to them,
but experience had taught me that in India indirect methods
often produce far better results than the visible and open use
of force. This, I think, was amply demonstrated by the fact
that when the Jats themselves had put their own house in order
and the troops returned to Meerut, there was no sign of any
resentment against the latter. The Jat can easily be aroused
against any Government, if he is under the impression that
its authority is weakening, but no man is more ready to acknowledge its existence and to accept it as one of the facts of
life when once this is firmly impressed on him.

Spasmodic trouble of a minor kind continued for some

time, with the students maintaining their nuisance value, rather more, it can be said, to the detriment of their own education than to that of the Government; but the thunder of the first fortnight of the rebellion was very muted by the end of a month. Certainly by the middle of September there were no further attempts at stirring up the masses into a concerted uprising, and all the towns of the District had returned to normal life. For Meerut the rebellion was at an end by the close of September. The eastern Districts, too, though by no means quiescent, were under control, so that Micky Nethersole was able to take a few days' leave from his arduous and unpleasant duties. On his way to the hills he stopped at Meerut, and since I, too, had been allowed ten days' casual leave, we travelled together to Mussoorie where in the peaceful cool of the Himalaya my wife and children had been since the previous May, far from the sound and fury of the last six weeks in the plains six thousand feet below. But by this time the fires were dying down rapidly throughout the Province, until by the end of the year the Chief Secretary could report to the Government of India that 'the rebellion is now regarded as a thing of the past and attracts little interest'—a factually correct, though somewhat superficial judgement. The rebellion had left a deep scar.

XI

Reflections on the Rebellion

THE OUTBREAK of war presented New Delhi with an admirable opportunity of winning over the Congress to its side, for despite the latter's pacifist wing under the Mahatma, the organisation as a whole was in no intransigent mood. Unhappily, the chance was thrown away—almost deliberately, it seemed—by the ruling power, so great was the psychological gap between ruler and subject.

That an agreement was possible has been emphasised by Desmond Young, who records in his *Try Anything Twice* a conversation with Pandit Jawaharlal Nehru in September. 'His [Nehru's] conditions for whole-heartedly supporting the war effort seemed to me to be reasonable,' he wrote. ' "We would want to be represented in the Government of India," ' said Jawaharlal, ' "but we would not presume to ask for any part in the direction of the war. That is a technical business of which we know nothing. We would not object, for example, to Indian troops serving overseas. But we would expect to be *consulted* before they were sent. The same would apply to recruitment for war industries. Granted that, we would be 100 per cent behind you. Most of us are quite as anti-Fascist and anti-Nazi as you are." ' Desmond Young goes on to record that the Governor of the U.P. (Sir Harry Haig) was sufficiently impressed to arrange for a special interview with the Viceroy. The Viceroy's Private Secretary, Sir Gilbert Laithwaite, however, when shown the text of the interview, 'instantly poohpooed it' with a ' "surely you don't believe a word these fellows say. You're only wasting your time." ' Lord Linlithgow questioned Desmond Young for half-an-hour and 'appeared at least half-convinced' but as the latter sadly writes: 'But Laithwaite went in as I came out, and I feared that the last word would rest with him and the violently anti-Congress members of the Viceroy's Council. So it turned out. I heard no more of my paper. Nor could I publish it, for I had promised Jawaharlal not to do so unless the Government were willing to meet him half-way. The Government of India

then came out with what still seems to me one of the silliest
official offers on record. It was proposed to form an unwieldy
Consultative Council to represent all classes of Indian opinion.
Members would be nominated by the Viceroy. It would be
called only when he felt himself in need of their advice. It
would have no powers of any sort. In this way India was to
be associated with the war. It need hardly be said that Indians
refused to take the offer seriously.'[1]

The complete lack of understanding on the part of the
British in India, not to mention the authorities in London,
was only too obvious in many ways. No one seemed to realise
the importance Indians attached to status, simply as status,
the desire for equal treatment with the white Dominions
without being expected to sit up and wag their tails with
pleasure, as it were, at the thought of entering a war which
was not of their making and which in 1939 appeared to many
as being merely the second round of the European Civil War
of 1914-8. Thus India's largest and most influential political
party was not consulted, and India was dragged unceremoniously into the war on the constitutional ground that whenever the King Emperor chose to go to war India must automatically accompany him. So much for the Dominion Status
(even of Mr Churchill's 'ceremonious' variety) which had
been officially promised a decade earlier.[2] Then, too, the
endless propaganda gushing out from New Delhi was as inept
as the manner in which India had been brought into the war
was high handed. 'We are fighting,' announced the Viceroy
on October 17th 1939, 'to resist aggression, whether directed
against ourselves or against others. We seek no advantage for
ourselves. We look beyond victory to the laying of the foundation of a better international order, and the establishment of
real and settled peace.' All very true, no doubt, but to one
like myself who had heard precisely the same high-toned
sentiments on countless occasions between the years 1914
and 1918, and had then seen their beauty tarnished in the

---

[1] *Try Anything Twice* (Hamish Hamilton, 1963). The text of the paper is
on pp. 245-6. The paper is of the greatest historical importance, although it cannot figure in the official archives, and it is to be hoped that it will not be ignored
by British historians when they get around to dealing seriously with Indo-British
relations during this period.
[2] See p. 92 above.

succeeding four, such propaganda only represented the old distillation of Lloyd George cum Northcliffe, the sleeping mixture as before. Many Englishmen added weight to this impression by openly expressing the view that the war would be a short one and by implying that England could do very nicely without India's assistance. In the very early days of the war a senior I.C.S. officer said to me that 'the war would be over within a few months, because Hitler would not be able to last out'. And stories of German tanks being made of wood and painted over to represent steel were current coin, along with foolish jokes like the one that a German tank had collided with a monkey which had escaped from a zoo and was upended as a result! It may all have been promising propaganda from the patronising heights of the New Delhi secretariat. But it sounded very odd to a man who exactly twenty five years earlier had heard innumerable times that 'the boys will be back by Christmas.' It was also odd that the man who expressed similar views in 1939 had himself seen four years active service in the First War. This kind of facile optimism continued for many months, and it was not until the unexpected collapse of France and the switching on of heat in North Africa that the 'couldn't care less about you, but just keep quiet' attitude changed almost overnight with the changed circumstances. Both London and New Delhi now suddenly realised that India came into the picture after all, and the Indian Government hastily commenced the expansion of the Indian Army 'as it ought to have been expanded ten months ago' in the frank words of the then Chief Secretary of the United Provinces.[1]

This complete lack of understanding, and a generally nursery governess attitude towards India and Indians all combined to exacerbate Indian distrust of British sincerity, and simultaneously British policy in regard to Burma was scarcely directed towards removing this lack of faith; for in 1939 all that the Burmese asked for was a guarantee of Dominion Status *after* the war, and even this very moderate request was not granted.[2] Yet, although it was certainly not

[1]The remark was contained in a letter of July 1940 from the Chief Secretary in reply to a request from me to join the Army.
[2]In *The Discovery of India*, p. 531, Pandit Jawaharlal Nehru has referred to this.

surprising to an Indian that the British paid the penalty in
Burma in 1942, some British officers resolutely refused to
shoulder the blame. I once heard an English officer of the
Burma Police deliver an address in which everyone save his own
countrymen came in for severe strictures for bringing about the
débâcle.

What all educated Indians, *without exception*, asked for was
a positive, clear advance towards the promised land, coupled
with an unambiguous guarantee of full Dominion Status as
enshrined in the Statute of Westminster immediately after
the war. What India actually received was a rigid, imperial,
Curzonian posture from Lord Linlithgow, an unpopular
Viceroy at the best of times, who was totally unsuited by
temperament and his heavy, Brontosaurian approach to touch
the hearts of sensitive subject peoples possessed of a very
low emotional flashpoint. When he chanced to visit Meerut in
the cold weather of 1940-41 for a partridge shoot—incidentally
incurring thereby the displeasure of his compatriots, who held
that there was a war on, he displayed no interest whatsoever
in the District, despite its importance as one of the best
recruiting grounds in the country. Doubtless his natural taci-
turnity had not been mellowed by the almost complete
absence of partridge, but that apart, he gave the impression
of being a weary, bored and rather unhappy man.[1] Thus
did the Imperial Power cast aside its only opportunity of
gaining the real goodwill of its subjects; as, indeed, it missed
it next door in Burma; and goodwill there certainly would
have been on the very practical ground, if no other, that none
foresaw in 1939 the near possibility of an invasion of England
itself and a long series of military disasters to follow.

The insensitive reactions of the British to the feelings of the
camp followers of the Empire contrasted strongly and strangely
with the attitude towards Eire.   It was common knowledge
that the Dublin Government had declared its neutrality on
the outbreak of war, although Eire was England's back door

---

[1] K.P.S. Menon in *Many Worlds*, p. 263, has referred in very strong terms to
Lord Linlithgow's unpopularity. This last was more than a mere lack of popular
appeal—no human being in India can ever have popular appeal unless he can
talk for an hour or so off the cuff without coming to the point, if any. Lord Wavell,
Lord Linlithgow's successor, lacked this kind of popularity for this reason; but
at the same time was greatly respected and trusted for his straightforwardness and
sincerity.

and, in fact, would have been in the gravest peril herself in the event of an invasion of Great Britain. The bitterness of the Dublin Government towards Great Britain was far greater than of the Congress in India, and, although perhaps its full extent was not known at the time, everyone in India realised that Eire's neutrality was positively hostile. Yet I never heard the smallest criticism of the Southern Irish for not jumping into the war as an ally of their next door neighbour. Condemnation was reserved solely for the Congress, and this despite the fact that 'Ireland was a hotbed of Axis espionage, that the lights of Irish cities were used as check points by the Luftwaffe for air attacks on England and that in the words of Sir Winston Churchill later, de Valera "was quite content to sit happy and see us strangled." '[1]

Nevertheless, after all criticism of the British has been exhausted, it does not seem to me that the diplomacy of the Congress in relation to the practical offers of the Government between 1940 and 1942 which culminated in the Mission led by Sir Stafford Cripps scintillated with brilliance, being clearly calculated to take advantage of each military reverse in turn as a means of pressurizing the British into an immediate handing over of the whole loaf. That each of the three political offers came in the wake of military disasters was not relevant to the actual political situation in India; for by this time it was obvious that British policy had altered. But with the military position precarious, especially on the borders of India itself, with the openly admitted need for India's great resources in men and material for the winning of the war, with the claim of the Congress to represent the whole of India in clear dispute and the ever-present possibility of communal anarchy, it

---

[1]Louis L Synder, *The War, A Concise History 1939-45* (Dell Publishing Co. Inc. New York, 1960), p. 313. See also Churchill's *The Second World War*, vol. ii, pp. 529-37. As early as 1st December 1940 Mr Churchill complained in a minute to the Chancellor of the Exchequer of 'the straits to which we are being reduced by the actions of the Dublin Government', and referred to 'public indignation' (p. 534). On another occasion in his correspondence with President Roosevelt he was almost apologetic: 'The Cabinet propose to let de Valera know that we cannot go on supplying him in present conditions. I am sorry about this, but we must think of our own self-preservation. You will also realise that our merchant seamen and public opinion take it much amiss that we should have to subsidise them when de Valera is quite content to sit happy and see us strangled.' (letter dated 13th December, pp 535-36). The English seaman's anger at the Irish attitude has also been noted more than once in Nicholas Montserrat's novel, *The Cruel Sea* (Cassell, 1951).

appeared to me unreasonable to expect the British to make an outright transfer of full power to one political party alone, however great its influence.

Since India's long term interests did, in fact, coincide with those of Great Britain, it has always appeared to me that a temporary agreement with the British was dictated by self-interest. Such an arrangement would not have committed the Congress to cooperation afterwards, and with the latter back in office in most of the Provinces and represented in the Central Government at New Delhi, its final position would have been impregnable, even against a possibly hostile Westminster later. Racial recrimination would have been avoided, and the formation of the Indian National Army, with its surprising appeal to Indian emotions, would have been sidetracked. Now, however, that its turn to be Laithwaitean had arrived, the Congress saw the position in a different light, and with the passage of the *Quit India* resolution reached the point of no return. Thus were two golden opportunities for a settlement rejected by the respective parties to the dispute; and had there been a Puck to circle India at the time, doubtless his only comment would have been 'Lord, what fools these mortals be.'

The rebellion will naturally always loom larger in Indian than in British eyes. In his History of *The Second World War* Sir Winston Churchill has poured a cold douche on it in a few not entirely accurate words.[1] His statement that 'The Viceroy's Council upon which *there was only one Englishman* (my italics) proposed unanimously to arrest and intern Gandhi, Nehru...' was incorrect in its detail, for out of the sixteen members of Council at the time four were Englishmen, excluding the Viceroy himself, namely Lord Wavell, Commander in Chief and Military Member, Sir Jeremy Raisman I. C. S., Finance, Sir Reginald Maxwell I.C.S., Home, and Sir Edward Benthall, War Transport. More important and of greater historical significance, it was an appraisal of very doubtful validity to assert that 'they (the measures proposed) proved the superficial character of the Congress Party's influence upon the masses, among whom there was deep fear of being invaded by Japan and who looked to the King Emperor to protect them.'[2] The

[1] Vol. iv, pp. 454-56.
[2] Ibid., p. 454.

exact contrary was the case, for the hold of the Congress on the masses was admitted on all sides, British and Indian, to be very strong. And so far as my personal experience went, I never came across any real fear of Japan.

A. J. P. Taylor, too, in his *English History, 1914-45* makes only a casual and passing reference to events in India in 1942. 'The failure of the negotiations with Cripps,' he remarks, 'thwarted Nehru's patriotism. He joined with Gandhi, and Congress proclaimed *passive disobedience* [my italics] against the British authorities. There were fresh disorders. *In September* [my italics] Gandhi and many other Congress leaders were again imprisoned, this time for the duration of the war.'[1] Here again it may be noted that 'passive disobedience' was not a term ever used in India for any of the various political movements of the last quarter of a century of British rule, even by the Congress itself. Nor, in fact, was the *Quit India* resolution intended to produce passivity. It should be added also that the arrests were made in the early part of August, and that by September the worst of the disorders had been tided over everywhere.

This post-war complacency was certainly not in evidence in war-time India, where the British correctly regarded the *Quit India* resolution and the widespread uprising that ensued as a grave menace both to the prosecution of the war and to the internal security and stability of the country. Quite apart from this, however, four aspects of the rebellion merit consideration; its purpose, its nature, its effect on the final British decision to leave India, and its mode of expression.

The precise purpose is difficult to gauge. If the *Quit India* resolution was intended only as a weapon for pressing the Government into further negotiations, the straightforward language of the concluding paragraphs did not suggest this; and the British could hardly have been expected to emulate the normal India approach to urgent problems, namely vacillation and lack of positive action. That the British would take preventive measures to forestall a mass movement was a certainty, and on the information at present with the public it is impossible to assess what the Congress hoped to gain. That a rebellion was doomed from the start has been admitted

[1]Clarendon Press, p. 545.

by Maulana Abul Kalam Azad, who was Congress President at the time and who was convinced that 'at this stage of the war the Government would not tolerate any mass movement', and would 'act swiftly and drastically'.[1] Nor was Pandit Jawaharlal Nehru's opinion different. 'It was a foolish and inopportune challenge,' he has written, 'for all the organised and armed force was on the other side, and in a greater measure, indeed, than at any previous time in history.'[2] Nevertheless, it was with this full knowledge of the certain British reaction that the Congress entered on a course which by the end of the year led to over 60,000 arrests, 26,000 detentions under the Defence of India Rules and an unknown number of casualties varying from the official figures of 940 fatal and 1630 non-fatal, to the popular estimate of 25,000 and Pandit Jawaharlal Nehru's figure of 10,000.[3] The precise number of casualties, however, is not of great consequence in my present context, since the really important fact is that, apart from the sabotage and material damage, these were the results of an upheaval which was admittedly a forlorn hope, foredoomed to failure and which could have been avoided.

As was inevitable in a mass movement of this kind the measures taken to deal with it led to excessive action in some cases, but in fairness two points should be made clear. First the administration had broken down temporarily in a few areas, and its speedy restoration was essential; and secondly, the policy of the Government as distinct from that of some local authorities was definitely preventive and not punitive. This was specifically stated in the factual and studiously moderate speeches of the Home Member, Sir Reginald Maxwell. The remarkable fact that the Central Assembly was permitted to discuss the situation more than once, with the generation

[1] *India Wins Freedom*, p. 76. 'I was convinced that in this critical stage of the war, the Government would not tolerate any mass movement. It was a question of life and death for the British. They would, therefore, act swiftly and drastically.'
[2] *The Discovery of India*, p. 592.
[3] The official figure of the number of times on which there was firing was 538; but certainly not everything was reported. The average number of deaths in Meerut District was five per firing, and on this basis the All-India figure would be less than 3000. There were, however, many areas far more disturbed than Meerut, and where the mobs were larger. In any case official figures would not take into account unreported deaths from military action, or the five occasions when aircraft were used for the dispersal of mobs engaged in sabotage, or such items as '200 rebels shot'.
My own rough estimate would be around 8000.

of much heat, not only emphasised the point, but was also proof that even at so critical a time the Government was liberal enough not to deny the fundamental rights of freedom of speech and criticism—for which credit has never been given by Indians.[1] In many instances of alleged excessive action enquiries were ordered, and I personally know of a case where an English Police Officer was compelled to pay monetary compensation from his own pocket to an innocent man whose house had been burnt down. I would not hesitate to say that throughout my service in the I.C.S. of the British régime the general discipline and efficiency of the magistracy and police were maintained at a far higher level than was to be the case after independence; and now that the British Empire has passed into history the fact should be honestly admitted. Situated as they were in 1942, the British could not have been expected to behave with the delicacy and self-effacement of the woodland violet. Indeed, their reactions to the rebellion might have been far more drastic, as India's Russian friends were to demonstrate later in Hungary, with less cause and without any conspicuous protest from the Indian Government.

Even the war-effort was not actually broken. It was temporarily dislocated in a few areas through the sabotage of rail communications, but no more; and recruitment to the Armed Forces continued unabated. In a communication to the Government of India the Chief Secretary of the United Provinces was soon to report that 'the villager never took much interest in the war, and at the moment is probably wondering what to do with his money. The war is not a thing about which the ordinary man need worry. The countryman would like it to last. The townsman would like it to end; but there is nothing much that either can do about it.'[2] Nevertheless, interest or not, there was never any dearth of recruits either

---

[1]The situation was debated more than once in the Central Assembly, the longest debate being from February 12th to 18th 1942.

'It has already been made clear in the Government communiqué of August 8th that the purpose of the Government is preventive rather than punitive, and that is the principle that has governed and will govern action.'—The Home Member in the Assembly on September 15th 1942.

'Government do not suggest that there may not have been cases when in a serious disturbance as this, there may not have been some excessive force or that innocent persons may not have suffered.'—Sir Sultan Ahmad, Law Member, on 24th September 1942.

[2]Report for April 1943.

for the commissioned or other ranks or for the ancillary services. At one Selection Board of which I was a member shortly before August 1942 no less than forty seven candidates appeared from the Meerut Division alone for emergency commissions, despite Congress propaganda over a long period, while surprising though it may seem, with the rebellion at its height the District supplied 1104 other ranks in August and 876 in September. Even after an upheaval which one would have thought would have had the opposite effect the rush continued. So much so that six months later the Provincial C.I.D. commented on the 'considerable rush to secure some employment, preferably safe, which will count as war service and qualify for jobs after the war.' To anyone unacquainted with the endless paradoxes India can produce out of its hat at any time, it might appear incongruous that many of our Meerut recruits came forward from places where their friends and relations were earnestly engaged in attempted sabotage!

As to its nature, the rebellion seems to me in retrospect to have been essentially a negative movement. For a variety of reasons it could not be classed as a national uprising in the true sense of the term. The civil and military services did not join it, though in doing their official duty Indians were placed in a difficult and unhappy position. On the other hand, the Congress attitude to them was ambivalent, for, since the Indianization of the services had been one of the main demands from 1885 onwards, it was paradoxical to go back on it after it had largely been achieved and to attack government servants for being where they were. The Muslims, too, as a community, remained passive spectators. For this reason, if for no other, the movement was embedded neither in a common national memory nor in a common desire to achieve new ends together, the final objectives of Hindus and Muslims being different.[1] Its basic racial memories were Hindu, the legacy of a distant, though over-glorified past, and were soon proved to have been regional, linguistic and rooted in caste. On a detached, unromantic assessment, it could, I think, be

[1]'Ce qui fait que les hommes forment un peuple? C'est le souvenir des grandes choses qu'ils ont faites ensemble et la volunté d'en accomplir des nouvelles.' —Renan, quoted by C. Delisle Burns in *Political Ideals* (Humphrey Milford, Oxford University Press, 1917), p. 178.

classified as an All-India, anti-British, non-Muslim movement with two nebulous and ill-considered aims: one negative, the prevention of the war-effort, and the other, the immediate transfer of full power by the British to one political party at the most critical period of the war, positive but admittedly unattainable.

This, of course, is an unorthodox view; for in general a great deal of glamour is now attached to the rebellion as being the main, if not the only, factor in the grant of independence. 'Thanks to two decades of training in non-violence under Gandhiji,' wrote Pyarelal recently, 'which opened up before us a new dimension of action when a granite wall stared us in the face, *independence came to us five years later as a result of the Quit India movement*'[1] (my italics). This, a common view, is often expressed even more emphatically by Indian members and ex-members of the former I.C.S. Writing of his memories of the Service one of the latter has referred to '*the year of grace 1947 when the mighty British Empire crumbled before the assaults of the Indian National Congress*'[2] (my italics). I was present, too, when an official, now very senior and in a responsible position, but with only four years service in 1942, recently affirmed very strongly that in his opinion 'the English were booted out of India'; and he genuinely regarded any other ideas as not only unhistorical and unpatriotic, but also, quaintly enough, as savouring of a dash of the C.I.A!

Such statements twenty five years after the event are seriously made and sincerely believed in, and if I venture to hazard a different view, it is not with any idea of forestalling the detached verdict of history nor as an attempt at refutation, but merely as an indication of how differently the same events can be interpreted when seen through another pair of spectacles, albeit also Indian.

The rebellion and the grant of independence should not, in the first place, be isolated from the general international position at the end of the war, to be treated in a vacuum. In Great Britain itself idealism combined with realism to produce an entirely new outlook. War weariness; the desire to rebuild a

---

[1]Article in *The Times of India* of August 6th 1967. The writer had been Mahatma Gandhi's Private Secretary for many years.
[2]C. C. Desai in *The Civil Servant in India*, p. 80.

country shattered by a long, savage war; the realisation that an empire, the outward appearance of which had been solid, but which had not been able to retain the loyalty of its subjects, was not worth the effort to retain by force; the earnest desire to redeem war time promises; were all inextricably interwoven. To which must be added two other influential factors, the sympathy of the U.S.A. and the changed attitude of the Indian Armed Forces. The continued loyalty of the latter which along with 'the firmness of the Viceroy stood between the country and anarchy'[1] in 1942 could no longer be taken for granted, as the mutinies of naval units and growing discontent in the Army and Air Force plainly indicated.[2] Had the British at the end of the war provoked an armed uprising of the two million men under arms together with another Civil Disobedience campaign in the countryside, and then made a vain attempt to suppress both, the theory of the crumbling of the Empire and of its eviction would hold good. But, as the facts stand, there is no sound reason why due credit should not be given to the British Government and the British people as a whole for recognising the winds of change for what they were before they became a hurricane, and for their political wisdom as well as for their liberalism, neither of which was in evidence in the case of the other two European empires in the East.

The rebellion should also be correlated with the campaigns which preceded it and which in the perspective of history may prove to have played a greater role in the events leading to freedom than is accorded to them at present; for it was the phenomenal success of the mass movements of the early and late twenties which killed the long-standing British axiom that the Congress stood apart from the masses. Certainly by 1939 the British in India were well aware of the Mahatma's almost hypnotic influence over the whole country, and it did not

[1]Sir Arthur Bryant, *The Turn of the Tide, 1939-43. A study based on the Diaries and Autobiographical Notes of Field-Marshal Viscount Alanbrooke* (Fontana Books, 1965).

[2]These mutinies were political and nationalist, and were of a very different nature from the quite numerous mutinies which took place in 1919 in many of the war-time units of the British Armies. In one of these a battalion of the Civil Service Rifles (a Territorial Regiment) chased their Colonel off the parade ground. But these were the direct result of delays in the demobilization of civilian armies, and of the unfair manner in which releases were carried out, men with little active service being 'demobbed' first, if considered essential for industry, while men with two and more years on the various fronts were held back.

require 1942 to drive the fact home. The rebellion, it is true, focussed immediate attention on India, widely discussed as it was in the House of Commons, in the British Press, in the U.S.A. and even in Chiang Kai-Shek's China;[1] but it did not bring to light anything the British did not know before. 'Make no mistake about it,' said Lord Linlithgow to Louis Fischer two or three months *before* the outbreak, 'the old man [Mahatma Gandhi] is the biggest thing in India. . . . Make no mistake. His influence is very great.'[2] And again: '. . . we are not going to remain in India. Of course, the Congress do not believe this, but we are not going to stay. We are preparing to leave.'[3] Sir Reginald Maxwell was even more explicit in his prescience when in the same month he prophesied to Louis Fischer: '. . . we shall be out of here two years after the end of the war.'[4]

Lower down in the hierarchy the position was similar. Early in 1941 I attended a recruiting meeting along with the Commissioner of the Division (my old friend the Senior Wrangler). The latter said to me before the gathering was under way, 'You can tell them that they'll get swaraj at the end of the war.' And when I demurred on the reasonable ground that we had no authority to say any such thing, his candid reply was, 'Well, we've promised it, and I don't see how we can get out of it.' Later, on August 22nd 1942, in the middle of the rebellion, I myself officially reported, 'There is not the least doubt that the movement will be entirely crushed, but its repercussions will continue. On the moderate Hindu side, and even among

---

[1] Copious extracts from the British Press and others have been given in *India Unreconciled*, pp. 56-74. While there was no sympathy at all for the actual rebellion there was general agreement on all sides, irrespective of political colour, that a 'constructive' policy was necessary (*The Times*, August 12th). The left-wing *Daily Herald* wrote on October 9th: 'the British Government's refusal to negotiate with Congress unless the civil disobedience campaign is abandoned has the support of public opinion in this country. But there is no public support for political paralysis.' *The News Chronicle* on August 13th suggested that 'there is no reason why leading members of the United Nations—the United States, Russia and China—should not be associated in some way with a settlement of Britain's pledge to India of full self-government after the war.' And the King's Speech proroguing Parliament on November 10th reiterated the pledge of full freedom and independence within the British Commonwealth immediately after the termination of hostilities. But Sir George Schuster, a former member of the Viceroy's Executive Council undoubtedly hit the nail on the head from the Indian angle in a letter to *The Times* of October 14th in which he put the question plainly: 'Have we given a right and inspiring leadership in the war?'

[2] Louis Fischer, *The Life of Mahatma Gandhi* (Jonathan Cape, 1951), p. 394.
[3] Ibid.
[4] Ibid.

kherkhuas (loyalists) there is much sympathy for the Congress, although they by no means sympathize with the methods, and a general feeling that the country has not been treated fairly in the past. What is more important, however, is the general feeling that it never will be justly treated. What is even more surprising is that a local Muslim League leader told me very recently that, though the Muslims would keep aloof, they, too, had a sneaking sympathy for the Congress. Other Muslims, not of the League, have said much the same thing. I think these feelings are of importance for the future.' In his own comments in his forwarding report, the Commissioner's view was: 'I should say that a large proportion of the people have lost sight of Japan. They look on these disturbances as *the third round* [my italics] of a long duel between the Congress and the British Government. They may not approve of the methods, but they certainly do not like the Government well enough to regard its difficulties with dissatisfaction.'[1] The reference to the 'third round' emphasises by implication the significance of the two earlier movements; and taking the evidence as a whole it seems to me to add up to the fact that the rebellion was by no means as crucial an element in the ushering in of August 15th 1947 as contemporary propaganda would suggest.

Considered as a widespread, mass experiment in non-violence the rebellion gave clear proof only of the ease and rapidity with which the 'new dimension of action' could slide into violent disorder. There had been examples of this in the previous campaigns, but in 1942 another most important fact was brought into prominence. The large scale campaign of organised sabotage of all kinds and the great destruction of property showed that special cadres of Congressmen had trained themselves and others in these techniques. In his article to which reference has been made, Pyarelal, however, has taken a very different view. 'Misled by B.B.C. broadcasts,' he claims, 'which poured into credulous ears what were given out as Congress instructions, quite a number of youths resorted to a campaign of sabotage. In Midnapore District of Bengal and

---

[1]Commissioner, Meerut Division, to the U.P. Government, August 25th 1942. Although it did not occur to me at the time, this was another example of the British characteristic of not resenting honest reports from their Indian officers. Indeed, considering the time at which my report to the Commissioner was written, it was an outstanding example.

in parts of Maharashtra parallel administrations were set up lasting for months. The bulk of the masses remained non-violent, and *on the whole care was taken to avoid injury to persons*'[2] (my italics).

One may leave aside the bizarre notion that the B.B.C. of all organisations set out to sabotage India's war effort, the question whether parallel administrations anywhere lasted for months—in east U.P. they certainly did not, and it is very doubtful if there were any administrations at all in view of the widespread looting that occurred—and the equally intriguing statement that the students received guidance by assiduously tuning in to London. In regard to this last my information for my own District was that city and town students greatly preferred Berlin and Tokyo to the B.B.C., while in the rural areas the number of receiving sets was negligible and of no importance from the standpoint of propaganda. But all this apart, it must be said that a magistrate involved in the situation on the spot was presented with a far more murky picture. Even if allowance is made for the possibility of the non-violent wood being obscured by the shaking of the large number of violent trees, violent disorder was everywhere conspicuous. There were 49 fatal casualties among the police and 1363 non-fatal, the corresponding figures for military personnel being 14 and 70. The free use of crude bombs was the cause of severe, sometimes fatal, injuries to innocent persons, and there were miscellaneous cases of men being tortured for not joining in the rebellion. In Monghyr District in Bihar, for example, rioters captured several men who had refused to go along with them. Three of the victims had an eye each dug out by a spear; the eye of a fourth was burnt out; the fingers of four were cut off, and five were branded. Damage to, and destruction of, government buildings and installations were on an impressive scale. The figures up to the end of 1942 presented in the Central Legislative Assembly were: Police Stations destroyed or severely damaged, 192; other government buildings, 494; Railway Stations, 318; tracks sabotaged, 102; rolling stock, 254; Post and Telegraph offices, 309; sabotage of cables, 11,285 cases. These figures do not include such items as cut and/or stolen signal wires and

[1] Article in *The Times of India* dated August 6th 1967.

damage to canal banks. In my own District at least, it was impossible to keep pace with and tabulate such cases.[1]

The application, however, by the masses, of such highly metaphysical abstractions as *satyagraha* and *ahimsa* must automatically produce eventual violence. If, for example, an organised crowd marches in a solid block to take possession of a government office, the magistracy and police can either surrender peacefully or carry out their protective duties—which, in fact, is the only proper course open to them. This being so, the irresistible force comes up against the immoveable mass with violence inevitable. In the same way moral persuasion will not succeed in collecting land revenue from villages which have been educated into the pleasant belief that payment is either immoral or unpatriotic or both; and Caesars everywhere, irrespective of their political colour, are obviously justified in garnering their legal dues. When Pyarelal's 'dimension of action' is further expanded by the authorised inclusion of the sabotage of communications, bridges, railways and the like, its only apparent intention in the possibly jaundiced eyes of a magistrate is to provoke the official side into defensive action with the object of throwing the blame on to it for any trouble that may ensue.

Twenty five years later a knowledgeable commentator observed that 'everyone knows today, though few would admit it openly, that our non-violence was far from that of the strong. It was far more an expedient than a principle. We used it against the British ruler against whom we just could not fight otherwise. And the violence that erupted now and then—which was duly disowned by Mahatma Gandhi—showed up the fact that we were not after all as strong as we imagined.'[2]

Essentially correct though this statement is, the country continues to be inoculated with other beliefs, so that *satyagraha* and *ahimsa* have been elevated into the most moral as well as effective form of political pressure, for use at all times. That the Indian reaction to the concept of non-violence is wholly ambivalent is never noticed, or if it is, it is passed over, and

[1]Corresponding figures for the United Provinces were:
Railway stations, 104; Other government buildings, 250; Derailments, 16; Sabotage of tracks, 15 cases; Sabotage of Telephones etc., 400; Bomb Explosions, 65.
[2]'Mihira' in *The Financial Express*, August 19th, 1967.

non-violence and political murder, though the one is the antithesis of the other, are both eulogised at one and the same time. The number of political murders in India probably never reached the commanding heights of those in Ireland, but there were several from 1900 onwards. In the nineteen-twenties alone three District Magistrates of Midnapore District in Bengal were assassinated in quick succession, while shortly afterwards on the other side of India in the Punjab a young English Assistant Superintendent of Police was murdered by Bhagat Singh, who followed this up with the throwing of a bomb into the Legislative Assembly. One of the most astonishing examples of inconsistency is provided by the recent case of the Government of India itself. In the first week of October 1968 the Gandhi centenary was celebrated with the usual tributes, official as well as non-official, to the apostle of non-violence, and with the customary meed of praise for the country as a whole for its devotion to this principle. Almost simultaneously the Postal Department announced the issue of a special stamp to commemorate the 'martyrdom' of Bhagat Singh. While it must be conceded that political murders of this type were motivated by patriotism and the desire to free the country from foreign rule, India must be the only country to glorify *ahimsa* and political assassination at one and the same time.

The consequences, therefore, of the doctrines of Truth and non-violence being stretched far beyond the immediate political object of their inventor have already proved to be dangerous in independent India, and may yet turn out to be a calamity; for violence masquerading as saintly non-violence can be a dangerous weapon in the hands of ambitious men seeking to exploit the discontents of an inflammable democracy consisting of several hundred millions of have-nots. If, as is the consistent theme of contemporary propaganda, so powerful a Raj as the British could succumb to the non-violence of the *Quit India* movement, the only probable lesson which the Mahatma succeeded in driving home was that there is nothing impossible of achievement by the same means in the face of indigenous regimes compounded of weakness, vacillation, lack of true national purpose, and an apparently ineradicable aversion from positive action in any sphere of government.

One last thought—a sobering one—will be a fitting end to these random reflections. It was not so much the British who suppressed the rebellion as Indians themselves on behalf of the former. Indian troops were largely used in dealing with it. Some of the higher magistracy and police were Indians and the subordinate executive and police were wholly Indian. How the historian or social psychologist will deal with this phenomenon I do not know; but I can say with confidence that, were he here now, Aristophanes would have a wonderful time once more at the expense of all of us, including the Congress itself.

XII

The Shape of Things to Come

IN MARCH 1944, when I had completed four years in Meerut, I received orders to proceed to Lucknow to take charge of the vacant post of Secretary, Local Self-Government, Medical and Public Health Departments. The prospect of a spell in the Secretariat had no charms for me, but I had no option in the matter. A mild bleat from my side elicited an equally polite riposte from the Chief Secretary to the effect that His Excellency the Governor could think of no one more fitted for the post, and—here was the sting in the tail—would I now make it convenient to take over charge without further correspondence? I made it so accordingly; for the time had yet to arrive for officials high and low to have unpleasant orders cancelled by the simple process of canvassing support from a friendly Minister or prominent local politician who would testify to the particular individual's absolute indispensability in the post he happened to be holding at the time. In the post-independence era this has become an accepted convention in all branches of the Administration, so much so, indeed, that in the Foreign Service positions have remained unfilled for many months just at the time when the presence of an ambassador has been essential.

At this period the United Provinces consisted of forty-nine Districts, each with its own elected District Board. In addition City and Municipal Boards numbered well over one hundred, and for the smaller townships with populations between ten and five thousand there were councils designated Notified and Town Areas. The District, City and Municipal Boards possessed wide powers of taxation and covered a wide area of administration, including education, and in the municipalities, public health. Long experience as a District Officer had given me considerable knowledge of the inner working of local bodies, their special characteristics, their communal antipathies, caste influences and party factions. All of which was of great value to me as Secretary of the Department, and often simplified the work at the top level.

It was Lord Bryce, I think, who once said that the essence of modern democracy lay in Local Self-Government. In India the foundations had been laid in 1884 during the viceroyalty of Lord Ripon, but the original structure raised on them had undergone many changes before my term as Secretary sixty years later. The controls once exercised by the District Officer and the Commissioner had gradually been whittled down with the passage of time, and even the guiding hand of these two officials, if used at all, had to be applied with gentle care and tact. Ever since the Government of India Act of 1919, local self-government in the Provinces had been the responsibility of elected Ministers responsible to the Legislatures, and the general feeling, official as well as non-official, was that there should be as little interference as possible with the growth and working of democracy at the grass-roots. Consequently the Government took action by way of supersession of a Board only in cases of gross maladministration or bankruptcy. Here was the people's training ground in the art of self-government, and even official guidance and control were kept to the minimum since they were liable to misinterpretation, and were always greatly resented by the vocal section of the literate public as being a thinly veiled method of using local institutions for official, and therefore non-democratic and anti-national, ends.

With Independence, the efficiency and integrity of the Boards, far from improving, have steadily deteriorated. Even in the five largest cities of contemporary Uttar Pradesh where the former City Boards have been converted into Corporations, with the complete panoply of Mayors (with robes to match the title), Aldermen and Corporators, standards which were always low have descended even lower. The blame for the vagaries of the elected representatives of the people at the roots of democracy, and for their constant deviations from the path of administrative rectitude, was inevitably, but falsely laid by the nationalist politician on the shoulders of the British— which in effect narrowed down to the I.C.S. About the time that I entered the Service Pandit Jawaharlal Nehru was serving his administrative apprenticeship as Chairman of the Allahabad Municipal Board. In his Autobiography he has devoted a chapter to the development of local self-government, and as the first Prime Minister of the future independent India his remarks are of more than academic interest. In general he did not find the Boards to be corrupt. 'They are,' he observed, 'just inefficient, and their weak point is nepotism, and their perspectives are all wrong. All this is natural enough; for democracy to be successful must have a background of informed public opinion and a sense of responsibility. Instead, we have an all-pervading atmosphere of authoritarianism, and the accompaniments of democracy are lacking. . . . Inevitably public attention turns to personal or communal or other petty issues.'[1]

My personal experience, covering a large number of local bodies in various Districts, entirely bore out Pandit Jawharlal Nehru's estimate of the general nepotism and inefficiency, but not of the lack of corruption. Corruption was common, although it was not so wholesale and widespread as it was to become later. There was no local activity in which an unscrupulous member could not make money, and the Taxation, Public Health, Public Works and Education Sub-Committees in particular presented members with wide opportunities for graft. In one U.P. city, for example, with a large meat-eating population, the Slaughter House with its licence fees was worth in 1930, I was told on unimpeachable authority, Rs. 10,000 a year to the member in charge. And this was only one example out of many.

The remedies proposed by Pandit Jawaharlal Nehru for this sorry state of affairs were two. First, it was essential for the whole system to be made democratic; and secondly the right men should be given the opportunity of being elected to local bodies and thus control them solely in the public interest. 'The Government has made every effort,' he wrote, 'even to the extent of passing laws, to keep out these people. It prefers and pushes on the lap-dog breed, and then complains of the inefficiency of our local bodies.' And the right type in Pandit Jawaharlal Nehru's judgement could only be Congressmen, because 'during the last fifteen years Congress workers. . . have shouldered heavy responsibilities. . . . This hard course of training has given them self-reliance and efficiency and strength to persevere; it has provided them with the very qualities of which a long and emasculating course of authoritarian government had deprived the Indian people. . . . But I have no

---

[1] *Autobiography* (John Lane, 1936), p. 145.

15

doubt whatever that an average Congress worker is likely to be far more efficient and dynamic than another person of similar qualifications.'[1] It was on this assessment of the régimes preceding the British and of the qualities inherent in the Indian character, with particular reference to the special virtues of Congressmen, that independent India was soon to be built.

I spent eighteen months in the Secretariat before receiving my promotion as Commissioner of the Benares Division, where I remained until July 1946. Benares City, or Varanasi as it now is, needs no description here. A *must* for every foreign tourist, it has been painted in colour, etched in black and white, and depicted in vivid words on innumerable occasions. The most venerable and important of the citadels of the Hindu faith, here religion is not merely centred in processions and festivals necessitating special arrangements for the preservation of the peace, but a daily matter. Benares lives round, in and to a large extent off, the waters of the sacred river which washes the steps of its eighty *ghats* and countless temples.

The Congress leaders had all been released from detention or prison before my arrival there, and in the cold weather of 1945-6 general elections were held throughout the country. As far as the Hindu-majority Provinces were concerned—which included the United Provinces—the results were a foregone conclusion. In the U.P. the Congress swept in everywhere with no opposition in the general constituencies, the Muslim League doing the same in the Muslim seats. On March 27th a Congress Ministry was formed under the leadership of Pandit Govind Ballabh Pant (Pantji to us all). Four members of this Cabinet were to join the Central Ministry at New Delhi within the next few years, Pantji himself, Rafi Ahmad Qidwai, Kailash Nath Katju and Hafiz Muhammad Ibrahim. Shrimati Vijaya Lakshmi Pandit was destined for a prominent role on the international stage, and of those lower down the political ladder at the time, Lal Bahadur Shastri was to be a future Prime Minister of India. The U.P. Cabinet thus consisted almost wholly of Congress leaders who were in the front rank of the Party, and whose influence and status covered the whole country. When to this galaxy of stars was added Pandit Jawaharlal Nehru himself, who belonged to the U.P. by adoption, though his

[1] Ibid., p. 146.

heart may still perhaps have been in Kashmir, it was not surprising that the Province shone brilliantly in the Indian firmament just at the time when the air was thick with rumours of an impending settlement with the British.

A few months after the formation of the new Government I was selected for the post of Chief Secretary. This was the only post in the Secretariat which I had ever coveted; for up to that time the Chief Secretary had always been a key man, the administrative head of all the Services, the right-hand man of the Government who was expected to know everything that was afoot everywhere, and whose advice previous Governments had been accustomed to treat with respect. This, however, was not to remain the case for long. Times were changing very rapidly, and the Chief Secretary was soon to become only one of many Secretaries to the Government, including for political reasons the private and parliamentary secretaries of Ministers who managed to obtain for themselves extensive, though un-written and unofficial, powers. My pleasure, therefore, at my elevation rapidly began to wear thin as month by month I found that the change in Government was accompanied by a complete change in the whole approach to administrative principles and practice. What I had taken for granted to be the foundation of sound administration was now not merely to be questioned but to be cast aside as unsuitable for the new India which was clearly at hand. Both the basis and the superstructure of the Administration were now to undergo a rapid and complete metamorphosis.

'The British political system,' it has been said, 'is remarkable among the democracies for the strongly hierarchical traits which it has succeeded in keeping; for the Administrative Class in the Civil Service, representing as it does an aristocracy of talent, has hitherto retained its pre-eminent position under govern-ments of all colours. To this extent the British system allows place for the idea that government is a special and rare skill, and that along with other special skills this one must be culti-vated and fostered in the national interest. In other words British democracy has been as successful as it has been largely because it succeeded in being so undemocratic.'[1]

---

[1] Prof. Max Beloff in *Encounter*, June 1954, p. 56, in the third of a series of articles entitled *Democracy and its Discontents*.

This fundamental British theory of administration I had unconsciously absorbed long before it had been formulated in so precise a fashion. In so far as India was concerned, it was not that I did not realize the need for changes in the structure of all the Services, including the residual I.C.S., for it was obvious that the old type of administration had to be attuned to new conditions. My ideal, however, would have been a strictly non-political Service, firmly rooted in the integrity, efficiency and sense of public duty of the former I.C.S. This Service would have been bound together by the code of public and personal conduct handed down by the British, a Service in which the individual would have been subordinated to the whole, un-amenable to political pressures and seeking neither political patronage nor, through it, special favours.[1] In my imaginary Service, recommendations based on private and personal consid-erations would have been at a discount. In addition, it was essential that neither the Government nor the heads of the Service should overlook the prime importance of the District as the basic unit of administration.

There were general points, too, which appeared to me to be necessary for the new type of administrative establishment. First, if the Indian residue of the old I.C.S. together with the new Service under creation were to be debarred from taking part in politics and political faction, it was equally basic that all political parties, including the Congress Party organization, should be prevented from interference in the routine of adminis-tration. To this end it would have been necessary for a firm and unbreakable line to be drawn between the duties of the District Officer and the local District Administration in general and the powers and functions of individual politicians and political cadres. Secondly, the District Officer must remain the chief representative of the Government within his jursdiction, irrespective of the particular Government's political colour. His function and that of other local heads of Government Depart-ments should be only the implementation of the Government's policy. Provided this was the case, the Government ought to protect its administrative representatives from political attacks.

---

[1] 'Civil servants are rightly forbidden to take any part in Party politics.' Viscount Norwich, *Old Men Forget* (Rupert Hart-Davies, 1953), p. 106.

Thirdly, it should be impressed on all political cadres that policy and execution should be kept distinct as two different aspects of government. As long as the Government's official policy was being carried out no interference whatsoever with local officials should be permitted, on pain of disciplinary action at the hands of the Party organization, since the correct place for attacking policy as such was the Legislature. Lastly, only if local officials failed in their duty of implementing official policy should complaints from local politicians be entertained by the Government, and in all cases such complaints should be founded on facts and figures.

I jotted down a few notes and headings of this kind for my private use, to be considered in greater detail at leisure, but the rapid march of events in the opposite direction soon proved that my ideas were either anachronistic or utopian. In either case they were quite out of line with both political and Service attitudes. Nevertheless, although I myself gave up the idea of formulating any scheme for the consideration of the Government, it was clear that there was need for some principles, not necessarily precisely the same as mine, to be laid down. In the early months of 1947 the Under-Secretary of State for India came out to wind up the I.C.S., and men were now being recruited for the new Service which would finally replace it, the Indian Administrative Service. Some guide lines were necessary, some administrative and Service ethos should have been formulated, so that India's masses would have been made aware of the administrative road on which they were soon to travel.

The need for a sound foundation for the new administrative set-up was emphasized by the conditions of the time. For the whole of my tenure as Chief Secretary the political and communal situations continued to deteriorate day by day, and the general instability was enhanced by extraneous factors. Discontent in the Armed Forces was reflected in serious mutinies in naval units. The glare of dramatic publicity which the higher military authorities ineptly turned onto the trial of the leaders of Subhas Chandra Bose's Indian National Army had the opposite effect of what had optimistically and rashly been expected, for it put into the background the great achievements of the true Indian Army, and converted the Indian National

Army into a band of heroes and martyrs in the national cause.[1]
Public emotions—always inflammable in India—were rapidly
aroused, and public enthusiasm mounted as the trials in the
Red Fort at Delhi proceeded. In the United Provinces the
released leaders toured the Districts and were greeted everywhere with great acclamation. So widespread, indeed, was
their influence that a Parliamentary Secretary emphatically
declared at a departmental meeting that 'what the country
needed was more young men with *the missionary spirit of the I.N.A.*'
(my italics). Side by side with ever-growing political and
communal tensions went industrial discontent, which was
openly fostered by political parties of all shades of opinion
and by ambitious individuals seeking to obtain control over
an assorted collection of mushroom Labour Unions. The
student community too, which for two decades had been
eulogized as the 'backbone of the country and its future leaders',
was naturally not slow to join in any movement that was afoot,
or to create a movement where there was none before. Cinemas,
shops, bus drivers, and, of course, police stations were all targets
for their energies, and in almost all Districts students engaged
themselves in activities not usually considered to be a part of
higher education.

In the circumstances a policy of hastening slowly in the
abandonment of the old traditions and the reconstruction of the
Administration on new lines would have been advisable; but
at the same time it must be admitted that both Congress and
Service opinion as a whole favoured rapid and fundamental
changes. Among other reasons for this was the fact that leading
Congressmen, nurtured on the pure milk at least of the theory
of non-violence, appeared to hold the sincere belief that the
violence of the time would automatically die out completely
with the full transfer of power by the British. In the United
Provinces they were certainly pained when the weapon used
against the British was turned against themselves. In this
stage of blissful political and administrative ignorance the
first step to be taken for the democratization of the Administra-

[1] The same view is expressed in *An Advanced History of India* by R. C.
Majumdar, H. C. Raychauduri and K. Datta, p. 992. 'This was a highly
impolitic step on the part of the Government, as it gave the Indian people a
complete picture of an organization of which they had hitherto known very little.
A wave of enthusiasm swept the country.'

tion in accordance with Pandit Jawaharlal Nehru's well-known philosophy was the grant, undefined and all the more dangerous for that reason, of extensive authority to members of the Legislature and politicians all the way down the ladder to the basic cadres with their roots in the villages.

Although the intention may have been to bring District Officers and others into closer touch with the political representatives of the Government at all levels, it unfortunately misfired, the only result being constant, and often even illegal, interference in the daily routine of administration. The handful of members of the Services who attempted to resist political pressures became the targets of bitter criticism and hostility as the alleged servile instruments of British imperialism. So harmful were the immediate consequences that I was compelled to make a report to the Cabinet on the dangers of a too rapid erosion of the old values. My Report contained detailed examples from a large number of Districts. In many cases—far too many in my view for good administration—local Congressmen had taken the initiative in criminal offences, inflicting fines (in one instance in a case of reported rape), drawing up inquest reports contrary to the provisions of the law, and putting every kind of illegal pressure on the magistracy and the police. There was an illuminating case where a body of Congressmen seized a cart suspected of carrying illicit grain, and fined the cartmen, though what happened to the money collected remained a mystery. In another District the District Magistrate, under strong pressure from the local Congress Committee, had the house of one of his subordinate magistrates searched, the allegation being that the latter was in possession of illicit cloth. The information was found to be false, but despite the District Magistrate's asking for action to be taken against the complainants nothing was done. So far as I could see the general objective of Congress cadres in the Districts was to bring local administrations into disrepute, and simultaneously to impress on the mind of the villager that real administrative power rested with the local Congress Committees.

On the other hand, allegations of blatant corruption on the part of Congressmen were winked at in the highest quarters. The District Supply Committees, the ostensible object of which

was to assist District Officers in the equitable distribution of
controlled commodities, were now dominated by Congressmen
as the representatives of the people. Here again, though
based on Pandit Jawaharlal Nehru's view that the average
Congressman was far more dynamic and efficient than others,
the new arrangements were a lamentable failure; and very
unsavoury stories soon became current that the members of
these Committees were indulging in hoarding and blackmarket-
ing for their own and their relations' benefit. Many of these
cases were brought to the notice of the Cabinet, but I was
never able to persuade any Minister to take action against
a fellow Congressman. Indeed, the reverse was the case. One
Commissioner, an Englishman, was actually told to mind
his own business (I did not pass this instruction on to him!)
for reporting that during his tours in his Division he had been
inundated with complaints against Congressmen for these
and similar unvirtuous activities. In another case, a long,
signed petition was sent to me in which a detailed complaint
was made against a certain Parliamentary Secretary. Whether
the allegations were correct or not, I could not have said—
the making of false allegations or the inflation of true ones out
of proportion to their importance is common enough in India—
but the petitioner should certainly have been examined on
them. Instead, the Chief Minister's simple orders were that
he had 'the greatest regard' for the Parliamentary Secretary
in point, and that the petition 'should be passed on to him,
as he would be interested to see'. In fact, the process had
already commenced on the eve of Independence Day which was
to gather momentum year by year until its culmination in the
admission of the Congress President himself in 1963 that
'one of the reasons for the loss of [Congress] prestige was that
Congressmen who were paupers in the pre-independence era
had become millionaires, some of them owning many cinema
houses, huge properties, a fleet of cars and many transport lines'.[1]

[1]Shri D. Sanjivayya, President of the Congress, speaking at Indore on
August 1st, as reported in *The Times of India*.
    And five years later another President, Shri S. Nijalingappa, was reported
in the Press to have publicly said that 'amassing of wealth by some Congress
Ministers had tarnished the image of the party and contributed to its defeat in some
States. There were a few such cases in Mysore, but complaints were many in
other States and this was a matter of shame.'—Report in *The Times of India* of
June 29th 1968.

Pseudo-democratization touched all aspects and all levels of the Administration. Its application to the assignments given to magistrates and police officers at a time when the political, communal and industrial situations were rapidly and simultaneously deteriorating made for weakness and procrastination instead of the firm administration that was required. The old procedure was that proposals would be drawn up by the Chief Secretary on the basis of the known fitness of a particular official for a particular District. These would then be discussed with the Governor and a few selected members of the Government before the issue of final orders. This procedure could have been successfully adapted to new conditions by the substitution of a small Cabinet Committee in place of the Governor and his chosen colleagues. Instead, the former method was wholly abandoned in favour of the *open conference system*, with the Chief Secretary's secret draft postings being placed before, and openly discussed by, a kind of public *panchayat*. The Chief Minister, other Ministers, Members of the Legislature, Private Secretaries to the Ministers and Parliamentary Secretaries were usually present, and often smaller fry would drop in uninvited. It was open house. The proceedings throughout were pleasantly informal, friendly and not infrequently inconclusive; and inevitably the question of appointments became the subject of personal likes and dislikes and the source of canvassing. The administrative merits of officials ceased to be the criterion, and one Minister even went so far as to pass orders to me that no postings should be made to his home District without his specific consent. Even when it was explained to him that, if all Ministers were to pass similar orders, no postings could ever be made, it was doubtful whether he understood the position. The postings of key men to the Districts thus became shuttlecocks between a number of politicians motivated solely by their own personal idiosyncrasies. So much so that in some cases it became impossible to make appointments at all without considerable delay, and important and heavy Districts were left in the hands of junior and inexperienced staff at a critical time.

It finally became incumbent on me to bring to the notice of the Cabinet in a memorandum dated August 22nd that it was impossible for all the inhabitants of a particular District to

like all the officers sent to them all the time, and that the
Government could only make the best use of the material at
hand. The four proposals which I made seemed to me to
be reasonable at the time, although events were soon to show
that they were not feasible in the context of the new administrative ethos. The most important of the recommendations
was the first, that the practice of approving postings or transfers
for personal or political reasons at the request of political
leaders, big or small, should be abandoned. The second and
third followed as corollaries. The second was that members
of all Services should be forbidden on pain of disciplinary
action to approach Ministers either direct or through their
friends for special favours; and the third stressed what ought
to have been self-evident, the need for the absolute maintenance
of discipline in the Services: officers must obey orders and not
be under the impression that they could safely circumvent
instructions which might be unpalatable. I added, lastly,
that the incessant, indiscriminate and often quite unjustified
attacks on the magistracy and the police in sections of the
Press and from the platform were irretrievably damaging
the morale of the Administration as a whole. I suggested steps
for their prevention since 'the Government has now
to face the possibility of an administrative breakdown...and
we cannot expect the Police Force to give of their best if they
are attacked in this way. We may grant that the police need
great improvement, but as things are we have to work with
them.'

To members of the Services including the I.C.S., apart
from a few individuals, the new administrative concepts were not
as unpalatable as I had assumed they would be. With the
liquidation of the I.C.S. as a British Service clearly close at
hand, the residual few hundred Indians were automatically
released from the discipline, conventions and inhibitions of
what was essentially an exotic Service with an exotic code
of conduct. A few perhaps desired to retain something of this
imported administrative *dharma*, but I began to realize at this
time that the majority sought a definite break from the immediate past. Two decades of independence in the course of
which there have been numerous reports on the need for
what is called 'toning up the Administration', and even more

ministerial assurances that 'good, clean, efficient' administration is round the corner, have now merely proved that platitudinous theory does not necessarily go hand in hand with practice.

There were instances of I.C.S. officials demanding their own terms in a manner which would not have been contemplated, and certainly not tolerated, when the Service was a close-knit British organization. And in at least one case a wife took unto herself an official importance (combining it with importunity on behalf of her husband) which had never been in evidence hitherto, which was an administrative nuisance and with which I was temperamentally unfitted to cope, especially on the telephone. Two senior officers of Commissioner's rank refused to go to the Divisions to which they had been appointed, although the orders had been approved by the Cabinet, and a month of argument followed before they could be persuaded to do the Government the favour of accepting the postings. One of them, I might add, went one better by introducing an entirely novel principle into the former Service code of obeying orders. He wrote an indignant complaint to me that as he had not achieved either of the two Divisions he had wanted, '*this method of dealing with such matters is not conducive to the peace of mind of government servants or to administrative efficiency*' (my italics). Comment is unnecessary. Political patronage, too, now became the rule rather than the exception and dabbling in politics together with lobbying for special favours a pastime. Sometimes high provincial politicians were approached, but canvassing one's claims for posts in the Government of India was equally common. In particular the new Foreign Service which was under contemplation became a favourite goal for those with a *wanderlust* to see the world.

The formation of factions was a further result of the mixture of politics with the business of administration. Most Indians enjoy party faction and manoeuvring for power in whatever sphere of life they happen to be placed. Everywhere the game is played with zest, be it for election to the committee of a social or sporting club, for the selection of a hockey team, or for membership of the Managing Board of a school or college. Not infrequently such contests find their way into the Law Courts, with the added spice of legal writs and injunctions.

When one such powerful faction was formed in the Secretariat under the aegis of a senior I.C.S. officer with strong political affiliations, I was asked by the representative of a younger group to head a rival one, and was assured of some support. This proposition I turned down. Apart from having neither the time nor the inclination for such extraneous pursuits, I lacked all the qualities and attributes necessary for the working of a political party within a Civil Service, namely political skill, temperamental flexibility, an ability to oblige everyone indiscriminately and simultaneously, and above all the support of a powerful Minister. To be all things to all men was far beyond my capacity, and in such circumstances discretion seemed to me to be the important requirement—certainly more so than a pretence of valour!

Many other factors began to overshadow public duty at this time. Personal friendships, family relationships and caste affiliations have always held a particularly high place in Indian estimation, but the tendency to indulge them at the expense of official duty had been kept in the background as long as the I.C.S. remained a British Service. Now, however, the tides of change broke through the weakened barriers and with the passage of time became so powerful that even in a public generally in favour of the exercise of extraneous influence in administrative matters a good deal of criticism has been aroused.

The replacement of a sense of public duty by the superior claims of personal friendship was brought to my notice personally by the action of a senior Secretary to the Government when a very necessary bill for the Maintenance of Public Order was framed in my Department. Some members of the Congress Party itself were strongly opposed to the bill (it contained among other preventive methods, a provision for temporary detention without trial for a fixed period in certain circumstances), and among them was an old friend of the Secretary in point. Late one evening the latter dropped in at my house, and in the course of casual conversation informed me that the reason for his having been delayed so long in office was that he had spent the evening drawing up amendments to the Bill for the use of his friend, and the opposition. That he had been conscientiously working *against* the Government of which he was an important administrative unit had escaped his notice. Nor did he appear to think it at all out of place for the Chief Secretary to be working out measures for the maintenance of public peace and order, while a colleague a few doors down the corridor should busy himself—outside his own sphere of work—in drawing up amendments designed to nullify its maintenance. It was again impressed on me strongly that the new administrative tide was surging in very rapidly.

It was only natural that the effects of the changed attitudes at the top should be felt all the way down the administrative ladder. The work and discipline of the clerical staff deteriorated considerably, the process being accelerated by the habit of Ministers, their personal and Parliamentary Secretaries, listening sympathetically to sad tales from those who may have been unfortunate enough to have received reprimands or to the importunity of others who sought promotion out of turn. All rules were ignored on both sides, and general conditions soon became so lax that the Governor of the Province himself was constrained to issue several directives, which, however, were broken with impunity almost as soon as I had issued them. One such ran as follows:—'I have dozens of times drawn attention to the laxity prevailing in most departments of the Secretariat in not complying with rule 13 of the Rules of Executive Business. This is a particularly blatant example, and I think the Chief Secretary should see the file. If his repeated circularizing of the departments has proved useless—and it looks like it—then perhaps a lecture to Secretaries and Deputy Secretaries would help.' Since the case in point related to finance and was, therefore, of importance, it is of melancholy interest to note in retrospect that what was later to be termed 'financial indiscipline' had raised its head even before the complete transfer of power into Indian hands.

That the situation had gone far beyond the possibility of being remedied by a course of lectures from me was clear, but my failure at the time to appreciate the deeper reasons for the emergence of Indian administrative ethic led me in March 1947 to make a well-intentioned, though admittedly mistaken, and for that reason infructuous, attempt to emphasize the need for the preservation of all that was good, as I saw it, in the traditions and principles of the Indian Civil Service of the British. The outcome of my having been asked to commit my views to writing was a memorandum to the Cabinet which included the examples already mentioned and which purported to show how the democratization of the administration and the new methods were adversely affecting the machinery and working of government. The relevant portion for my purpose here was contained in the first and penultimate paragraphs. 'During the last six months,' I wrote, 'I have been watching with great apprehension the deterioration that has been going on not only in the quality of work of officers but also in general standards and morale. I have often brought this to the notice of the Cabinet in individual cases, but there have now been so many of these that *I view the future of the Administration with concern.* Officers are now so concerned with pushing their own interests, fighting for this or that job, looking after the interests of their friends and lobbying for support... that discipline and efficiency have been impaired. *The British régime may have been good, bad or indifferent, but its officers certainly worked better for it than they are working now.*' The penultimate paragraph once again stressed the importance of that favourite hobby-horse of mine, the District as the basic administrative unit, without the good administration of which, 'no scheme drawn up at headquarters can be successfully implemented, however well planned it may be on paper. The great importance of the District in these precarious days is not properly understood by officers, who in some cases have spent several years in the Secretariat.... Similarly it is not understood by M.L.A.'s, Congress Committees and others. Continual vilification of the magistracy and the police does not make a bad officer good, and it may well make a good officer bad.... Furthermore, in the case of the Police Force, it should be remembered that this consists of Indians, and if it is a defective Force, the fault lies in our own character.... I suggest it would be a good thing if the Hon'ble Premier were to call a meeting of Commissioners and senior Collectors and give them a short address on the necessity for maintaining reasonable standards in administration.'[1]

---

[1] This memorandum was 'Top Secret' and intended only for the Cabinet. It soon became public, however. Save for the mention of individual names, it was

As the next twenty years were conclusively to prove, such ideas were impractical in Indian conditions and were not in consonance with the objectives India had in view. All shades of opinion at the time, political, public and Service, certainly favoured a politically aligned Civil Service at all levels in which the official would be not so much the instrument of the Government as a cog in the machinery of the Congress Party organization. In looking back at the events of the period I think I was justified, as Chief Secretary, in bringing to the notice of the Cabinet the potential dangers, as I saw them to be, of the new policy; but I should have been wiser to have realized that even in the Services there were only a few instances where British ethos had seeped in deep enough not to welcome its reversal. In my own case Macaulay had certainly done his work too well, for at this time I did not realize that my desire for political emancipation coupled with a simultaneous expectation that British administrative practice would be retained was fundamentally a contradiction in terms. In the context of the general outlook, and in particular of the fact that Indian life in all its aspects is dominated specifically by caste, community and personal relationships and friendships, both could not exist together. Other factors, too, as I mentioned in my various notes to the Cabinet, had commenced to impinge on the Administration. Writing in 1963, another I.C.S. left-over noted that 'a new class amongst the I.C.S. sprang up. Instead of devoting their time and energy to the work entrusted to them, their sole aim was to please their Ministers.' And later the same writer frankly says: 'I can say without fear of contradiction that the Party in power, with some notable exceptions, assiduously worked to undermine the prestige of the Services in general and the I.C.S. in particular.... No opportunity was lost in depriving them of the powers they had enjoyed in the past. This had the natural consequence of decline and decay in their morale. I leave it for future historians to apportion the blame

---

reprinted in full in a Muslim daily, *Dawn*. Copious extracts have also been quoted by the late Lieut.-General Sir Francis Tuker in his *While Memory Serves*, pp. 254-5. An interesting sidelight on the fundamental differences between English and Indian attitudes to the business of administration is the fact that while General Tuker has given full and generous approval to the purport of the ideas contained in the memorandum, Indian reaction varied from strong to mild disapproval, but always disapproval.

for this tragedy, as between the Party in power and the Civil Service.'[1]

I have given this somewhat lengthy quotation not because I agree with all the views expressed in it. Much of the former power of the I.C.S. had of necessity to be reduced, but it was not this clipping of wings that was the cause of the decline in prestige and morale. It was the changed attitude of the residue of the Service to its former ethic, for within my own knowledge even where power and trust were reposed in it, both were often misused or abused. Owing to a certain lack of mental flexibility—to put it at its best—the basic contradiction which I have mentioned above took time to sink into my consciousness, but when it did I ceased to criticize free India's administrative *dharma*. Whether this is the best instrument for the creation of a twenteth century Welfare State—which is said to be the objective—for stable governance or for the wholly western political philosophy enshrined in the Constitution of 1950 is not relevant. The people of every country are entitled as of right to select for themselves the type of governmental and administrative apparatus which they consider best suited to their aptitudes and circumstances. To me, as I look back on two decades of independence, there does not appear to be any tragedy for the historians to consider nor any blame for them to apportion. A free people, with free institutions, makes its own Government. A freely elected Government makes its own Civil Services. And the Civil Services make their own image.

Incongruous though it may seem, many of the points raised in my memorandum of March 1947 to the Cabinet of the U.P. were endorsed almost verbatim by no less a person than Mahatma Gandhi himself, and I had actually forestalled him by several months. That conditions similár to those which I had described prevailed throughout India, with the natural local variations, was admitted by the Mahatma on 12th January 1948, only a fortnight or so before his assassination. Before entering upon his last fast as a final attempt to bring about a reconciliation between India and Pakistan, the Mahatma made a detailed statement in the course of which he referred at length to other matters such as corruption among Congress-

---

[1] C. N. Chandra in *The Civil Servant in India*, p. 300 and p. 301.

men and the general maladministration.[1] He referred in particular, to a letter received from 'an aged friend, no other
than Deshbhakta Konda Venkatappayya Garu', who had
complained bitterly of 'the moral degradation into which
men in Congress circles had fallen', and who, said Mahatma
Gandhi, continued with the words:

'In my province the conditions are very deplorable. The
taste for political power has turned their heads. Several of the
M.L.A.'s and M.L.C.'s are following the policy of make-hay-
while-the-sun-shines. *Making money by the use of influence, even
to the extent of obstructing the administration of justice in the criminal
courts presided over by magistrates. Even the district collectors
and the other revenue officials do not feel free in the discharge of
their duties on account of the frequent interference by the M.L.A.'s
and M.L.C.'s on behalf of their partisans. A strict and honest officer
cannot hold his position, for false reports are carried against him to
the ministers, who easily lend their ears to these unprincipled self-
seekers* [my italics].... The situation is growing intolerable
every day with the result that Congress as well as the Congress
Government have come into disrepute...the factions in the
Congress circles, the money-making activities of the M.L.A.'s
and M.L.C.'s, and the weakness of the Ministers have been
creating a rebellious spirit among the people at large. The people
have begun to say that the British Government was much
better, and they are even cursing the Congress.' The Mahatma's
comment on this letter was: 'Let the people of Andhra and the
other provinces measure the words of this self-sacrificing
servant of India. As he rightly observes, the corruption described by him is no monopoly of Andhra. He could only give
first hand evidence about Andhra. Let us beware.'

The Mahatma, indeed, had given a previous warning
to the leaders of the Congress which, though less detailed, was
equally pointed. Speaking at Bikram in Bihar on 21st May
1947, only a few weeks after the arrival in India of the last
of the Viceroys, he told his audience that he had heard from
various quarters that the Congress was now fast becoming
an organization of selfish power-seekers and job-hunters.

---

[1] The text of the statement is given in D. G. Tendulkar, *Mahatma, Life of
Mohandas Karamchand Gandhi* (Probstain 1954), vol. viii. The quotation is from
pp. 302-03. In his *Mahatma Gandhi, The Last Phase* Pyarelal gives a summary of
the text on pp. 675-76, vol. ii.

Instead of remaining the servants of the public it had become
its overlords and masters.... The Congress had won their
(the people's) confidence through years of service. If it betrayed
them, he was afraid they would fall a prey to the white-robed
goondas of society into whose hands all power would pass.[1]

Since no heed was paid to the warnings of the greatest
Indian of the age, it was only natural that similar ideas from
a civil official should miscarry—and in some circles even be
resented. What was surprising, however, was the fact that the
Mahatma himself appeared not only to have underrated the
strength of India's legacy from the ancient past but also to have
overrated the effects of British rule. Great Britain's effective
dominion of about a century and a quarter was only one of
the many stones cast by destiny into the 4,000-year-old pool
of India's history. Its first consequences, it is true, went deep,
though not wide, but with the passage of time they became
more and more superficial as the ripples and circles spread
outwards. While as Chief Secretary I did not fully comprehend
this process, it was daily brought home to me that I was not
a suitable incumbent for the post in a fast-moving situation
which was evolving in a manner which seemed to me to be
against both the canons of good administration and the true
interests of India. I mentioned this aspect of the case tentatively
to Pantji, and one evening he and Rafi Ahmad Qidwai came
over in person to my house to discuss the matter. They caught
me with my evening whisky and soda, but generously turned
a blind eye to this mild deviation from the strict Congress
path of rectitude. I was very surprised, indeed touched, when
they asked me to continue in the post, and requested my wife
to use her good offices to this end! At the time, however,
I wanted a few months' leave to take my son to England for the
completion of his education, and I felt that while I was there it
would be possible for me to think over the matter in a more
restful atmosphere than the overheated conditions of India
permitted. Towards the end of April I sailed for London and
during my leave I came to the conclusion that I would be more
useful to the Government as Commissioner of a Division in
the time of troubles now ominously close. It was with
real regret that I wrote to inform the Government of my

[1] Tendulkar, vol. vii, p. 472.

decision, for Pantji had always treated me with consideration, despite the wide divergence between our respective approaches to, and opinions on, the business of administration. In the circumstances, however, it would have been improper for me to have remained the Government's chief adviser on administrative and service matters, and it would have been equally unfair on the many old Service colleagues of mine who also differed radically from me in their attitude to these subjects.

Thus, in just under one brief but exciting year, ended my direct contact and work with the second Congress Ministry of the United Provinces.

XIII

Last Experiences

AUGUST 15th opened up a new horizon for India, despite the turmoil, the bloodshed and the uprooting of fifteen million people from their ancestral homes which were its accompaniment. To the townsmen of all classes and to the country people in their villages, where many years of assiduous propaganda against the alleged evils of the British Raj had produced the desired results, the sun was rising on a new and free India, suffusing the future with the roseate hue of unformulated hopes. The vividly glowing words of Pandit Jawaharlal Nehru's speeches and writings were heard and read everywhere with a surprisingly uncritical enthusiasm. Supplanting all else, their effects were to last, though not entirely undimmed, for many years.

'Long years ago,' he told the Constituent Assembly on August 14th, 'we made a tryst with destiny, and now the time comes when we shall redeem our pledge, not wholly or in full measure, but very substantially. At the stroke of the midnight hour when the world sleeps, India will awaken to life and freedom. A moment comes, which comes but rarely in history, when we step out from the old to the new, when an age ends and when the soul of a nation, long suppressed, finds utterance. It is fitting that at this solemn moment we take the pledge of dedication to the service of India and her people, and to the still larger cause of humanity.' One day later the grandeur of the Prime Minister's vision and the wide range of his ideals again shone in his message to the Press on the inauguration of Independence: 'The appointed day has come, the day appointed by destiny, and India stands forth again after long slumber and struggle, awake, vital, free and independent. The past clings on to us still in some measure and we have to do much before we redeem the pledges we have so often taken. Yet the turning point is past, history begins anew for us, the history we shall live and act and others will write about. It is a fateful moment for us in India, for all Asia and for the world. A new star rises, the star of freedom in the East, a new hope comes into being, a vision long cherished materializes. May the star never set and that hope never be betrayed!'[1]

Although as a result of my experiences as Chief Secretary only a short time before, my own expectations did not rise to such heights, there can be no doubt that the Prime Minister's views were an eloquent expression of the general outlook of the intelligentsia. The new India of Mahatma Gandhi, went the theme in a variety of different words, was to be a spiritual example to the world after her long 'slavery' under the British, a beacon light for all, a model both for the decadent West and for all new nations rising from the ashes of western colonialism. The peoples of the West, too, at least those who had been at the business end of modern warfare, were by now weary of strife, wholesale destruction and genocide in gas-chambers, and were quite ready to take India at Pandit Jawaharlal Nehru's valuation. This kind of divine afflatus was again in evidence a few months after the Independence Day celebrations when the Prime Minister addressed the Constituent Assembly on March 8th 1949. 'Then again,' he said, 'not only were we revolutionaries and agitators and breakers up of many things, but we were bred in a high tradition under Mahatma Gandhi. *That tradition is an ethical tradition, a moral tradition and at the same time it is an application of those ethical and moral doctrines to practical politics. That great man placed before us a technique of action which was unique in the world which combined political activity, and political conflict, and a struggle for freedom with certain moral and ethical principles. Now, I dare not say that any of us, not all of us, lived up to those ethical and moral principles and I do dare to say that in the course of the past thirty years or so, all of us, in a smaller or greater degree, and the country itself in a smaller or greater measure, was* [sic] *affected by those moral and ethical doctrines of the Great Master and Leader*' (italics mine). Remarkable for their coruscating idealism these words were even more noteworthy for having been delivered only about

---

[1] Extracts from the speeches of Pandit Jawaharlal Nehru have been taken from the official volumes issued by the Government of India from time to time. That they have a special importance and significance has been made clear in the foreword to the first volume which states: 'Here is the story of India and the world by India's most eloquent, sensitive and knowledgeable spokesman. These speeches are much more than the utterances of the head of a Government.'

two months after the Mahatma's solemn warning to the
Congress in January just before his assassination and only
five weeks after it. But all in all, it was a picture painted in
brilliant colours and on a vast canvas which was presented
to, and readily accepted by, the peoples of India in the first
years of independence. Criticism of it as a work of art was
frowned on in all literate strata of society.

I remained in official service for nearly nine years after
August 15th 1947, although not all of it was in the I.C.S.
During this period I was able to see at close quarters more of
the application of the 'moral and ethical principles' in which
the Congress and modern India had been bred, and was also
well positioned to watch from the inside the new theory of
administration which had long been advocated by the Prime
Minister.

After a short spell, on return from leave, as Commissioner
of Rohilkhand Division in Uttar Pradesh (the new designation
of the former United Provinces), I was seconded to the Government of India for duty in the newly established States Ministry,
the function of which was to deal with the integration of the
554 former feudatory States into the fabric of the Indian Union
and to look to their administration thereafter. My year in the
Rohilkhand Division, which comprised six Districts with
headquarters at Bareilly, coincided with the civil war following
on the partition of the sub-continent. Of this period I need
only say that my experience did nothing to lessen the fears I
had expressed previously as Chief Secretary regarding dangers
facing the Government; for quite apart from the temporary
problems and difficulties caused by the mass migration of
millions of people, the civil Administration was clearly beginning to show permanent signs of wear and tear.

With the actual integration of the one-time ruling States—
the one really remarkable administrative achievement since
independence—I was not personally concerned. It was carried
out without the use of force, save in the cases of Kashmir and
Hyderabad, and its successful accomplishment was entirely
the work of two men, Sardar Patel, the Minister in Charge,
and his Secretary-General, V. P. Menon, a man of considerable ability, who combined a deep, expert knowledge of
constitutional affairs with an equal capacity for patient diplo-

macy and skilful negotiation. The feudatory States, with the temporary exceptions of Kashmir, Hyderabad, Mysore and Bhopal, now lost their separate identities, and were grouped together into Unions as a preliminary step to their complete absorption into the Union of India. It was to one of these, the United State of Vindhya Pradesh, that I was sent as the Government of India's representative with the deceptively imposing title of Regional Commissioner and Adviser.

Born in April 1948, the Union consisted of 35 States situated in the heart of the Vindhyan Hills, in some of the wildest and most beautiful country in India, and with its capital at Rewa, 32 miles from the nearest railway station. Stretching from Rewa in the east to Orchha and Datia in the west, the long, narrow, strip was sandwiched between Uttar Pradesh and Madhya Pradesh (the former Central Provinces). It represented a medieval India, scratched here and there on the surface by the twentieth century, and the history of the constituent States had been as chequered as that of any portion of India. Originally held by the Chandel clan of Rajputs, the whole area had fallen later to the Baghel and Bundela clans. Both Baghelkhand and Bundelkhand had subsequently been overrun by Muslim conquerors at various times from the Tughlaks to the Mughals, who gave way in the eighteenth century to Mahrattas, who in their turn surrendered power to the British at the Treaty of Bassein in 1802. It was some time, however, before the newcomers were able to turn their serious attention to the full pacification of the country, which in the interval continued to be ravaged by bands of Pindaris and other marauders.

The total area of the Vindhya Pradesh Union was 24,600 sq. miles, with a population of over $3\frac{1}{2}$ million and a revenue of nearly Rs $2\frac{1}{2}$ crores. Only four of the former ruling States, Rewa, Orchha, Datia and Samthar, had been in treaty relations with the British before the lapse of paramountcy, the title of the remainder being dependent on *sanads* granted by the East India Company and confirmed later by the Crown. The States varied not merely in status but also considerably in size. Apart from Rewa State with an area of 12,000 sq. miles, the only two slightly exceeding 2,000 sq. miles were Orchha and Panna. Chhatarpur, where the famous eleventh century temples of

Khajuraho are situated, was a little over 1,000 sq. miles, and
Bijawar and Datia just under. The rest descended into almost
microscopic units, no less than nineteen being well under
an area of 100 sq. miles, and two only 8 and 5 sq. miles
respectively.

From its inauguration the Union was under an unhappy
star. Reflecting the mutual rivalries inherited from their history,
its two halves, Baghel and Bundela, were never able to see
eye to eye, and the composite, allegedly democratic, Congress
Ministry under the genial and amusing leadership of a Congressman of the former Rewa State, was far more actively engaged in
esoteric personal matters than in public affairs. It was into this
interesting set-up that I descended in September 1948, unasked
for and solely at the behest of New Delhi. On my arrival in
Rewa I was certainly not in a condition of primeval innocence—
no one who had been Chief Secretary of the United Provinces
only two years before could be that, but I confess that I was
somewhat unprepared for what I found. The parting instructions of the Secretary-General had been, 'We want you to act
as our watch-dog,' and while this was an excellent order in
itself, it was apparent from the commencement that the last
thing desired by the Ministers was a watch-dog. A sleeping
dog, or better still a lap-dog, yes. Anything more dangerous,
definitely no. Inevitably, therefore, Ministry and watch-dog
tended to look askance at each other, and I fear that I was
never a popular pet with the former. The general public, on
the other hand, who were not ostentatiously enamoured of
their Ministers, had no particular objection to my presence,
their only complaint being that I had no power to do anything
concrete for them.

The Ministry and I consequently started on our journey
together out of step. One of the terms of my contract was the
provision of a furnished house. I obtained the house, but the
Ministry by a series of seemingly unending subterfuges avoided
supplying most of the furniture, presumably in the hope that
I would eventually depart in disgust. The upshot of our first
skirmish was that I finally commandeered a truck and took
whatever I required from the Government's own storerooms.
Since the whole operation was conducted with reasonable non-
violence, it went down well with everyone. The public was on

my side, and the Ministers, accustomed to the vagaries of their previous ruling Princes, acquiesced in the *fait accompli*.

Other matters, however, could not be disposed of so simply. From the outset of my work I was inundated with complaints from the public of both portions of the Union, the people of Rewa even begging for the return of their late ruler, Maharaja Gulab Singh, who had been deposed by the British in 1942 for an assortment of sins of both commission and omission and who in 1948 was under house detention in Dehra Dun several hundred miles away. It was embarrassing, indeed somewhat invidious, to be forced by circumstances to report every fort-night to the Congress Government at New Delhi that the Congressmen of Vindhya Pradesh were even more unpopular for their corruption and maladministration than a former ruling Prince whose misdemeanours had brought about his removal from his throne. At the same time the Ministers, too, had their own difficulties, and since they were naturally averse as a body from having their numerous offences brought to the notice of New Delhi, the impasse between us led to amusing episodes. For example, they suborned local postal clerks to try to obtain my reports to the Central Government before their dispatch. This I had to counter by making special arrangements with the Postmaster himself, an outsider who disliked Rewa and all its works, and who was only too ready to be of assistance. The Ministry also controlled their own secret police, who kept a wary eye on what they thought I was doing; and I, in turn, was helped by a Central Intelligence Officer who maintained a dossier on the activities of the Ministry. Then, too, every month the Chief Minister, or one of his colleagues, or some-times the Ministry in a body, would rush to Delhi to complain against the Regional Commissioner for his 'anti-national' attitude, while almost simultaneously the latter would be summoned to give his version of what was afoot. As to the effect on the Government of India, the policy appeared to be to give the Ministers plenty of rope; but much depended on who pushed in his report first.

Had the desire been present, the Ministry, despite its inexperience, could have done a great deal of good work in this backward and completely undeveloped area. When the administration of the former Rewa State had been taken over

from the deposed Maharaja, some experienced officials had been
sent there from British India, and the Chief Medical Officer
had seen many years of service in the State before service in the
Indian Army. All were men of capability and integrity. In addition the States Ministry had deputed two I.C.S. officers apart
from myself for service with the Union, one as Chief Secretary
and the other as Commissioner of Bundelkhand. Unfortunately,
the Congressmen of Vindhya Pradesh failed to make the best
use of their services. Indeed, no use was made of them at all to
any purpose.

From the commencement the Ministers and I thought and
worked on different lines, and the Government as a whole
never attempted to achieve what seemed to me first essentials,
an assessment of the Union's resources, a reasonably correct
budget and the framing of development schemes. Although
Cabinet meetings were held regularly, I never succeeded in
coaxing a consolidated budget out of the Ministry, let alone
anything else, because the figures were always manipulated to
suit particular ends and the delaying tactics used were both
ingenious and of infinite variety. On one occasion, for example,
the proposals of the Medical Department were postponed in-
definitely over the apparently insoluble problem whether the
pay of the head washerman at the Victoria Hospital should be
Rs 25 per month or only Rs 20. Then, too, the most entertain-
ing side issues were sometimes introduced, such as that arising
from the Chief Minister's desire to hold a rank in the Indian
Army. The Chief Minister, previous to his political career, had
been a captain in the Rewa State Forces, a quaint assortment
of no military value at any time, and at one Cabinet was
stirred into action by the recollection that during the war General
Smuts, then Prime Minister of South Africa, had been awarded
a Field-Marshal's baton in the British Army. On the same
analogy, why should not he, a fellow Prime Minister as it were,
be given a rank in the Indian Army? Granted this, the problem
was: what rank? The Chief Minister himself was modest,
doubtless in view of his State's obscurity, and suggested that
the rank should be not less than Lieut.-Colonel. The pros and
cons of this weighty idea dominated the morning's discussions to such an extent that after the motion had in parliamentary jargon been talked out, with much ribaldry, we

retired for luncheon without a decision on anything at all!
Which, indeed, may have been the Chief Minister's shrewd
intention from the start.

Nevertheless, despite the general atmosphere of burlesque
and comic opera, the Ministers were serious enough in many
personal matters, and these activities eventually led to their
downfall, since the wait-and-see policy of the Government of
India could not continue for ever. Interesting anonymous
pamphlets and *Black Books* were circulated publicly from time
to time containing surprising allegations and disclosures, most
of which I found on investigation to be substantially correct.
My own secret reports to New Delhi contained details of every
variety of maladministration, and showed that financial irregu-
larities (to use a mild word) were the rule rather than the
exception. The State Bank of Baghelkhand was completely
under the control of the Ministers, who in some cases maintained double accounts in their own names, public and private
being mixed up. One Minister made simultaneous collections
for the Gandhi Memorial Fund and for Congress Party funds for
which he opened an account in his own name to be operated by
himself. He issued orders to the Bank that 40 per cent of the
collections should be credited to the Memorial Fund and 60
per cent to a fund marked 'P'. But this conflicted with a later
order from another Minister, who, amongst other 'persuasive'
(as he called them) methods, instructed colliery owners to pay
into the fund Rs 2 per ton on the average raisings for the previous ten days and who further passed a direction that his
collections would be dealt with by himself. He would decide
how much would be given to the Memorial Fund and how much
to Party funds. When, after the dismissal of the Ministry, I was
appointed Chief Minister for a short period and examined the
bank's registers, I found in the Ministers' personal accounts a
large number of most interesting and damaging items.

The actual dismissal of the Ministry took place in April
1949 when the position was summed up later by the Secretary-
General as 'one of widespread corruption and nepotism,
continued dissensions and mutual recriminations among the
Ministers resulting in a most distressing situation, which reached
its climax when one of the Ministers was caught red-handed
in Delhi accepting an illegal gratification from the representa-

tive of a mining concern'.[1] The ministerial fiasco reminded me
of E. M. Forster's remark in *The Hill of Devi* regarding the then
Maharaja of Chhatarpur: 'I do not think he misgoverned his
kingdom, as my friend did his (Dewas Senior). . . . He merely
omitted to govern it.' But here in Vindhya Pradesh there
was a difference. The Vindhya Pradesh Ministers managed
to combine both, for sometimes they misgoverned and sometimes they let the business of government slide altogether.

I have mentioned my adventures in Vindhya Pradesh in
some detail for the insight I gained into the possible future of
the Indian Republic, as the Dominion was soon to become.
I now possessed personal experience of the most sophisticated of
the State Governments, that of Uttar Pradesh, as well as that
of the most inexperienced, though none the less worldly; and
as I pondered over the general state of affairs which I had seen,
my earlier apprehensions as Chief Secretary were increased
rather than diminished. My thoughts, too, often turned to
Pandit Jawaharlal Nehru's dictum that 'the average Congressman was more efficient and dynamic than anyone else'.

The ignominious collapse of the Vindhya Pradesh Ministry
was generally held, very charitably and, indeed, inconsequently,
to be the result of 'immaturity and lack of proper training in
democracy',[2] but at the same time mild forebodings for the
future of Indian democracy were apparent. 'Vindhya Pradesh
carries with it a warning for the rest of India,' was the opinion
of one daily newspaper, 'both for the Provinces and the States. . .
For Ministers to accuse one another of corruption, inefficiency,
nepotism and misrule is to touch the nadir of administration
and degradation.'[3] That conditions in Vindhya Pradesh differed
little from those elsewhere and that this was an ill omen for the
future was also emphasised by others. 'While the centre is
solid under Sardar Patel,' was the comment of a Calcutta
daily, *Amrita Bazar Patrika*, 'the provincial and union Ministries
are shakier than an autumn leaf in the storm. Madhya Bharat,
Madras and East Punjab have recently seen changes in régime,
and they have merely followed what happened in Bengal
some time ago. What is really alarming is that all these chang-

---

[1] V. P. Menon, *The Integration of the Indian States*, p. 217.
[2] *The Times of India*, April 19th, 1949.
[2] Ibid.

es do not indicate changes in policy. They indicate merely changes in fingers who [*sic*] will manipulate power-strings. Personal cupidity, rivalry and ambition are at the bottom.' Cautionary voices of this kind, however, were at a discount, although the near future was to justify them. General opinion at the time, both Indian and foreign, held that democracy in India had got off to an excellent start, and the inauguration of the new Constitution on January 26th 1950 greatly increased the prevalent optimism.

I remained in Vindhya Pradesh for only a few weeks after the dismissal of the Ministry. After acting as Chief Minister for a month, I was transferred (for reasons never disclosed to me, but which I could guess) to Bhopal to take over, as Chief Commissioner, the administration of the last of the Princely States. Bhopal, though much smaller in area and revenue than Hyderabad, was next in importance among the Muslim States. In May 1949 protracted negotiations between the Government of India and the Nawab had ended in an agreement under which the State would be taken over by the former for a period of five years, at the end of which a final decision on its future would be taken. This arrangement, satisfactory though it was in the existing conditions, appeared to have given the Nawab the erroneous impression that, if he played his cards with the diplomatic skill with which he was credited, he might with a little luck succeed at the end of the stipulated period in keeping the State intact, and possibly under the guise of constitutional governorship retain his pre-eminence in it.

The Nawab, therefore, took a long time to adjust himself to the altered circumstances and to retire gracefully into private life. In actual fact there were no grounds whatsoever for the idea which always seemed to be at the back of his mind, for the principle of the abolition of the State had already been settled, and the only remaining question was whether it should be divided between two of the constituent units of the Union of India or be bodily incorporated into only one of them. Finally, on the reorganization of the country in the middle fifties and the formation of new States on the basis of language, it was incorporated in the State of Madhya Pradesh. The future of the State, however, was not of great moment to me,

for I had completed twenty-five years in the I.C.S. and had
decided to resign from the Service, though not necessarily from
the Government, as soon as a suitable opportunity presented
itself. This was not long in coming; and after one year as Chief
Commissioner I resigned from the Indian Civil Service to
become Chairman of the recently established Public Service
Commission, Hyderabad.

My premature resignation from the highest executive
post open to a member of the Service at the time and my
acceptance of a position which was a dead end, when I still
had ten years of service before me with still greater possibilities,
was certainly contrary to normal Indian standards and conventions. In some circles it was considered unpatriotic; but
more generally, I think, it was criticized as being a combination of excessive anglicization, perversity, folly and above all
lack of worldliness. The last item of this fairly heavy indictment was probably most in evidence, for it must be confessed
that Hindus as a whole, despite their constant claim to a higher
degree of spirituality than others and the reiteration in the
Bhagavad Gita that all action must be for action's sake alone
and without any attachments, are very sophisticated indeed
in their ambition to get the most out of the material, man-
made world.

The point, if any, at which a civil servant ought to resign
can be decided only by the individual concerned, and depends
entirely on the individual's angle of vision. There is, however,
one thing which no civil servant is entitled to do: he cannot
rightly remain in official service and simultaneously insist on
the general tone of the Administration's being what *he* thinks
it ought to be. It is not for him to sit in judgement; and this,
as I now realised, was precisely what I was attempting. The
doubts and fears which I had expressed as Chief Secretary
a few years earlier had by this time become certainties. The
conversion of the Administration into a playground for political
parties together with its re-orientation towards largely personal
ends, even under the guise of socialism or social democracy, did
not seem to me to be in the true interest of the country any
more than the corruption, nepotism, inefficiency and regionali-
sm which were openly fostered by all parties after Independence.
Nor was I in agreement with the apparent ease with which so

many of my Service colleagues rejected the old in favour of the new values. This being the case, and since I found myself unable to fit snugly into the altered administrative ethic, resignation was the only straightforward course. One should not attempt to march with the battalion and at the same time be out of step with it.

From the practical, worldly standpoint it was certainly true that I lost materially through my action, for all prospects of lucrative employment at a later stage as a high executive in a foreign industrial or commercial firm receded for ever into the background. Big business does not concern itself anywhere in the world with the administrative or financial morals of the Governments with which it has to deal. It merely adapts itself to them, and quite reasonably and understandably would look askance at a former official who himself regarded with distaste many ministerial activities in particular and some aspects of the new system of government in general. That mine was an attitude which lent itself to easy criticism, and even outright condemnation on the 'Rome and Romans' principle, was, however, irrelevant. I have mentioned my resignation from the Service and the reasons leading to it merely as facts; and I defend it only on the personal ground that rightly or wrongly I found more peace of mind in the quiet, generally unsought backwater of a Public Service Commission than in continuing to swim against the current in what appeared to me, again not necessarily rightly, to be very unpleasant administrative waters.

Sixteen years after my resignation *Seminar*, through the pens of its seven contributors, launched the devastating barrage of criticism against the Indian residue of the Indian Civil Service to which reference has already been made. In retrospect, particularly in the light of the adverse opinions expressed at the time both against my misconceived actions as Chief Secretary and against my resignation a few years later, several of its articles make interesting, though strange, reading. Of particular interest to me is 'Observer', who in a conversation with an Indian left-over of the I.C.S. pointed out that no one should have allowed himself to be bothered about salaries or official prospects where integrity was concerned. This is certainly a laudable proposition, with which I personally have always agreed, but I confess that I never heard it in 1950. 'How strong, one is tempted to ask,' continues 'Observer', 'was the tradition of independence of judgement among Indian members of the I.C.S., and how many of them were willing to pay the price for it?' 'In fact,' he adds, 'in a few public enquiries the part played by them has not done them credit. I am thinking in particular of the Mundhra case in which many I.C.S. men were involved.'[1] 'Observer' was not alone as an example of how opinion had changed by 1966, at least in a few circles. Mr. H. K. Paranjape joined him with the view that 'there have been very few resignations, even from the top category of civil servants, for the reason that they have found it difficult to function as the result of wrong decision-making.... They have bowed down to what they consider inevitable.' In his conclusion, Mr. Paranjape hopes that in future 'merit will be the sole criterion for top appointments', though the thorny question of what constitutes merit has been sidestepped.

This special number of *Seminar* raised the precise issues which faced me for decision, without the benefit of its assistance, at the time of my resignation. But this is only a personal matter. The real problem, the issue of real public importance, has not been touched by any of the contributors, all of whom have based their arguments and criticisms on an unverified premise. They have not merely accepted the traditions of integrity and independence, of justice and impartiality, which were the hall-marks of the I.C.S. of the British Raj as desirable in themselves, but have assumed, contrary, I think, to the evidence, that these qualities are considered equally desirable in practice, as distinct from theory, by India's democratic rulers, and are actually expected of the latter by India's democracy.

Among many other points raised by *Seminar*, the question of merit was one that came before me daily in my work on the Hyderabad Public Service Commission. What actually constitutes merit is incapable of definition, and for its assessment a degree by itself is not a sure guide, for merit can assume different forms for different spheres of work, especially in the higher

[1] A financial scandal involving an industrial magnate and his dealings with the Life Insurance Corporation of India—a nationalised concern—and with the Finance Ministry of the Government of India.

posts. This is one of the most difficult of all the problems which come before selection bodies in every country where impartiality in the choice of personnel for administrative services is desired, and for which no perfect answer has so far been found. But here again, standards of impartiality differ from country to country according to custom and convention, and in this respect British and Indian standards can hardly be placed in the same category.

Public Service Commissions as institutions in India's administrative apparatus require some comment. A Commission for the Government of India had been established as early as 1920 under the provisions of section 96(C) of the Government of India Act. Its first Chairman, Sir Ross Barker, of the Home Civil Service, worked it on the lines and traditions of the Civil Service Commission in London, than which no better pattern could have been found in any country in the world. Sixteen years later, with the constitutional reforms of 1935, the principle was extended to the then Provinces. With independence, the integration of the former feudatory States, and the splitting up of the country into linguistic regions, there were further extensions as each unit of the Republic was formed, and a consequential plethora of Commissions followed in the ordinary course of India's political nature.

The Commissions were endowed with a separate and independent existence under the Constitution, which, while guaranteeing the status and salaries of members, debarred them from further employment under the Central and State Governments on the expiry of their terms of office, except that this ban did not apply to service with another Commission. In theory, therefore, Public Service Commissions were intended to be free from executive interference and pressures. In practice everything depended on the men who worked them; and in general the respect given to a Commission in the estimation of the public was in inverse ratio to its popularity with the Government.

During my tenure of six years I was very fortunate in, and happy with, my colleagues. My first two were the ex-Rector of Osmania University, who had been at Oxford six years or so before me, and a former professor of English Literature. We thus formed a nice blend of the 'Police State left behind by the

17

British' and the higher culture, and worked together as an excellent team. No doubt we made errors in our estimates of the worth of candidates. Nor could it be claimed that all our selections turned out as well in service as we had hoped; but no extraneous factors ever entered into our calculations. The permanent debarment of some candidates at an early stage from further appearances before the Commission for such misdemeanours as the obtaining of special recommendations from influential friends, tampering with certificates and the like, was widely publicized and its salutary effect greatly eased our work.

It was interesting to watch from this quiet little niche the development of the new India, especially the ever-growing gap between theory and performance. Public Service Commissions are purely advisory bodies. It is not incumbent on a Government to accept their recommendations, nor are Commissions empowered to enforce their decisions. Although the number of instances of the various Governments rejecting the advice of their respective Commissions was not large, at least in the early days of independence, my experience was that whenever the Hyderabad Government felt strongly in favour of a particular person our advice was overriden, despite our loud protests. Almost all Public Service Commissions in their Annual Reports deplored this tendency on the part of the Executive. Often, too, ingenious methods were adopted to bypass the Commission. One of the most common related to temporary appointments not exceeding one year—such appointments, reasonably enough on paper, being outside the purview of the Commission's functions. When a Department was determined to push in its own favourite, the appointment would be made for one year in the first instance. It would then be abolished and recreated for another year, the first incumbent again being appointed. After this game had been played for three years or so, the Commission would be requested to appoint the holder of the post permanently on the ground that he had gained experience in it! Then, too, it was the Government that laid down the terms and conditions for a post, the sole duty of the Commission in the first instance being to issue the public advertisements before making the actual selection. It was not uncommon for Heads of Departments to ensure the success of their own candidate by specifying conditions to suit only a particular person.

One Head of a Department was so adept in the art that it was almost impossible to circumvent him when he really set out on this course. That he subsequently rose to a very high position in the Government of India, and for some years was in great favour with Ministers, may perhaps have been only a coincidence.

I found Hyderabad a most pleasant place in which to work. The State was intact on my arrival, but it was during my stay there that the decision to break it up was taken. These six years, as I look back on them, seem in many respects to have been crucial for the future of the whole country, for it was then that the trends so manifest in 1946 began to crystallize into strong, solid forces, and widespread signs of instability increased. Crime figures everywhere were increasing, with criminals taking to the use of modern arms for the commission of gang robberies. Corrupt practices were intensified in every sphere of activity, and corruption seeped even into educational institutions on a wide scale, while Pandit Jawaharlal Nehru himself was constrained on a visit to Hyderabad severely to criticise those who had indulged freely in corruption at the time of elections to the Congress Committee. Nor was this all. Student indiscipline and a general spirit of violence were on the increase, and a strong warning was delivered by Pandit Jawaharlal Nehru in a speech at Sanchi in Bhopal State on November 29th 1952. Taking communal organizations to task, he said that 'if they continued to create disruption and indulged in misguiding people, strong action would have to be taken.' Almost four years earlier he had given an even more spectacular warning to the student community on January 28th, 1949, in an address at the Silver Jubilee Convocation of Lucknow University. 'No Government can take risks with violence,' he asserted with reference to some recent trouble from the side of the students, 'and I can tell you from such accounts that I have heard, the United Provinces Government has been too weak in dealing with the situation here. There has been a lot of shouting about what happened. *If I had been in charge, I would have taken stronger action against those who have been misbehaving in the streets of Lucknow. What is this business of young men and women going and attacking the police and slapping them and throwing bombs and playing about with lathis?*' (my italics). Later in the same address he asked the question: 'Is this the idea of freedom? I want you to think about it. Where are we going? Because no Government in the wide world can tolerate this kind of thing. . .' Whether Pandit Jawaharlal Nehru was entirely serious, in the light of the events of his long Prime Ministership, is, of course, anybody's guess. In fact, similar warnings continue to be given, similar denunciations continue to be made at regular intervals by a large variety of authorities almost as a matter of routine, and it is doubtful if they are taken seriously. The last was delivered by the Congress Committee set up to examine the nature and causes of communal disturbances only a short time ago, but the effects of words unaccompanied by action have still to be seen.

It was during this period, too, that the reorganization of the whole country on the basis of language and region was undertaken—a reorganization born of a month's rioting in Madras and elsewhere culminating in the self-immolation of an Andhra Congressman, Potti Sriramulu; and after this had been accomplished, one began to hear a great deal about a 'crisis of character', a phrase which was soon to be bandied around freely. 'National integration' and 'emotional integration', too, were now added to the long list of popular clichés which abound in India. Nor were these the only highlights of the time. There was now a general realization in high quarters that administration and the business of government were progressively deteriorating everywhere. Committees were, therefore, set up from time to time to 'tone up' or alternatively to 'stream-line' the machinery of the Administrations both at the Centre and in the States, and lengthy and detailed Reports followed in due course. A. D. Gorwala, a retired member of the I.C.S., produced two such, one on Hyderabad and another on Mysore. Dr Appleby, an expert from the U.S.A. produced a third in 1953, and V. T. Krishnamachari yet a fourth, while an Organisation and Methods cell was set up in the Government of India. The spate of such reports continued unabated for many years, and since the Administrations continued to deteriorate everywhere despite them, another such Committee was set up in 1966 or 1967 to start the process of 'toning up' all over again. This last, very high-powered, a veritable mountain of eminence, if ever there was one, is still in labour; but there is no reason to suppose that it will be the end of the series. In addition to these matters, economic and financial problems were coming to the forefront, but their dangerous aspects were neglected, and were covered over with thick layers of optimistic jargon on a 'developing economy' and much misdirected and very much misunderstood flattery from foreigners.

The work of a Public Service Commission differed from that of the numerous Departmental selection committees on which I had often sat during my official service, and my new posting was both novel and interesting. After having spent twenty-five years in executive and administrative posts, I was now able to look with a detached eye on the actors in the new drama. It is not necessary for me to enter into the details of my experiences on the Commission, since these are to be found in the Annual Reports. These last were not confidential documents. They were laid on the table of the Legislature for the information of members, and were always sent to the Press. A few points, however, are worth my mentioning for their bearing on certain aspects of the new administrative principles which were now being put into force.

That caste and community would soon play an important role in free India was often brought to our notice; for we used to receive applications for employment in Hyderabad from Brahmins of Mysore who frankly admitted to us that as Brahmins the scales were heavily weighted against them, and that they had little hope of employment in their native State. So great was the antagonism between Brahmins and Non-Brahmins that the sins of the twice-born ancestors of the former were now to be visited on their descendants with real vengeance. At the same time the Hyderabad Government for their part had made it a condition for all appointments other than certain technical ones that preference must be given to Hyderabadis ('Mulkis' in official parlance and 'sons of the soil' according to the journalists). The unfortunate applicants from Mysore were thus between the devil of anti-Brahmin antipathy in their own home State and the deep sea of local patriotism in Hyderabad. Not, indeed, that there was any excess of brotherly love for the Brahmin among the generality of Hindus in Hyderabad, since the most influential local caste was not of that community. A decade or so later, in addition to the pulls exercised by caste and community, local patriotism was to make itself even more powerful throughout the country with the formation of Senas, or associations, the sole object of which was to keep one's own State pure and, as far as possible, undefiled by intruders from outside. By 1968 the principle of employment to 'sons of the soil alone' had been given even greater impetus in many States. The Mysore Government asked Central Government undertakings in the State to give preference in recruitment to Mysoreans. In Maharashtra the official demand was that 90 per cent of such recruitment should be the share of local people. The Government of Orissa decided to tighten up the State's Industrial Employment Rules in such a way as to compel employers to give preference to residents of the State, and the State's Minister for Labour went so far as to issue a warning to Public Sector Corporations and the like that action would be taken against them in the event of non-compliance. The Chief Minister of Andhra Pradesh went one step ahead of his colleagues elsewhere, for *his* ambition was that permanent residents of Andhra should be given preference even in the matter of promotions.[1]

Personal factors also, such as friendships, have always been a strong, and by no means healthy, influence on Indian administrative life. They are so pervasive and carry such weight that their exercise is not only often unconscious, an automatic, reflex, mental reaction to a certain set of circumstances, but also leads to the genuine belief that indulgence in one's own brand of nepotism has actually been dictated by the merits of the particular case. Strong criticism is often expressed in public and privately, in the Press, in the Legislatures and on the platform against the prevalence of nepotism and favouritism of all kinds, but it would be true to say that this is usually not directed against the principle. More often than not it is sparked off by a feeling of resentment on the part of the critic that it is *his* son or relation who has been overlooked in favour of another's with greater influence in the corridors of power. The ramifications of personalities, friendships, personal likes and dislikes in the fabric of Indian life resemble the branches of a tree which is for ever producing new shoots. In the extreme form in which they exist in contemporary India they affect every aspect of

[1] Whether these and similar reports in the daily press are correct or not, I do not know; but they have never been denied.

the Administration adversely. I have often been reminded of the experience and reactions of an old I.C.S. friend of mine in the British days. He was a very slow worker and, by no means brilliant at the best of times, added to his difficulties by being a very late riser. Although he was by way of being on friendly terms with his Commissioner, the latter's estimate of his worth as a man contrasted strongly with that of his capacity as a District Officer. With the normal British habit (so incomprehensible to Indians) of keeping personal feelings out of assessments of a man's official work, the Commissioner maintained a careful balance in his confidential annual report. He eulogized my friend's qualities of heart, but as regards the latter's head his brief comment was: 'He would find his work less of a burden, if he got up earlier in the morning'! In short, my friend was a 'good chap', and that was all. The comment, being adverse, was in due course sent down for perusal and remedial action. Whereupon my friend's aggrieved remark to me was: 'And I thought XYZ was a friend of mine!' I fear that I was unable to soothe his ruffled feathers, for it never occurred to him for one moment that he and not the Commissioner was the one at fault.

One particular instance of a similar kind selected from my experience at Hyderabad is a good illustration of how Indians often manage genuinely to delude themselves. A very high judicial dignitary of the State quietly appointed his nephew to a particular post. The Commission, their attention having been directed to the appointment, took strong objection to it, not merely on the ground that the post should have gone by promotion but also that, if the post had to go to an outsider (of which the Commission was the judge), it should have been thrown open by advertisement. The dignitary in point saw the matter in a different light. Deeply offended, he strongly contended that the position was an important one involving a certain amount of confidential work, and that therefore his nephew was the only man in the whole of Hyderabad suitable for it! The case caused a good deal of excitement, with the Government, according to a news agency report, 'considerably perturbed at the publication in the Press of this and other extracts from the Annual Report'. The local Press, on the other hand, 'welcomed the observations of the Commission which only go to confirm the doubts and suspicions that are deepening'. Of course, it must be admitted that even if the honours of war were with the Commission, the victory was not, for all that we had succeeded in doing was to lock the stable door after the horse had been stolen. I mention this particular case out of many similar ones because of the light it throws on the much neglected question of what in fact, and not in theory, constitutes the criterion for merit in India.

The last point is more personal and merits attention only for its general implications. On the eve of my departure from Hyderabad the local English daily gave me a generous measure of praise in a leading article for 'being extremely impartial and fair' and for not being amenable to outside pressures.[1] The great significance of this leader certainly did not lie in the personality of the individual concerned, though I hope the newspaper's opinion was correct. The important lesson to be learnt was that the most influential daily newspaper in the region should have considered it necessary to have singled out the qualities in point. Impartiality and a capacity to resist external pressures ought surely to be the essentials of any Civil Service or Public Service Commission, and normally a Chairman or Member would deserve attention for departing from these principles rather than for acting up to them.

In April 1956 my six years' tenure of the Chairmanship ended. It happened to coincide with a vacancy in the Chairmanship of the Union Public Service Commission in New Delhi, and my name, supported by two former Service colleagues, was considered for the post. In different circumstances I should probably have been given the appointment; but by 1956 the new administrative ethos had completely superseded the old. That I was not considered suitable was not unexpected, and I have never had any reason for complaint, since every Government the world over is entitled to select for its top positions those whom it considers to be the best instruments for its purposes and policies. No Government can reasonably be expected to choose men who, right from the start, are out of tune with its practices and methods. On April 11th, therefore, my official service of thirty-one years under two completely different types of Governments and civil Administrations, with antipathetic

[1] *Deccan Chronicle*, Saturday, April 7th, 1956.

codes of conduct in the business of government, came to its close.

After a short interval, the next four years saw me the Secretary of the Upper India Chamber of Commerce in northern India's largest industrial and commercial city, Kanpur (Cawnpore of the British era). This Chamber of Commerce, one of the oldest in India, is still a constituent member of the Associated Chambers of Commerce, Calcutta, and its secretaryship, though a humble post, enabled me to keep in close touch with the movement of the economy. These were the years when the new economic policy flourished unchecked, the so-called 'mixed'—often in fact confused—economy embodied in the socialistic pattern of society fathered by Pandit Jawharlal Nehru and enthusiastically wet-nursed by the Congress Party. I now had the opportunity of attending the annual meetings of the Associated Chambers, and of hearing the Prime Minister and the Finance Minister of the day speak—admittedly always in vague terms—on the economic and financial issues of the time. The discussions, too, of the delegates sent by the various constituent units of the Associated Chambers on the resolutions to be put before the Government for consideration gave one an insight into the attitude of big business and industry.

It is doubtful if the deliberations and resolutions of the Chambers of Commerce had any marked effect on either the policies or the decisions of the Government. During these four years it was clear that the political leaders and civil servants in charge of economic affairs in New Delhi had aligned their sights on the affluent society of the West as an attainable target in the near future without considering the intermediate stages necessary.[1] Hence vast projects of all kinds were undertaken which proved to be neither economical in their construction nor efficient in their administration afterwards. Business men and officials talked freely of a 'developing economy' without appreciating the fact that real economic progress depended not so much on the haphazard establishment of new industries

---

[1] *Rostow on Growth*, p. 1. Professor W. W. Rostow places all societies in one of five categories; the traditional; the transitional; the society in the crucial take-off stage; the maturing; and finally the society which has achieved the stage of high mass consumption. This pamphlet is an abridgement of Professor Rostow's lectures at Cambridge in 1958 on *An Economic Historian's Way of Envisaging the Sweep of Modern History*. The London *Economist* prepared the abridgement in collaboration with Professor Rostow and published it in pamphlet form in August 1959.

with foreign collaboration as on building up a growth and reinvestment rate sufficient for the country to pass from one stage of development to another without undue strain. If the misinterpretation of Keynesian theories of money finally produced the economic contradiction of inflation coupled with stagnation, it was in the four-year period from 1957 to 1961 that signs of both were already in evidence but were ignored. Resolutions, therefore, impressing on the Government the need for balancing agricultural with industrial development and for increasing food production in the face of an ever-expanding population had little effect on the Government, until near-famine in the sixties forced a more realistic attitude towards India's basic problems. Similarly, suggestions for greater efficiency in the Administration failed to evoke any more practical response than the reiteration of pious platitudes on 'toning up' the whole system and the eventual setting up of the Committee to which reference has been made.

The middle of the year 1961 saw the close of my connexion with the Upper India Chamber of Commerce, and thereafter I settled down in the foothills of Dehra Dun and the cool lower slopes of the Himalaya at Mussoorie. Here in retirement, but not complete solitude, I retained a connexion with, and interest in, the progress of the economy as a member of the Board of Directors of two public companies, one engaged in the Cinderella of Indian industry, the manufacture of sugar, and the other in engineering. This, I hasten to add, has not converted me, unfortunately, into a member of that happy class which is so often alleged to be growing richer day by day; but it has enabled me to keep in touch with political and economic developments, and to watch the further impingement of political factionalism on economics in the same way as I had once seen the impact of politics and politicians on the administrative machine.

Now, however, the 'sound and fury' had ended and the excitement of being in the game was over. Hinduism divides life into four ashramas or stages, those of the student, the house-holder, the hermit and the ascetic. I had passed through the first two, and was ready for my own version of the third and fourth, contemplation: contemplation in comfort, admittedly, and 'without tears'; contemplation not of the future, not of that Ultimate Reality of Hinduism which is the soul of the Universe, but contemplation of India's recent past, of the British Empire in India, its nature, and, in the light of what was going on around me, the quality of its rule.

XIV

Looking Back at the Past

As THESE words are being written, the last garrisons of the
British Empire are being gradually withdrawn from the
residue of the vast possessions their rulers chose to retain after
the great renunciation of power in 1947. But when I was taken
to England the British Empire covered both hemispheres and
much of the map of the world was coloured in red. Out of
my thirty one years of service twenty two belonged to the
British period of Indian history. By 1947 the emotional enthu-
siasms and reactions of the angry young man of 1927 and earlier
had disappeared, and by 1967 I had acquired through other
experiences sufficient detachment to take another look at
British rule in order to find out for myself whether or not there
is an element of truth in the claim of its defenders that fundamentally it had a more meaningful purpose than the mere
expression of power for power's sake.

An examination of this question is all the more necessary
in view of the sedulous indoctrination of free India with the
idea that British rule stood in the way of that rapid development
and progress on modern lines which presumably, it is assumed,
would have been initiated by the various indiginous powers
arising from the ruins of the Mughal Empire, had they not
succumbed in turn to the British 'usurper'.

Regarded from one angle, it must certainly be admitted
that British supremacy was from the beginning a barrier
against India's natural line of evolution. All the numerous
contestants for power in the eighteenth and early nineteenth
centuries, except the East India Company, were native to the
country. Whether any one of them, Hindu, Muslim or Sikh,
would have succeeded in imposing his supremacy on the others
and in giving even the semblance of physical unity to the sub-
continent is most unlikely; but this apart, the rapid expansion
of a Power which was both foreign and western, constituted a
strong, though not complete, catalytic element in India's natural
course of political, and even cultural, development by diverting
it into an extraneous channel. It is possible that to some

extent and in a slightly different manner India may yet revert, if only partially, to her own nature as the effects of the temporary catalyst wear off; for centrifugal and divisive tendencies have risen rapidly to the surface during twenty years of independence.

This danger, always foreseen by the British and always made light of by Indians in the past, had been noted many years ago by the percipient authors of *The Rise and Fulfilment of British Rule in India* in dealing with the prospects of a future Federation. 'We may expect,' they wrote, 'a vigorous provincial life, with threats of secession, if the Central Government is too domineering. Already such slogans as Bengal for the Bengalis have made themselves heard. ... The greatest immediate danger is that the long period of internal peace has induced the belief that there will always be an outside authority ready to restore order, while the politician unable to redeem his pledges will be tempted to raise constitutional questions and to revive racial or religious animosities.'[1] If it is borne in mind that these prophetic words were written in the early thirties, when an independent Republic was hardly even a distant dream, it must be admitted that their authors displayed a political acumen and foresight far more accurate than those of any Hindu astrologer. This, of course, is not to suggest the imminent break-up of the country into independent units; for against the pull of diversity and the absence of true national feeling there certainly exists an All-India sentiment of some strength, fostered by a common religion with common deities on the one hand and by modern communications on the other which is likely to be a barrier against this. Doubtless there will be permanent weaknesses, stresses and strains, political, administrative and economic, and the world's attitude to India as well as India's reaction are likely to be conditioned by these factors; but wholesale Balkanization does not appear to me to be round the corner.

---

[1] p. 653. The opinion of the two authors makes interesting reading when placed alongside that of Pandit Jawaharlal Nehru: 'Britain's supremacy in India brought us peace, and India was certainly in need of peace after the troubles and misfortunes that followed the break-up of the Moghal Empire. Peace is a precious commodity, necessary for any progress, and it was welcome to us when it came. But even peace can be purchased at too great a price, and we can have the perfect peace of the grave and the absolute safety of a cage or prison. Or peace may be the sodden despair of men unable to better themselves. The peace which is imposed by an alien ruler has hardly the restful and soothing qualities of the real article' (*Autobiography*, p. 436).

The British left behind a triple legacy: novel political and administrative principles, equally novel constitutional doctrines, and finally a western educational system based on western science. All were foreign importations unknown, indeed repugnant, to India's true political and cultural heritage. The whole legacy was embodied in the English language, which was the cementing element between the various sections of the intelligentsia of a country proudly devoted as much to its diversity as to its unity; and furthermore was enshrined in a republican Constitution. This last, lifted bodily from the West, is here for all to see, and some few even to read, with its two holy books, also in English, Erskine May on *Parliamentary Practice* and Sir William Anson on *The Law and Custom of the Constitution.*

That the legacy has been twisted and garbled is not surprising in the light of India's far more ancient inheritance, but this is a phenomenon requiring separate examination and is outside my purpose here. It would not be out of place, however, to suggest that two problems basic to India's future appear to stand out. First, to what extent have western, particularly English, ideas percolated into the Hindu mind? Are they merely a veneer or someting more? And secondly, since India is also Bharat, what is the extent of the influence of the still living concept of Bharat Mata on an India, which willy-nilly is a part of the modern, scientific, and electronic age? But British dominion as a catalyst and its effects on the future of an India that is Bharat have no connection with British rule, as such, and now that independence is no novelty, the time is ripe for a reassessment of Indo-British relations in general and of British rule in particular.

So far as attitudes had a bearing on the question of race relations, I had seen little outward change during my short visits to England during the thirties. I was thus quite unprepared psychologically for what I found in 1947, when my 'Discovery' of a new England completely eroded within a few weeks my easy assumption that the outlook following on victory would be a replica of that of 1919 on my leaving Dulwich for Oxford. Changes, almost incredible in my eyes, had been wrought by the trials and sufferings of a war out of all proportion to the First World War and as a result of the lone, courageous and defiant stand for nearly two years against an apparently all-powerful European enemy together with disastrous defeats at the hands of an Asiatic power. There was a self-questioning, an insidiously attractive introspection which I had never known in the twenty one years I had spent in the country and which often took the external form of questions unheard of in the 'good old days'. 'Are the English a cruel race?' I was once asked to my astonishment by a perfectly normal young English woman in her early thirties; astonishment, because even the most jaundiced critic of the British, an essentially kindly people, could hardly have thought up this line of attack after having seen what others could do under the spur of racialism on really getting down to action. Racial theories apart, sustained and consistent scientific ruthlessness based on political ideology seems inconceivable to me in the case of the British. Nor did the heart-searching cease there; for the eighteen year old daughter of an I.C.S. friend of mine was accustomed to argue with her father (to his not unnatural disapproval) about the evils of imperialism, British included. I was often asked, too (once much later by the daughter of a former Cawnpore industrial tycoon), whether it was correct that the British had been 'very arrogant' in India. There was certainly no arrogance in the England of 1947, the arrogance so rightly chastised in *Must England Lose India* and in the statement of Sir Dinshaw Petit, the Parsee millionaire, who explained the revolt of the Burmese and their assistance to the Japanese as being 'the result of British colour prejudice and superior ways. All orientals hate the British for this stupid bias. It has done more harm than anything else. It is at the bottom of the whole trouble.'[1]

The wheel had come full circle. There was, I found, a great deal of the 'humble and contrite heart' advocated by, but not present in, Kipling many years before, a real feeling that the Empire could not have come up to its pretensions. An earnest desire, unformulated in precise terms, for better human relationships was everywhere apparent, and was evidence of the correctness of Louis Fischer's appraisal expressed to Mahatma Gandhi as early as June 1942. 'There is,' he told the latter,

---

[1] Edgar Snow, *People on Our Side* (1944), p. 56. Compare also *Must England Lose India?* quoted on p. 51 above.

'a vast popular ferment going on in England. ... The mass of the people are resolved not to be ruled after the war by the sort of people who ruled them before the war and brought on this war'.[1] There was, I also found, much genuine goodwill towards India. The former indifference, the long-standing tradition that India was far away, of interest only to the expert, and that in any case Hindus were really rather impossible people, had given way to a thirst for information.[2] So deep, indeed, was the reaction that the people in general tended to forget in a cloud of self-denigration the past greatness of their country and the great quality they themselves had shown during the war. I was thus soon compelled to realise that the 'little learning' of my long residence in England had proved to be dangerous. I was living anew, and the time had come for me to learn anew; and one of the earliest of my new lessons was the further realization that almost all the criticisms which I had once so readily levelled against the British could rebound against Indians. Take, for example, racial and colour prejudice. 'No culture was ever so fanatically colour-sensitive, so racially exclusive, so inhumanly rigid in its social stratification as India was . . . and still is.' So has written a recent observer who is by no means unsympathetic to India. 'Africans,' he continues, 'are frankly told by their Afro-Asian brothers that they can go back where they belong—into the trees. Fair girls are marriageable; dusky girls are left on the shelf. And these are not aberrations such as an Act of Parliament can cure. They are rooted, far more deeply than the equivalent prejudices in the West, in that impenetrable thicket of Hindu tradition.'[3] This is, of course, an oversimplification and overstatement. There are equally 'impenetrable thickets' in

---

[1] *A Week with Gandhi*, p. 16 (International Book House, Bombay, 1944).

[2] 'The real truth,' said the Duke of Wellington, 'is that the public mind cannot be brought to an Indian subject.' And in my boyhood in England it used to be said that the quickest way of emptying the House of Commons was to have a debate on India.

[3] John Mander in *Encounter*, June 1965, p. 52. The stress laid on a fair complexion is confined to northern and central India, and even here all girls, whatever be their hue, succeed in getting married in the end. India may be many things, but it is certainly not a land of disgruntled, dusky spinsters. As for the rest of what John Mander says, I can vouch for the remarks on the Indian attitude towards Africans, for I have heard Indians make comments on the latter which would have sent Indian blood-pressure sky high had they been made about themselves in London fifty years ago, when even relatively mild remarks were wont to cause an appreciable rise.

the U.S.A. and South Africa, to mention merely two western countries; and the reference to the competitive merits of 'fair girls' and 'dusky girls' in the marriage market is doubtless due to misunderstood research into the matrimonial columns of the newspapers. Nevertheless, there is truth in the passage, and even before 1947 I had seen for myself that all that glittered in India was not even tinsel, let alone gold; but the process commenced late and had been slow. When, for example, I read the following in Radhakrishnan's *Indian Philosophy*, it did not strike me in the late 1930s that I was reading a perfect defence of that same colour prejudice which we all resented and which we never supposed was ours as well. 'Caste,' wrote the future President of India, 'was then the salvation of the country. . . . The only way of conserving the culture of a race which ran the risk of being absorbed by the superstitions of the large numbers of native inhabitants was to pin down rigidly by iron bonds the differences of culture and race. . . . Only caste made it possible for a number of races to live side by side without fighting one another. . . . India solved peaceably the inter-racial problem which other people did by a decree of death.'[1] This, of course, was just about as close to the doctrine of apartheid as it could be without actually being stigmatized as such, and the only comment now necessary is that I read the passage quite uncritically at the time.

To what extent the changed climate of opinion in Great Britain during and shortly after the war was prevalent among the British in India, is impossible for an Indian to estimate. It was, of course, recognised on all sides that a return to the pre-war situation was out of the question, but how far Lord Linlithgow, Sir Reginald Maxwell and some others among the very senior service men whom I knew represented the general British view I do not know. Probably by 1945 there were three schools of thought in the Services: the first holding that the time had arrived for the immediate liquidation of the Empire in India, the second accepting this but advocating a gradual withdrawal by clearly defined dates and stages, and a third (small and perhaps not very influential) which sought to postpone

[1] *Indian Philosophy* (George Allen and Unwin), vol. i, p. 113. First published in 1927, the two volumes have been reprinted several times. The theory as worded would serve as a panacea for all countries today where a number of races have to live together without fighting. Presumably this was not the author's intention.

18

the day as long as possible—ten years at the most, one Governor
of a Province is alleged to have said.

In looking back, however, I think it should be admitted
that in the last few years of British rule—always excluding the
rebellion of 1942—there existed a more friendly, certainly
more realistic, attitude towards India and Indians than I
realized at the time, or, to be honest, was ready to concede.
I do not know if it was widespread, but it was present at both
ends of the I.C.S. spectrum, the very senior and the very junior.
Among those of the former was Philip Chichele Plowden, together with his wife, Edith. Plowden was District and Sessions
Judge at Meerut for two out of my four years there. Belonging
to a very well-known family with roots deep in the India
of the East India Company, many of his forebears had attained
high positions in the Company's civil and military services
(and some in England afterwards). His immediate relations
had been in close contact with Gladstone, and Plowden
himself, imbued with the Gladstonian tradition, believed, like
G. T. Garratt before him, that Great Britain had fulfilled
her destiny and purpose in India and that it was now for
Indians to govern or misgovern themselves according to their
own wishes. One of the kindliest of men, Plowden had judicial
peculiarities of his own specific brand, and some of his unexpected acquittals were certainly apt to cause mild alarm
and despondency in magisterial hearts. His wife, Edith, combined charm, presence of mind and a nice sense of humour in
equal proportions. On one occasion as she cycled home after
a shopping expedition—in the days of petrol rationing there
were no extra coupons for anyone except the Governor of the
Province—she was held up by a procession chanting the popular
slogan of the time, 'Quit India'. Unperturbed at what looked
like an unpleasant situation, she cheerfully retorted, 'But I
can't quit India on a bicycle, can I?' The crowd roared with
laughter and passed her on her way.

Ian Bowman was at the other end of the ladder, having
entered the I.C.S. only two years before the outbreak of war,
and was no Gladstonian. A socialist and an incorrigibly
adventurous spirit, he possessed no marked capacity for adher-
ing to convention. Under the guise of casual leave he left the
United Provinces in the early months of the war, having been

refused permission to join the Army, and arrived in Pondicherry. There he enlisted in the French Foreign Legion. The Government managed to entice or lever him out of this, but neither threats nor persuasion could induce him to return to the ordinary routine of the I.C.S. and the conclusion of hostilities found him with the Assam Rifles in the north-eastern jungles. In 1945 he was District Magistrate, Mirzapur, where his uninhibited socialism and sympathy for the underdog—which not infrequently had to be toned down for obvious administrative reasons—greatly endeared him to the factory workers when they indulged in their habitual strikes. A great worker and always out for new experiences, his first act on retirement was to enlist as a miner in his native Scotland in order to see for himself exactly what it was like to be one. For how long he remained underground, I do not know, but in 1948 I received a letter from either the Gold Coast or Nigeria where he had exchanged his mining excavations for a post at a University College. During his Mirzapur days he was, it need hardly be said, a bachelor, with his mother keeping house for him. When I said good-bye to them preparatory to leaving for Lucknow, Mrs Bowman wished me luck and added: 'Please remember, Mr Bonarjee, that we are not all diehards, and there are many of us who wish India well.' I often recalled these words later when I started to do my homework again. These, the Plowdens and the Bowmans—the unorthodox, may I call them?—were the salt of the I.C.S. adding just that pinch of savour to its traditionally conventional outlook and intellectual inhibitions which was so necessary.

The importance of racial relations in the Indo-British confrontation really requires no special emphasis, but even if it did, there is the remarkable testimony of no less redoubtable an imperialist than the late Sir Winston Churchill. Lord Moran has recorded that in a conversation on August 8th 1953 with Lord Salisbury, Mr (as he was then) R. A. Butler and himself, Sir Winston referred to India. 'He told us,' recounts Lord Moran, 'that some Indians had been treated with contempt. *"If we had made friends with them,"* he said, *"and taken them into our lives instead of restricting our intercourse to the*

---

[1] Lord Moran, *Winston Churchill, The Struggle for Survival, 1940-1965* (Constable, 1966), pp. 449-50.

political field, things might have been very different"[1] (my italics).
This was wisdom seventy or eighty years too late, for the proper
time for it would have been when the infant Indian National
Congress earnestly sought a friendship that was consistently
refused until its early moderation evaporated.

And yet why should Indians not admit, particularly at this
distance of time, that the British alone could not be blamed,
since it was the general European attitude that was at the root
of the trouble. If the colour prejudice of the Anglo-Saxon
vitiated his outlook, the Latin races, especially the French,
though free from it to a large extent, were not slow to display
their sense of cultural superiority towards Asia in general.
But who are we to cavil at the colour bar, the practice of
racial inequality, and other nations' feeling of cultural
superiority, we, many of whom are the descendants of a far
earlier band of conquering invaders, who designated themselves *Arya* or noble because of their fair skin, who raised
inequality to a fine art, who treated the native Dravidian,
dark-skinned peoples with the greatest contempt, and who by
pinning down their supposedly higher culture with the 'iron
bonds of caste' in order to preserve their original racial purity,
resolutely opposed any form of racial, political, or social
equality? Fifty years ago I did not realise (and many Hindus
still do not) that history had caught up with the sins of the
Vedic Aryan and was visiting them on their posterity far beyond
the third and fourth generations.

I have dealt with this controversial question of race relations
at length for two reasons: first, because it was impressed on me
at an early age, and secondly because one of the worst consequences of the unhappy relations between the two races has
been a distortion on the Indian side of the picture of British
power expressed in terms of governance and administration.
For a balanced appreciation of British rule, considered solely
as rule, racial difficulties and personal quarrels of the past
should be excluded. It is no longer enough to judge the quality
of British rule only by racial attitudes or by isolated episodes
such as the methods used in the suppression of the Indian
Mutiny and in the martial law administration of 1919; for
quite apart from a change for the better in the British outlook

[1] See note on p. 112 above.

from the palmy days of Seton Kerr[1] and Kipling, neither will give a complete or accurate picture of the panorama of British rule in its more noteworthy aspects. British rule was not all dark. There was a great deal of light which should be taken into account along with the shade.

The author of *The Guardians* was not the first to draw a parallel between the I.C.S. and the guardians of Plato's imaginary Republic. That had already been done some thirty years earlier by Sir Herbert Fisher, Warden of New College, Oxford, in a series of lectures at Glasgow University; and the short appraisal of N. C. Roy has already been quoted.[1] The analogy is an apt one inasmuch as the education given in the English Public School at the beginning of the century approximated in many respects to that recommended by Plato. It was not tailored specifically for Plato's political purposes and it was not formulated precisely in Platonic terms; but certainly up to the end of the first World War, the English professional, upper-middle classes were trained, almost unconsciously, for their imperial duties under a system which stressed the humanities while simultaneously laying equal importance on physical fitness (excessive emphasis on games to the hypercritical), on the development of corporate spirit (class consciousness to the same critics) and on the inculcation of a high sense of duty and responsibility.

Contemporary Indian opinion does not accept as valid such eulogies of the former I.C.S., and owing to the highly-developed Indian propensity to self-deception the great quality of the Service as a governing and administrative corporation has been intentionally blurred. The popularisation of the glowing romance of India's past, whether mythical or factual, has induced a firm belief in the minds of the intelligentsia that all the country's ills could be fathered on to the British. Despite the warnings of western well-wishers that 'there can be no evasions now, no blaming it on to the West, no looking for outside scapegoats,'[2] indulgence in all three continues unabated; and as a starting point what could be more gratifying to Indian self-esteem than to place the whole responsibility for Indian

---

[1] See p. 100 above.
[2] Barbara Ward, *The Rich Nations and the Poor Nations* (W. W. Norton and Company, Inc., New York, 1962), p. 143.

failings onto the I.C.S. as an essentially British institution?

Take a glance at the views expressed by Pandit Jawaharlal Nehru in his *Autobiography* and in his later *Discovery of India*, both of which contain word pictures of the I.C.S., vivid and mainly derogatory. The men of the Service in his estimation were 'helpless and incompetent. They had no training to function democratically, and they could not gain the good-will and cooperation of the people, whom they both feared and despised; they had no conception of big and fast moving schemes of social progress, and could only hamper them by their red tape and lack of imagination.'[1] Running through all the Pandit's writings is the theme of the emasculation of India's life by British rule through the I.C.S., of the greater efficiency of the Congressman and of the suppressed desire of a traditional and hidebound society for rapid social change. 'The British conception of ruling,' went one vigorous indictment, 'was the police conception. . . . India is a servile State, with its splendid strength caged up. . . . The I.C.S. must disappear completely as such.'[2] Two decades later, with fully democratic Governments, Central and State, and completely new administrative establishments throughout the country, contemporary critics of the British continue happily to go through the same exercises in cloud-cuckoo land. 'Why,' asks Mr Patwardhan as a preface to his recent lectures, 'had the actual progress of the country not been commensurate with the high purpose and vision with which Pandit Jawaharlal Nehru worked so strenuously? Why on the eve of the fourth Plan was there so much disappointment and confusion all round? Why was there so much indiscipline, inefficiency and corruption?' And the one answer given to these intriguing questions is not that the vision *was* merely a vision and far beyond the capacity of the people, nor that Indians as a whole are at fault, nor even that the stars in their courses have been

---

[1] *The Discovery of India*, pp. 451-52.
[2] *Autobiography.* The first part of the quotation is on p. 435: 'The British conception of ruling India was the police conception of the State. Government's job was to protect the State and leave the rest to others'. The second part on p. 437: 'India is a servile State, with its splendid strength caged up, hardly daring to breathe freely, governed by strangers from afar.' And the third on p. 445: 'Therefore it seems to me quite essential that the I.C.S and similar services must disappear completely.' Again on p. 446: 'The I.C.S. and similar services should cease to exist in their present form.'

against India. It is that 'Pandit Jawaharlal Nehru ultimately depended on the bureaucracy or steel frame created by the British to *maintain a Police State to enable it to carry on the economic exploitation of India*.'[1] (my italics). It is as simple as that.

Critics working on these and similar lines are not in short supply. Says the author of the introductory note to the I.C.S. number of *Seminar*: 'Those who were trained in the collection of taxes, in the maintenance of law and order, in the art of keeping aloof from the masses, cannot run a complex steel plant or feel the needs of citizens or sense the frantic urgency of a positive health policy or a dynamic education policy.' Nor are the daily newspapers far behind the experts in the propagation of the new gospel. The influential *Times of India*, for example, in a recent analysis of the extraordinary proliferation of the bureaucracy throughout the country, referred to the fact that 'the task of *transforming the Police State into a Welfare State* [my italics] is not an easy one.' And the same newspaper in another series of articles referred to the attitude of the Police (in Delhi) as being 'a hangover from the British days and is resented'.

But why, it may be asked, should Pandit Jawaharlal Nehru of all people have fallen so completely under the spell of the residual bureaucrats of the old regime? Why have officials trained in the collection of taxes and in the maintenance of law and order been so conspicuously unsuccessful in both? In what precise way have former members of the old services hampered the new educational and language policies, both of which are the creation of the democratic leaders of the people and which certainly lack neither 'boldness' nor 'dynamism'? Indeed, there are even *diehards* who hold that it would have been better for the country if the Services *had* stood in the way of these, and similar, bold policies. What possible connection can there be between the I.C.S. of the British and the 'all round indiscipline, inefficiency and corruption' which form the burden of Mr Patwardhan's lamentation? And why after two decades of freedom has democratic India been unable to rid herself of the so-called Police State and to construct a better system of administration out of a new generation guided by freely elected leaders, who in the words of the Prime Minister

[1] Mr P. H. Patwardhan in the *Financial Express*, note on p. 103 above.

constituted the most efficient and dynamic element in the country?[1]

Such queries, though apposite, are of little significance in the prevailing climate of opinion. In many countries there are mental postures which are considered axiomatic and which are necessary for the bolstering of national morale. Although they are proof against argument and must be accepted as an integral part of the national outlook, acceptance does not preclude a closer look at the Indian position. The obsession that the British bequeathed to India an apparently irremoveable Police State seems to me to be no more than a convenient belief which is soothing to the national ego; but there is a large body of evidence to the contrary which, neglected though it is in contemporary India, is likely to carry weight with future historians.

India under British dominion saw an impressive, though not flashy, tally of progressive administration which in some respects was more advanced than that of Great Britain herself. Macaulay's famous Minute on Education was certainly open to criticism, but from it was developed an Education Service which helped to modernise the country and did yeoman service in its own sphere. No doubt this Service was established in the first instance mainly to produce subordinate staff for the new type of government office, but within a short time it was turning out judges and magistrates. By 1920 it had certainly moved a long way from its starting point, for by then the Government Colleges were sending young Indians into all the higher Services, including the I.C.S. Ironically enough, I have no doubt that many of the most ardent critics of the British were themselves the products of this same Educational Service!

More or less coincidental in time was the Public Works Department for the construction and administration of civil engineering works of various kinds. Even earlier was the foundation of the Thomason College of Engineering at Roorkee,

---

[1] In the light of Mr Patwardhan's strictures on Pandit Jawaharlal Nehru, it is interesting to glance at the latter's views only a decade or so earlier. 'Individual members (of the I.C.S. and similar services), if they are willing and competent for the new job will be welcome, but only on new conditions. It is quite inconceivable that they will get the absurdly high salaries and allowances that are paid to them today. The new India must be served by earnest, efficient workers who have an ardent faith in the cause they serve, and are bent on achievement, and who work for the joy and glory of it and not for the attraction of high salaries. The money motive must be reduced to a minimum.' *Autobiography*, p. 445.

the first of its kind in Asia, and the model for others in India. The Sanitary Boards of 1864 were expanded into Public Health Departments—a very novel experiment in a country still not noteworthy for its devotion to public hygiene—and Agriculture and Forest Departments were soon to be added to the list of official activities. Rapid expansion in every sphere was the keynote of the fifty years following the end of the Mutiny. Agrarian legislation continued at regular intervals up to the 1930's, and labour and industrial legislation followed the development of industry. The foundations of Local Self-Government were laid during the viceroyalty of Lord Ripon, to be followed twenty years later by the establishment of the Cooperative Department, while the construction of a railway system which with the passage of time was to cover the whole country had been commenced in the middle of the nineteenth century. As to this last, Pandit Jawaharlal Nehru's criticism that the construction was undertaken in 'an enormously wasteful manner' because the Government guaranteed 5 per cent on the capital investment and because all purchases were made in England sounds odd; and the surprising charge of waste is even more odd in the context of the general financial extravagance and mismanagement in India since 1947.

Some of the new Departments were understaffed, it is true, and others were often short of funds; but all came under the reforming zeal of Lord Curzon, who, for all his amusing Pomposities and habit of doing the right thing in quite the wrong way, was certainly one of the ablest and most energetic administrators to come to India. All this activity, considerable though it was, admittedly did not spell perfection, but it was an excellent start for a country whose peoples were sunk in a morass of stagnation, ultra-conservative tradition and only too frequently in plain superstition.[1] India was fortunate to have been left with such wide and sound foundations on which to build in 1947.

That India is now being carefully educated into another belief, in fact into make-belief, is most unfortunate in its psychological consequences. The idea that in the nineteenth

---

[1] There are several references to this in *The Discovery of India*, as for example, p. 155. And the Great Revolt of 1857 is described as 'essentially a feudal outburst'—which, of course, it was.

century the whole country was clamouring for radical change and reform, with the British acting as a brake on its zeal, is a pleasant delusion and no more. It was actually to the credit of the ruler that he moved as rapidly as he did after the Mutiny—a rebellion which had largely been precipitated by the reforming policies of the British and which in the judgement of Pandit Jawaharlal Nehru himself was a reactionary, conservative movement. The abolition of the practice of suttee had always been unpopular with the orthodox majority. There was widespread suspicion that the British were trying to tamper with the caste system, the sheet anchor of Hindu society. The Religious Disabilities Act, designed to protect the civil rights of converts from Hinduism, and the Hindu Widows Remarriage Act which went so far as to permit such unholy unions, were both bitterly opposed. The extension of inventions such as the electric telegraph and the construction of railways alarmed both Brahmins and lower castes by the implication that the foreigner was possessed of more wisdom than the twice-born, and neither approved of Mother Ganges being assiduously tapped for irrigation canals. In short Mother India was seriously perturbed at the actions of the unspiritual foreigners from the West who were attempting to seduce her so unceremoniously.

The British, therefore, might well have been pardoned if, after having caused one upheaval by their passion for reform and modernization, they had slowed down the pace, since it was only a small minority which sought progress on modern lines. The country as a whole remained sullen and indifferent, and had to be pushed into modernity by the British, aided and abetted by a handful of reformers, mainly from Bengal, whose lot, as has been seen, was an unhappy one in their own communities. The mid-nineteenth generation of Indians did not rush into their modern age with the enthusiasm and alacrity which their great-grandchildren have rushed into patterned bush-shirts, jeans and drain-pipes. In this difficult and arduous business, the spadework of reform, the most important role, was played by the I.C.S. since nothing could have been accomplished without the constant prodding, guidance and assistance of the District Officer and the Divisional Commissioner.

It is unnecessary to enter into the details of all the progressive legislation between 1857 and the second World War. They can be found in innumerable blue-books, annual Reports and the like. The legislation itself may not have been as comprehensive as present-day critics would have liked, but there is one thing that can be said for it. It was generally lucid, and so far as Indian apathy permitted, efforts were made to enforce it—a sharp contrast with conditions in independent India, where there is a plethora of complex legislation on every subject, some of which is badly drafted and a great deal never properly implemented by action. Indeed, it might truthfully be said that the only law which is scrupulously observed by all Governments in India is the one that should not be—Parkinson's.

One further point in this connection deserves mention. Once the tide of war had turned in favour of Great Britain in 1944 and it was clear that victory was only a matter of time, the need for rapid development and for the expansion of existing welfare schemes on modern lines was promptly recognised, and both the Government of India and the Provincial Governments turned their serious attention to the framing of plans for post-war development and reconstruction. In 1944 in the United Provinces the Development Departments, Medical and Public Health (of which I happened to be Secretary at the time), Education, Agriculture, Irrigation, drew up comprehensive schemes for the future, and an Indian officer of the I.C.S. was placed on special duty for their consolidation and for making the necessary financial arrangements. While it may be conceded that they could not compete in magnitude, breadth of vision and financial grandeur with the vast Five Year Plans of independence, their deficiencies were more than balanced by their practical possibilities. Although they were soon to be thrown on the scrap heap, they illustrated three points. First, if placed in their proper perspective in the panorama of British rule, they represented a continuation of the long and varied series of reforms initiated a century or more before. Secondly, again in their correct perspective, they furnish more evidence that British rule went beyond the negative purpose of the maintenance of law and order and the collection of taxes. And lastly, the fact that these blue-prints for planned development were largely the work of the I.C.S., takes the pith out of the criticism that those whose duties included attention to stability and security and the maintenance of sound finances could not see farther ahead and 'feel the needs of citizens'.

The I.C.S. was not directly concerned with the commercial exploitation which was the theme of strong Indian criticism in the twentieth century, and the men in the Districts saw none of it. It was subtle, and doubtless always present up to a point—there has been no empire in history which did not try to benefit from its conquests. But the criticisms can be, and have been, overdone, and here, it seems to me, is another good example of the pot and the kettle. Indians would do well to remember that they, too, have been tarred with the same brush. In Burma, Africa and in other parts of the former British colonial empire, Indian traders and capitalists became the targets of bitter hostility for indulging in a species of sub-colonialism under the protective umbrella of the imperial power. To such an extent, indeed, that in the course of the last twenty years they have been unceremoniously ejected by one ex-colonial territory after another not merely for their alleged exploitation of the host country but also for indulging in precisely the same racial exclusiveness which always constituted one of the main Indian complaints against the British. So far as the British in India were concerned, I doubt if exploitation, pure and unadulterated, was the only purpose of British rule. More detailed examination would probably show that in addition to leaving behind solid constitutional foundations for the construction of a sound democracy, the British bequeathed to India an industrial base, capable of expansion and backed by a tradition of sound finance, a stable rupee and the sum of Rs 1200 crores in the till.

That this is a controversial matter, I am well aware; but a more balanced appreciation of the charge that the British not only failed to develop Indian industry but actually stood in the way of its growth might emerge, if the picture were considered from another angle. British performance should not be treated in a vacuum, but should be compared with that of other empires in their own spheres. Secondly, a comparison between industrial and commercial conditions in India at the time of the handing over of political power by the British and the achievements of underdeveloped but independent countries by 1947 would be both interesting and instructive. For example, the figures for the production of cotton textiles, coal, iron and steel and consumer goods, not to mention Indian monopolies such as jute goods and tea, for the period from 1920 onwards might be compared with those of Russia, China and the Latin American Republics. Thirdly, the idea that from 1857 on India was bursting with a Japanese zeal to learn and was faced with insuperable opposition from the side of the British requires, I think, closer examination. Indeed, certain industries such as the plantation, for example, might never have got off the ground at all had it not been for British enterprise and British capital—capital sunk for many years without any return. Despite his strong criticisms of the British for having created a 'servile State' in India, and for having stifled India's growth, Pandit Jawaharlal Nehru himself has hinted that there can be a slightly brighter side of the medal in his admission that 'there have been great changes in India also, and the country is very different from what it was in the eighteenth century—railways, irrigation works, factories, schools and colleges, huge government offices etc, etc.'[1] Lastly, it should be remembered that India made tremendous industrial strides during the second World War.

From the angle, therefore, of progressive legislation, much of which was entirely foreign to the Hindu inheritance from history, and the natural consequence of which was often imitation rather than absorption, the British State in India, whatever its defects may have been, could not in my view correctly be classified as a Police State. And what, after all, do the critics of the I.C.S. as a British Service mean by the term 'Police State'? If the intention is to convey the number of times on which the Police fire on their fellow citizens or the occasions on which policemen run amok to the detriment of human life and property, the democratic Indian State established by law in 1950 would be well in the running for inclusion in that category. But it seems to me that the term itself is misunderstood in India. The Police State, the Welfare State, the Affluent Society, ideas which are now bandied around freely and loosely, are very modern inventions, and were not in existence in dictionaries of western political terminology fifty years ago. The last two were invented after the second War, and

[1] *Autobiography*, p. 437.

the Police State was the quintessence of the totalitarian régimes in Russia, Germany and Italy after the first World War. There is, moreover, a certain amount of confusion of thought in classifying the Police State as the antithesis of the Welfare State, when the four largest totalitarian States of modern times can all lay claim to have achieved a considerable amount of welfare for their peoples. The Police State is linked to the political conditions of a nation; the Welfare State to its social and economic conditions, and to that extent are distinguishable from each other.

The Police State, therefore, which was the alleged creation of the British in India and their legacy, requires examination from two angles, distinct from any material achievements, the legal and political. As a general proposition it can be said without any fear of contradiction that the whole trend of English constitutional history from the thirteenth century onwards is by itself clear proof that the Police State of the modern age has always been foreign to the English (and later British) way of life, and that the I.C.S. as a British Service could neither have been nurtured in so un-British a tradition nor expressed it in action. Apart from the general proposition, two basic features of the State in India clearly differentiated it from the Police State, namely the rule of law and the gradual but regular advance towards responsible self-government, concepts entirely foreign to Hindu tradition and the Hindu way of life. 'The establishment of the great principle of the equality of all before the law in a country where under Hindu doctrine a Brahmin could not be punished on the evidence of a Sudra, where even punishments varied according to caste, and where according to Muslim Law testimony could not be given against a Muslim, was in itself a legal revolution of the first importance.' So has written the Indian historian, the late Sardar K. M. Panikkar. Indeed, he has gone a step farther with his reference to the 'imposing and truly magnificent legal structure which has changed the basis of society in a manner which few people realise.'[1] Indians, in fact, have become so accustomed to this

---

[1] The first quotation is from *A Survey of Indian History*, (Asia Publishing House, 1964), p. 257; and the second from *Asia and Western Dominance* (George Allen and Unwin, 1959), p. 497.

The ancient Code of Manu (the *Manu Smriti*) is of great interest in this context. Under it, for example, the penalty for the murder of a Brahmin by a Sudra was death, but of a Sudra by a Brahmin only a fine. Of course, inequalities

'magnificent structure' that they have come to believe that it has been theirs from time immemorial and not a recent western innovation. Yet no Indian interested in the beginnings of the Police State and in the ancient Hindu concepts of law, crime and punishment can do better than glance at Kautilya's advice on *The Institution of Spies* and *The Creation of Wandering Spies* in Chapters 12 and 13 of Book 1 of the *Arthasastra* and at the punishments—mutilation and torture in a variety of ingenious ways—listed in Chapters 10 and 11 of Book IV. It should be remembered in this connection that the Mauryan Empire from the time of Chandragupta to the death of his grandson, Ashoka, is for the purposes of modern propaganda one of India's many golden ages before the British take over.

Nor was the rule of law the only novelty imposed on a conservative society inured to the vagaries of despotic, and very often tyrannical, rule. Hindu thinkers down the ages have devoted themselves generally to the study of religion and metaphysics. Political philosophy, the political sciences, the science of jurisprudence, the comparative examination of political institutions, are British importations, and concepts like freedom of the subject and of speech and association, representative government, responsible government, parliamentary democracy are entirely foreign to Hindu thought.[1] The paternal State established by the British in India in the nineteenth century was in fact the liberal State of the Victorian age—liberal not merely in the narrow sense of party politics, but, more significantly, in its wider connotation. It embraced the State of the Tory Disraeli and of John Stuart Mill. It was the State that stemmed from the English Revolution and from Locke's Essay on Civil Government, the State which re-

---

have existed in all legal systems, but this is a somewhat glaring one, and, what is more, existed in what is now regarded as India's golden age.

The Code recently figured in the Upper House of Parliament in a debate on December 24th 1968. Mrs Yashoda Reddy pointed out that Manu had denied property rights to women. Mr. B. K. P. Sinha capped this by adding that the *Manu Smriti* also laid down that 'a person who did not pay his debts would be reborn *either as a dog or a pig or a woman*!'

[1] This is only a broad generalization. Political ideas are to be found in the *Rig Veda* and other ancient works, most important of which perhaps are the *Dharmashastras* (legal treatises). Then, too, there is the *Arthasastra*—though this is more in the nature of a Manual on the art of Government than a work on Political Science. By and large, however, there was no systematic study of such concepts as sovereignty, the origin of the State and so so, as there has been in the West from the time of the Greeks up to the present time.

presented the supremacy of Parliament and the supremacy of
Law. To place this liberal State in the category of Police States
is an error arising not merely from a confusion of thought but
also from an effort both to show that India had nothing to
learn from English political principles and to exaggerate the
quality of India's performance after independence. Yet by
contrast with the British State in India, the varied assortment
of autocracies and tyrannies which preceded it and the five
hundred odd Princely feudatories (excluding a handful like
Mysore, Baroda, Travancore and Gondal) which flourished
during it, had far more in common with the Police State than
the State administered by the I.C.S. ever had.

Of course, the Victorian State in India was a paternal
bureaucracy. But at the same time it was an amalgam of the virtues as well as the faults of the Victorian paterfamilias; and the paternalism was not a permanent feature. During the last forty years
of its existence British rule divested itself by stages of its original
character, and bureaucratic paternalism was watered down at
regular intervals. That it gave India good government throughout was implicit in the dictum so often voiced by Indians in the
past that 'good government is no substitute for self-government'.
But the term 'good government' covered more than stability,
security and sound finance, and inasmuch as Indians had been
encouraged from the start to think in terms of the free and
liberal political institutions they had never possessed before, it
automatically ruled out the existence of the Police State. In
brief, British dominion, despite its occasional lapses (from the
Indian point of view) in the sphere of political agitation, was
disfigured neither by the arbitrary nor the tyrannical nature of
the Police State.

Apart from the rule of Law two other aspects of the British
Raj merit more objective consideration than has been given
them. First, Police States neither concede political reform,
unless they are overthrown by revolution, as in the case of
Tsarist Russia, nor do they permit political agitation to that
end. Secondly, the British Empire is the only example in history
of an Empire which not only set out from its inception deliberately to educate its subjects in its own constitutional and
political doctrines, thereby foreshadowing its eventual demise,
but also tried to train them in its own administrative and even

military principles. I cannot think of another Empire which manufactured its own rebels in the same way.

In retrospect, too, the pace of political reform on the road to self-government, though not as rapid as political India desired, was by no means slow. All Indians born in 1885, the year of the first session of the Indian National Congress, and short of premature death, lived to see independence sixty-two years later. Agitation from the side of the subject was inevitable, since no Empire will concede political rights without some pressure being exercised on it. Equally inevitably a certain amount of repression was certain. But when the worst has been said, the four stages of political progress at intervals of approximately ten years stand out as clear landmarks, 1909, 1917-20, 1930-35 and finally 1946-47. The British certainly had their fits of fright and sought to procrastinate, but the four stages are there and cannot be ignored; and if length of time is any yardstick for the acquisition of political rights, free, democratic India could do worse than remember that over ten years elapsed before the right of the Assam Hill peoples to a measure of autonomy was recognised in 1968—a belated decision which may or may not be a final solution for the problems that beset this troubled area.

The story of Indo-British political relations must surely be one of the most fascinating paradoxes in the history of empires. Every constitutional advance, whatever may have been the compulsions behind each, included an invitation to Indian Oliver Twists to ask for more, and no empire, ancient or modern, ever gave its subjects so much freedom of criticism both in the Legislatures and outside coupled with so much scope for propaganda throughout the world. Short of advocating the removal of the British by armed rebellion, there were few, if any, limits to the constitutional pressures allowed. In this connexion a comparison between what constituted sedition under British rule and what is held today to be sedition in totalitarian States as well as between their respective legal procedures would be an instructive line of research. In India it was not sedition, nor an offence of any kind, to advocate and press for full swaraj by any constitutional method; and even in 1943 the Supreme Court, with an English Chief Justice at its head, held the detention of Mahatma Gandhi to be illegal. The

19

alleged Police State came into action—apart from the possibility
of an armed uprising—only when there was the likelihood of
stability and security breaking down under actual violence.
History may well comment also on the nature of the clash
between Mahatma Gandhi and the British. *Ahimsa,* by virtue
of its basic theoretical character, naturally suited the British
imperial book inasmuch as it restrained the Congress as a whole
from taking the path of violent revolution. At the same time it
appears to have appealed to an indefinable trait in the British
character, for the British have always had almost an affection
for their rebels; not merely their own Pyms, Hampdens, John
Wilkeses and even atheistic Bradlaughs but also others like
Michael Collins and many other Irishmen who at various times
have been in rebellion against British power. How others
would have dealt with the Mahatma is, of course, pure speculation; but one may be sure that their methods would not
have been gentle. The Germans, whether of the pre-Hitler
or Hitler era, would doubtless have shot him outright, and the
Russians, Tsarists, early Bolsheviks and certainly Stalinists,
would have been equally drastic. Even the French, who were
by no means as enthusiastically liberal and democratic in their
Empire as in their own republican homeland, would probably
have incarcerated him, unhonoured and unsung, in their Devil's
Island.

By contrast, the British positively encouraged him, and no
other imperial race would have done so much on its own account
to invest him with a Mahatma's halo. A combination of saint
and extremely shrewd political leader, he possessed an uncanny
and intuitive insight into British reactions, and in his first role
he was almost sanctified by the Imperial Power itself for the
simplicity of his life and for his work on behalf of the lowly
and downtrodden. At his first trial in 1922 for sedition, the
presiding Judge, C. N. Broomfield of the I.C.S., in sentencing
him to six years imprisonment, addressed him as follows: 'The
determination of a just sentence is perhaps as difficult a proposition as a judge in this country has ever had to face. The law is
no respecter of persons. Nevertheless, it is impossible to ignore
the fact that you are in a different category from any person
I have ever tried or am ever likely to try. It is impossible to
ignore the fact that in the eyes of your fellow-countrymen you

are a great patriot and leader. Even those who differ from you in politics look on you as a man of high ideals, and of noble, even saintly, life. If the Government see fit to reduce the sentence, no one would be better pleased than I.'[1] The Government, it may be added, did see fit to reduce the sentence considerably, and for the next twenty years it was only when the Mahatma transformed himself from the saintly social reformer into the political leader of mass movements against a 'satanic' Government with its '*Kala Qanun*' (black law) that he was put behind bars, and then, too, only to be released in due course to start all over again. In the intervals, the Prime Minister of Great Britain, Secretaries of State for India, Cabinet Ministers, Viceroys and a host of lesser lights parleyed with him as the uncrowned king of India. Honoured in many ways by the British of a 'Police State', he ended his life violently at the hands of the independent and democratic India for which he had worked, and which continues, despite the mass of evidence to the contrary, to consider itself devoted to non-violence. His assassination by a fellow Hindu was the final paradox of his career.

Of the Mahatma's uncanny insight into the British character and of his instinctive knowledge of the fundamentals of British rule, the following little story is a good illustration. In the early twenties the Mahatma was accustomed to stay with a certain nationalist family in Allahabad. One of the sons of the family who had recently been commissioned into the Indian Army (he rose to be a General after independence) once asked him whether he really felt that non-cooperation would have the slightest effect on the British. To which the Mahatma's reply was (my italics): '*My boy, I know my Englishman; and if you once persuade him that what you are asking for is true and right, he will give it.*' As remarkable a testimonial as could ever have been given an imperial race at the apparent zenith of its power by one of its subjects.

In the light of a certificate of this kind the persistent criticism of British rule that is so prevalent to-day might seem out of place, but it is not as odd as it appears to be on the surface. In addition to the general desire, already noted, to find excuses

---

[1] Louis Fischer, *The Life of Mahatma Gandhi* (Jonathan Cape, 1951), pp. 225-26.

for Indian inadequacies, there is another important factor which blurs the picture of the Empire in India, namely the strong Hindu reaction against the foreign disciplines and the foreign ethos which were imposed on the country, and which were basically repugnant to the Hindu way of life and thought. The long period of near anarchy preceding the rise of British power had produced a natural craving for the restoration of internal stability and for ordered government, foreign or native. But by 1947 the effects of a century or more of stability under the foreigner had lost both their justification and their former charm. The result has been the creation of a dangerous amnesia in the Hindu mind as a whole coupled with a partly uncon- scious desire, generated by the over-glorification of India's history, to return to the ancient ways. Order, stability, security, have different meanings to the Englishman and to the Hindu, so that good government in the British sense on the basis of British precept is not the objective of contemporary India. Or if it is, the latter is unable to put the desired principles into practice.

In emphasising what appear to me to have been some of the unique aspects of British rule I have been influenced by the consistent efforts now made to pass them over for the greater glorification of Mother India. A balance, however, has to be struck, if history is not to be falsified on both sides of the hill, and it is, therefore, necessary for the value of the Indian connection not to be underrated and slurred over by the British. How the last thirty or forty years of the Indo-British confrontation will be treated in the schools and universities of Great Britain is only a matter of guess work, but if present indications are pointers, there is every likelihood of a partial and one-sided view being as acceptable in the future as in the past. The conse- quences flowing from the British Raj did not work only for the benefit of India. They constituted a two-way traffic; and if it is for Indians to be honest enough to admit at least some of the virtues of British rule, the Englishman should return the compli- ment with a measure of gratitude to his erstwhile subject. I am not referring to the solid commercial gains accruing from the possession of a vast and easy market on the doorstep and cap- able of measurement in pounds, shillings and pence, but to an aspect of the Indo-British connection which has been given little recognition in Great Britain, namely the military.

Is it generally known, for example, that in October 1914 an Indian Division, ill-equipped though Indian soldiers were for the rigours of a European winter, was hastily despatched to France to assist in pushing the Germans back from the vicinity of Paris and in holding the fort until the formation of Kitchener's new armies? Or that by the end of 1914 nearly ten per cent of the men on the western front were Indians— 24,000 out of 270,000—and that Indian casualties in three months amounted to 6,500? Nor does this complete the story, for while Indian troops were fighting with distinction in the battles of 1915, at Loos and Neuve Chapelle, another 180,000 were sent overseas from India to East Africa, the Persian Gulf and Egypt.[1] Three years later Mesopotamia and Palestine were conquered largely from India and by India entirely for the benefit of others; for the Arabs obtained their freedom, the Jews a national home and the British themselves an addition to their Empire in the shape of a unique collection of mandates. India admittedly was granted a measure of political reform but its sweetness had already been soured by the passage of the Rowlatt Act for the suppression of political agitation and by a very unfair gift in the form of Brigadier-General Dyer. Admittedly also, the mandates soon proved to be very hot potatoes indeed, and a source of considerable inconvenience to the mandate-holder for the next thirty years; but in 1919 there was no writing on the wall of the future for anyone to see.

Between the years 1914 and 1918 India raised over a million combatants and half-a-million non-combatants for the Empire's service, to end in being the main instrument in the dismemberment of the Ottoman Empire with which she had religious ties and no cause whatsoever for enmity. Total casualties amounted to 106,594 and India bore on behalf of the Empire the costs of her troops overseas. In addition she made a free gift of £100 million sterling to the imperial exchequer, and by 1918 had supplied stores and material worth another £80 million.[2] All this constituted no mean contribution from an Asiatic country which was one of the poorest in the world, and which

[1] Major-General Sir George Aston, *The Great War* 1914-18 (Home University Library), p. 63; *The Rise and Fulfilment and British Rule in India*, p. 600; and the *Encyclopaedia Britannica*, 23rd Edition, vol. xii, pp. 172-73.
[2] *Encyclopaedia Britannica*, 23rd Edition, vol. xii, p. 177.

was connected with Europe's domestic quarrels only vicariously by virtue of being a subordinate appendage of the Empire.

The convention—almost a tradition—of taking India for granted whenever London chose to involve itself in war continued after 1918, and this doubtless accounts for the general lack of appreciation in Great Britain of the magnitude of India's war effort between 1939 and 1945, although it far surpassed her earlier contribution, and of the great role played by India in the final victory. Out of the 130 pages devoted to the Second War by Taylor in his *English History* 1914-45, the Indian Army receives no mention beyond a two-line footnote on p. 515. Most significant of all was the Victory Broadcast by Great Britain's war-time Prime Minister on May 13th 1945. After referring to 'the sense of envelopment which might at any moment turn to strangulation owing to the action of the Dublin Government' and to 'the restraint and poise with which we left the Dublin Government to frolic with the German and later the Japanese representatives to their heart's content,' Mr (as he was then) Churchill went on to pay a generous and graceful tribute to Australia, Canada and New Zealand. 'They came to our aid in dark times,' he said, 'and we must not leave unfinished any task which concerns their safety and future.' Indeed, he went even farther; for handsome tribute was also paid to 'those southern Irishmen who hastened to the battlefront to prove their ancient valour'.[1] Australia, Canada, New Zealand and a handful of Irishmen. From this it would appear that it was only India that did not come to Great Britain's aid in the time of darkness, although she provided more in men and material than the rest put together.

In much the same manner India's material contribution to victory tends to be slurred over. Writes Taylor again on pp. 545-46: 'The British insisted on defending India against the will of her political leaders, and paid for the privilege of doing so. *All the costs of the war in India were debited to Great Britain*

---

[1] The text of the Victory Broadcast is given in appendix F to volume vi of Churchill's *The Second World War*. The reference to Eire and the tribute to the Irishmen who fought is on p. 667. The tribute to Australia, New Zealand and Canada is on p. 672. It is only fair to add, however, that due acknowledgement has been given to the Indian Army on p. 182 of volume iv. But out of the millions who heard the Victory Broadcast, how many have read the fourth volume of Churchill's History?

(my italics) and produced sterling balances at the rate of one million sterling a day.' This statement is calculated to give the idea, erroneous, so far as I am aware, that India contributed nothing in hard cash towards the war effort. Actually, India's defence budget rose by almost ten times between 1939 and 1945 to £300 million sterling, and my impression has always been that it was only the vast amount of material supplied to the *general cause* (my italics) that produced the sterling balances. Then, too, quite apart from the general budget, individual Districts regularly contributed both in cash and kind. My own District, Meerut, provided cash on one occasion for the purchase of five armoured cars and a large sum towards the purchase of an aeroplane on another. In January 1942 one Sub-Division alone of the Muzaffarnagar District presented the Governor of the U.P. with Rs 83,000 for war funds. And these are merely a few examples out of many. Later, in 1944, the Government of the U.P.—bent, it seemed, on seeking unpopularity—introduced a more or less compulsory war loan in the rural areas, a scheme which at a meeting of senior officials called to consider the matter I strongly but vainly opposed on the ground that it would do far more harm than good. All this added up to a very great and effective effort on the part of India. The statement, too, regarding India's defence, appears to me to be misleading; for the British did not defend India (mainly with Indian troops, it may be added) solely for the sake of India, but very largely in order to make India an assault base for the war in the Far East.

May one hope, therefore, that at some future date the compilers of text-books for the schools of Great Britain will remember the 24,438 Indian soldiers killed in the second World War, the 11,754 missing, the 64,345 wounded, the 79,589 prisoners of war, together with the 6,500 naval and merchant service personnel who lost their lives, even though they find no place in the Victory Broadcast, and not merely take them for granted as being the legitimate price paid for India's being a second class component of the Empire? The Indian Army was expanded from 190,000 men in 1939 to two and a half million by the end of the war, the largest voluntary army ever to have been raised anywhere; and even as early as 1941 India had sent nearly a quarter of a million men to the Western

Desert and the Middle East. Her armies fought in Libya, Syria, Tunisia, Malaya, Burma, Greece, Sicily and Italy; and out of the one million men under the S.E.A.C. nearly 700,000 were Indians.[1] It was from India, too, that the lost portions of the British Empire were reconquered, for without India as a vast, consolidated assault base, reconquest would have been impossible. As Field-Marshal Sir William Slim has remarked, 'India was our base, and three-quarters of everything we got was from there. The campaign in Burma was largely an Indian Army campaign. The bulk of the fighting troops and almost all those on the lines of communication were soldiers from India; and magnificent they were. India, too, trained and sent us our reinforcements.'

So much for the eastern theatre of war. What of the western? Here is Lord Wavell's generous tribute. 'It was due to the soldiers that India sent,' he said, 'that we held the Middle East, and *that debt must not be forgotten*'[2] (my italics). Only a few specialists and a handful of men concerned with the old Indian Army—a diminishing band every year—have appreciated India's great contribution to the final British victory. But perhaps it should be added that before a debt can be forgotten it first has to be known; and it is here that British historians ought to make their presence felt.

These facts and figures covering two global wars, the long list of casualties and of countries either defended or set free or in some cases conquered in the service of the Empire, in particular the defence of the Middle East for two years before the Japanese had forced a reluctant U.S.A. into the war and the conversion of India into the base for final victory in the East are all as deserving of record in British history books as the rebellion of 1942, the general story of British rule, constitutional reform and the development of self-governing institutions. From the British angle they are not as romantic as the hoary stories of the Black Hole and the Cawnpore Well, those notable landmarks in the history books of Great Britain. They are not coloured with the glamorous overtones of the capture of Seringapatam and the death of Tipu Sultan in the breach of the walls of his fortress, of the fall of the fort at Jhansi, of the defence of

---

[1] *While Memory Serves*, appendix 3, pp. 578-79.
[2] *Asiatic Review*, April, 1946.

the Residency at Lucknow by a small band of resolute men, but they are historical facts nonetheless, however much they may be pushed aside, or even completely ignored, as being of no importance to the British Isles. While from a detached standpoint I would admit that India owes much to her connection with Great Britain in general and to the I.C.S. in particular, history may not inconceivably come to the finding on the evidence of the first two global wars of the twentieth century that the debt has been repaid in full—in Indian blood—and that this, too, deserves its recognition on the other side of the medal.

I have emphasised these details because of their relevance and importance in the wider context of the history of Indo-British relations, but they are not germane to my concluding point, the nature of the British Empire in India. No detailed, comparative study of the aims and methods of modern imperialism has so far been made, and it is not possible to predict exactly how another ruling power would have acted in India—there were considerable variations within the British Empire itself[1]—but it would not be unreasonable to take as a guideline the attitudes and policies adopted by each in its own special sphere.

On the assumption that the general international ethic of the eighteenth and nineteenth centuries made it inevitable that an India torn with internal dissension would succumb easily to foreign conquest, and that the only issue was who would be the lucky foreigner, I should say that we were fortunate to have drawn the British in the lottery. But if one may judge from the numerous criticisms put out during two decades of independence, this would not be the opinion of all, and perhaps not even of most, Indians. The point is worth some consideration, because British rule is never looked at from this angle; and if Asiatic invaders like the Persians and Afghans are left out of account, who were the possibles? The British being on

---

[1] Viscount Norwich, *Old Men Forget*, p. 287: 'I fear that our relations with Burma do not form one of the proudest chapters in British imperial history. I was surprised to find that my views were shared by the Governor, and old House of Commons friend of mine, Reggie Dorman-Smith, who had formerly been Minister of Agriculture. He surprised the company at dinner that evening by saying that he could see nothing we had done to the benefit of Burma since we took over, no roads, no schools, no health plans, no drains, no agriculture development.'

the spot were the likely winners, their nearest rivals, the French and the Dutch, having fallen far behind in the race as a result of the European wars culminating in Great Britain's undisputed supremacy after the defeat and final abdication of Napoleon. Nevertheless, at one period both had a chance, and the only three possible tickets from which to select were the British, the French and the Dutch.

Certain important differences between British imperial rule and that of the others stand out clearly—practical, visible, differences in addition to the basic, elemental qualities already mentioned. The British left behind a sound administrative base (sound, of course, according to British concepts, though not necessarily sound in the estimation of contemporary India), together with a fully trained personnel, a judiciary of equally good standing and trained in principles of jurisprudence and justice far higher than those of either the ancient Hindu or more modern Islamic systems, constitutional ideas unknown to India, the second stage of parliamentary democracy, and the twenty seven year old foundations of a national army.

Neither of the other two European empires in the East could rightly put forward similar claims. The French, whose freedom from Anglo-Saxon colour prejudice gained them much goodwill, made no attempt to train their dependencies in free institutions or for political emancipation. To be linked with French culture, to be educated at the Sorbonne so as to be a part of it, was held to be a sufficient reward for being a subordinate unit of Metropolitan France. But for the subject to demand political rights from his republican ruler was almost an impertinence. Was it not Clemenceau, France's war time Premier for most of the First War, who on a visit to India in the twenties was reputed to have stated that the British committed two great errors in India? The first was the failure to grant social equality; and the second the conceding of political rights. The French, moreover, did not hesitate to wage long, savage, bitter wars, complete with modern military gadgetry, in order to regain the imperial power which they had lost with their own freedom in 1940. North Africa and Indo-China were not granted independence after three rounds of political agitation on the basis of Truth and Non-Violence—neither of which would the French have permitted in practice, however much their Romain Rollands admired such concepts in theory. The Dutch, too, took the would-be tough line. They had not prepared the Indonesians for self-government; nor were they ready to concede it without a fight; and they made a determined effort to reimpose themselves on their Asiatic possessions through the same military force which had failed to defend their own homeland for more than a few days in 1940.

It is one of the ironies of history which has not been appreciated in contemporary India that the nation which fought stubbornly, and for nearly two years alone, to uphold its principles gave the largest and most important unit of its empire its freedom in accordance with those principles, while the defeated imperial powers denied to their colonial possessions the freedom which they themselves had been able to regain only through the sacrifice of others. In contrast to both the French and the Dutch, the British handed over power with grace. Save for the Kashmir problem, where British responsibility is heavy, though not total, India's many ills are hereditary and not of British manufacture.[1] Indeed, in 1947 Edmund Burke no longer needed to turn in his grave, if that was what he was doing; for August 15th must surely have rejoiced his heart as an outstanding example of great empires and great minds going hand in hand.

Next in point of time came the Russian expansion in Central Asia which gave the appearance of being directed against India as its final objective. It is unlikely that Indians would have preferred Russianism to Victorian liberalism despite its close resemblance to many of the autocracies which once flourished in India, and the eulogies heaped on the U.S.S.R.

---

[1] I consider British responsibility very heavy because a section should have been inserted in the Act setting up the two separate Dominions so as to ensure that where the religion of a Feudatory Prince differed from that of the majority of his subjects, the question of accession should be decided by a referendum, or in the alternative by laying down that Muslim areas would be given to Pakistan and Hindu areas to India. A referendum could certainly not have been opposed by the Congress, since it would have been based on democracy; and the alternative would merely have followed the principle adopted for British India. It is an historical irony that the Kashmir trouble arose out of the accident that the State was not part of British India. Either of the alternatives would have surmounted the religious and political arguments put forward by Pakistan and the legal technicalities later established by India on the complexities of aggression and the need for the adoption of the secular principle. This last was an entirely extraneous argument in the light of the fact that the partition of the sub-continent rested on religion. A British decision on the above lines would also have settled the Hyderabad issue without protracted negotiations ending in Police Action.

(until its recent backsliding in the matter of arms to Pakistan) by all and sundry from Ministers of External Affairs to those at the bottom of the political ladder. But one thing is certain. Tsarist Russia was the precursor of the modern Police State in its denial of political and constitutional rights, and in its expert methods of consistent repression; and had India fallen to it, Indians would have been in a better position to appreciate the nuances between the true Police State of fact and the Police State of an overheated imagination.

Of other western imperialisms, some Indians under the heavy influence of a short visit to the home of the European renaissance might perhaps have chosen the Italian variety; but whether this would have been a good selection is open to doubt. Italian rule in Ethiopia, forcibly imposed on a practically defenceless people by the lavish use of aircraft and mustard gas, was certainly accompanied by some material improvement, but equally certainly was not actuated by any higher purpose than the ambition to acquire a modern Roman Empire. 'It is a great pity that the Italians did not treat us with a little kindness and decency,' remarked an Ethiopian nobleman to Desmond Young later, 'for we would have responded: for we realise that we are a primitive people and have much to learn from Europe.'[1] Other Indians, under the misapprehension that all Germans were embryonic Max Müllers, might have accorded preference to imperial Germany, despite that country's dismal record in the small portions of Africa which it had managed to grab, and its full-throated, undisguised militarism both in theory and in practice. But German rule in South-West Africa, at least, was not a good advertisement for German imperialism. Serious trouble in 1893 with a Hottentot Chief, Witbooi, had followed its acquisition a decade before. The Germans wiped out Witbooi's village, killing 150 men, women and children. A second rebellion by another tribe in 1903 was quelled by General von Trotha by methods which reduced a tribe of 80,000 to 15,000 starving refugees who escaped into British Bechuanaland and sought protection there. As a side issue it may be added that the near extermination of the Hereros provided the British Press with some excellent

---

[1] *Try Anything Twice* (Hamish Hamilton, 1963), p. 275.

propaganda material when the annexation of the German colonies became a recognised war aim in 1915.

Most interesting of all, perhaps, would have been rule by the U.S.A.—a State which rapidly grew into the largest and most powerful of Europe's colonial experiments, and which developed a messianic imperialism entirely of its own brand. As has been noted earlier, Indian independence owes a debt to American sympathy over a long period of time, and one should not look a gift horse in the mouth. Nevertheless the persistent hostility of Americans to British rule in India is an interesting study in the light of the history and development of the United States itself; and it is permissible, I think, to speculate on the shape American rule might have taken had the U.S.A. entered the Indian stage and taken the place of the British. There has always been little awareness of the historical fact that, although Americans have strongly opposed the smallest sign of European influence in the Americas, they not only took over European imperialism bodily but in some ways even improved on the latter's methods of dealing with 'inferior' and coloured peoples. The U.S.A. was, in fact, born of a vast, expansive colonial movement at the expense of the original inhabitants, and this great colonising movement, once consolidated, was the precursor of a number of experiments in that same imperialism which, when indulged in by others, was the target of much adverse criticism.

'The White Man's Burden' of Europe was transformed by the U.S.A. into a crusade for the salvation of all mankind. A contemporary historian, William Miller, has called the process of transformation 'the Messianic impulse' and he concludes his *New History of the United States*[1] with the words: 'Our values remain humane; we cherish the preservation of the single life, the individual spirit, voluntary unity. The preservation *and extension of American ideals is the task of our maturity*' (my italics). About seventy years earlier George Bancroft in his ten volume *History of the U.S.A.* maintained the thesis that 'the political and *social system* [my italics] of the U.S.A. represented the highest point reached at that time in man's quest for the perfect State.'[2] Comments on

---

[1] Published by George Braziller, New York, 1958. Miller devotes a special Chapter—Chapter 12—to what he calls the Messianic impulse.
[2] See article on George Bancroft in *The Encyclopaedia Britannica*, 23rd Edition. Other Studies of American imperialism can be found in *Modern Imperialism*

such notions are hardly necessary beyond the remarkable fact
that Bancroft was writing at a time when the American Indians
had been finally suppressed and when both they and the
American negroes were outside the American social system,
while William Miller's thesis coincided with the boiling up of
the black-white issue and forestalled the American adventure
in Vietnam by only a few years.

The American attitude to coloured races was made clear
early on in the treatment both of the native Indian tribes and
of the black Afro-Americans. The story began with a systematic
and continuous attempt to destroy the former by a process which
would now be damned as genocide and which would doubtless
evoke some nasty comments in the U.N. The policy originally
laid down in the North-West Territory Ordinance of July 13th
1787 and subsequently enshrined in the legislation of 1789
verbally ensured that 'the utmost good faith shall always be
observed towards the Indians. Their lands and property shall
never be taken from them without their consent, and in their
property, rights and liberty they shall never be invaded or
disturbed, *unless in just and lawful wars authorised by Congress* [my
italics]. But laws founded in justice and humanity shall from
time to time be made for preventing wrongs being done to
them.'

This paper morality was immediately thrown onto the
scrap heap, and for the next hundred years the most ruthless
forms of coercion backed by overwhelming military force were
used in order to deprive the Indian tribes not merely of their
lands but often of their lives in addition. Rebellions—always
mercilessly suppressed, took place at regular intervals up to the
grande finale as late as 1890, when, as an interesting sidelight,
the U.S.A. forestalled the British in India by producing an
American version of General Dyer in the shape of the commanding officer of the 7th Cavalry Regiment who shot more
than 200 *men, women and children* in cold blood.

As a result of this series of wars of extermination and of
Reservation Acts, the residue of the Indian tribes lost 86 million

by R. S. Lambert (Longmans Green & Co, 1928), Chapter IV, and in Ludwell
Denny's *America Conquers Britain* (Alfred A Knopf, New York, 1920). This last
deals in detail with the American search for oil, rubber and the like. Lastly,
there are various articles in the *Encyclopaedia Britannica*.

acres out of the 138 million they possessed prior to the Act of 1887. The policy now pursued by the American Paramount Power was one of neglecting and pauperising the remnants of the harmless people to whom the country had once belonged in the confident expectation that the latter would die out in the face of superior 'culture'; and for some years American hopes ran high. The population of the Californian Indians which numbered 100,000 in 1853, dropped to 50,000 a decade later and to as little as 19,000 in 1906, while epidemics were allowed free scope among tribes like the Pawnees, the Chees and the Blackfeet. Yet, despite vigorous efforts by the American Government the Red Indian refused to oblige his master by dying out, and imperial America was finally compelled to recognise his existence. *In 1934, one year before the penultimate Government of India Act, one hundred years after Macaulay's Minute on Education in India, and seventy years after the establishment of Sanitary Boards by the British, Washington passed an Act for the education and health of America's own dispossessed and displaced natives.*[1]

Meanwhile the American economy flourished until the end of the Civil War on the institution of slavery; and racial equality, despite a mass of legislation, remains something of a myth even in the second half of the twentieth century, if the evidence of negro writers, of racial riots, flourishing organizations like the Ku Klux Klan and the recent emergence of a Presidential candidate on the anti-Black ticket, has any meaning. Lust for gold, oil and rubber, and trade, and the natural instinct of a young and powerful nation to go one better than its European forebears led to imperialist ventures like wars against Mexico ending in the annexation of vast tracts of Mexican territory, and the forcible intimidation of the Japanese into trade relations under threat of invasion by a naval squadron under Commodore Perry. Other similar acts of aggression followed, such as the annexation of the Philippine Islands after three years of fighting and the crushing of a rebellion under Auguinaldo, who only sought for the islanders the independence for which the Americans themselves, with the assistance of the French, had successfully fought the

---

[1] The above facts have been taken mainly from the article on the USA in the Encyclopaedia Britannica (23rd Edition).

British, and the forcible occupation of Hawaii by American
Marines which was followed by the deposition of Queen
Liliuokalami, whose crime lay in her demand, 'Hawaii for the
Hawaiians'.[1]

I have mentioned these few examples—the list could be
enlarged, not by way of criticism. The Americans have acted
as all other strong races have acted towards their weaker
opponents in the past, and it is not suggested that their attitude
towards, and treatment of, the American Indian and the Afro-
American would necessarily have taken the same forms elsewhere. But facts speak more strongly than theories, and
American criticism of British imperialism has always appeared
to me to be very incongruous in the light of the history of
American expansion and development.

There are ample indications that India under American
domination might have been considerably worse off than under
the British Raj. From the facts of the treatment meted out to
the American Indian tribes it would not be unreasonable to
conclude that the lot of the vast tribal areas of India would not
have been a happy one; for these are largely the plantation
areas and the oil bearing tracts, the areas, in short, which have
a magnetic attraction for commercial enterprise. The ruthless
manner in which rebellions were everywhere suppressed was
not a good augury for political agitation in India, and it is
doubtful if a nation nurtured in war and violence from the
commencement of its history could have understood the complexities of *satyagraha* and *ahimsa* or have permitted either to
interfere with its domination. The suppression, as part of a deliberate policy of colonial domination, of the American Indian
and Afro-American, until resistance from the latter became too
strong to be ignored, is an indication that liberalism and
tolerance were not as basic to the American way of life as they
are sometimes thought to have been, and might well not have
flourished under American rule. Then, too, the neglect of the
health and education of their own coloured peoples and of
their general betterment was not a good advertisement for

[1] In 1933 I chanced to be travelling to Europe on the Italian liner, *S. S. Conte
Verde*. Among the passengers was a Filipino delegation en route to the U.S.A. via
Europe, to demand a fixed date for independence. Although the members of the
delegation were not perhaps as critical of their American masters as Indians
were of the British, they were by no means enthusiastic. They did not actually
gain their independence for another thirteen years.

imperialism of the messianic brand. If, therefore, in spite of the high tone of the Declaration of Independence, the Americans were unwilling to give tolerant, enlightened and beneficient rule to the coloured races of their own continent—and political and social charity should begin at home—it is difficult to see how they could have given it to those of another, with an ancient civilization deeply rooted in the past. Of course, this would not have been impossible; but on the evidence it appears to me to have been unlikely. Indians have always been prone to accepting at face value western eulogies of Hindu spirituality, and during the age of British imperial power, Americans for a variety of reasons were greatly impressed by the saints and sages of India from early times to the era of Vivekananda and Mahatma Gandhi. Whether this solicitude would have survived for long the strains of closer proximity and the stresses imposed by America's inherent colour and racial feeling is an open question. It certainly did not in the case of the author of *Mother India*; and I imagine that American administrators would more probably have been hard-headed business men than scholars or medical missionaries.

Thus after a long journey of nearly fifty years I have arrived at my conclusion, a personal estimate of the quality of British rule, an unsentimental, unromantic estimate which I should not have dreamt of making in 1920, and which perhaps only a handful of Indians would openly make in 1967. The early performance of the East India Company, except from its own commercial standpoint, was certainly not auspicious, but with the growth of British Dominion from the chrysalis stage into a full imperium, its horizons widened, and a deeper purpose projected itself, to go hand in hand with trade and commerce. The record of the Empire in India when set against that of other western empires elsewhere or of previous indigenous autocracies would not bear out the indictment that its object was to keep India a 'servile State' or to clamp down rigid bonds on her 'splendid strength'. The British imperium was, I should say, the only empire in India's long history which has been distinguished by a higher purpose than power for power's sake or commerce for the sake of commerce alone. The Mauryan Empire could perhaps have made a similar claim, but only for a short period spanning the life of one man, the Emperor

20

Ashoka. The Mughal Empire, too, might have been in the running, but here again only during the reign of an individual
Emperor, Akbar, with his attempt to weld together his heterogeneous peoples into a unity and to cement them through a
composite, eclectic, universal religion of his own fashioning.
Both these, however, were personal and exceptional cases,
representing the policies and ambitions of particular rulers.
On a detached view, the British Raj seems to me to stand in a
category of its own, because it reflected the general political
ideal of a whole nation over a long period of time, through
Governments in London of different political colours and
through its administrative machinery in India. That the deeper
purpose and ideal, good government, justice, the unity of India,
the training of a conglomeration of peoples in the art of liberal
self-government and in free institutions, were cften blurred,
sometimes even disfigured, does not negative their existence.

In the entrance hall of the Victoria Memorial in Calcutta,
inset into one of the walls, is a marble tablet. Engraved on it
are the words of Queen Victoria's Proclamation after the suppression of the Great Revolt of 1857.[1] May it always remain

[1] The Proclamation announced the end of rule through the East India
Company, and granted an amnesty to all who had taken part in the rebellion save
those guilty of actual murder. The noteworthy portions for the purpose of my
conclusion ran as follows:— 'We hold ourselves bound to the natives of our Indian
territories by the same obligations of duty which bind us to all our other subjects,
and those obligations, by the blessing of Almighty God, we shall faithfully and
conscientiously fulfil.

Firmly relying ourselves on the truth of Christianity, and acknowledging with
gratitude the solace of religion, we disclaim alike the right and desire to impose
our convictions on any of our subjects. We declare it to be our royal will and
pleasure that none be in any wise favoured, none molested or disquieted, by reason of their religious faith or observance, but that all shall alike enjoy the equal and
impartial protection of the law; and we do strictly charge and enjoin all those who
may be in authority under us that they abstain from all interference with the
religious belief or worship of any of our subjects on pain of our highest displeasure.

And it is our further will that, so far as may be, our subjects of whatever race
and creed, be freely and impartially admitted to office in our service, *the duties of
which they may be qualified by their education, ability and integrity duly to discharge* [italics
mine].

We know and respect the feelings of attachment with which the natives of India
regard the lands inherited by them from their ancestors, and we desire to protect
them in all rights connected therewith, subject to the equitable demands of the
State; and we will that generally in framing and administering the law due regard
will be paid to the ancient rights, usages and customs of India. . . . .

When by the blessing of Providence internal tranquillity shall be restored, it is
our earnest desire to stimulate the peaceful industry of India, to promote works
of public utility and improvement, and to administer the government for the
benefit of all our subjects resident therein. In their prosperity will be our strength,
in their contentment our security, and in their gratitude our best reward. And may
the God of all power grant to us, and to those in authority under us, to carry out
these our wishes for the good of our people.'

there, long after every road has been renamed and all the
statues of Englishmen have been removed and lost to memory,
even as the rock edicts of the Buddhist Emperor, Ashoka,
remain. It is silent testimony to the basic ideals which under-
pinned the British Raj. Indian political, social and religious
history has many facets. Some are merely dull. Many are dark
and blood-stained. Very few of the countless empires which
have waxed and waned in the sub-continent possess a lustre
which at least in parts shines brightly throughout. The impartial
and objective historian writing in the future about the past may
quite possibly arrive at three conclusions at present quite
unacceptable, it seems, to Indian opinion: that India's
greatest enemies for many centuries have been Indians themselves; that the British, despite the human blemishes in their
rule, brought to India a liberal, tolerant, efficient, enlightened
administration; and lastly that in doing so they meant well by
India and the Indian peoples.

The portion italicized is very important. It must be remembered that the
British sought to carry on their administration on British principles and on British
administrative ethic. It was inevitable that they should have assessed Indian
capacity on those and not Indian principles.

This Proclamation may well be compared with that issued by Queen Victoria's
grandson, King George Vth, on the inauguration of the reforms under the
Government of India of 1919. It dwelt on the greatness of the changes that had
taken place, and the demands which would now be made on all concerned with the
working of the Act. 'There will be need', said the Proclamation,' of perseverance
and mutual forbearance between all sections and races of my people in India. . . .
I rely on the new popular assemblies to interpret wisely the wishes of those whom
they represent. . . . I rely on the leaders of the people to face responsibility and to
endure misrepresentations, to sacrifice much for the common interest of the State.
Equally do I rely on my officers to respect their new colleagues, and to work with
them in harmony and kindliness, to assist the people and their representatives in an
orderly advance towards free institutions; and to find in these new tasks a fresh
opportunity to fulfil, as in the past, their highest purpose of service to my people.'

Anyone who has read Harold Nicholson's *Life of King George Vth* will be able to
see the imprint of the King himself in this Proclamation.

Epilogue

It will be one of the functions of historians, when they get down to work, to decide on the place of the British Raj in Indian history; and it is quite likely that their assessments will differ according to the nationality and outlook of the individual. My purpose in writing has been only to make a personal estimate from the empirical angle, of the quality of British rule and not of its ultimate value or significance in India's evolution. But in the true Hindu setting, the Hindu view is unlikely to be empirical, and since the Hindu perspective is important, I venture to give a sketch of it as it appears to me.

In the Epilogue to *The Guardians* it has been suggested that only after the lapse of perhaps two centuries will it be possible to assess correctly the ultimate value of the British incursion into India, since that would be the length of time required to judge whether English ideas have bred with Indian as Roman did with Gaulish. The length of time—two centuries—coupled with the use of the terms 'ultimate' and 'incursion' might almost suggest that the author of *The Guardians* himself had in mind the great importance of the Hindu view of life. One thing at any rate can be said with certainty. The analogy between Great Britian and India on the one side and Rome and the Gauls on the other cannot actually hold good; for the Gauls at the time of the Roman conquest were still in the tribal stage, without a well-developed identity of their own, without an elaborate and highly developed metaphysical system, without a way of life, and an attitude to life, buttressed by several millenia and handed down through the ages. The Gauls had no four Vedas, no Upanishads, no Ramayana, no Mahabharata.

Within the framework of Hindu thought, culture and daily outlook British dominion would wear a very different appearance from what it would to the western empirical eye. It would be governed by the eternal cosmic cycle of creation, preservation, dissolution and again creation, and so on *ad infinitum*, the cycle personified in the Hindu *Trimurti* (Trinity) of Brahm, Vishnu, Shiv: and behind the personification is the eternal cosmic universal soul, *Brahman—Atman*, the self-creating, self-preserving, self-dissolving and immanent, of which the individual human soul is only a small part.

While a detailed examination of Hinduism, whether philosophical or popular is neither possible nor necessary here, it can be correctly said, I think, that the essence of the general Hindu outlook is contained in this belief in the Universal Cosmic Soul, final absorption into which is the objective of every individual human soul in the mundane world of the senses.[1] This is the foundation of the Hindu claim to the possession of a greater degree of spirituality than that of any other people, although this spirituality has nothing in common with morality or ethics as western philosophies know them.

Certain other beliefs follow as axioms from the main faith. First, all empiric existence in the world of perception is in itself an evil, inasmuch as it is only partial and incomplete like the world in which it is. Secondly, empiric existence involves a chain of deaths and rebirths, the chain of *samsara*, or the course of earthly existence. Thirdly, the circumstances into which one is reborn are determined by the law of *karma*, or the effects of one's actions in the past life. Fourthly, release, or *moksha*, from this seemingly endless chain is the desirable goal, and this can be reached more rapidly by devotion (*bhakti*) to the Cosmic Soul and knowledge of it (*jnana yoga*). The fifth and last is that devotion and knowledge are attainable through a process of deep contemplation, for which the last two of the four *ashramas* previously mentioned are necessary, that of the hermit and ascetic.

This is a very summarized assessment of the Hindu outlook, and inevitably suffers from all the defects of over-simplification. There are six recognized schools of Hindu philosophy, the Nyaya, the Vaiseshika, the Samkhya, the Yoga, the Purvamimamsa, and the Uttaramimamsa or Vedanta; possibly even a seventh, Kashmir Saivism. In addition, mention must be made of the *Tantras*, or semi-philosophical dialogues between the deity, Shiv, and his consort, Parvati, which are the specific for dealing with the Kali Yug, or age of evil. It is, however, almost impossible to sort out with any certainty the faith of the average educated Hindu, because the latter's beliefs are a compound of legend, mythology, astrology, some philosophy of the

[1] 'Verily this whole world is Brahma. Tranquil, let him worship It as That from which he came, as That into Which he will be dissolved, and as That in Which he breathes.' The *Chandogya* Upanishad as quoted by A. C. Bouquet, *Hinduism*, p. 50, (Hutchinson's University Library, 1948).

Vedantist variety and much worldly wisdom: and over and above the beliefs, ceremonial and ritual count for as much as, if not more than, anything else.

At the risk again of over-simplification one can perhaps hazard the view that every Hindu believes, to a greater or lesser degree, in the doctrines of reincarnation, the rebirth of the individual soul, *karma*, or retribution according to one's deeds (or misdeeds) in this life, and in *moksha*, or final release of the soul from the unpleasant cycle of rebirths. But even here, general faith in the third, *karma*, appears to have been so diluted by the pressure of modern circumstances that its influence on the majority of the intelligentsia is small. The doctrine entails a descent in caste in the next rebirth appropriate to the number and quality of one's misdeeds in the present—the Harijans of today are theoretically supposed to be expiating the sins of the past—on which basis India of the future bids fair to being almost exclusively peopled by very low castes, with the politicians as a class, though no doubt with a noble exception here and there, at the bottom of the ladder.

If detailed examination of such questions is left aside, what is of significance is the fact that the general spirit of Hinduism lives on not merely among the masses but also in the minds of the intelligentsia. The spectacle of any large religious festival on the banks of the Ganges or at any sacred place, the daily life at Benares or a similar city, will drive this point home to the disinterested observer. The well-to-do educated classes can be seen driving in jeeps to the holy places in the recesses of the Himalayan snows, while the masses trudge along on foot for a less comfortable pilgrimage, or cram themselves into buses and trucks; and literate and illiterate both have an abiding faith in the efficacy of ritual in warding off the allegedly evil effects of an eclipse of the sun or moon, or of the inauspicious movements of the planets through the signs of the zodiac. 'I myself have all my life seen,' observes Nirad Chaudhuri, 'professors of physics loaded with amulets; secularists poring over horoscopes and palms; and politicians refraining from submitting their nomination papers except on "auspicious days"'.[1] Whether such an outlook on life is scientific in the em-

---

[1] *The Continent of Circe*, p. 103. Pp. 103-4 deal at length with this interesting subject.

pirical sense, whether the doctrine of determinism has not been stretched beyond what it can bear, is not material. The most important corollary of the five fundamentals—as they appear to me to be, of the Hindu faith—is that the Universal Cosmic Soul alone is True, Real, and Infinite. All else, our earthy world of perception through the senses is *Maya*, or non-true, non-real, finite, and therefore of no great importance in the light of Truth and Reality. *Maya*, which hinges on the doctrine of *Advaita* or Non-Dualism, is found in the Vedanta, but is probably the most commonly accepted part of Hindu philosophy. The Bhagavad Gita, which is a portion of the heroic poem, the *Mahabharata* and which is the Bible of the modern Hindu, is, as *The Lord's Song* or *The Song Celestial*, more spiritual in content than philosophical. The doctrine of *maya*, as such, is not an integral part of it; and as an interesting sidelight the Gita is very far from being founded on *ahimsa*.[1] In essence an outlook based on *maya* is inevitably the complete antithesis of western philosophical thought, rooted as the latter is in the world of perception, the world that is and not the world of the spirit.

As a small part of *maya* and of the *Kali Yug*[2] the British Empire in India pales into relative insignificance. What to the Englishman was, at its highest level, a great adventure, with purpose and meaning behind it, loses much of its colour and historical importance. The British Raj becomes merely one of the many empires which have arisen, waxed, and then waned in the long history of the sub-continent, just a chapter, and that, too, only a short one in the unending story depicting how

> 'Sultan after Sultan with his pomp
> Abode his destined hour, and went his way.'

Indeed, it may well be that independent India is merely pre-

[1] There are a few casual (not basic to the theme) references to non-violence as being one of the numerous attributes of Shri Krishna such as humility, freedom from anger and pride, patience, truth and so on. See Discourse X, shloka 5: Discourse XIII, shloka 7: Discourse XVI, shloka 2.

[2] In Hindu tradition the four stages of the world are the Satya, Treta, Dvapara and Kali, the whole forming the Mahayug. According to the glossary in *Hindu Philosophy* (Theos Bernard: Jaico Publishing House, Bombay), the respective durations are 1,728,000, 1,296,000, 864,000 and 432,000 years each, the descent in numbers marking a corresponding moral decline. In the Kali Yug, virtue and morality are at their lowest, twenty-five percent. The Kali Yug is supposed to have started on February 17th/18th 3120 B.C. and thus has a long way to go. At its end the world will be destroyed, presumably to be recreated out of the Brahman. The theory is a curious one. It contradicts the doctrine of retribution in a way, since one's misdeeds become just things that must happen in such an age. Secondly, India's many golden ages before the advent of the British have always been in the

paring the ground for another Sultan to arrive and abide his
hour or two—a Sultan, this time, of a different variety, and
possibly even welcome to some, a Sultan who will be commercial
and economic, with perhaps military undertones in addition.
And if the new Sultan is prepared to share the shaking of the
Pagoda tree equitably with its native owners, present indications
are that there will be little or no opposition from all those who
count in India's life.

The impact, then, of Great Britain and the West may not
have gone as deep into India that is Bharat as is often thought.
Which brings me to the point raised earlier in a general way,
the tug-of-war, as it were, between an India compelled by
force of western influences and power to live, politically free,
in the modern, empirical age of electronics and space research
and a Bharat living in *maya* and hoping at some very distant
date to be absorbed for ever in the Eternal, All-Pervasive,
Universal Self, *Atman,* so as to be at one with Truth and
Reality. Bharat Mata, as she manifests herself today, lives on in
the hearts and minds of millions of Hindus, and appears to be
fighting back not merely against the extremes and abnormalities
of the technical age, not merely against its crudities, but even
against the scientific outlook of the modern era which is very
much concerned with conditions in the world of human
existence.

One consequence of her resistance is the emergence of many
anomalies which sometimes assume unpleasant forms. Anyone
interested in the fascinating discrepancies between India and
Bharat can find examples almost daily in the newspapers. A
very recent one reported in July 1968 is worth attention because
it involved both the new temples of technology and the ancient
ones of superstition, a combination of modern engineering and
ancient lore. A twenty eight year old Assistant Engineer of
Jagadalpur was sentenced to life imprisonment for strangling
his minor son and offering him as a sacrifice to Sidhi Baba in
the belief that this would bring him wealth, prosperity and
supernatural powers. Since then there have been two other

---

worst age; and lastly, if the durations are taken at face value, the two best ages of
the world go back to the age of Australopithecus, if not to the Pliocene and
Pleistocene geological eras. To what extent the tradition carries any weight is
impossible to say; but the Tantric school of thought was specially designed as a
method of coping with the Kali Yug.

cases of the same kind, one involving a contractor who sacrificed the small son of one of his workmen in order to ensure the success of his undertaking, and the other a trader. Both were well-educated—in the ordinary sense of the term.

While these are extreme cases, and cannot be taken to be the rule, the dictum of Surendranath Banerjea, 'Scratch a Hindu and you will find him a conservative',[1] holds good today, as it held good in the past: and religious conservatism, religious sentiment, queer superstitions masquerading as religion can easily be turned into political channels. As long ago as 1896 Lokmanya Tilak, who had already revived Mahratta nationalism, turned his attention to using religion as an instrument of politics. His paper *Kesari* fomented the ill-feeling aroused by the measures taken to combat a wide-spread outbreak of plague to such an extent that the Commissioner in charge of anti-plague operations, W. C. Rand of the I.C.S., was assassinated, along with one of his assistants, Lieutenant Ayerst. The two culprits, the Chapekar brothers, belonged to a society 'for the removal of obstacles to the Hindu religion' and the line taken was that the anti-plague measures outraged the religious susceptibilities of the people. Fourteen years earlier, Swami Dayanand had founded the Cow Protection Association for the defence of that animal not against its daily, and normal, maltreatment, but against the Muslim practice of using it for sacrificial purposes. The problem of the cow, the problem of its preservation rather than of its low production of milk, is, of course, a hardy annual in free India.

Although Hinduism and the Hindu outlook have always shown a marked capacity for adaptation to the outward circumstances of a given period, adaptation is different from the absorption of its spirit. Nothing indicates this more clearly than the history of caste, which over a period of three thousand years or more has successfully adapted itself to every political,

[1] *A Nation in Making.* (O.U.P. Bombay, 1925), p. 367. More important than the examples given is the case of the Shankaracharya (High Priest) of the temple at Puri in 1969. The Shankaracharya had inaugurated a campaign for the retention of the caste system including the doctrine of untouchability. He was prosecuted for breach of the article in the constitution which specifically prohibits untouchability, but was acquitted by the Magistrate on the technical ground that the constitution prohibits only the practice of untouchability and not propaganda in its favour. The Shankaracharya with a crusading zeal worthy possibly of a better cause has stuck to his guns; and on the 23rd June 1969 is reported to have told a meeting at Amritsar that he was prepared to leave India if anyone could prove that his view of the Hindu scriptures was incorrect.

economic and social change, and which continues to be an influential political factor in democratic India. Gautama, the
Buddha, the early Sikh Gurus, Swami Dayanand, the founder
of the Arya Samaj, and lastly Mahatma Gandhi all tried to
eradicate it, either wholly or in part, while the Constitution of
1950 abolished it *in toto*. And all failed. India that is Bharat, it
would appear, is once again adapting herself to a new age
without actually absorbing as much of it as is really necessary
for rapid progress in the modern world; for adaptation is
compulsory, dictated by circumstances and mimetic, whereas
absorption and assimilation are the products of an active
desire not merely to accept change as a necessary evil but also
so to alter the national outlook as to bring it into line with,
and to help in moulding, the modern era.

How this interesting struggle, as I see it, between India and
Bharat will end is purely a matter for speculation; but if an
onlooker may hazard a guess there may well be no actual
winner. The tug of war is likely to continue, with the heave
going now to one side and now to the other, and with only a
comparatively small gain each time in favour of the few who
seek to become a part of the technical age. Modernism demands
a scientific attitude of mind as well as methodical efficiency,
neither of which appear to me to find a place in the legacy
from the ancient past. Yet even if the pull of Bharat acts as a
brake on rapid progress and as a bar against India's being in the
forefront of the advanced nations of the immediate, and for
that matter the distant future, what, after all, does the contest
signify? Very little, I should say, in a country whose inhabitants as a whole would regard it as being merely a part of
maya, the world of illusory phenomena, the world of fleeting
appearances.

Index

Administration, basic British principles, 100-2, 227, 228; difference between British and Indian ethic, 102-6, 111, 234, 237, 240, 249-53, 256; changes in after 1946-1947, 146, 223, 227, 231, 232, 236-9, 254, 259, 260, 261, 264; possible dangers in changes, 179, 180, 238, 241, 292; need for reforms in, 228, 229, 240; need for retention of virtues of former system, 238, 239; toning up of, 260, 266; extraneous factors in, 235, 236, 261-4; politics in, 231, 233, 239-41

Ahimsa, 189, 218-22, 311

Allen, Sir George, 9

Alleyn, Edward, 31

Amritsar, effects of massacre at, 62, 74-80

Anomalies in India, 17, 18, 20, 114-17, 121, 160, 214, 221

Aristophanes, 116, 222

Azad, Maulana Abul Kalam, Congress President, 175 and note, 176

Bandyopadhyays of Kanyakubja, 1, 2

Bandyopadhyay, Pitambar, 3, 4

Bhagavad-Gita, 90, 167, 254, 311

Bharat, Bharat Mata, 105, 155, 157, 158, 167, 177, 269, 270, 282, 292, 310-14

Bhopal, 253-4

Bonarjee, Debendranath, 9, 10, 12, 16, 17, 21. See also chapter VIII

Bonarjee, Dorothy, 34, 59

Bonarjee, Janet, née Sirkar, 12, 16, 22, 58

Bonarjee, Neil, schooldays in England, 37, 38, 40-4, 46, 47, 53, 54; effects of World War 1914-18 on, 58, 59, 62; absorption of English ethic, 88, 89, 121, 122, 228, 229, 238; religious attitude of, 14, 61, 62, 169; emotional nationalism of, 58-60, 117; Oxford, 67-9, 81; school-master, 81-3; London School of Economics, 85-87; passes into I.C.S., 87; District work, see chapter VII; in Government of India, 138-41; District Magistrate, Meerut, 108-13, 194-204; Secretary to Government, United Provinces, 223; Divisional Commissioner, 226, 246; Chief Secretary to Government, 227 and foll; attempts application of British principles to Indian conditions, 228, 229, 234, 237-9, 242; experiences as Regional Commissioner, 247-56; Chief Commissioner, Bhopal, 253; resignation from I.C.S, 254-6; Chairman, Public Service Commission, Hyderabad, 257-65; Secretary, Upper India Chamber of Commerce, 266; revision of former ideas, 270-2, 274, 276

Bonarjee, Shib Chunder, son of Pitambar Bandyopadhyay, 4, 6-8

Bonnerjee, Girish Chunder, son of Pitambar Bandyopadhyay, 4

Bonnerjee, Womesh Chunder, first President of National Congress, son of Girish Chunder, 4, 5

Bowman, Ian, 274, 275

Bowman, Mrs, 275

British Raj, early Indian admiration of, 96 (note), 187; growth of Indian distrust, 78-80, 91, 93, 207; lack of sensitivity of, 79, 92, 93, 205-8; legacy of, 270; Nehru and others on, 278, 279; criticism of examined, 280-8; progressive legislation during, 159, 160, 280-3; political progress during, 289; qualities of, 289-91, 298; comparisons with other imperialisms, 297-305; assessment of, 305-7 (see also Indian Civil Service)

Centrifugal forces, 179, 185, 269

Christian Missions, 13, 14

Churchill, Sir Winston, 92, 93, 210, 294 and note

Collins, Major, 22

Communalism (Hindu-Muslim), personal experiences of, 167-70, 178, 179; composite culture, 170-3; All-Parties Conference of 1928, 174; British position, 172, 175, 182; political basis of, 173; Cabinet Mission of 1946, 175; Congress reactions to,